Beckett's Voices / Voicing Beckett

Themes in Theatre: Collective Approaches to Theatre and Performance

Series Editor

Peter G.F. Eversmann (*University of Amsterdam, The Netherlands*)

Editorial Board

Elaine Aston (*Lancaster University, UK*)
Jacqueline Lo (*Australian National University, Australia*)
Karen Fricker (*Brock University, Canada*)
James Harding (*University of Maryland, USA*)
Milija Gluhovic (*University of Warwick, UK*)

VOLUME 12

The titles published in this series are listed at *brill.com/tt*

Beckett's Voices / Voicing Beckett

Edited by

Laurens De Vos
Mariko Hori Tanaka
Nicholas E. Johnson

BRILL

LEIDEN | BOSTON

Cover illustration: Pan Pan's *Embers* in the Samuel Beckett Theatre, Dublin, 2013. Directed by Gavin Quinn. Designed by Aedín Cosgrove. Skull by Andrew Clancy. Used with permission. Photo © Ros Kavanagh.

Library of Congress Cataloging-in-Publication Data

Names: De Vos, Laurens, 1978- editor. | Tanaka, Mariko Hori, editor. | Johnson, Nicholas E., 1981- editor. | International Federation for Theatre Research. Samuel Beckett Working Group.
Title: Beckett's voices–voicing Beckett / edited by Laurens De Vos, Mariko Hori Tanaka, Nicholas Johnson.
Description: Leiden ; Boston : Brill, 2021. | Series: Themes in theatre: collective approaches to theatre and performance 1871-8736 ; 12 | Includes bibliographical references and index.
Identifiers: LCCN 2021022004 | ISBN 9789004468399 (hardback) | ISBN 9789004468382 (ebook)
Subjects: LCSH: Beckett, Samuel, 1906-1989–Dramatic works. | Voice in literature. | Voice (Philosophy)
Classification: LCC PR6003.E282 Z57278 2021 | DDC 842.914–dc23
LC record available at https://lccn.loc.gov/2021022004

Typeface for the Latin, Greek, and Cyrillic scripts: "Brill". See and download: brill.com/brill-typeface.

ISSN 1871-8736
ISBN 978-90-04-46839-9 (hardback)
ISBN 978-90-04-46838-2 (e-book)

Copyright 2021 by Koninklijke Brill NV, Leiden, The Netherlands.
Koninklijke Brill NV incorporates the imprints Brill, Brill Nijhoff, Brill Hotei, Brill Schöningh, Brill Fink, Brill mentis, Vandenhoeck & Ruprecht, Böhlau Verlag and V&R Unipress.
All rights reserved. No part of this publication may be reproduced, translated, stored in a retrieval system, or transmitted in any form or by any means, electronic, mechanical, photocopying, recording or otherwise, without prior written permission from the publisher. Requests for re-use and/or translations must be addressed to Koninklijke Brill NV via brill.com or copyright.com.

This book is printed on acid-free paper and produced in a sustainable manner.

For
Julie Campbell
and
Mary Bryden

Contents

Preface and Acknowledgements   XI
List of Figures   XIII
Notes on Contributors   XIV

'All the dead voices': Introduction   1
    Laurens De Vos, Mariko Hori Tanaka, and Nicholas E. Johnson

Listening to the Inner Voice in *Watt*: Innovations in Narrative Form   11
    Julie Campbell

PART 1
Musicality of Voices

Sound Matters in Beckett   25
    Linda Ben-Zvi

Revealing the Limit of Language in Relation to Music   42
    Michiko Tsushima

Embers: A Polyphonic Piece for Radio   56
    Jürgen Siess

PART 2
Voices of an Absent Other

Samuel Beckett, Quickening the 'dead voices': From *Waiting for Godot* to *That Time*   67
    Llewellyn Brown

Scratching the Surface: The Dramaturgical Oxymoron in Beckett's Silences   85
    Laurens De Vos

Why Is 'Listener' Named '*Souvenant*'? The Role of the Spectator in a Bilingual Reading of *That Time/Cette fois*   97
    Kumiko Kiuchi

Un-bodied Voices, the Thing Itself and Beckett's Neural Theatre 111
    S. E. Gontarski

PART 3
Voices of the Vulnerable

Pacing as Repressed Memory of Embodiment and Enactment in *Footfalls* 127
    Svetlana Antropova

'Rock her off': The Paradoxical Tension of the Split Voice in *Rockaby* 143
    Teresa Rosell Nicolás

Technology and the Voices of the More than Human in Beckett's *All That Fall* 158
    Anna McMullan

A Creamy Work: Schiller and Beckett 175
    Arthur Rose

PART 4
Cinematic Voices

Filmic Perspectives in Speaker's Narrative of *A Piece of Monologue* 193
    Mariko Hori Tanaka

Cinematic Adaptations of Beckett's *Breath* 208
    Anna Sigg

Translating Silence: Ashish Avikunthak's Cinematographic Version of *Come and Go* 221
    Thirthankar Chakraborty

PART 5
Enacted Voices in Performance and Media

Without Colour: Beckett and the Stage Voice 237
    Nicholas E. Johnson and Cathal Quinn

Beckett in Performance: The Body of a Beckettian Actor 250
    Melissa Nolan

Translating Beckett's Voices in Different Cultures   267
    Yoshiko Takebe

Articulations of Voice and Medium in Beckett's Screen Work   280
    Jonathan Bignell

All That Fall as a Case Study in the Possibilities and Problematics of Re-routing Samuel Beckett's Radio Plays for Performance in Other Media   295
    Everett C. Frost

Bibliography   311
Index   331

Preface and Acknowledgements

Preface: The Samuel Beckett Working Group

This book results from the past several meetings at the Samuel Beckett Working Group under the auspices of the International Federation of Theatre Research. It is the first book for our working group to be included in the Themes in the Theatre Series.

The Samuel Beckett Working Group first met at the 1997 IFTR in Israel when Linda Ben-Zvi gathered several Beckett scholars, including distinguished academics such as Ruby Cohn and Martin Esslin. Since then, Ben-Zvi convened the working group several times until she handed the baton to Julie Campbell and Mariko Hori Tanaka in the 2011 IFTR held in Osaka. The Samuel Beckett working group constantly met and kept its existence not only in the IFTR's annual conferences, but also in sub-meetings (in 2012 in both Southampton and Tokyo and in 2017 in Budapest). Today it is the only working group focused on a single author (Beckett having outlasted Shakespeare, in this case).

This book will be the fourth volume of collected essays presented at the Samuel Beckett Working Group. The seeds of the publication plan were planted back in 2012 by Julie Campbell. Unfortunately, she passed away in May 2014, just before we met at the IFTR congress at the University of Warwick. As her succeeding co-convenors (2014–18), Nicholas Johnson and Hori Tanaka decided to pursue her project. Julie Campbell provided the first approach for what was to become this book's central theme. We then invited contributors from the meeting attendees. In the meantime, we also included another editor, Laurens De Vos, who has been a regular participant of the Working Group since the 2015 IFTR annual conference.

We hope our working group will prosper and make a significant contribution to future Beckett studies. As it is one of the longest active working groups in the IFTR, its membership is constantly renewing, with dynamic early-career researchers working alongside senior scholars. The global reach of IFTR enables the gathering of various academics and practitioners from many cultural and linguistic backgrounds, widening the scope of our research. In our past meetings, we have been honoured to be able to exchange our ideas with people encountering Beckett in classrooms and theatres all over the world. We hope this book, which features researchers from nine countries, will be an impetus for people interested in Beckett to pursue their studies with a broadened intercultural and intermedial perspective.

Acknowledgements

This book would not have been possible to finish without the support of our many collaborators and affiliated institutions. We thank the IFTR executive committees and Working Group coordinators over the last decade, whose stewardship of our international gatherings has proved so enriching. We are especially grateful to Linda Ben-Zvi, our honourary convenor and founder of the Samuel Beckett Working Group. All the essays collected in this book are based on the papers that were presented at the past Samuel Beckett Working Groups, though some were revised to fit the theme of voice. We thank the many members of the Samuel Beckett Working Group whose essays may not appear in this volume, but whose feedback at our meetings has helped to shape our thoughts about the field, as well as refining individual essays. The editors wish to thank our home universities, our academic colleagues, and our students, for providing the environment for our research to grow. Along with his colleagues, Peter Eversmann, editor of the Themes of Theatre series, overlooked the publication of this book with Brill and has dispensed wise advice throughout its development. We thank Pan Pan Theatre Company, Gavin Quinn, and Ros Kavanagh for permission to reproduce their *Embers* image for the cover. We thank Courtney Grile for her help with indexing.

The impetus for this project came from Julie Campbell, whose warmth touched many members of the Working Group in the course of her career. Because the Beckett community also lost Campbell's colleague and friend Mary Bryden during the making of this book, the editors would like to dedicate this volume to them both. We also thank Sam Campbell, daughter of Julie Campbell, to have let us include her essay 'Listening to the Inner Voices in *Watt*' which was originally delivered at the Osaka meeting. Julie and Mary spoke to so many students and colleagues within their lifetimes through their writing, teaching, and collaboration; we offer this volume as evidence that their voices will endure.

Laurens De Vos
Mariko Hori Tanaka
Nicholas E. Johnson
February 2021

Figures

1. Melissa Nolan in *Footfalls*, photo © Futoshi Sakauchi   253
2. Melissa Nolan in *Not I*, photo © Bob Dixon   256
3. Melissa Nolan and Colm O'Brien in *Catastrophe*, photo © Cathal Quinn   259
4. Geraldine Plunkett, Melissa Nolan, and Jennifer Laverty in *Come and Go/Teacht Is Imeacht*, photo © Futoshi Sakauchi   261
5. Melissa Nolan in *Play* (dress rehearsal), photo © Matthew Ralli   263

Notes on Contributors

Svetlana Antropova
is currently a full-time professor at Centro Universitario Villanueva, affiliated with the Complutense University of Madrid, Spain. She completed her PhD in English and North American Literature at the Autonomous University of Madrid. Her doctoral thesis was entitled 'Staging Memory and Trauma: Past Voices and Bodies Haunting the Present in the Theatre of Samuel Beckett'. She was a member of the steering group at the interdisciplinary conference 'Trauma: Theory and Practice' in 2014–2015. Her recent contribution 'Filming Trauma: Bodiless Voice and Voiceless Bodies in Beckett's *Eh Joe*' (*What Happened? Re-presenting Traumas, Uncovering Recoveries*, 2019, ed. E. McInnes and D. Schaub) is the result of her research on disembodied voices which function as *acousmêtre* in Beckett's theatre.

Linda Ben-Zvi
was twice elected president of the International Samuel Beckett Society, founded and chaired the Samuel Beckett Working Group of the International Federation of Theatre Research (IFTR) for fourteen years, and initiated and still chairs the Annual Beckett Lecture at Tel Aviv University. She has authored and edited thirteen books, including four on Beckett (*Samuel Beckett, Women in Beckett, Drawing on Beckett*, and *Beckett at 100*, co-edited with Angela Moorjani), and four on American playwright and novelist Susan Glaspell, including the biography *Susan Glaspell: Her Life and Times*, winner of the Jury Prize of the American Theatre Library Association. In addition, she has authored more than 100 articles in books and journals on modern world theatre.

Jonathan Bignell
is Professor of Television and Film in the Department of Film, Theatre & Television at the University of Reading. His current research is on the technologies and aesthetics of space in TV drama. His book *Beckett on Screen: The Television Plays* (Manchester UP) was published in 2009, and his previous work on Beckett includes articles on Beckett's TV drama in the *Journal of Beckett Studies* and *Samuel Beckett Today/Aujourd'hui*. He was also a contributor to Linda Ben-Zvi's *Drawing on Beckett* (2003). He is a Trustee of the Beckett International Foundation at the University of Reading.

Llewellyn Brown
teaches French literature at the Lycée international de Saint-Germain-en-Laye. He has published *Figures du mensonge littéraire: études sur l'écriture au XXe siè-

cle (2005), *L'Esthétique du pli dans l'œuvre de Henri Michaux* (2007), *Beckett, les fictions brèves: voir et dire* (2008), *Savoir de l'amour* (2012), *Beckett, Lacan and the Voice* (2016), *Beckett, Lacan and the Gaze* (2019), *Marguerite Duras, écrire et détruire: un paradoxe de la création* (2018). He is a member of the editorial board of publisher Lettres modernes Minard, for whom he directs the 'Samuel Beckett' series.

Julie Campbell

who passed away in May 2014, was Senior Lecturer at the University of Southampton. She published many articles on Beckett in journals and collections of essays. Her latest essay entitled 'Beckett and Trauma: The Father's Death and the Sea' was published in *Samuel Beckett and Trauma* in 2018. She co-convened the Samuel Beckett Working Group under the auspices of the International Federation of Theatre Research in Osaka (2011) and convened in Southampton (2012) and Barcelona (2013).

Thirthankar Chakraborty

is Assistant Professor in the Department of Liberal Arts at the Indian Institute of Technology Bhilai, India. He wrote his PhD on 'Samuel Beckett and Indian Literature', sponsored by a University of Kent 50th Anniversary Scholarship. Funded by the Centre for Modern European Literature, he co-organised the 'Samuel Beckett and World Literature' conference at Kent in 2016 and later co-edited the volume on *Samuel Beckett as World Literature* (2020). He won the BCLT bursary for participating at the Institute of World Literature in 2015 and was recipient of the Samuel Beckett Summer School's international bursary in 2014.

Laurens De Vos

is Associate Professor in Theatre Studies at the University of Amsterdam. He obtained his PhD in 2006 from the University of Ghent. He is the author of *Cruelty and Desire in the Modern Theater. Antonin Artaud, Sarah Kane, and Samuel Beckett* (Dickinson Fairleigh UP, 2011) and *Shakespeare* (Lannoo, 2016) and editor of *Sarah Kane in Context* (Manchester UP, 2010). He has published articles on English contemporary playwrights such as Harold Pinter, Mark Ravenhill, and David Greig, and on theatre makers such as Jan Fabre, Ivo van Hove, and Milo Rau. To his research topics belong the dynamics of the gaze in theatre and arts.

Everett C. Frost

produced and directed the award-winning American national broadcast premieres of Samuel Beckett's radio plays. Projects developed through his independent production company Voices International included a year-long SoundPlay series of radio dramas, a mini-series of Native American myths and rituals, and the "Hörspiel/USA" series of collaborations with German radio. As an Executive Producer and Project Director at WGBH, Boston, he developed series adapting American Literature and Greek mythology for broadcast. Frost is Professor Emeritus (Film, Television, Radio), New York University, and continues to write about, among other things, Beckett.

S. E. Gontarski
is Robert O. Lawton Distinguished Professor at Florida State University. He has recently published: (with Paul Ardoin and Laci Mattison) *Understanding Bergson, Understanding Modernism* (2013) and *Understanding Deleuze, Understanding Modernism* (2014,) both from Bloomsbury. He has, in addition, edited *The Beckett Critical Reader: Archives, Theories, and Translations* (2012) and *The Edinburgh Companion to Samuel Beckett and the Arts* (2014), and published two recent monographs, *Creative Involution: Bergson, Beckett, Deleuze* (2015) and *Beckett Matters: Essays on Beckett's Late Modernism* (2016) — all from Edinburgh University Press. *Beckett's Happy Days: A Manuscript Study* was reissued by The Ohio State University Press in 2017, and *Revisioning Beckett: Samuel Beckett's Decadent Turn* appeared from Bloomsbury in 2018.

Mariko Hori Tanaka
is Professor of English at Aoyama Gakuin University. She has published essays on the reception of Beckett's works in Japan and influences of haiku on Beckett in *Samuel Beckett Today/Aujourd'hui*, as well as chapters in collections of essays on Beckett. With Yoshiki Tajiri and Michiko Tsushima, she co-edited *Samuel Beckett and Pain* (Rodopi, 2012) and *Samuel Beckett and Trauma* (Manchester UP, 2018). In Japanese, she authored *Beckett Pilgrimage* in 2007 and *Revised Versions of* Waiting for Godot: *Beckett as Director* in 2017, which was awarded the 28th Yoshida Hidekazu Prize.

Nicholas E. Johnson
is Associate Professor of Drama at Trinity College Dublin. Books include *Experimental Beckett* (Cambridge UP, 2020) and *Bertolt Brecht's* David *Fragments* (Bloomsbury, 2020). With Jonathan Heron, he co-edited the *Journal of Beckett Studies* special issues on pedagogy (29.1, 2020) and performance (23.1, 2014) and founded the Samuel Beckett Laboratory in 2013. He is a founding co-director of the Trinity Centre for Beckett Studies and co-convened the Beckett Working Group for IFTR, 2014–2018. He works as a dramaturg for Pan Pan and Dead Centre and has held visiting research positions at the Freie Universität Berlin and Yale University.

NOTES ON CONTRIBUTORS

Kumiko Kiuchi

is Associate Professor at the Institute for Liberal Arts, Tokyo Institute of Technology. She has published several articles on Samuel Beckett in English and Japanese, mainly on his exploitations of literary sources and on his cross-genre experiments to address the questions of language, image, and sound in his work. Her recent publications include *Landscapes in Time: Patrick Keiller's Robinson Trilogy* (2015), 'Finding a Form for the Speechless' (*SBT/A* 29, 2017), 'Gender, Position, Spectacle' (*FLS Studies in Language and Culture* 2, 2018 [in Japanese]). She is a regular contributor to *Snow lit rev*.

Anna McMullan

is Professor in Theatre at the University of Reading and co-director with Mark Nixon of the Beckett International Foundation. She is author of *Performing Embodiment in Samuel Beckett's Drama* (2010) and *Theatre on Trial: The Later Drama of Samuel Beckett* (1993), and co-editor of *Reflections on Beckett* (2009) with Steve Wilmer. She has co-edited with David Pattie a special issue of *Samuel Beckett Today/Aujourd'hui* on Staging Beckett at the Margins (29.2, 2017) and, with Graham Saunders, a special issue of *Contemporary Theatre Review* on Staging Beckett and Contemporary Theatre and Performance Cultures (28.1, 2018).

Melissa Nolan

is a theatre-maker. She holds a H.Dip in Theatre and a Masters in Performance Drama from University College Dublin. She co-founded Mouth on Fire Theatre Company with Cathal Quinn (Head of Voice, The Lir, Trinity College Dublin) in 2010. Since then they have produced over twenty of Samuel Beckett's works, travelled internationally and translated five of his plays into Irish.

Cathal Quinn

is the artistic director of Mouth on Fire Theatre Company, which he co-founded in 2010 with producer and performer Melissa Nolan. He is also Head of Voice, The Lir, Trinity College Dublin. He has directed over twenty innovative yet highly respectful productions of Samuel Beckett's poetry, prose and drama as well as plays by Yeats and Shakespeare, and has written dramas about Keats, Yeats, and Wilde. Mouth on Fire Theatre Company has performed Beckett in prisons, hospitals, for the homeless as well as at Tullow church Foxrock, for the President of Ireland at Áras an Uachtaráin and in theatres all over Ireland. The company commissioned and performed translations of Yeats's and Beckett's plays and poetry in the Irish language, transcreated by world-renowned translator Gabriel Rosenstock. Mouth on Fire toured Beckett's works to the UK, Spain, India and Japan. *Before Vanishing*

(*Ohio Impromptu, Footfalls, That Time, Come and Go/Teacht is Imeacht*) won awards at the Kot Bayun Literary Arts Festival in Russia.

Arthur Rose
is a vice-chancellor's fellow in English at the University of Bristol. His publications include *Literary Cynics: Borges, Beckett, Coetzee* (2017), *Theories of History* (2018) with Michael J. Kelly, and *Reading Breath in Literature* (2019) with Stefanie Heine, Naya Tsentourou, Peter Garratt, and Corinne Saunders. His essays have also appeared in *Modern Fiction Studies, Ariel: A Review of International English Literature, Twentieth Century Literature* and *Samuel Beckett Today/Aujourd'hui*. His forthcoming monograph considers literary responses to asbestos.

Teresa Rosell Nicolás
is Assistant Professor of Literary Theory and Comparative Literature at the University of Barcelona. Her lines of research centre on hermeneutics, dramatic theory, aesthetic representation in the post-war period, and comparative literature in the European intellectual space. She has published widely on these topics and on authors like Samuel Beckett, Claude Simon, Herta Müller, or Jorge Semprún. She has lately co-edited *Comparatistes sense Comparatisme* (2018, with Antoni Martí Monterde) and *El Comparatisme en els Escriptors Catalans* (2019).

Jürgen Siess
is Associate Professor in Comparative Literature at the University of Caen, France, and has taught literature in France, Germany, and Israel. He has co-organised colloquia at the Cerisy-la-Salle centre and at various universities. He is an active member of the ADARR Research Group, at the Porter Institute Tel Aviv. He has been an active participant in the International Samuel Beckett Working Group (recent publication: 'Beckett's *Posture* in the French Literary Field'). He is the editor of an important collective work in epistolary studies, *La lettre, entre réel et fiction*. In a comparative perspective he has published on Rilke and Voltaire.

Anna Sigg
holds a PhD in English literature from McGill University and is a full-time English literature instructor at John Abbott College, Montreal. She also works as a part-time lecturer at Bishop's University, Concordia, and McGill. Her articles on Beckett's *Krapp's Last Tape* and *Embers*, as well as her book project, *Therapeutic Theatre: Trauma and Bodily Articulation in Post-War European*

Drama, explore the link between trauma, body, and silence in post-war European drama (Beckett, Artaud, Brecht, Bond, Kane). She recently started her own theatre company ('Steal the Void Theatre') and works as a director, acting coach, and music director.

Yoshiko Takebe

is Associate Professor in Translation and Interpreting Course at the Department of Practical English, Shujitsu University in Japan. Her research focuses on the correlation between nonverbal and verbal forms of expressions with respect to drama and theatre. She studied Drama and Theatre in Research at Royal Holloway, University of London. She has worked as a Japanese–English interpreter and translator in Tokyo.

Michiko Tsushima

is Professor in the Faculty of Humanities and Social Sciences at the University of Tsukuba, Japan. She is the author of *The Space of Vacillation: The Experience of Language in Beckett, Blanchot, and Heidegger* (Peter Lang, 2003) and *Hannah Arendt: Reconciling Ourselves to the World* (in Japanese, Hosei UP, 2016). She has also published a number of articles on modern literature and contemporary thought including articles on Beckett and Arendt. Her articles on Beckett appeared in *Samuel Beckett Today/Aujourd'hui*, *Samuel Beckett and Pain* (Rodopi, 2012) and *Samuel Beckett and Trauma* (Manchester UP, 2018) co-edited by Mariko Hori Tanaka and Yoshiki Tajiri.

'All the dead voices': Introduction

Laurens De Vos, Mariko Hori Tanaka, and Nicholas E. Johnson

The concept of 'voice' presents productive ambiguities that are grounded in its etymological origins. Its earliest appearance in English is attested from the late thirteenth century, when it referred to the sounds made by the human mouth (the voice of a *person*); within a century, it had already gained its more political meaning, the sense of a feeling or expression (the voice of a *people*). Around 1600 its meaning referring to musical ability arrived, though it did not become a technical term in linguistics (for when the vocal cords are engaged in the utterance of a letter-sound) until the 1860s. The nineteenth century also elaborated the rhetorical, stylistic, and grammatical dimensions of 'voice' as writing training became more standardised and widespread. Appearing sporadically from 1579 but substantially expanded in the twentieth century, concurrent with the revolution of interior consciousness sparked by psychoanalysis, is the voice as invisible spirit or daemon, especially in the context of 'hearing voices' within. It is in keeping with his habits that Samuel Beckett drew on nearly every one of these diverse, sometimes divergent meanings in his sixty-year career, not only using these different denotations across his works in all genres and media, but also excavating their specificities, experimenting with them, and performing them.

Beckett's thematic engagement with the idea of voice resonates with his attraction to ontological slippage, and he often exploits the phenomenology of voice, which of course varies based on which definition is adopted. Many of the anatomical, musical, and linguistic notions of voice have a haptic character, as sound resonates within and beyond a body, physical yet invisible. The more inward and abstracted voices of memory, madness, conscience, duty, franchise, representation, empowerment, or even narration also appear across the oeuvre, gaining special influence in the space of Beckett's prose. The refrain 'I say it as I hear it' from *How It Is* offers a textual formulation in which there are (at least) two voices implied, while *The Unnamable* uses a voice identified as singular to fracture the narrator: 'I strained my ear toward what must have been my voice' (*Three Novels*, 309). *Molloy* uses the terms 'lesson' and 'pensum' to refer to what 'you think you are inventing' (32), ideas which are then re-localised in *The Unnamable* into an infection within the vocal apparatus itself:

I emit sounds, better and better it seems to me. If that's not enough for them I can't help it. If I speak of a head, referring to me, it's because I hear it being spoken of. But why keep on saying the same thing? They hope things will change one day, it's natural. That one day on my windpipe, or some other section of the conduit, a nice little abscess will form, with an idea inside, point of departure for a general infection. (353)

The seeds of Beckett's long engagement with the voice in broadcast media can also be traced to the use of 'transmission' in *The Unnamable*, where the narrator declares, 'I shall transmit the words as received, by the ear, or roared through a trumpet into the arsehole, in all their purity, and in the same order, as far as possible' (349), and later comments that 'This transmission is really excellent. I wonder if it's going to get us somewhere' (351). Provocative enough on the page, such a passage would have gained immeasurably when spoken in the voice of Patrick Magee on the BBC in 1959: 'But it's entirely a matter of voices, no other metaphor is appropriate' (325).[1]

The creative leap from the prose voice into the voice of the stage, the radio, and the screen — the remarkable affordance of being able to split the embodied actor in one space from a voice coming from or going elsewhere, and for the actor's own capacity to moderate their instrument — provides the impetus and a kind of map for the present volume. This book explores the theme of the voice in relation to silence, language, music, imagery, physicality, and space in Samuel Beckett's dramatic works, including his radio and television plays, as well as some adaptations. It is this intermedial breadth that distinguishes this volume, since many before us have noted that voice is one of the central recurring themes in Beckett's oeuvre. Foundational texts such as Jonathan Kalb's *Beckett in Performance* (1989) and Enoch Brater's *The Drama in the Text* (1994) clearly reveal how voice — 'orality' in Brater's terminology — links Beckett's world of theatre to the realms of his prose. Eric Levy called his study of the late prose *Beckett and the Voice of Species* (1980); thirty years later, Sarah West published her monograph *Say It: The Performative Voice in the Dramatic Works of Samuel Beckett* (2010). As Ackerley and Gontarski noted in a long entry in their *Companion*, from the beginning of his career, '[a] voice (word, and perhaps image) from the dark', that is, coming from nowhere, 'would provide [Beckett] with a compelling metaphor for his art of aporetics,

---

[1] Julie Campbell was one of the first scholars to investigate the BBC broadcasts of the prose systematically, in her essay 'Beckett and the Third Programme' (2013); see also Matthew Feldman's 'Beckett's Trilogy on the Third Programme' (2014) for more detail specific to *The Unnamable* on radio.

fragmentation, and disintegration' (Ackerley and Gontarski, 608). The origin of the voice remains elusive and inaccessible: it is unclear from where exactly the voice originates or to whom precisely it speaks. It is often located in the head of the protagonist, the character, the narrator, or an absent Other in the Lacanian sense. These mysterious voices become especially prominent after *Watt*, his novel written during the Second World War. Julie Campbell, in the first essay of this book, aptly argues that 'In much of Beckett's work from *Watt* onwards, the protagonists' awareness, even hyperawareness, of the inner voice is a crucial factor' (13).

The voice in Beckett first and foremost represents suffering and incomprehension; it lacks an origin and inflicts pain. Many characters, particularly in his post-war works, hear or perceive unknown voices. Llewellyn Brown notes the voice's imperative nature, quoting Steven Connor's phrase: 'a voice without a visible source is — precisely because it manifests itself as voice — endowed with a particularly imperative force, with "the power of a less-than-presence which is also a more-than-presence"' (11). The voice does not have an identity; therefore, in that sense, it has 'the power of a less-than-presence', but it targets the listener's 'essence of being' manifesting itself as 'a more-than-presence'.

In fact, such unidentifiable voices and their relation to being are fully explored by Jacques Lacan and his successors. Many contemporary analyses of the voice have been informed by Lacan's psychoanalytical seminars, on which other critics such as Slavoj Žižek or Kaja Silverman in film studies have later expanded. Lacan's theory is embedded in the poststructuralist ideas that emerged in the second half of the twentieth century, and since then, Beckett's work, in its preoccupation with the multiplication and dislocation of the self, repetition and bodily fragmentation, has given rise to a substantial body of critical work that recognises in his texts a deconstructive poetics. This perspective has offered a fruitful gateway to classify Beckett as a poststructuralist writer, although we cannot deny that many arguments may be brought in to side him with the modernists. Much closer to the truth is that Beckett escapes these easy categorisations, by moving to and fro between different linguistic and ideological positions. His characters exist neither here nor there but in limbo (or perhaps purgatory). In this sense, it may come as no surprise that the voice, as the oxymoronic representation of the presence of absence, is a predominant motif in Beckett's work, and serves as an excellent metaphor for this ambiguous position between being and non-being.

In line with Lacan's update of Freud based on Ferdinand de Saussure's linguistic semiotics, self-alienation in Beckett seems rooted in the implementation of the symbolic order and the subject's appropriation of language. Within the process of differentiality that structures the operations of the signifier, the voice is considered the leftover, the last signifier of that which cannot be symbolised. Signification is always postponed due to the incessant process of referral among signifiers. Meaning, in other words, crystallises in the void between the signifiers, rather than being inherently attached to them. In this play of circulation where signification exists (or ex-sits) due to absence, it comes across as somewhat paradoxical that the voice — nothing but air and vibrations — as what Lacan calls an *objet a*, exemplifies the halt from where this mill is set in motion, the 'real' presence in a world of absence. And yet, despite redefining the concept of the *objet a* many times in the course of his career, Lacan holds fast to its imaginary nature, thus not attributing it entirely to the realm of the Real. Therefore, the voice stays in its ambiguous nature as seen in Beckett, resonating a presence that has irredeemably been lost. Through the voice, language becomes possible, giving birth to the subject and to desire, yet also to its lack.

Echo holds up a mirror to our own restrictions, as we, as linguistic beings, can only make use of the words that we have at our disposal (Clov: 'I use the words you taught me'), but that will always remain external and alien to ourselves (Vladimir: 'What is terrible is to have thought'). In his highly idiosyncratic writing in between English and French, Beckett fights this battle at the cutting edge. Language presents itself as the enemy that needs to be overcome by its own means. Self-translation from English to French or French to English, with the 'deconstruction' of grammar and the ambiguous use of punctuation (or lack thereof), is a way to make it possible for Beckett to set one language against another, or words against other words, in order to escape the rationality of language and touch upon the sensuality of sounds.

Beckett was also well acquainted with psychoanalysis due to his own sessions with Wilfred Bion and his numerous readings in the matter. Along with the gaze, another ungraspable *objet a*, from which a subject flees from themselves, the voice functions in his work as an important origin of his characters' development of self-alienation. Hence, amidst the fragmentation of the self, the question of who is speaking is one of the most urgent ones in Beckett (*Texts for Nothing*: 'What matter who's speaking?')

Closely related to self-alienation as a result of the subject's introduction in the symbolic order is the idea of loss. Beckett's texts express a strong sense of nostalgia for what has gone for good. Because this longing for the past is, however, only very rarely identified, it is perhaps more useful to speak of melancholy, a state of mind in which, according to Freud, the subject has primarily lost itself. For even when the characters' loss is concretised, as in *Krapp's Last Tape* or *That Time*, underlying this search of lost time is always the lingering anxiety of the trauma of birth, and the unnamable desire that has sprouted from it. Hence, the wish of what one might call self-authorship conflicts with the expulsive, even excremental nature of the human that breaks up any initial harmonious unity.

Not only does the voice exemplify the presence of the subject; its ephemeral nature equally points at the subject's perpetual disappearance. Moreover, even before the voice serves as the vehicle for the foreign body called language, it is made up of nothing but air, which is necessary in order to live but transient and intangible at the same time. *Breath* probably best exemplifies the traumatic ambiguity on which human existence is built. The mechanical amplification of the breath in this playlet enhances the sense of one's own foreignness. The first breath when a human being breathes at his/her birth marks the onset of being-in-the-world, a world that is moreover filled with rubbish, nothing like the harmonious and perfectly clean isolation of the inside of the womb. Illumination in the play does lead to the presence of a voice, but it is inarticulate: the 'vagitus' of the newborn, a cry that is an instinctual response to the state of being (Hamm: 'You're on earth, there's no cure for that!').

In such an inharmonious world, one becomes hesitant to speak language, being swayed by the sense of foreignness. Beckett pushes this hesitation to the denial of wording, in other words, silence or silencing, as he gropes towards what he calls, in the 'German Letter' of 1937, 'a literature of the unword'. However, the narrator of Beckett's work cannot 'silence' a voice coming from nowhere, when it is ungraspable whether it is an inner voice or a voice outside. It annoys the listener, so that he gets obsessed with his desire to kill it; Beckett calls it 'Mental thuggee' in *Eh Joe*.

The narrator in the post-war prose works, such as *The Unnamable* and *Texts for Nothing*, struggles to locate this voice in vain. The narrator of *Texts for Nothing* tries to hear 'the voice of silence, the voice of my silence' (Text 10, 125); however, simultaneously, the voice just 'murmurs' without any sense so that the narrator longs for the 'silencing of silence', silencing 'the voice which is silence' (Text 13, 139). Therefore, the narrator is destined to hear and narrate a story by naming the unnamable: an *a priori* impossible task. Beckett's ongoing struggle with language and form in his writing is the challenge to this impossibility, such that he must 'fail better' again and again to progress 'worstward'.

During the same period that Beckett was wrestling with a voice in his prose works, he wrote *Waiting for Godot*. In the theatre, he seemed to discover more possibilities to express even without language, instead using actors' bodies, other media, lighting and sets. However, his challenge to language and form was still explored within his theatre pieces, in which the narrative structure of a vocal bifurcation continues to play an important part. The spectators or listeners of Beckett's plays concentrate on the narrative that an actor transmits through his/her voice, sometimes through recorded voice. His post-war theatre work thus effectively enacts some of the schemes experimented within his prose, perhaps due to the fact that the performative voice he writes on the page can best be heard and listened to through an actor's body or a technological medium on stage. In other words, voice can be materialised through stage enactment. Thus, the theatre made it possible for Beckett to express his multi-layered voices through crossing various genre boundaries (novels/plays and radio/television), while always running the risk of destroying the constitutive ambiguity achievable in the 'invisibility' of the prose. When this ambiguity is preserved through careful directorial, scenographic, and performative strategies, the theatre audience, radio listeners or TV viewers hear an enacted voice in performance, but it could either be an inner voice or voices emerging from a place outside the character in the narrative.

Beckett crossed spiritual and metaphysical boundaries as well as those of genre. For example, Vladimir and Estragon in *Waiting for Godot* listen to 'all the dead voices' — the voices of the dead, and the protagonist of *Footfalls* hears the voice of her dead mother. Many characters in Beckett's later plays are either in the process of dying or dead, in a form of limbo in which they are often annoyed by an 'unnamable' voice they cannot silence, despite also fearing that same silence. Even still, the voice in Beckett does not necessarily manifest itself as language or words, but rather as a cry, a whisper, or just an utterance, a murmur — a vocal sound. It can also be music, as in his radio plays such as *Words and Music* and *Cascando*. The musicality of the voice is often as important as the words spoken in narrative form. In *Rockaby*, the musicality of the woman's voice follows the movement of a rocking chair that swings like a metronome.

Voices are also heard in relation to technology. Beckett was an early adopter of various new technologies not only as media for delivery of his work, but also as features within his theatre, from films to radios, televisions to tape-recorders. In the early stages of those media, they were thought uncanny and often regarded as something fearful because they allowed voices to come from the air; that which is seen or heard through machines has no physicality, unanchored from the mouth or the body, allowing an utterance without embodied origin. The affordance of a voice arriving from some unknown and invisible source particularly intrigued Beckett. Seeking for a language that might express the ineffable and unspeakable, Beckett found in new technology the possibility to convey the forgotten voices of the past or even the dead.

In one of the most widely cited examples of this temporal shift, Krapp in *Krapp's Last Tape* listens to his own voice that he tape-recorded himself decades ago. From the fact that technology rendered the voice's immateriality possible, Beckett perceived the drama of an absent voice or a ghostly past manifested through technological devices. The sense of absence or silence associated with these voices becomes particularly prominent through the realm of radio, television and film. Beckett's genre-crossing oeuvre makes it possible to transfer his works to other media, yet his ontological and phenomenological suspicion of a too-defined voice makes this inherently challenging.

This volume carries forward all of the debates addressed in this introduction so far, from Lacan and trauma to cinema, broadcast, technology, and adaptation. Julie Campbell's opening essay on the inner voice in *Watt* makes clear that Beckett's fascination with the voice manifested in *Watt* 'had a great influence on his decision to write plays, especially for the radio'. She especially focuses on the fact that the narrator of *Watt* is listening to his own inner voice, a feature which will be more deeply explored in Beckett's post-war drama. After this introductory section dedicated to the 'seed' of voice present in Beckett's prose, the rest of the book is divided into five sections.

The first section, 'Musicality of Voices', addresses how such inner voices of Beckett's protagonists express something important through their musicality and sounds, rather than by the meanings of words. Linda Ben-Zvi examines how Beckett deliberately calls attention to sounds, how they often structure his works, and how they provide the only sense possible. As she repeatedly quotes Beckett's own words, his work was 'a matter of fundamental sounds (no joke intended), made as fully as possible', while being at the same time a striving towards 'a literature of the unword'. Thus, what the voices in Beckett speak or utter often makes no sense, but nonetheless retains a poetic beauty and musicality, obtaining meaning through the force of sound. It is well-known that Beckett was intensely attuned to the enunciation of his text when he directed his plays. More than on the meanings of words, he focused on sound, pace, pitch, and tempo of speaking lines. He created his work as if it were a musical score, a metaphor still in use by the Beckett Estate today, and directed as if he were a conductor. Michiko Tsushima asks why sounds and music are more important than the meaning of words and notes how Beckett opts ultimately for music over words themselves. By using Schopenhauer, Tsushima focuses on Beckett's radio plays, particularly *Words and Music* and *Cascando*, that present the materiality of language as the finitude of language while music can express the immaterialised ineffable. In a linguistic approach, Jürgen Siess analyses the way Beckett fully exploits the possibilities of *Embers* to complexify the polyphonic structure as defined by Ducrot. In this radio play, Henry, an old man, is desperately looking for his lost interlocutors, but cannot control the voices in his head, which is why 'an incoherent discourse is produced that does not allow for the constitution of a self-identity'.

The second section pivots from the materiality of the outer voice to seeing voice as an immaterial absent Other. In Beckett, the inner voices and noises tend to grow alienated and lose their owners; in other words, they are in fact 'outer voices/noises' for the original possessors. The second section, entitled 'Voices of an Absent Other', therefore philosophises Beckett's subject from the starting point of the voices that are unidentified and absent as Other. Llewellyn Brown examines how 'the voice creates a void in the subject, caused by the absence of any guarantee from the Other' by overturning the Lacanian jouissance, breaking up syntactic structure and removing punctuation. Laurens De Vos, especially focusing on the background noise of the scratch on Krapp's tape-recorder, concludes that such noise conflicts with the silence spoken of in the narrative. Comparing Beckett's English text with his French translation, Kumiko Kiuchi analyses how Beckett's rereading of Proust's *À la recherche du temps perdu* and the 'depersonalised' stage figure in Beckett's German production influenced the change of the title from *That Time* to *Cette fois* and of names from 'Listener' to 'Souvenant'. S. E. Gontarski uses Gilles Deleuze's idea of 'a process, a constant becoming' or 'ghostly dimensions' seen in Beckett's 'un-bodied voices' to define 'in-betweenness' in Beckett's approach to any value in this world, whose 'neural theatre' ultimately opens up new theatrical possibilities in the future.

The third section explores the dimension of trauma both arising from, and expressed through, Beckett's voices. Beckett's protagonists are filled with inner voices and noises that express their repressed memories and trauma of birth and death. Often, such traumatic voices and existential noises are represented in non-verbal imageries, lighting, bodily movements, and even silences. Svetlana Antropova focuses on the repressed memory of birth and death emerging from May's pacing movement and theatrical lighting, while Teresa Rosell Nicolás, finding in the image of the woman in *Rockaby* similarities to paintings by Whistler and Van Gogh, observes the woman in a rocking chair as just a vulnerable object, who, as if she were a baby, can control neither her recorded voice coming from outside nor the rocking movement of her chair. Anna McMullan offers a new reading of the radio play *All That Fall* from an ecocritical perspective. The protagonist Maddy's voice is paralleled with animal sounds, which are 'voices of the more than human' transmitted through her perspective. Voices of both Maddy and animals are vulnerably victimised by the threatening world of machine and technology. Arthur Rose deals with the way Beckett attempts to approach Friedrich von Schiller, who has been often dismissed in Beckett studies because of Beckett's critical view of the eighteenth-century German writer. He demonstrates that Beckett's theatre through his post-war years continued to follow Schiller's aesthetics in playwriting by seeking for the beauty and harmony of visible forms and by emphasising feeling over rationality. In both Beckett's and Schiller' aesthetics, beauty emerges from the political and the ethical.

The section on 'Cinematic Voices' demonstrates that Beckett's plays are filled with both verbal and visual images that he studied in the mid-1930s through his readings of early film theories, and notes that such plays are therefore more adaptable to cinema. Mariko Hori Tanaka contemplates the narrative voice of the Speaker in *A Piece of Monologue*, which projects filmic images onto the mental screen within audience minds. She discusses how the narration of the Speaker reflects early film theories that Beckett must have been familiar with. Anna Sigg explores traumatic voices as Lacanian *objet a* in four different film versions of *Breath*, while Thirthankar Chakraborty tells us how Beckett's plays, which resist Western traditional forms and conventions, fit well in the postcolonial era with a detailed discussion of an Indian cinematic adaptation of *Come and Go*.

The last section, 'Enacted Voices in Performance and Media', explores the staging possibility of voices in Beckett's plays — whether faithful to the text or not — in theatre and other media. Nicholas E. Johnson and Cathal Quinn discuss how to enunciate Beckett's voice on stage through various training methods that have been developed recently, using the form of the dialogue to 'activate' a different scholarly voice. Melissa Nolan explores what happens to the actor's body during the rehearsal and performance process when performing Beckett. It is well-known from some testimonies by Billie Whitelaw, for example, that many Beckettian actors undergo physical and mental suffering and pain. Nolan, an actor who has performed many Beckett works, records her own experience of performing Beckett. Yoshiko Takebe considers the adaptability and intermediality of Beckett's plays, which can be exemplified through some Japanese staged versions of Beckett's theatrical pieces. Also explored in this section are the significance of the TV studio as a physical space in the production of Beckett's TV plays, and the possibilities and problems that arise when Beckett's radio plays are transported to other media. Jonathan Bignell probes into the former question of TV studio space where Beckett questioned ideas of technological progress and dwelled on outdated aesthetic forms by using actors' voices and bodies. Everett C. Frost records Beckett's reluctance to allow his radio plays to be produced on stage and offers some examples of staged radio plays produced without permission of Beckett and his heirs. He believes that there must be 'a visual way of conveying our indebtedness to Beckett's script and its radiophonic origins — re-routing without being imprisoned by them', which we believe should be applicable to any work of Beckett, not limited to radio plays.

Both for readers of this book who move from its beginning to its end in order, as well as for readers who read only one section, a feeling of multiplicity — that happy destabilisation one feels after leaving a crowded, multilingual conversation at the end of a conference or a working group dinner — would not be an unfortunate outcome from our editorial perspective. The oscillation between 'Voicing Beckett' and 'Beckett's Voices', the tension between legacies and origins, the diversity of strategies and range of methodologies, philosophical frameworks, and references: all this is a feature of contemporary Beckett Studies, not a bug. The book will focus on the theatrical oeuvre, but in so doing, it is impossible not to consider other media. In addressing how the voices in Beckett centre on ontological and psychoanalytical subjects in the realm of the inner life, it is not possible to exclude how they are related to cultural and theatrical circumstances and to today's burning philosophical issues in the outer life. Presented with such voices, our strategy has been mainly to listen as closely as we can, to seek a diverse range of academic and practitioner voices, some at close range and some far afield, some from the discipline's past and some from its future. We suspend these voices here and now, somewhere between digital evanescence and material certitude, in the medium of the book.

Works Cited

Ackerley, C. J. and S. E. Gontarski, eds. (2006), *The Faber Companion to Samuel Beckett*, London: Faber and Faber.

Beckett, Samuel (1994), *Three Novels: Molloy, Malone Dies, The Unnamable*, New York: Grove Press.

Beckett, Samuel (1967), *Texts for Nothing* in *Stories and Texts for Nothing*, New York: Grove Press.

Beckett, Samuel (1996), *Worstward Ho* in *Nohow On*, with an introduction by S. E. Gontarski, New York: Grove Press.

Brown, Llewellyn (2016), *Beckett, Lacan and the Voice*, Stuttgart: Ibidem.

Campbell, Julie (2013), 'Beckett and the Third Programme', *SBT/A*, 25: *Beckett in the Cultural Field / Beckett dans le champ culturel*, Amsterdam: Rodopi, pp. 109–22.

Feldman, Matthew (2014), 'Beckett's Trilogy on the Third Programme', *SBT/A*, 26: *Revisiting* Molloy, Malone meurt / Malone Dies *and* L'Innomable / The Unnamable, Amsterdam: Rodopi, pp. 41–62.

Listening to the Inner Voice in *Watt*: Innovations in Narrative Form

Julie Campbell

Abstract

This chapter clarifies how important the inner voice is in relation to Beckett's artistic practice, by tracing the ways in which Beckett's own listening to his inner voice is reflected in his novel *Watt*. Completed in 1945, *Watt* was written, in the main, during the Second World War, before Beckett began to write drama for the stage and for radio, where voices are made manifest, sounded, and listened by the audience. His fascination with the voice must surely have had a great influence on his decision to write plays, especially for the radio. In *Watt* there is an intriguing confusion concerning the position of the narrator (or narrators), which at times seems omniscient, at times first person, and also a perplexing mix of both. This essay will relate this procedure with Beckett's own, as the narrator of *Watt* can be interpreted as listening to his own inner voice.

∴

> [E]xpression of the within can only be from the within.
> Samuel Beckett to Aidan Higgins (2 April 1958)

∵

1 The Inner Voice

Watt marks a crucial place in the evolution of Beckett's work. It was his last work in English for a period of eleven years; he turned to writing in French, and did not return to English until he wrote the radio play *All That Fall* (completed in 1956). As he spent most of wartime in Roussillon, in unoccupied France (1942–5), his library of books and notebooks full of research was left behind in Paris, and thus he was forced to move away from his former method involving a plethora of erudite allusion, which is a salient feature of his earlier work such as *Dream of Fair to Middling Women* (completed in 1932) and

Murphy (completed in 1936). It marks a move away from the influence of Joyce towards a far more individual approach, which places a strong reliance on his inner voice.

A very significant element in Beckett's work, especially present in his work from *Watt* onwards, is the focus on characters listening to their inner voices. Recent cognitive theories concerning listening to the inner voice are pertinent to considerations of Beckett's presentation of the inner voice in *Watt*, and help to clarify Beckett's strong and prescient understanding of the phenomenon. Inner speech is, as Don Ihde clarifies, something that is a quite normal and necessary phenomenon: it is 'an *almost continuous* aspect of self-presence. [...] As an *accompaniment* to the rest of experience it is a most "inward" continuity of self-presence' (137; italics original). He describes inner speech as 'a special type of auditory imagination' (137). However, it is not always attended to, as it is 'hidden, fragile, and difficult to locate' (136). Daniel C. Dennett explains that sometimes the voice is silent, but at other times it is voiced, and sometimes there are only 'the faintest shadows or hints of words' (59). Inner speech can be an unconscious process, unheeded or intermittently heeded on a conscious level.[1] Clearly Beckett paid close attention to his own inner voice, as it was essential to his art: Martin Esslin wrote of how he

> once asked Beckett how he went about his work. He replied that he sat down in front of a blank piece of paper and then waited till he heard the voice within him. He faithfully took down what the voice said — and then, he added, of course, he applied his sense of form to the product. (206)

This process is not an easy one to master, as inner speech, Ihde explains, 'bursts forth in rapid tonalities which present themselves as an uneven "flow". And unless attended to specifically it may be hard to recount just what words have been used at all' (142). And yet, as Donald G. Mackay confirms, 'The experience of inner speech is virtually universal', and he recognises that 'units resembling those required for producing inner speech are said to underlie writing' (121).

Beckett was clearly conscious of the way that his inner voice underlay his writing, and this places listening as a crucial, primary activity in relation to his art. The aim of this essay is to show how this focus on listening begins to become specifically prominent in Beckett's novel *Watt*. It is of significance

---

1   Uri Margolin writes of how a good deal of cognitive processing is '"unconscious", not being accompanied by any self-awareness or self-consciousness' (285).

that listening is also a crucial aspect of reading. Reading is a kind of listening, for readers will 'hear' the words they are reading: the auditory imagination is involved in an inner voicing or sub-vocalisation of the words. This is clearly apparent when reading the words of a narrator or character with a strong accent or dialect, when the reader 'hears' the specific way or speaking, even when unable to reproduce this when speaking the same words out loud.[2] This happens even in silent reading: as the eye follows the words on the page an inner voice silently sounds the words that the reader 'hears'. Inner speech is also involved in 'memory, learning and reasoning', and is a 'basic tool in human thought and problem solving' (Smith, 170), and thus has an important role in the reading process as regards the long- and short-term memory involved, and an intellectual and emotional engagement with the narrative.

In much of Beckett's work from *Watt* onwards the protagonists' awareness, even hyperawareness, of the inner voice is a crucial factor. It is perhaps unsurprising that this heightened attention to listening to the inner voice should become such an essential element of his art: this is how his art comes into being, and the world it brings to light has the obscurity, ambivalence and hidden quality of that spoken by an inner voice, and the fascination of glimpsing the dark, unfathomable and ineffable mystery beyond our understanding. Beckett is alert to the slippery qualities of inner speech: how inner speech is elusive and 'hard to grasp directly', and how it 'bursts forth in rapid tonalities which present themselves as an uneven "flow"' and '"jumps" and "changes key" almost constantly' (Ihde, 141–2).

2   The Inner Voice and Schizophrenia

Louise A. Sass's fascinating discussion in *Madness and Modernism* generally keeps the artist and the schizophrenic distinct, whilst suggesting intriguing resemblances and 'affinities' in relation to the intense inner focus and the turning away from the external, shared world (9). Beckett's own relation to his inner voice, as described to Esslin — 'He faithfully took down what the voice said — and then [...] he applied his sense of form' — is one in which both acceptance and control are apparent. What needs to be stressed in this

---

2   Reisberg, Wilson, and Smith comment on the way it is possible to 'subvocalize sounds [...] that one cannot vocalize' (70). Clearly this is true: not only in relation to sounds like those made by a hammer or a musical instrument, but also when reading, for example, an Irvine Welsh novel, and 'hearing' the Edinburgh accent but being quite unable to voice it out loud as accurately as it is 'heard' in the head.

description is the shaping activity of the artist which comes between the inner voice and the text that the reader reads. Beckett spoke of listening to the inner voice as initiating the artistic process, but the following stage of applying 'his sense of form' is of enormous significance. It is an artistic control, and in relation to the novel *Watt*, a reading of the earlier versions in manuscripts and typescripts at the Harry Ransom Humanities Research Center in Austin, Texas gives a sense of the vast amount of time this shaping process took in this particular case, and how much work this application of a 'sense of form' involved. It is clear that the activity was one of control: editing, reshaping and subtracting elements. There is a great deal in the earlier versions of *Watt* that is no longer present in the published text, although the 'Addenda' does allow glimpses, if fleeting ones, of some of the excised material.

Beckett's creation of his characters' inner voices can be related to schizophrenia, but some caution is required. G. C. Barnard considers that the protagonist Watt is a schizophrenic, and even more precisely 'a catatonic schizophrenic' (17). Sass's opinion is that Watt has a schizoid personality (58), and Beckett is included in a list of modernist artists considered as 'markedly schizoid persons' (367). And yet, in Beckett's case, it is far more valuable to keep the author and his characters distinct in relation to such diagnoses, as Shane Weller does when he contends that Beckett can be seen as intent on producing a language that 'he himself understood to be "schizophrenic"' (32). This places the intention as an artistic choice, an act of volition. The distinction is an important one, and is telling in relation to Beckett's powers of observation, for example in relation to the patients that he met when he visited the Bethlem Royal Hospital where his friend Dr. Geoffrey Thompson worked in 1935. In a letter to Thomas MacGreevy of September 1935, he wrote of how he felt:

> I was down at Bedlam this day week & went round the wards for the first time, with scarcely any sense of horror, though I saw everything, from mild depression to profound dementia. (Beckett, 2009, 277)

It may well be that in place of horror he felt both fascination and compassion. That this experience stayed with him is clear in that he recalled, thirty years later, observing a schizophrenic patient, and how strangely he appeared: 'There was no one there. He was absent' (Knowlson, 209). At the Beckett Archives at the University of Reading there is a recording of Thompson discussing Beckett and his abiding interest in psychology and psychoanalysis. He spoke of Beckett visiting him at the Bethlem Royal Hospital, and how he was fascinated by the patients who were most isolated and turned inwards, which Thompson recognised, in retrospect, as having a strong resemblance to characters in Beckett's work, who are often so introverted as to be completely immobilised: 'all that goes on goes on inside their heads', comments Thompson, both in relation to the patients Beckett showed most interest in, and his fictional characters: they 'had not really entered the world' (RUL MS4985).

Beckett read books on psychoanalysis and psychology, and made many notes; this was in 1934–35, when he was undergoing therapy with W. R. Bion, yet, as Weller points out, 'there is almost nothing in any of [his notes] on schizophrenia and no mention at all of the "schizoid voice" or of schizophrenic language' (38) (See Beckett's Psychology notebooks, TCD MSS 10971/7 and 10971/8). Beckett's reading of the work of Friedrich Hölderlin in 1938–39 is also significant; this took place very soon before he started working on *Watt* (Weller, 40–41). The fact that *Watt* quotes poetry by Hölderlin supports the idea of Beckett's creation of a 'schizophrenic' voice. Weller contends that 'it is arguably in the course of *Watt* that Beckett begins — but only begins — to pass from the thematisation [in *Murphy*] to the actualisation of that voice' (40). Weller's discussion focuses on later Beckett texts, and only refers glancingly to *Watt*, whereas this discussion will consider this novel specifically, in relation to the presentation of the inner voice: the methods used and the effects produced. It is the beginning of an important transformation in Beckett's work, which privileges the listening activity: it becomes an essential feature in the inception, the artistic process, and the reception of his work, as well as an increasingly more significant focus within many of the prose and the dramatic works.

3   The Third-Person Narrative Voice

Focusing on *Watt* allows an exploration of how Beckett set about attempting to achieve the actualization of the voice. His notebooks and his library of books were left behind in Paris, but he had his inner world to take their place. The change in direction evidenced in *Watt* can only be seen as a beginning of an innovative artistic approach that will become even more apparent in later work, but it is a crucial and significant beginning. It was also a difficult project to successfully fulfil. With *Watt* he decides not to plunge the reader into the strangeness immediately. He takes the reader through a frame, in the way a Gothic novel or story makes use of a frame: situating the reader within an apparently conventional and familiar third-person objectivity before moving into the fantastic and improbable situations. *Watt* commences with a framing device which in many ways is a familiar, if parodied, entry to a novel, meeting the expectations of a reader accustomed to more traditional narratives. *Watt* begins with what seems to be a third-person narrator, but one that is not entirely omniscient. The narrative voice appears to be placed in a conventional heterodiegetic position outside the narrative world, knowing more of a character within than it could know.

Sass considers that 'In reading Beckett, we find ourselves inside a head, listening to a kind of inner speech' (197). This is a valid way to describe many later works, but with *Watt* it is difficult to speak with certainty in relation to where the reader is placed. The reader does share a great deal with Watt: the strange, meandering thought processes and his convoluted attempts at explaining the events that take place, while also being told of the voices he hears. It may well be that we are situated as if inside a head, but, as I will argue, Sam's rather than Watt's.

In *Watt* there are many voices, and many levels of voices, noisy and jostling, causing great confusion concerning whose voices they are and where they emanate from. There are not only inner voices but also what seem to be conventional narrative and characters' voices, but these are treated oddly, with the familiar codes flouted, and many difficulties are placed for readers trying to make sense of the world, the characters, the setting and the events that are being told. The exposition of Watt lacks any real substance; even though it results from Mr. Hackett's 'burn[ing] with curiosity, and with wonder' (Beckett, 1963, 15), he, and thus the reader, learn very little. However, at the beginning of *Watt*, the readers can feel as if they are on familiar ground, up to a point, with a third-person narrative voice and the character, Mr Hackett, as focaliser:

> Mr. Hackett turned the corner and saw, in the failing light, at some little distance, his seat. It seemed to be occupied. This seat, the property very likely of the municipality, or of the public, was of course not his, but he thought of it as his. This was Mr. Hackett's attitude towards things that pleased him. He knew they were not his, but he thought of them as his. He knew they were not his, because they pleased him. (Beckett, 1963, 5)

The narrator clearly has access to Mr. Hackett's thoughts, and thus so has the reader, who 'sees' with him, and is told about what he thinks, although there is a lack of knowledge shown about the actual ownership of 'his seat'. There are dialogues, between Mr. Hackett and the policeman, and between Mr. Hackett and Mr. and Mrs. Nixon, whose first and last names we only learn when they are spoken to (the attribution moves from 'the lady' and 'the gentleman' to 'Tetty' and 'Goff'). It seems that their names need to be 'heard' before they are known. Yet these conversations have no connection with the future narrative, until Watt is introduced, who will be the protagonist of the novel, albeit a very unusual protagonist. His introduction is also very unusual. Watt's presence is alerted by the sound of a voice: 'the voice of the conductor, raised in anger' (Beckett, 1963, 14). But abruptly, after seventeen pages spent with Mr. Hackett, the narrator leaves him on his bench, looking 'towards the horizon that he had come out to see' (22). He is left in silence and does not appear again, and neither do any of the other characters in this opening section; the narrative voice now focuses on Watt.

It is as if the reader has been, for a short while, in the traditional third-person narrative situation. It is a frame a reader will recognise, but it may well be there for the very purpose of demonstrating just what this particular narrative does not intend to do: lead us through a familiar narrative structure which will to a large degree appear invisible, with the focus very much on the story that is being told rather than the telling. *Watt* will focus on telling and on listening. The opening frame is presented and then disappears. The reader may have grown interested in Mr. Hackett, and may be on tenterhooks as to his future activities, but he is presented and then disappears. It is an odd beginning, but the oddness of the narrative increases as the play with narrative voices continues.

As the narrative carries on it still appears to be presented by a third-person voice, clearly having access to Watt's thoughts and those of others; the reader is told of the contentment aroused in the 'connoisseurs on whom the exceptional quality of Watt was not lost' (Beckett, 1963, 23). When Watt boards the train a garrulous Mr. Spiro introduces himself, and talks to Watt, who must have heard the questions — 'Where do you get down, sir?' and 'I beg your pardon?' — as he answers him (26). But Mr. Spiro's questions and answers about 'a rat, or other small animal [eating] a consecrated wafer' are not attended to:

> But Watt heard nothing of this, because of other voices, singing, crying, stating, murmuring, things unintelligible, in his ear. With these, if he was not familiar, he was not unfamiliar either. So he was not alarmed, unduly. Now these voices, sometimes they sang only, and sometimes they cried only, and sometimes they stated only, and sometimes they murmured only, and sometimes they sang and cried, and sometimes they sang and stated, and sometimes they sang and murmured, and sometimes they cried and stated, and sometimes they cried and murmured, and sometimes they stated and murmured, and sometimes they sang and cried and stated, and sometimes they sang and cried and murmured, and sometimes they cried and stated and murmured, and sometimes they

sang and cried and stated and murmured, all together, at the same time, as now, to mention only these four kinds of voices, for there were others. And sometimes Watt understood all, and sometimes he understood much, and sometimes he understood little, and sometimes he understood nothing, as now. (Beckett, 1963, 27)

Watt is not listening to Mr. Spiro, but to voices, obviously inner voices, but the reader does not have access to what they sing, cry, state, or murmur, only a lengthy statement about the diversity of their singing, crying, stating, and murmuring. It is significant that there are many voices: 'four kinds' and 'others', and that Watt's understanding of the inner voices he hears varies, and at present 'he understood nothing'. Perhaps it is their unintelligibility that prevents their communication to the reader. This unintelligibility is supported by Smith, who notes that inner voices are 'rarely loud and clear — they whisper, mumble, mutter' (172). Mr. Spiro's discourse, however, unheard by Watt, is summarised for the reader. Watt's voices prevent him from hearing Mr. Spiro's lengthy discourse, and this is made abundantly clear: 'Watt heard nothing of this' (Beckett, 1963, 27). This is strange in itself. But it is stranger still when the reader later learns about the way this narrative is mediated. Watt's story comes to the reader, it is claimed, through the act of listening: much of it is a retelling of what has already been told. The narrative comes to seem like the story of the Galls: 'ill-told, ill-heard, and more than half forgotten' (Beckett, 1963, 71). But this brings to the fore a crucial, unavoidable question: how can Watt tell what he hasn't listened to? There is a mystery here.

When Watt arrives at Mr. Knott's house he meets a gentleman in the kitchen, who is later named as Arsene. Arsene makes a 'short statement' which is not short at all; in fact, it lasts for twenty-five pages: twenty-five pages of a dense, puzzling, unparagraphed 'statement', seemingly recounted in all its detail (Beckett, 1963, 37–62). But later the reader is told that Watt did not listen to what Arsene was saying: Arsene's 'declaration had entered Watt's ears only by fits, and his understanding, like all that enters the ears only by fits, hardly at all' (77). Why did he not pay attention? — 'something had prevented him, perhaps his fatigue' (77).

4 Listening to the Inner Voice in the First-Person Narrative

In a traditional narrative with a third-person, external narrator, the narrator, and thus the reader, is often in a position of knowing more than any of the characters in the narrative world. It is on page 123 that this position is undermined: an 'I' — a first-person voice — enters the narrative. All that this narrator knows, he tells the reader, 'came from Watt, and from Watt alone' (123). The whole narrative, the reader is now informed, comes from what Watt told this narrator; the narrator listened to Watt, and the result is the narrative the reader is reading. It is admitted that there may be omissions, and there may be elaborations: 'it is difficult for a man like Watt to tell a long story like Watt's without leaving out some things, and foisting in others' (124). Watt, as the reader has been told, did not always listen to what he was told, and this seems to be true of the narrator, too, shown in his confession:

> It is so difficult, with a long story like the story that Watt told, even when one is most careful to note down all at the time, in one's little notebook, not to leave out some of the things that were told, and not to foist in other things that were never told, never never told at all. (124–5)

Any reliability that the narrative may have had has been exploded. It is now to be perceived as a narrative dependent on the listening capacity of Watt, who has been shown not to be an attentive listener, and on his memory, already shown as fallible; it is also dependent on the listening capacity alongside the note-taking skills of another, who confesses to possible omissions and elaborations. Thus, the reader is encouraged to regard the narrative in its entirety as 'ill-told, ill-heard, and more than half forgotten' (71).

A new surprise is sprung on page 130: Watt tells his tale in reverse: 'Spoken as he spoke it, back to front' (130). Part III of the novel provides examples of Watt's odd way of telling his story, but this only results in further bafflement. Listening, it is clear, can be a precarious activity, requiring attention, lack of interference, and a good memory or good note-taking skills to retain what is heard. The first-person narrator, who calls himself Sam and Watt, hardly ever meet, and when they do, they often do not converse (149–51). Sam tells that 'when Watt spoke, he spoke in a low and rapid voice' which would clearly problematise listening. Watt's 'voice *at once* so rapid and so low, is hard to believe' (154; italics original). This links his voice with the inner voice: Mackay writes of how internal speech is far more rapid than spoken speech (144); Smith reports on how inner voices are described as often 'soft and mumbled' (159), 'muffled' and mere 'whispers' (158). Watt's voice could be Sam's inner voice, and this would be a possible interpretation: a possible alternative to the method described, which is impossible to give credence to. Beckett is engaged in undermining the suspension of disbelief in the reliability of the narrative method that is claimed, and is taking this subversion to comic extremes. Sam tells us that 'of [Watt's] impetuous murmur much fell in vain on my imperfect hearing and understanding, and much by the rushing wind was carried away, and lost for ever' (154). Sam also retells Watt's reversed discourse, and this reversal is another phenomenon of inner speech reported by Smith (161). Here is the first example, which begins: '*Day of most, night of part, Knott with now*' (Beckett, 1963, 162). The inversion goes further: 'no longer the order of the words in the sentence, but that of the letters in the word'; he gives an example, which begins: '*Ot bro, lap rulb, krad klub*' (163). Five more examples of inversions follow, ending with the example which begins: '*Dis yb dis, nem owt*' (166). These inversions do not make reading easy, and would make listening extremely difficult, not to mention note-taking. And Sam's listening deteriorates, as he tells of how his 'hearing now began to fail' (167).

The telling of the whole narrative, the reader is to understand, is as a result of Sam listening (imperfectly) to Watt telling his story (imperfectly). But how does this explain the fact that the reader is told of things that Watt did not witness, for example, at the beginning of the narrative: Mr. Hackett desiring and gaining his seat, the conversation between Mr. Hackett and Mr. and Mrs. Nixon, and Mr. Hackett, left alone on the seat in the dark? At the end of the narrative Watt must have boarded the five-fifty-five train, but this is not clarified from the narrative. It tells of Mr. Case, Mr. Gorman and Mr. Nolan, and the goat, and the sound of the clatter if it is pale and chain, becoming 'fainter and fainter' (245). There is no Watt, just 'the long wet dream with the hat and bags' (246), so how would Sam be able to recount this? The reader is also told of very long speeches, which Watt either did not hear at all, or did not listen to attentively, such as Mr. Spiro's and Arsene's.

Angela Moorjani contends that Watt is 'Sam's inverted mirror image' (1982, 31) emerging and fading 'into the shadows' (34), but if the focus is placed upon the auditory rather than the visual imagery, an alternative proposition is possible: Sam as Watt's echo. It is useful to take this idea of his echo figure further, further than is proposed within the text, and put forward the idea of Sam as a representative of the author within the text, listening to the voices within his head. This would suggest that Sam listens to the voice of Watt, a voice that fades in and out of his auditory perception, as is delineated within the text, and Watt can also be considered as an inner voice of Sam who is in turn also able to listen: listening in to a yet lower level of inner voices, yet only to some of them, and failing to listen to others. This suggests a multiplicity of voices, and many of these could be being accessed by Sam, including those not attended to by Watt. There is a layering of voices: voices within voices, and a layering of listening. Moorjani has discussed, insightfully, the multiple narrative levels, as 'embeddings inside embeddings', and has also made references to the echoing of voices, discussing their vertical alignment: 'Hackett's voice echoes Sam's which echoes Watt's which echoes the voices within Watt and so on infinitely' (36),[3] whereas the suggestion here is that Sam is echoing all the voices, which are intermittently perceptible to him, and as such is the representative within the fiction of that other Sam: Samuel Beckett. The various voices are given names which, in relation to Watt (what?) and Knott (not or naught) summon up the idea of their namelessness. The arbitrariness of naming is present in the way that the names change during the process of shaping the narrative in the early drafts: 'Molloy' and 'Quin' to Knott, 'we' and 'Johnny' to Watt. *Watt*, especially when considered alongside the earlier versions, provides many intriguing insights into Beckett's artistic process at this stage, and anticipates his future experimentation regarding this focus on listening to inner voices which would become of even greater significance in later work.

Watt removes its readers from that seemingly safe, conscious, rational world of so-called objective reality and has them share in an 'escape into the spacious annexe of mental alienation' (Beckett, 1965, 32). One of the significant results is that the seemingly ordered world of so-called 'reality' now appears, in comparison, as a fictional construct. The reader is made aware of the effects of 'Habit' described by Beckett in *Proust* (1931) as the 'minister of dullness' which acts as 'a screen to spare its victim the spectacle of reality' (Beckett, 1965, 21). Beckett suggests that 'the only world that has reality and significance [is] the world of our own latent consciousness' (13). The novel leaves the rational world behind and enters an unknown and unknowable space, which resists attempts, however valiant, to foist upon it a sense of order, control and structure. Beckett's shaping process shows a strong awareness of the futility of such an enterprise, and the realisation that there is within 'our own latent consciousness' much that will never be known, that will never lose its strangeness. *Watt* has encouraged the reader to listen to many voices: inner voices, and even voices within voices, and in the process created a comedy out of failure — the failure to tell, the failure to listen, and thus the failure to communicate.

Works Cited

Barnard, G. C. (1970), *Samuel Beckett: A New Approach: A Study of the Novels and Plays*, New York: Dodd, Mead & Co.

---

[3] Moorjani discusses the layering of voices, describing the 'embedded narrative series' that occurs in *Watt*. She concurs with the idea that 'while Sam listens to Watt, Watt in turn listens to an inner, unidentified voice', citing Sam's observation that 'Watt spoke as one speaking to dictation, or reciting, parrot-like, a text, by long repetition become familiar' (1982, 28).

Beckett, Samuel (1984), *All That Fall*, in *Collected Shorter Plays of Samuel Beckett*, London: Faber and Faber, pp. 9–39.
Beckett, Samuel (1993), *Dream of Fair to Middling Women*, London: John Calder.
Beckett, Samuel (2009), *The Letters of Samuel Beckett* Vol. I, 1929–1940, ed. Martha Dow Fehsenfeld and Lois More Overbeck, Cambridge: Cambridge UP.
Beckett, Samuel (1973), *Murphy*, London: Picador.
Beckett, Samuel (1965), *Proust and Three Dialogues with Georges Duthuit*, London: John Calder.
Beckett, Samuel (1963), *Watt*, London: John Calder.
Beckett, Samuel, 'Watt, Composite T and Tccms/inc with A revisions and A note S', The Harry Ransom Humanities Research Center at the University of Texas at Austin.
Dennett, Daniel C. (1991), *Consciousness Explained*, Boston: Little, Brown & Company.
Esslin, Martin (1991), 'Telling it How It Is: Beckett and the Mass Media', in J. E. Smith, ed., *The World of Samuel Beckett*, Baltimore: The Johns Hopkins UP, pp. 204–16.
Ihde, Don (1976), *Listening and Voice: A Phenomenology of Sound*, Ohio: Ohio UP.
Knowlson, James (1996), *Damned to Fame: The Life of Samuel Beckett*, London: Bloomsbury.
Logie, Robert H., and Michel Denis, eds. (1991), *Mental Images in Human Cognition*, Amsterdam: Elsevier Science Publishers.
Mackay, Donald G. (1992), 'Constraints on Theories of Inner Speech', in Reisberg, pp. 121–49.
Margolin, Uri (2003), 'Cognitive Science, the Thinking Mind, and Literary Narrative', in D. Herman, ed., *Narrative Theory and the Cognitive Sciences*, Chicago: CLSI (U of Chicago P), pp. 271–94.
Moorjani, Angela (1982), *Abysmal Games in the Novels of Samuel Beckett*, Chapel Hill, NC: U of North Carolina P.
Moorjani, Angela (2004), '"Peau de chagrin": Beckett and Bion on Looking Not to See', *SBT/A*, 14: *After Beckett / D'après Beckett*, pp. 25–38.
Reisberg, Daniel, ed. (1992), *Auditory Imagery*, Hillsdale, NJ: Lawrence Erlbaum.
Reisberg, Daniel, Meg Wilson, and J. David Smith (1991), 'Auditory Imagery and Inner Speech', in Logie and Denis, pp. 59–81.
Sass, Louise A. (1992), *Madness and Modernism: Insanity in the Light of Modern Art, Literature, and Thought*, Cambridge: Harvard UP.
Smith, David J. (1991), 'The Auditory Hallucinations of Schizophrenia', in Reisberg (1992), pp. 151–78.
Thompson, Geoffrey, no date. Recorded talk on Samuel Beckett. MS4985. Beckett International Foundation, University of Reading.
Weller, Shane (2009), '"Some Experience of the Schizoid Voice": Samuel Beckett and the Language of Derangement', *Forum for Modern Language Studies*, 45:1, pp. 32–50.

PART 1

Musicality of Voices

Sound Matters in Beckett

Linda Ben-Zvi

Abstract

It is hard to think of another writer whose characters talk so incessantly about talking and yearn so vocally and vociferously for silence as do Samuel Beckett's fictive people. Like their author, they are acutely aware that the voice that pours out words will never part the dark, since 'nothing is sayable' (Beckett, qtd. in Juliet, 39). Therefore, if meaning is not the promised or hoped-for end, what better way to show the penury of language than to foreground how the voice sounds rather than what it says. Although there has been a proliferation of sound studies in numerous fields, they have tended to overlook Beckett's writing, despite the fact that he is, as this essay argues, the consummate creator of sound, whose finely-tuned ear and sense of musicality allow him to use alliterative repetitions of phonemes, tempos, rhythms, cadences, echoes, and noises to create works in which aurality ultimately becomes as powerfully evocative on the stage as on the page, ear often usurping eye in the sensory hierarchy. Discussing his works in relation to central theories of sound theorists, particularly Don Ihde, the essay traces Beckett's concern with sound, from his earliest fiction 'Assumption' to his later plays, particularly *Not I*, as well as his directorial work, to make the case that, as Beckett famously acknowledged, 'My work is a matter of fundamental sounds' (Harmon, 24), and that in all his writing sound matters.

The subject of sound in Beckett's writing has, over the years, received little discrete attention.[1] Despite an ever-increasing number of works across disciplines, including theatre and performance practices, such as Lynne Kendrick and David Roesner's edited collection *Theatre Noise: The Sound of Performance* and Mladen Ovadija's *Dramaturgy of Sound in the Avant-garde and Postdramatic Theatre*, a study which he describes as revealing 'sound and voice as the autonomous materials [that] led to the disruption of the logocentric rational framework of the traditional literary and dramatic form' (7), the former has only one essay related to Beckett; the latter does not even mention his name. The reason is apparent: their focus is on postdramatic theatre which, though denying the efficacy of language to convey meaning — as Beckett does —

---

1 For two early essays focusing on sound in Beckett, see Perloff and Ben-Zvi (1987).

traces its origins back to the theories and works of Antonin Artaud.[2] And just as the first iteration of Artaudian influence in the late 1960s through early 1980s, at least in the United States, drew a line between performativity and text, performer and playwright, and actions and words, these studies, following in the footsteps of Hans-Thies Lehmann and Erika Fischer-Lichte, assume that the centrality of sound in performance is found only in postdramatic not text-based theatre. They ignore the ways in which Beckett's uses and manipulations of sound in his writing animate and delineate his characters and their world, disrupting precisely what Ovadija calls 'the logocentric rational framework' (7), in the quote cited above.

It is not difficult to find evidence in Beckett's works of his skillful and purposeful use of sound as technique and theme. As the unnamed voice in *Text 13*, the last of the *Texts for Nothing*, says: 'there is nothing but a voice murmuring a trace. A trace, it wants to leave a trace, yes, like air leaves among the leaves, among the grass, among the sand' (Beckett, 1995, 152). Through the proliferation of *s* sounds created by *s* and *ce*, as well as the homonym 'leaves' as verb and noun, Beckett illustrates the condition that the speaker in the text describes: 'Whose voice, no one's, there is no one, there's a voice without a mouth, and somewhere a kind of hearing' (152).

Rather than creating units of language for the purpose of imparting specific meaning in such works, Beckett employs sound patterns that deny any fixity in words, while providing a 'kind of' visceral, auditory experience: 'something compelled to hear' (152). His writings, like musical compositions, provide an auditory experience, through the consummate use of tempos, rhythms, cadences, echoes, as well as alliterative phoneme repetitions — particularly sibilant *s*, voiced plosives *d* and *g*, and voiceless plosives *t* and *k* — to create works in which aurality in his fiction destabilises language and calls attention to its paucity, and sound in his plays, most noticeably in his later works, provides the means by which audiences experience the power of performance, ear often usurping eye, in that sensory hierarchy that traces back to Aristotle.

1   Sound Sense

Adam Piette begins *Remembering and the Sound of Words: Mallarmé, Proust, Joyce, Beckett* with an exchange between Shelley and Byron, reported in 1830

---

[2] For a discussion of the relationship between Artaud's theories and Beckett's dramas, and the difficulty of uniting them, see De Vos.

by Mary Shelley, in which Shelley argues that a line, as well as 'your outspread heroics, or a tragedy', might stand 'as a whole, beautiful in itself', because of its carefully chosen and balanced alliterative sound play, citing, as example, Shakespeare's, 'How sweet the moonlight sleeps upon this bank'. 'Heavens', Byron retorts, 'Do you imagine, my dear Shelley, that Shakespeare had any thing of the kind in his head when he struck off that pretty line? If any one had told him all this about your *p*'s and *s*'s, he would just have said, "Pish!" [...] The beauty of the line does not lie in sounds and syllables, and such mechanical contrivances, but in the beautiful metaphor of the moonlight sleeping'. But it is the '[c]adence', 'sound', and 'alliteration', explains Shelley, that 'provide the sense that the metaphor imparts', thus making it 'beautiful'. 'Well, then', replies Byron, resting his case: 'I'm glad I'm not a poet [...] It must be like making out one's expenses for a journey, I think, all this calculation!' (qtd. in Piette, 3).[3] In this debate Shelley might be taken for the book-keeping critic Beckett pilloried in his defence of James Joyce's *Work in Progress*, but as a poet he understands the potential of sound to animate an object, turning a moon into a metaphor of beauty, akin to Beckett's own sense of the inherent possibilities of sound to escape the snares of language and, like music, create an illusiveness that unfixes and overrides the limits of semantic sense.

Byron's disparagement of the significance of sound has a long history in Western culture, going back to the ancient Greeks who assumed that the eye was the central, and most important, sensory organ. As Don Ihde argues, quoting Theodor Thass-Thienemann, Greek thinking was 'conceived in the world of light, in the Apollonian visual world' (6), the word for sight grammatically conjoined with the word for knowing, a relationship Aristotle assumed when he stated, 'Above all we value sight [...] because *sight is the principle* [sic] *source of knowledge* and reveals many differences between one object and another' (qtd. in Ihde, 7). Ihde points out that ultimately sight was tied to a metaphysics of objects; vision becoming the 'objective sense' (7), an assumption that has remained virtually unquestioned down to the modern period. Descartes, for example, believed as well that 'all the management of our lives depends on the senses [... and] that of sight is the most comprehensive and noblest of these' (65). So did Francis Bacon who, in *The Plan of the Instauratio Magna*, proclaimed: 'I admit nothing but on the faith of eyes' (qtd. in Bull and Back, 37). Only in the middle of the last century was the hegemony of the eye seriously questioned, starting in the early 1940s with the seminal writings of John Cage, followed in the 1970s with influential sound studies by Ihde, music theorist

---

3   Piette uses the quote from 'Text for Nothing 13' quoted above as epigraph for his book.

Murray Shafer, film theorists Christian Metz and Michel Chion, and economics philosopher Jacques Attali, who makes the case most succinctly: 'For twenty-five centuries Western knowledge has tried to look upon the world. It has failed to understand that the world is not for beholding. It is for hearing' (qtd. in Bull and Back, 1).

This silencing of sound, Jeff Porter suggests in his book *Lost Sound: The Forgotten Art of Radio Storytelling*, may have been premeditated, '[t]o restrict aurality to the letter of language in order to pre-empt any slippage between sound and sense', the fear being that when 'sound calls attention to itself, it evokes a capacity to transcend its referent, resonating in ways that are closer to music than language. Such sound-centeredness ushers in other meanings, including unintended associations, and therefore possesses the power to disturb word-meaning, thus upsetting the semantic order of language' (7–8). In a long discussion on *All That Fall*, he credits Beckett with the ability to 'complicate, if not resist, the symbolic order of language, and to take revenge on the *logos* for having devocalized language' (11).

What Porter describes is not limited to radio drama. In Beckett's case, from the beginning of his career he illustrated that objects are not as objectively defined by words and through sight as Aristotle posited. Even a lowly pot, Watt's pot, alters and dissolves the more one looks at it, and the more one says its name (Beckett, 1959, 81): the seen becoming, as Beckett writes in *Worstward Ho*, 'Misseen', the said 'Missaid' (Beckett, 1983, 7, 12, 35, 36). Through the repetition of the word 'pot', with its plosive *p*'s and *t*'s, the eye is not allowed to pass over the pot quickly, but is made to continually return to it, and with each repetition, sound ultimately detaches the name from its object, Aristotle's theory of eye as the means of objectivity becoming questionable. So too the *t*'s in pot, Watt, and Knott blur, confuse, and conflate the distinct names they represent, denying that 'semantic succour' (Beckett, 1959, 83) — another sibilant phrase — that Watt, and all subsequent Beckett people seek.

2 'Assumption'

As early as his 1937 letter to Axel Kaun, Beckett pondered the possibilities of using sound to bypass the limits of language, as he does through the proliferation of *s*'s he illustrates below:

> Is there any reason why that terrible materiality of the word surface should not be capable of being dissolved, like for example the sound surface, torn by enormous pauses, of Beethoven's Seventh Symphony, so that

through whole pages we can perceive nothing but a path of sounds suspended in giddy heights, linking unfathomable abysses of silence? (qtd. in Cohn, 1983, 172)

'On the way to this literature of the unword, which is so desirable to me, some form of Nominalist irony might be a necessary stage' (173), Beckett suggests to Kaun, perhaps having in mind his first published fiction, the brief short story 'Assumption', written eight years earlier, in which aurality powers the narrative development. Critics have tended to overlook or disparage the work, focusing primarily on expositional details, without paying enough attention to the ways in which it presents Beckett's initial parry against the snares of language by employing sounds described later in his Kaun letter, that can serve as a parse for the story.

'Assumption' begins, 'He could have shouted and could not' (Beckett, 1995, 3–7)[4] the 'and' in place of the expected 'but', functioning like those Beckett commas Steven Connor describes, that are 'appositional rather than compositional [... bringing] about coordinated rather than subordinated syntax' (2014, 61–62), creating in this way structural balance but capriciously undermining clarity. Since the modal auxiliary verb 'could' carries several meanings — ability, desire, need — it requires a main verb to indicate action. Instead, the second 'could' remains merely a verbal echo, rendering the sentence open, porous, and unfixed, the effect Beckett most likely sought, given the dream he described to Kaun of 'finding a method by which we can represent this mocking attitude towards the word, through words' (Cohn, 172). The second sentence, 'The buffoon in the loft swung steadily on his stick and the organist sat dreaming with his hands in his pockets', seems to dangle its verbal images in front of the reader, as if to say: 'You want explication; I'll give you explication'. Although the sentence again provides grammatical conjunction and specific description, it too fails to provide clarity. Instead, it aurally and rhythmically points to the central struggle that marks the story: action battling stasis played out in sound. The breathy f's in 'buffoon' and 'loft', as well as the sensuous s's in 'swung', 'steadily', and 'stick' placed as initial word sounds, create a sense of propelling action 'stead/i/ly' on, thereby animating the buffoon, while the s's in the concluding words of the sentence are final sounds evoking the static state of the 'or/gan/ist' — a syllabic but not sonic parallel to stead/i/ly — whose enervation is reinforced by the tempo created by

---

4 Because of the brevity of the story, I have not included page numbers.

the double-syllable word 'pockets', even more attenuated than its parallel one-syllable word 'stick'.[5]

These double-clausal sentences, specific yet unclear as they are, also point to the doubleness of the unnamed protagonist, 'he', a whisperer, unable or unwilling, like the conductor/organist, to produce more than 'driblets of sound': 'driblets', a near-onomatopoetic word, its *d*'s and *b*'s playing with, and off, its sibilant *s*, the kind of word Krapp would have savoured in the saying. In 'Assumption', the speaker refers to this inner voice as 'it', 'his prisoner', 'the enemy', whom he struggles to keep in check lest this voice emits 'a wild rebellious surge that aspired violently towards realization in sound', again a sentence sighing with sibilant *s*'s. Beckett's choice of the word 'aspired', indicating both breath and ascension, as well as sound and assumption, is an early example of his love of wordplay as well as soundplay, illustrating the slippery nature of words and the expandable meanings they carry. Here the doubling and punning on the title 'Assumption' implies that the character is striving, seeking, and ambitious, as well as fearful, should the vocalic outpouring of his suppressed, inner voice reveal that he has nothing to say or, worse, that the words mimic the sounds of others, perhaps Beckett's bow to Joyce, whose literary place he may have secretly wished to 'assume'.

While it may be tempting to equate 'he' with Beckett in 1929, 'withdrawn [...] within that terrifying silent immobility' in response to the threat of the Apollonian force of Joyce, more important to this discussion is the way in which Beckett shift senses in mid-tale by upending the initial Marsyan preoccupation with sound for the Apollonian desire for sight. If the first two paragraphs of the story focus on aurality, the next two suddenly shift to visuality, precipitated by 'the Woman', also unnamed, who inexplicably appeared, 'turned on the light and advanced carelessly into the room'. Rather than struggling against his fear of sound, the character now becomes entranced by the power of sight engendered by the materiality of the woman's body: 'the extraordinary pallor of her lips', their shape and protuberance; the shadows, shape, and colour of her eyes as the light highlights them; even the colour and style of her clothing. No longer that fierce, silent, parodic warrior against the mundane 'pleasure of Prettiness', described earlier, he is now engulfed in the sensory world of sight. But not for long. 'Then it happened', the narrator announces, opening

---

5 Such syllable play used to ironise and indicate meaning through aurality can be seen in later Beckett writing. For example, in *Waiting for Godot* when Vladimir says, 'Down in the hole lingeringly the grave-digger puts on the forceps' (Beckett, 1954, 58a), the four-syllable 'lin/ger/ing/ly' rhythmically points to the unendurable span of life 'on this bitch of an earth' (25b).

the penultimate section of the story in which the woman 'was swept aside by a great storm of sound, shaking the very house with its prolonged, triumphant vehemence, climbing in a dizzy, bubbling scale, until, dispersed, it fused into the breath of the forest and the throbbing cry of the sea'. The story ends in this climax of sound: a profusion of *s*'s spiralling upward combining with plosive *p*'s and *b*'s creating a poetic soundscape, echoing or parodying Shelleyesque poetry, that frees the voice but kills the man.

I have focused at length on this youthful, brief fiction because, although awkward and uncontrolled in places, it already reveals three struggles related to voices that will run through Beckett's subsequent writing. First is the ever-present struggle described in his writing between a character and his or her voice. Published forty-seven years after 'Assumption', 'Afar a Bird' also has an *I* speak of a *he* who seeks a voice for a *me*: 'it's impossible I should have a voice and I have none, he'll find one for me, ill beseeming me' (Beckett, 1995, 232–3). In the last decade of his life, Beckett still foregrounded pronominal uncertainty in *Company*, which begins: 'A Voice comes to one in the dark. Imagine' (Beckett, 1980, 7), an indefinite pronoun for an indefinite place, space, and self, whose materiality at best can only be imagined but not fixed in words. Second is the struggle between voice and meaning. As early as 'Assumption' and the Kaun letter, Beckett did not confuse the two, a tendency that some critics make when they invoke voice and quickly shift to what the voice says.[6] Mladen Dolar warns how easy it is, and dangerous, to conflate and confuse them, arguing that voice needs to be distinguished from the language it speaks. As he puts it, voice is assumed to have 'an intimate connection with meaning; it is a sound which appears to be endowed in itself with the will to "say something", with an inner intentionality'. However, it is 'strangely recalcitrant' about doing so. 'If we speak in order to "make sense", to signify, to convey something, then the voice is the material support of bringing about meaning, yet it does not contribute to it itself' (Dolar, 14–15). In other words, if meaning and clarity are not possible, something Beckett was aware of as early as 1929 and even earlier, what better way to show the failure of words than to foreground the sounds the voice produces rather than what it says. Third is the struggle between sound and image, harkening back in certain respects to the Shelley/Byron debate about the role of sound in the materialisation and power of metaphor and illusion. In 'Assumption' Beckett employs alliteration and repetition to conjure up images, such as the 'great storm of sound', resonating in voice and nature. 'Afar a Bird'

---

6   For recent studies that focus on Beckett and voice, yet tend to make voice synonymous with meaning, see Ali and West.

begins with 'Ruinstrewn', Beckett's perfectly-constructed portmanteau word, repeated five times in the brief piece, sounding the ruin and strewn decay of the land as well as the man's ruinstrewn body: 'the little heap of hands and head, the trunk horizontal, the jutting elbows, the eyes closed and the face rigid listening [...] that image and no more' (Beckett, 1995, 233). In this last phrase, Beckett uses that slippery, 'now you say it now you don't', letter *h*, like the name H. Aspirate Haitch which he gives to his 'hearer' in *Company* (Beckett, 1980, 31), a sly reference to the pronunciation wars over this most elusive sounding letter — what Steven Connor calls, in his extended discussion of the 'h', 'the degree zero of consonance' ('Whisper Music'). What better name for a speaker who seeks a voice and has none, but only a sound and a breath.

3 Words as Vocal Events

These struggles may have been one reason that Beckett, after completing *Malone meurt*, turned to theatre, a medium in which a material body would — presumably — be present, a human voice would speak, and through his or her actions, connections between voice and meaning, sound and self, and time and place, might be concretised, certainly more so than in prose texts. Ruby Cohn makes this point in a discussion of the difference between Malone and his fictive predecessors, when she argues that, unlike them, it is Malone who 'virtually elides his identity into what he calls his present state. The art of the present state is theater rather than fiction' (Cohn, 2001, 175). Perhaps Beckett's turn to theatre after *Malone meurt*, she suggests, is that he could make it possible for his audience to hear the sounds of 'living through time'. She concludes that 'In dwelling on time, *Malone meurt* probes to the constituents of fiction, and *En attendant Godot* probes to the constituents of theater' (176). Don Ihde presents a similar idea. In his discussion of the phenomenologies of sound, he cites the distinction between written words, with their 'seriality or linearity', requiring that the reader 'follow the series', and voiced words, 'serial in a strictly temporal sense', but still able to create 'a gestalt in which the harmonics or disharmonics of voice occur' that transcend the grammatical (Ihde, 168). For him, such 'all-at-onceness' is found in theatre, in which the dramaturgical voice, its inflections, intonations, accents, and stresses, creates a 'second "grammar", sounded in the how, co-present with the what, of the saying' (169). One of his examples is *Krapp's Last Tape*, in which 'even when there is a "single" character [...] there is a minimal symphonic harmony to the monologue of time and tone in the voice on the tape. *What is* said, the discursive, in voice is never present alone but is amplified within the possibilities of how the voice says it' (170).

In his discussion, Ihde uses the Hebrew word *dabar*, that carries the meaning of speaking and the event of speaking, what he calls a '*word-event*' that is 'elevated above the ordinary' (167), similar to a dramatic event. The actor's '*voicing* is what allows his [or her] voice to bring to life the wider context of meaning which animates the drama' and thereby creates what Idhe describes as 'the embodiment of sounded signification beyond what is merely declarative, in which a whole range of unsuspected existential possibilities may come to life' (170). He might have also used the Hebrew word *shama* as well, which means to hear and to heed — another 'word-event' — and the opening word of a central prayer in Judaism.[7] Mary Bryden, describing how 'the aural nuances of Beckett's work are of paramount importance', uses a term similar to Ihde's, when she argues that Beckett's 'pitch, tone, duration, rhythm, and audibility were not optional extras, or embellishments [...] Rather they *were* that meaning, that vocal event' (Bryden, 43).

Beckett often indicated the importance of aurality in his work. To composer Morton Feldman, who created a one-act opera of Beckett's text 'neither' and composed the music for Everett Frost's radio version of *Words and Music*, he revealed his habit of repeating things aloud over and over to himself (qtd. in Frost, 51); to André Bernold he said, 'I have always written for a voice' (qtd. in Bernold, 77); and to Charles Juliet he admitted that 'hearing is becoming more important to him than sight' (qtd. in Juliet, 22, 27). While sound in theatre can be produced by many means, for example curtains on rings making a clacking sound as they are moved aside and metal ashcan tops scraping as they are raised and lowered — as Beckett carefully orchestrated and calibrated for the 1964 Aldwych and 1976 Royal Court productions of *Endgame* (McWhinnie, qtd. in McMillan and Fehsenfeld, 176) — it was the sound of human voices that most interested him. It is, therefore, not surprising that he chose to work with actors whose voices had a distinct timbre. James Knowlson reports that when Beckett first heard Patrick Magee reading extracts from *Molloy* and *From an Abandoned Work*, broadcast on the BBC Third Programme, he was so taken by the 'cracked quality' of that voice, that soon after he wrote 'Magee Monologue' that became *Krapp's Last Tape* (443–4).

He was also interested in tempo. When I interviewed Billie Whitelaw, the actor most associated with Beckett's plays, having appeared in ten directed or

---

7   The primacy of hearing rather than seeing is indicated as well in Deuteronomy 4.12: 'the Lord spoke to you out of the fire; you heard the sound of words but perceived no shape — nothing but a voice'.

assisted by him, she described how important it was to Beckett for her 'to get the music right', approaching lines metronomically. For the opening words of *Happy Days*, she explained, 'I thought Winnie would say "another happy day" sprightly. And Sam said — let me see if I can get it right — [flat monotone] "A-no-ther hap-py day"'. She explained that 'with these plays the music and tempos are essential. If you get them right, everything else falls into place' (qtd. in Ben-Zvi, 1992, 6). In interviews, she often described herself as the instrument through which or on which Beckett plays the notes. David Warrilow, another Beckett favourite blessed with an unforgettable vocal sound, echoed Whitelaw: 'If I get it right, if I sing it "on key", "in tune", it's going to vibrate properly for somebody else' (qtd. in Kalb, 224).

Beckett's sense of the musicality of words is not surprising, given that he came from a musical family, as his nephew Edward Beckett — himself a well-known professional flautist — testifies. From his youth, he studied piano, becoming 'quite a proficient pianist, favouring Beethoven and Haydn sonatas [...] as well as Chopin and Schubert', and kept pianos in both Paris and Ussy (Edward Beckett, v–vi). Ann Atik describes how, as a ritual after every dinner Beckett had with her and her husband Avigdor Arikha, at their home, they would listen in silence to recordings of works by these composers, chosen by Beckett, and sometimes also Webern (Atik, 21).[8] 'Music, precisely, was our greatest bond', Atik writes, and 'poetry was part of that bond, the other half of the heart, as it were' (21). A poet herself, she relates how Beckett loved to recite poetry, and would do so at every opportunity: walking with her down a street, the two sitting in a café, even in hospital when a cataract operation made it impossible for him to read, and near the end of his life, in a nursing home, when 'Even in delirium [he] recites poetry' (127).

What is surprising, given his directorial demand that his actors use 'no colour', is Atik's description of how Beckett recited, singing or crooning lines, as well as his tendency to pronounce long and short vowels in end rhymes following 'historical rhyme' rather than 'eye rhyme', for example, giving the *i* in 'Wind' a long sound in order to rhyme with 'behind', in Shelley's 'O, Wind/ If Winter comes, can Spring be far behind?' (54). Atik's comments about Beckett's pronunciation of, and attention to, sounds in others' poetry, brings home the fact that, while it has become commonplace for people, as those quoted above, to speak of how Beckett wrote what he heard in his head, there are virtually no recordings to indicate how those words sounded to him.

---

8   For a discussion of the relationship between Webern's music and Beckett's writing, see White.

There is no possibility, therefore, to experience 'the tissue of sounds', the term Christopher Ricks used, in a fascinating lecture on the poetry of T. S. Eliot, in which he played recordings of Eliot reading his poems to illustrate the poet's idiosyncratic pronunciations and surprising rhythms that were central to 'that auditory imagination which is everywhere the condition of his art, and which is laid upon him and which he lays upon his listeners and readers' (Ricks). Although Beckett scholars have no such recordings, one means available to determine how he may have heard his texts for theatre is through his directorial comments to actors about how his words were to be spoken.

Ihde, in his discussion of the dramaturgical voice, positions it 'between the enchantment of music, which can wordlessly draw us into the sound so deeply that the sound overwhelms us, and the conversation of ordinary speech, which gives way to a trivial transparency that hides its sounded significance' (167). In Beckett's case, it is the very ordinariness of everyday speech, raised through his acute sense of tempos, rhythms, tones, pauses, silences, and phonetic repetitions that create a musicality and aural significance. Those actors who have had the opportunity to work with him, and those assistants and critics who have attended rehearsals and have written accounts of his directorial methods, provide important insights into how a Beckett text through voice becomes a 'word-event', thereby activating and replicating his unique auditory imagination and transmitting it to an audience.

4   The Sound Stage

In *Beckett in the Theatre*, Dougald McMillan and Martha Fehsenfeld offer invaluable descriptions and interviews with those connected to the English, French and German productions of Beckett's early plays *Waiting for Godot*, *Endgame*, and *Krapp's Last Tape*; and many of these observations relate to sound. Roger Blin, the director and Pozzo in the 1953 premiere of *En attendant Godot* at the Théâtre de Babylone, for example, suggests that Beckett's changes in the English version of the name-calling dual between Didi and Gogo in Act 2 of *Waiting for Godot* 'were as much determined by the repetition of sounds and cadences as by the meanings of the paired couplets as in the French original' (McMillan and Fehsenfeld, 76).[9] Looking closely at the words, it is possible to see that even this early in Beckett's writing for theatre, he was

---

9   Since the following quotations are from the same source, I have indicated only page numbers.

conscious of structuring sound patterns. For example, the end rhymes /n/ in the two-syllable words 'Moron!' and 'Vermin!' are followed by the three syllable 'Abortion!' and 'Morpion' [crab louse], also ending in *n* creating an escalating sound rhythm rising to that jarring, emphatic riposte 'Sewer-Rat' that serves as a pause leading to the double *c*'s in 'Curate!', and 'Cretin!', finally climaxing in 'Crritic!', an echo of the previous opening and closing *c*'s and, more important, an aural conflation of 'Crritic' through its double *r*'s with 'Sewer Rat', Beckett's ultimate jab.

It says more about the nature of *Godot* as a written text than Beckett as a nascent director that his *Regiebuch* (directorial book) for his 1975 *Godot* production in German at the Schiller-Theatre, Berlin concentrates primarily on visual elements, much less than on sound or delivery, whereas *Endgame*, written later but his first solo direction of one of his plays, also done at the Schiller-Theatre eight years earlier, focuses extensively on vocality. Blin, to whom the play was dedicated and who directed the 1957 premiere of *Fin de partie*, points out that in this play Beckett was more adamant that words and phrases be voiced in exactly the same tone, creating an echo, 'like a note of music played in an invariable way by the same instrument' (171).[10] Michael Haerdter, Beckett's German assistant on the Schiller-Theater *Endgame* production, whose extensive rehearsal diary is printed in *Beckett in the Theatre*, agrees, writing that this repetitiousness gradually reveals itself as one of the formal principles of what he calls Beckett's '"musical" direction' (222).

'*Piano, piano*' (210) Beckett would tell his German Hamm, Horst Bollmann, and Clov, Ernst Schroeder, even advising them in certain speeches to whisper, as he had suggested to Pat Magee, an earlier Hamm (178), reminding Schroeder that his first soliloquy was to be held back to the 'limits of audibility' (216); and exhorting his Nell, Gudren Genest, and Nagg, Werner Stock, to 'speak almost without voice and colour', explaining that 'Once the right tone is found [...] then it will be possible to send the voice out' more strongly (210). Tempo was also vital. Haerdter describes how Beckett would mark it with 'a tok tok tok tapping', similar to how he later conducted Billie Whitelaw, noting that 'Beckett's ear is like a seismograph for stresses and tempos' (214). Even more important, Beckett told his actors — as he did in productions he directed — to speak in a monotone, with no colour, assuring them that the musicality of

---

10 When Donald McWhinnie, director of *All That Fall* on radio, directed *Endgame* in 1964 and 1976 at the Royal Court, he, too, pointed out these repetitions of word sounds, likening them to a 'music guide [...] more important than the interpretation', since Beckett 'wants to get it as exact as the human instrument can get it' (McWhinnie, qtd. in McMillan and Fehsenfeld, 176).

the sounds would take care of itself, as long as they did not get in the way by acting.

To have the audience also focus on sound, Beckett required that there be a clear separation between action and speech: 'Never let your changes of position and voice come together' (211), he admonished actors and directors, the better for the audience to listen and not be distracted by the movements they see. Haerdter describes this 'phonetic separation of echoes' in *Endgame*, when Hamm knocks on the 'hollow wall' of his cell with a clearly scanned sequence of three short strokes and then says 'Do you hear?' (215–6), the three knocks echoed by the three single-syllable words.

Whereas early Beckett plays balanced, though separated, sound and movement, in the later works, as characters become more visually arresting but more physically static — as in *Not I*, *That Time*, *Rockaby*, and *A Piece of Monologue* — their vitality derives increasingly from the sounds they, their recorded voices, or the voices of unseen others utter rather than from what they do. This gradual shift from the visual to the aural can be seen as early as *Krapp's Last Tape*, in which the multiple characters in *Godot* and *Endgame* give way to one figure, barely moving, whose primary actions entail speaking and listening to an earlier self, designated by recorded sound, the speaker's age determined and differentiated by the timbre and tone used to mark the passage of time. In *Happy Days*, Winnie's voice becomes progressively faster-paced, the words of Act 2 fragmented and abbreviated echoes of those uttered in Act 1, aurally replicating her visual sinking into her mound, whereas *Play* begins with its three characters already encased in urns, their 'voices toneless except where an expression is indicated', speaking in 'Rapid tempo throughout', beginning 'faint, largely, unintelligible' and their opening, closing, and *da capo* opening and closing speeches delivered simultaneously, 'largely unintelligible' (Beckett, 1984, 147), their voices audibly replicating the fading light that prompts them to speak.

This ascendancy of sound and diminution of movement climaxes in *Not I*, in which the embodied voice must be imagined since the material body is hidden, 'whole body like gone' (Beckett, 1984, 220) with only the apparatus of speech — lips, tongue, saliva, and teeth — visible in vivid closeup in the television version, a tiny blur in the theatre, a mouth suspended eight feet above the stage in surrounding darkness. In both versions, the speaker, shorn of perceptible body, is shorn of a name. She is called Mouth, calls herself 'She', five times vehemently denying the personal pronoun 'I'. Mouth is reduced to words that begin, unintelligibly before the curtain rises, end, unintelligibly, after it descends, and between are articulated clearly but in an almost impossibly fast tempo, as Beckett required, Billie Whitelaw's fourteen minutes far ahead of Jessica Tandy's twenty-two, now eclipsed by Lisa Dwan's incredible nine.

When staged as written, the only actions, other than the writhing mouth, are the Auditor's four arm movements of supplication, prompted by, and diminishing with, each of Mouth's five denials of first-personhood. There is, however, an inner voice, unheard by the audience, that speaks only to Mouth, not the enemy or prisoner, as in 'Assumption', nor Mother or other in *Footfalls*, but, rather, a prompter or director, who periodically stops Mouth's flow, correcting her errors and omissions, precipitating, as well, her third-person assertions, and questions 'what?' 'who?', a possible echo of the audience's bewilderment when trying, like Mouth, to understand 'what she was saying! ... imagine! ... no idea what she was saying!' (Beckett, 1984, 219). Although Mouth mentions 'certain vowel sounds ... she had never heard ... elsewhere' (219), and Beckett in other works plays with vowel sounds (think Bam, Bem, Bim, and Bom in *What Where*) consonants dominate *Not I*, particularly sibilant *s*'s, used more than 200 times in the short play, their proliferation creating less a buzzing than a hissing.

It is revealing to study revisions of *Not I* in English to see how consciously Beckett worked on this soundscape.[11] For example, 'Unbroken stream' became 'steady stream'; 'any subsequent time' became 'any subsequent stage'; 'winter mostly' became 'always winter some strange reason'; while the phrase 'No sooner done his devilish work' became 'no sooner buttoned up his trousers', and finally 'no sooner buttoned up his breeches', the double *o*'s in 'sooner' echoed by the double *e*'s in breeches, set off by the two voiced plosive *t*'s in buttoned. The phrase was made even more rhythmical once Beckett exchanged the three-syllable de/vil/ish for the two-syllable trou/sers, and then syllabically made it echo the two-syllable bree/ches.[12] In addition, Mouth first wandered in 'Croker's Meadows'; but perhaps since 'Meadows' mitigates the strong sound sense of 'Croker', it became in revision 'Croker's Acres', both words with long sounds, emphasising the end rhymes, the alternations similar to what Shelley describes about how sound shifts can alter the power of the metaphor or image of a line.

While *Not I* is Beckett's consummate sound play, his shortest is the thirty-five second *Breath*: the cry of vagitus signalling birth followed by the same cry announcing death, an example of Beckett's 'all I can manage, more than

---

11 See Rosemary Pountney, pp. 252–8. Appendix VII provides tables of the two Holographs and six typescripts of *Not I* indicating changes Beckett made in the process of composition.
12 Gontarski (p. 147) cites this change, but focuses on its allusion not its sound.

I could' (qtd. in Harmon, 24). Yet, seemingly not enough for directors in the thirty-two years since his death, who often have been unwilling or unable to follow Beckett's meticulous instructions concerning the sounds and rhythms of his texts. One has only to think of Peter Brook's direction of an evening of short Beckett plays under the heading *Fragments* at his Théâtre des Bouffes du Nord, with two of the three spectral women in the delicate, haunting *Come and Go* played by men in drag, saying the words broadly for laughs; and *Rockaby*, in which the woman says the recorded words herself, uninflected, as she stands and finally sits in a straight-backed chair. When questioned about the changes, Brook responded that the writer's words are always sacrosanct, but that the stage directions 'can legitimately be modified' (2008), not noting that in Beckett's plays the words are wedded to the stage directions, and meaning is derived from sounding not merely saying the words as written. Certainly, no one would want directors and actors to slavishly follow Beckett's directorial work, turning his plays into those 'Masterpieces' against which Artaud railed. Beckett himself made changes, recognising that each production has its own life, but always in order to make the essential visual images and aurality of his plays more powerful. One can only hope that directors in the future have sensitive enough ears to hear and understand that in a Beckett play, as in Shakespeare's plays and in poetry, meaning is a matter of fundamental sounds.

Works Cited

Ali, Khaleem Nafeez Mohammed (2014), 'Impossible Voices: Phenomenologies of Sound in Beckett', PhD diss., Harvard University.
Atik, Anne (2001), *How It Was: A Memoir of Samuel Beckett*, London: Faber and Faber.
Beckett, Edward (1998), 'Foreword', in Mary Bryden, ed., *Samuel Beckett and Music*, pp. v–vi.
Beckett, Samuel (1954), *Waiting for Godot*, New York: Grove P.
Beckett, Samuel (1959), *Watt*, New York: Grove P.
Beckett, Samuel (1980), *Company*, New York: Grove P.
Beckett, Samuel (1983), *Worstward Ho*, London: John Calder.
Beckett, Samuel (1984), *The Collected Shorter Plays*, New York: Grove Weidenfeld.
Beckett, Samuel (1995), *Samuel Beckett: The Complete Short Prose, 1929–1989*, ed. S. E. Gontarski, New York: Grove P.
Ben-Zvi, Linda (1987), 'Phonetic Structure in Beckett: From Mag to Gnaw', in Alan Warren Friedman et al. eds., *Beckett Translating/Translating Beckett*, University Park, PA: Pennsylvania State UP, pp. 155–64.
Ben-Zvi, Linda, ed. (1992), *Women in Beckett*, Urbana: U of Illinois P.

Bernold, André (2015), *Beckett's Friendship: 1979–1989*, Dublin: The Lilliput P.

Brook, Peter (2008), Interviewed by Paul Taylor, *The Independent*, 5 September 2008, rpt. http://www.newspeterbrook.com/tag/fragments/.

Bryden, Mary (1998), 'Beckett and the Sound of Silence', in Bryden, ed., *Samuel Beckett and Music*, Oxford: Clarendon P, pp. 21–46.

Bull, Michael and Les Back (2003), *The Auditory Culture Reader*, Oxford: Berg.

Cohn, Ruby, ed. (1983), *Disjecta*, London: John Calder.

Cohn, Ruby (2001), *A Beckett Canon*, Ann Arbor: U of Michigan P.

Connor, Steven (2007), 'Whisper Music', available online at: stevenconnor.com/whisper-music.html.

Connor, Steven (2014), *Beckett, Modernism and the Material Imagination*, Cambridge: Cambridge UP.

Descartes, René (1965), *Discourse on Method, Optics, Geometry, and Meteorology*, trans. Paul J. Olscamp, Indianapolis, IN: Bobbs–Merrill.

De Vos, Laurens (2011), *Cruelty and Desire in the Modern Theater: Antonin Artaud, Sarah Kane, and Samuel Beckett*, Madison, NJ: Fairleigh Dickinson UP.

Dolar, Mladen (2006), *A Voice and Nothing More*, Cambridge, MA: MIT P.

Frost, Everett (1998), 'The Note Man on the Word Man: Morton Feldman on Composing the Music for Samuel Beckett's *Words and Music* in *The Beckett Festival of Radio Plays*', in Bryden, ed., *Samuel Beckett and Music*, pp. 47–55.

Gontarski, S. E. (1985), *The Intent of Undoing in Samuel Beckett's Dramatic Texts*, Bloomington: Indiana UP.

Harmon, Maurice, ed. (1998), *No Author Better Served: The Correspondence of Samuel Beckett and Alan Schneider*, Cambridge, MA: Harvard UP.

Ihde, Don (2007), *Listening and Voice: Phenomenologies of Sound*, Vol. 2, Albany: State U of New York P.

Juliet, Charles (2009), *Conversations with Samuel Beckett and Bram van Velde*, trans. Tracy Cooke et al., Dublin: Dalkey Archive P.

Kalb, Jonathan (1989), *Beckett in Performance*, New York: Cambridge UP.

Kendrick, Lynne and Roesner David, eds. (2011), *Theatre Noise: The Sound of Performance*, Cambridge: Cambridge Scholars Publishing.

Knowlson, James (1996), *Damned to Fame: The Life of Samuel Beckett*, London: Bloomsbury.

McMillan, Dougald and Martha Fehsenfeld (1988), *Beckett in the Theatre*, London: John Calder.

Ovadija, Mladen (2013), *Dramaturgy of Sound in the Avant-garde and Postdramatic Theatre*, Montreal: McGill–Queen's UP.

Perloff, Marjorie (1982), 'Between Verse and Prose: Beckett and the New Poetry', *Critical Inquiry*, 9:2, pp. 415–33.

Piette, Adam (1996), *Remembering and the Sound of Words: Mallarmé, Proust, Joyce, Beckett*, Oxford: Clarendon P.

Porter, Jeff (2016), *Lost Sound: The Forgotten Art of Radio Storytelling*, Chapel Hill: U of North Carolina P.

Pountney, Rosemary (1988), *Theatre of Shadows: Samuel Beckett's Drama 1956–76*, Gerrards Cross: Colin Smythe.

Ricks, Christopher (2014), 'Lecture on T. S. Eliot's Auditory Imagination', Harvard College, 2 September, 2014, available online at: https://www.youtube.com/watch?v=zhkcrQo9YdU.

West, Sarah (2010), *Say It: The Performative Voice in the Dramatic Works of Samuel Beckett*, Amsterdam: Rodopi.

White, Harry (2008), *Music and the Irish Literary Imagination*, Oxford: Oxford UP.

Whitelaw, Billie (1990), 'Interview', in Linda Ben-Zvi, ed., *Women in Beckett*, Urbana: U of Illinois P.

Revealing the Limit of Language in Relation to Music

Michiko Tsushima

Abstract

Beckett's critique of language in his early period is related to his strong interest in music. He regards music as an idealised model for literature that transcends the limits of language. This essay examines how the relation between language and music is presented in Beckett's radio plays, *Words and Music* and *Cascando*, in terms of his idea of 'materiality' and 'immateriality'. Both plays present words and music as characters in their own right (Joe and Bob in *Words and Music*, and Voice and Music in *Cascando*).

By juxtaposing language with music, *Words and Music* discloses the limit of language. The limit of language implies the materiality of language. The play suggests that whereas music can express what Schopenhauer describes as 'that which of its essence can never be representation' or the ineffable, language fails to do so. In *Cascando*, Voice is gradually immaterialised by the help of Music and becomes more and more self-reflexive. In this movement language reveals its own finitude.

In both radio plays Beckett reveals the limit of language in its relation to music. He shows the possibility that only by returning to and showing the finitude of language, language can get access to the ineffable.

Beckett's interrogation of language in his early period is related to his strong interest in music.[1] In a famous letter written in 1937 which can be regarded as his artistic manifesto, Beckett's critique of language and literature is shown with his aspiration towards a state of music. In the letter he expresses his contempt for 'an official English' and its style and grammar, as he writes, 'more

---

1 This article is a revised version of the article, 'Language and Music in Beckett's Two Radio Plays' published in *Journal of Modern Languages & Cultures* 15, 2015, pp. 89–101. It is based on my paper 'On the Boundaries between Materiality and Immateriality: *Words and Music* and *Cascando*' presented at the annual meeting of International Federation for Theatre Research in 2011. The Japanese article, 'Between Materiality and Immateriality: *Words and Music* and *Cascando*', also based on this paper, was published in *Samuel Beckett To Hihyo No Enkinho* [*Samuel Beckett and the Perspective of Criticism*], ed. Kojin Kondo and Yoshiyuki Inoue, Tokyo: Michitani, 2016, pp. 201–17.

and more my own language appears to me like a veil that must be torn apart in order to get at the things (or the Nothingness) behind it' (1984b, 171). Then he says that while music and painting have already found ways to represent 'the Nothingness' or silence, literature is still caught in 'the old lazy ways' (172). He thinks that literature which remains behind other arts should find its way out of the present situation, and that literature should move towards what he calls a 'literature of the unword' (173). The 'literature of the unword' has a paradoxical meaning. It attempts to eliminate language through language. It is an attempt to, by using language, 'bore one hole after another in it [language], until what lurks behind it — be it something or nothing — begins to seep through'. And it is in Beethoven's music that Beckett finds a model for this literature:

> Is there any reason why that terrible materiality of the word surface should not be capable of being dissolved, like for example the sound surface, torn by enormous pauses, of Beethoven's Seventh Symphony, so that through whole pages we can perceive nothing but a path of sounds suspended in giddy heights, linking unfathomable abysses of silence? (172)

The similar aspiration towards a state of music has already been expressed by Beckett through Belacqua, the protagonist in *Dream of Fair to Middling Women* (1932) (1992, 102, 137–8).

Thus, in his early period, Beckett regards music as an ideal other of language or an idealised model for literature that transcends the limits of language, as Catherine Laws rightly suggests: '[T]he literary and philosophic conception of music as the "beyond" of language persists from its nineteenth-century idealist envisioning. To an extent this is reflected in Beckett's work, with music sometimes idealised as a model for what literature might be or do if freed from the banalities of language, and sometimes providing a refuge from the very struggle with meaning' (179).[2] This chapter will examine how the relation between language and music is presented in Beckett's radio plays, *Words and Music* and *Cascando*, in terms of his idea of 'materiality' and 'immateriality'.

To return to his letter written in 1937, we notice that what Beckett criticises in language is its materiality. As we have seen, he writes, 'Is there any reason why that terrible materiality of the word surface should not be capable of being dissolved, like for example the sound surface, torn by enormous

---

2   Laws adds to these sentences: 'However, this is not straightforward; music is by no means a singular entity in Beckett. It is manifested in different ways', and presents different ways in which music is thematised in Beckett. See Laws, pp. 179–80.

pauses, of Beethoven's Seventh Symphony [...]?' (172). The 'terrible materiality' of language here means the fact that language can never be completely free from describing material things in the phenomenal world and expressing their meanings. It also means that language in its nature conceals the (non-)existence of what cannot be represented, as shown in his view that language is 'a veil that must be torn apart in order to get at the things (or the Nothingness) behind it' or 'a mask' (171). We could say that throughout his career as an artist of language, Beckett continues to fight with the 'terrible materiality' of language.

For Beckett, music is an ideal other of language which can move beyond the materiality of language. In the coda to *Proust*, he states that music is the 'most immaterial art of all the arts' (1999, 92). This suggests that when Beckett regards music as an idealised model for literature, what he recognises in music is its immateriality, and that on the model of music, he pursues the possibility of an immaterial art. It is well known that in his youth Beckett greatly admired Schopenhauer, finding in his thought 'an intellectual justification of unhappiness' (Beckett, 2009, 32–3). Beckett's early work, including *Proust*, was written under the influence of Schopenhauer's work, especially *The World as Will and Representation*. In the coda to *Proust*, Beckett tries to explain Schopenhauer's view on music and writes, 'music is the Idea itself, unaware of the world of phenomena, existing ideally outside the universe, apprehended not in Space but in Time only' (92). Then Beckett shows the similar understanding of music found in Proust's work: 'In one passage he [Proust] describes the recurrent mystical experience as "a purely musical impression, non-extensive, entirely original, irreducible to any other order of impression [...] sine materia"' (93). We could see how this immaterial quality of music is very important to Beckett, when he condemns the distortion of the immaterial quality of music by the listener. He says, 'This essential quality of music is distorted by the listener who, being an impure subject, insists on giving a figure to that which is ideal and invisible, on incarnating the Idea in what he conceives to be an appropriate paradigm. Thus, by definition, opera is a hideous corruption of this most immaterial of all the arts' (92). He thus severely criticises the materialisation of music.

It is true that in the coda to *Proust* we find distortion in Beckett's presentation of Schopenhauer's idea of music, as Pilling argues.[3] However, the immateriality of music which Beckett emphasises in the coda to *Proust* undoubtedly

---

3   Pilling writes, 'Much of *Proust* borrows from Schopenhauer, whether tacitly or by acknowledgement, and expresses the philosophy of *The World as Will* with little or no distortion. But this is not the case in the coda, and it remains a moot point whether Beckett was sim-

comes from Schopenhauer's philosophy of music presented in *The World as Will and Representation*. It is found in Chapter 52 of Volume I and Chapter 39 ('On the Metaphysics of Music') of Volume II.

Schopenhauer argues that music differs from and is superior to all the other arts, for it is independent of the materiality of the phenomenal world and directly expresses the inner nature of the will itself.[4] He writes, 'music [...] is [...] independent of the phenomenal world, positively ignores it, and, to a certain extent, could still exist even if there were no world at all, which cannot be said of the other arts' (Vol. I, 257). What music expresses is not a particular phenomenon but 'the innermost soul of the events and occurrences':

> [...] [music] never expresses the phenomenon, but only the inner nature, the in-itself, of every phenomenon, the will itself. Therefore music does not express this or that particular and definite pleasure, this or that affliction, pain, sorrow, horror, gaiety, merriment, or peace of mind, but joy, pain, sorrow, horror, gaiety, merriment, peace of mind *themselves*, to a certain extent in the abstract, their essential nature, without any accessories [...] Nevertheless, we understand them perfectly in this extracted quintessence. Hence it arises that our imagination [...] tries to shape that invisible, yet vividly aroused, spirit-world that speaks to us directly, to clothe it with flesh and bone, and thus to embody it in an analogous example. This is the origin of the song with words, and finally of the opera. (Vol. I, 261)

We can see how Schopenhauer's idea about the origin of the opera turns into a severe critique of the opera in Beckett. In his philosophy of music,

---

ply working from a fallible memory, or whether his own developing creative vision [...] was beginning to generate its own refractory music' (177–8).

4 By 'will' Schopenhauer means 'the innermost essence, the kernel, of every particular thing and also of the whole'. It shows itself in 'every blindly acting force of nature, and also in the deliberate conduct of man'. It is recognised not only in the phenomena in the realm of men and animals. It is also found in 'the force that shoots and vegetates in the plant, indeed the force by which the crystal is formed, the force that turns the magnet to the North Pole', 'even gravitation, which acts so powerfully in all matter, pulling the stone to the earth and the earth to the sun', and so on (Vol. I, 110). Schopenhauer conceives 'will' as 'every force in nature' or 'the innermost essence of everything in nature' (Vol. I, 111). He also stresses that 'will' is 'entirely free from all the forms of the phenomenon into which it first passes when it appears' (Vol. I, 112). 'All representation, be it of whatever kind it may, all *object*, is *phenomenon*. But only the *will* is *thing-in-itself*; as such it is not representation at all, but *toto genere* different therefrom. It is that of which all representation, all object, is the phenomenon, the visibility, the *objectivity*' (Vol. I, 110).

Schopenhauer repeats the view that music is 'not a copy of the phenomenon, or, more exactly, of the will's adequate objectivity, but is directly a copy of the will itself, and therefore expresses the metaphysical to everything physical in the world, the thing-in-itself to every phenomenon' (Vol. I, 262). For him, music is characterised by 'its complete indifference to everything material in the incidents' and 'never assimilates the material' (Vol. II, 449). He presents an example of Beethoven's symphony: 'all the human passions and emotions speak from this symphony; joy, grief, love, hatred, terror, hope, and so on in innumerable shades, yet all, as it were, only in the abstract and without any particularisation; it is their mere form without the material, like a mere spirit world without matter' (Vol. II, 450). Schopenhauer considers music as our most direct method of knowledge of the world or the movement of the will itself. This is the reason why 'music makes every picture, indeed every scene from real life and from the world, at once appear in enhanced significance [...]' (Vol. I, 263). We could clearly see the influence of Schopenhauer's view on music in Beckett's aspiration towards the state of music and pursuit of the possibility of an immaterial art.

Although Beckett attacked language and admired music, he continued to create his work with language. In a sense, his attempt was a paradoxical attempt to immaterialise language that can never be free from its own materiality. Beckett's use of radio can be discussed in terms of this attempt. Bryden points out that 'throughout Beckett's long writing career, one can trace an extended preoccupation with compositional boundaries: between light and dark, audible and inaudible, perceptible and imperceptible — and, above all, between sound and silence' (39). To these words, we can add 'between materiality and immateriality'. We could say that Beckett tried to compose his work on the boundaries between materiality and immateriality by making the best use of the qualities of radio as an artistic medium.

Beckett's experimentation with the radio medium was a way out of a logjam that he had experienced after writing the trilogy and *Texts for Nothing*. His use of radio introduced an important innovation in his creative process. Starting from *All That Fall*, which was first broadcast on the BBC Third Programme in January 1957, Beckett's radio plays were broadcast in English, French, and German; *Embers* in June 1959; *Words and Music* in November 1962; *Cascando*, written in French, by RTF in Paris in October 1963 (its English version was broadcast in October 1964). Two other radio plays were written in French in the early 1960s: *Rough for Radio I* (*Esquisse radiophonique*) and *Rough for Radio II* (*Pochade radiophonique*). The latter was broadcast as *Rough for Radio* on BBC Radio 3 in April 1976 (McDonald, 51–2).

Thus, Beckett explored new possibilities of the radio medium characterised by the absence of physical space. Rónán McDonald writes, 'Just as he had taken stagecraft back to its elementals, broadening and reinvigorating the possibilities of live theatre, so with the radio Beckett stretches and tests the form, exploiting the absence of a visual dimension and deploying the ethereality of the medium to create a tension between aural presence and physical absence' (52). He also states that 'the essence of radio is insubstantiality: the *air*waves are by definition ephemeral' (53). In radio, the substantial or phenomenal world that we can actually see is absent. In that sense, the radio medium is ethereal and ephemeral. Here we recall that the immateriality that he discusses in the coda to *Proust* involves the absence of physical space or spatial extension. In *Proust*, Beckett argues that music is the 'most immaterial of all the arts' by saying that it is 'unaware of the world of phenomena, existing ideally outside the universe, apprehended not in Space but in Time only' (92). If we apply Beckett's idea of immateriality to the radio medium, we could say that the essence of radio is immateriality. Although radio works evoke the imagined space in the mind of the listener, they do not exist in an actual space. Indeed in radio plays the listener does not see actors' bodies that he or she sees on the stage in theatrical plays. Instead the listener hears voices. In this sense, the radio medium is characterised by the absence of the material bodies and spatial extension.

The absence of the physical space in the radio medium is related to its power to bring the drama in the darkness of the interiority of the self (or in the head, in the skull) revealing the internal processes directly to the listener. This evokes the function of the eyelids to close the world that we see in front of our eyes. Jacques Derrida speaks of Aristotle's distinction between blinking and unblinking animals:

> In his *De anima* (421b) [Aristotle] distinguishes between man and those animals that have hard dry eyes [*ton sklerophtalmon*], the animals lacking eyelids, that sort of sheath or tegumental membrane [*phragma*] which serves to protect the eye and permits it, at regular intervals, to close itself off in the darkness of inward thought or sleep. What is terrifying about an animal with hard dry eyes and a dry glance is that it always sees. Man can lower the sheath, adjust the diaphragm, narrow his sight, the better to listen, remember, and learn. (Derrida, qtd. in Connor, 1992, 96)

Here the eyelids are considered as that which serve to 'protect the eye and permits it, at regular intervals, to close itself off in the darkness of inward thought or sleep' and help man's act of listening, remembering, and learning.

We could say that the radio medium has a similar function, and that Beckett exploited in his radio plays this nature of closing the visible world and letting us enter the inner darkness.

Now we shall see how his two radio plays, *Words and Music* (1962) and *Cascando* (1963), present the relation between language and music on the boundaries between materiality and immateriality. Especially, we will examine how Beckett depicts the materiality of language in its relation to music. Both plays present words and music as characters in their own right: they are called Joe and Bob in *Words and Music*, and Voice and Music in *Cascando*. They also present a third voice which invokes words and music: Croak in *Words and Music*, and Opener in *Cascando*.

In *Words and Music*, an old man named Croak comes to his two servants, Words and Music named Joe and Bob.[5] Words and Music are called 'My comforts!' or 'my balms!' by Croak, which suggests that their roles are to mitigate the old man's pain and suffering. At the beginning of the play, Words and Music are presented to be on bad terms. Especially Words exhibits hatred towards Music. In the play, Croak shouts at Words and Music, commanding them to portray themes like 'love' and 'age'. They perform, first separately, and later together. At the end of the play their collaborative performance evokes the memory of a woman whom Croak loved in the past and cannot forget. And Croak is overwhelmed by the explicitness of that memory and shuffles off.

This is what happens in the play, but we should note that this does not take place in the outside phenomenal world. In a sense, it is an allegorical play of what takes place in the darkness of the interiority of the mind. We could say that Words and Music symbolise the linguistic faculty and the non-linguistic or musical faculty respectively. Daniel Albright holds that Beckett uses technology to 'chop apart human faculties', for example, 'with memory demoted to tape recording in *Krapp's Last Tape*, with imagination demoted to microphonic voice in *Eh Joe*' (26). In *Words and Music*, we find the technique of not only chopping apart human faculties but personifying them as characters in the play. We could also say that this play is essentially a self-reflexive work, as Ruby Cohn argues that it is 'a composition about composition' (268).

The play begins with Music and Words, Joe and Bob, tuning up while waiting for Croak's arrival. From the very beginning, Words shows his loathing for Music. Irritated by the tuning sound of Music, Words says, 'Please! [*Tuning.*

---

5   This play was written in English for collaboration with John Beckett, for the BBC. It was completed towards the end of 1961. In a letter dated February 12, 1961, Beckett writes about this play: 'Next job will be with John Beckett [a cousin] — a text-music tandem for the BBC. Beginning to have a few ideas' (qtd. in Zilliacus, 99).

Louder.] Please! [*Tuning dies away.*] How much longer cooped up here in the dark? [*With loathing.*] With you!' (1984a, 127). Words can no longer bear the situation in which he is locked up with Music in the dark space. Croak arrives with the sound of shuffling slippers. He is late, because he saw the face on the stairs of the tower. He announces that tonight's theme is 'love'. With the thump of a club, Croak orders Words to speak. Words starts, 'Love is of all the passions the most powerful passion and indeed no passion is more powerful than the passion of love. [*Clears throat.*] This is the mode in which the mind is most strongly affected and indeed in no mode is the mind more strongly affected than in this. [*Pause.*]' (128). Here he uses abstract and general words similar to philosophical language. These words indicate the connection between language and reason. Yet they are presented as nonsensical words that Hugh Kenner calls 'scholastic garbage' (170). Then with violent thump of the club Croak commands Bob to perform. While Music is playing soft music melodically, Words groans and protests. Music grows louder and drowns Words' protestations. Words fails to interrupt Music.

Next, Croak announces the second theme, 'age', and tells them to play together. He shouts with a violent thump, 'Together, dogs!' (129). This time Music leads Words by playing musical phrases and giving a suggestion for Joe's words that follow him. Then Words follows Music's lead and tries to sing to Bob's music. Here we recognise a harmony between language and music as well as the mutual transformation in which music is becoming language and language music. Music also plays air alone, invites Words to sing and finally accompanies Words' singing. Words sings softly:

> Age is when to a man
> Huddled o'er the ingle
> [...]
> She comes in the ashes
> Who loved could not be won
> Or won not loved
> Or some other trouble
> Comes in the ashes
> Like in that old light
> The face in the ashes
> That old starlight
> On the earth again. (131)

Unlike the abstract language that he uses in trying to define 'love', Joe's words here describe a particular situation which shows what it is like to have aged.

After a long pause, Croak murmurs, 'The face' repetitively. It is not clear whether Croak announces the third theme, 'The face' or not, but Words and Music take Croak's words as the announcement. Again Music gives a suggestion for Words, but this time, Words disregards it. In a cold and composed manner Words depicts an image of a man's eyes observing the face of a post-coital woman. Words gives a detailed description of the face. This description makes Croak relive the lost moment with his lover and brings him pain. He utters in an anguished voice, 'Lily!'. By this point Croak becomes passive to their performance, and he no longer gives orders to Words and Music. When Music plays, Words tries to interrupt his music with protestations — 'Peace!', 'No!', 'Please' — but again Words fails to stop Music. Music reaches 'Triumph and conclusion'. After this victory of Music, Words resumes the portrait of the woman in post-coital recuperation; Words describes the facial features of the woman who is awakening, including the opening of her eyes. His description grows concrete. Then Words starts depicting the movement of eyes exploring her eyes in a poetic tone. Clas Zilliacus recognises here the motif of 'intensely probing eyes', or 'the motif of eyes trying, in eyes, to perceive something more than eyes' as in *Murphy* and *Krapp's Last Tape* (110). Words again starts to follow the suggestions and invitations given by Music. They play separately, but later, with their efforts put in harmony, they perform a song about the 'wellhead'.

> Then down a little way
> Through the trash
> Towards where
> All dark no begging
> No giving no words
> No sense no need
> Through the scum
> Down a little way
> To whence one glimpse
> Of that wellhead. (133–4)

Zilliacus sees in this poem 'a penetration through worldly paraphernalia toward a point of absolute rest' (111). In this context, we could say that this poem suggests the possibility of a penetration through material things towards the realm of absolute immateriality where there is no word, no sense, or no need and where complete darkness prevails. Being shocked and dropping the club, Croak shuffles off. After Croak leaves, Words begs Music to play again, this time calling him Music, not Bob. The deep sigh made by Words at the very end of the play indicates that Words admits his own defeat and acknowledges the victory of Music.[6] We could guess that from the beginning Words already knows that he is in the subordinate position. This is why he feels irritated by Music's existence and reacts to Music in childish ways. But Words' attitude towards Music gradually changes, and after much meandering he eventually accepts Music's superiority and his own limitations.

Thus *Words and Music* thematises the relation between language and music. In the play both Words and Music are told to portray abstract themes like 'love' and 'age' which are not particular things that we see in the phenomenal world. In carrying out that task Words cannot surpass Music. It is because while music is independent of the phenomenal world, language cannot be completely free from its own tendency of particularisation in describing things, that is, free from the phenomenal world. In a sense, the superiority of music to language that Schopenhauer argues is realised in this play. In this play, we recognise Beckett's attempt to reveal the limits of language, to be more precise, the materiality of language, by placing it in a relation with the immateriality of music. The play indicates the importance of returning to the finitude of language instead of disregarding it.

In *Cascando*, language and music are called Voice and Music. A third voice, Opener opens and closes Voice and Music separately or together. Voice has 'two strands — self and story'.[7] The strand of the self is made of Voice's self-reflexive words which show his desperate desire to tell the right story and reach the end of his storytelling. For example, Voice says at the beginning of the play:

> —story ... if you could finish it ... you could rest ... sleep ... not before ... oh I know ... the ones I've finished ... thousands and one ... all I ever did ... in my life ... with my life ... say to myself ... finish this one ... it's the right one ... then rest ... sleep ... no more stories ... no more words ... and finished it ... (1984a, 137)

Besides uttering self-reflexive words, Voice also narrates the story of Woburn (called Maunu in the French original) who takes journeys. For example, Voice narrates:

---

6 Beckett himself said to Katharine Worth, 'Music always wins', when she played him her new version of *Words and Music* with music by Humphrey Searle (Worth, 16).
7 According to Cohn, Beckett 'indicated in his letter [... that] Voice has two strands — self and story' (2001, 272, 402). Zilliacus also holds that 'Voix is not regarded by its author as one indivisible story but as a compound of two, made up of an *élément soi* and an *élément histoire*' (129).

—down ... gentle slopes ... boreen ... giant aspens ... wind in the boughs ... faint sea ... Woburn ... same old coat ... he goes on ... stops ... not a soul ... not yet ... night too bright ... say what you like ... he goes on ... hugging the bank ... same old stick ... he goes down ... falls ... on purpose or not ... can't see ... he's down ... that's what counts ... face in the mud ... arms spread ... (138)

In Voice's words, we hear the alteration of the self and the story. As the play moves on, the proportion of the self gradually increases and that of the story decreases. While with the strand of the story language narrates particular characteristics of Woburn's movements, particular places or things, with the strand of the self, language does not have any referential content and depicts Voice's own desire which exists in the inner realm severed from the phenomenal world. Language in the self becomes immaterial. Zilliacus observes, 'the words of Voix in *Cascando* gradually approach the fundamental quality of Musique: they rid themselves of their anecdotal content, of *histoire*. Voix, in conjunction with Musique, moves away from the figurative and is actualized as *soi*' (136).

Indeed, only when Voice is with the thread of the self, Music accompanies Voice. Speaking of the situation in which Voice and Music are put through simultaneously by Opener, Zilliacus argues that it is 'operatic in a very superficial sense only. Voix does not particularise Musique; in conjunction with Musique, Voix is de-particularised. The less Voix particularises, the more Voix and Musique agree' (136). For our purpose, we could say that in conjunction with Music, Voice becomes immaterial. Here we see Beckett's paradoxical attempt to immaterialise language that cannot be free from its materiality. Music in *Cascando* is presented not as what is triumphant in its superior relation to language as found in *Words and Music*, but as what accompanies Voice and helps Voice's de-particularisation or immaterialisation.

Unlike Croak, Opener does not command Voice and Music to speak or play. He switches the continua of Voice and Music on and off. Zilliacus holds that Voice and Music 'run incessantly' and 'emit continua which Ouvreur, at the receiving end only, renders discontinuous'; 'Ouvreur disconnects them, puts them through, and then disconnects again, at will. Voix does not emit lines, nor Musique movements' (128). This movement of opening and closing Voice and Music recalls the image of an eye which repeats opening and closing in Beckett's later prose works including *Ill Seen Ill Said*. In 'Between Theatre and Theory: *Long Observation of the Ray*', Steven Connor discusses the structure of blinking and introduces Derrida's assertion that reason 'must [...] learn how to wink at itself, to close itself off from the hard, dry continuousness of sight, and catch at the possibility of observing its own observation'. He quotes from Derrida:

> The time for reflection is [...] the chance for turning back on the very conditions of reflection, in all the senses of that word, as if with the help of a new optical device one could finally see sight [...] The chance for this event is the chance of an instant, an *Augenblick*, a "wink" or a "blink", it takes place "in the twinkling of an eye". (19–20)

Connor then writes, 'Beckett's long observation in his work of the processes of looking, thinking and imagining may aptly be thought of as belonging to this attempt to capture this interstitial sight within vision' (97). This observation leads us to think that Opener's movement of opening and closing which repetitively severs the continua of Voice and Music in *Cascando* catches at the possibility of turning back on the very conditions of creation. Further, we could say that this play, *Cascando*, itself is 'the time for reflection', the chance for turning back on the very conditions of creation. Indeed Beckett wrote about this work: 'It is an unimportant work, but the best I have to offer. It does I suppose show in a way what passes for my mind and what passes for its work' (qtd. in Zilliacus, 118).

While *Words and Music* foregrounds the tension between language and music, *Cascando* emphasises Voice's desperate desire to tell the right story which would enable him to reach an end and his repetitive failure to do so. The same motif is also found in *The Unnamable*. As we have seen, in *Cascando* the words of Voice gradually move away from the material world and become self-reflexive in conjunction with Music. At the end of the play, Opener says, with Voice and Music, 'As though they had linked their arms' (143), and we hear the sounds of Voice and Music together. Together with Music, Voice's words run:

> —this time ... it's the right one .... finish ... no more stories ... sleep ... we're there ... nearly ....
> .... just a few more ... don't let go ... Woburn ... he clings ....
> .... on ... come on ... come on —
> .... [Silence.] (144)

Although throughout the play Opener speaks in a calm and composed voice, here his voice turns to a fervent one. Opener says 'Good!' in an excited voice, responding to the sounds of Voice and Music. It is as if both Music and Opener joined in Voice's frantic attempt to catch Woburn 'this time'. Yet, Voice can never catch Woburn and reach the end. The repetition of 'this time' in Voice's words throughout the play emphasises the never-ending nature of this attempt and the interminably repeated failure. Thus *Cascando* reveals the finitude of language.

Both *Words and Music* and *Cascando* turn back on the very conditions of creation. In that self-reflexive movement they return to the limit of language or the finitude of language on the boundaries between materiality and immateriality. By juxtaposing language with music and letting them compete with each other, *Words and Music* discloses the limit of language. The limit of language here implies the materiality of language. The play suggests that whereas music exists as the representation of 'that which of its essence can never be representation' or as 'the copy of an original that can itself never be directly represented' (Schopenhauer, Vol. I, 257) and can express the ineffable, language fails to do so. Language cannot completely separate itself from the phenomenal world and in its essence conceals the ineffable. This is seen especially at the end of the play where Words admits its defeat in its relation to Music. In *Cascando*, language is gradually immaterialised by the help of music and becomes more and more self-reflexive. In this movement language reveals its own finitude. Voice tries to catch Woburn (i.e. the ineffable) and tell his story, but repetitively fails. The phrase 'this time' is repeated throughout the play. This repetition indicates the infinite deferral of the final point.

In both radio plays Beckett reveals the limit of language in its relation to music. But this does not mean that he merely criticises language. He does not try to transcend its limits. He repetitively returns to the finitude of language. Both *Words and Music* and *Cascando* show the possibility that only by returning to and showing the finitude of language, the materiality of language, or the failure of language in catching the ineffable, language can get access to the ineffable. In '"On Such and Such a Day ... In Such a World": Beckett's Radical Finitude', Connor writes, 'To say that Beckett's work constitutes a radical finitude is to say that it strives to permit itself the very least remission it can manage from this awareness of always having to live, move and have its being "in such a world" "on such and such a day ..." never in the world in general, or "as such"' (47). In relation to this remark, we could say that as *Words and Music* and *Cascando* show, language in Beckett's work always stays with the 'awareness of always having to live, move, and have its being' in its materiality, however 'terrible' it is.

The recurrent image of Woburn's movement of falling down (for example, falling into the mud, the sand or the stones) in *Cascando* might be evocative of the ceaseless movement of Beckett's language falling down to its materiality.

> ... he goes down ... falls ... on purpose or not ... can't see ... he's down ... that's what counts ... face in the mud ... arms spread ... that's the idea ...

already ... there already ... no not yet ... he gets up ... knees first ... hands flat ... in the mud ... head sunk ... then up ... on his feet ... huge bulk ... come on ... he goes on ... he goes down ... (138)

Works Cited

Albright, Daniel (2003), *Beckett and Aesthetics*, Cambridge: Cambridge UP.

Beckett, Samuel (1984a), *Collected Shorter Plays*, London: Faber and Faber.

Beckett, Samuel (1984b), *Disjecta: Miscellaneous Writings and a Dramatic Fragment*, ed. Ruby Cohn, New York: Grove P.

Beckett, Samuel (1992), *Dream of Fair to Middling Women*, ed. Eoin O'Brien and Edith Fournier, Dublin: Black Cat.

Beckett, Samuel (2009), *The Letters of Samuel Beckett*, Vol. I, 1929–1940, ed. Martha Fehsenfeld and Lois Overbeck, Cambridge: Cambridge UP.

Beckett, Samuel (1999), *Proust and Three Dialogues with Georges Duthuit*, London: Calder.

Bryden, Mary (1998), 'Beckett and the Sound of Silence', in Bryden, ed., *Samuel Beckett and Music*, Oxford: Oxford UP, pp. 21–46.

Cohn, Ruby (2001), *A Beckett Canon*, Ann Arbor: The U of Michigan P.

Connor, Steven (1992), 'Between Theatre and Theory: *Long Observation of the Ray*', in John Pilling and Mary Bryden, eds., *The Ideal Core of the Onion: Reading Beckett Archives*, Reading: Beckett International Foundation, pp. 79–98.

Connor, Steven (2008), '"On Such and Such a Day ... In Such a World": Beckett's Radical Finitude', *SBT/A*, 19: *Borderless Beckett/Beckett sans frontières: Tokyo 2006*', pp. 35–50.

Derrida, Jacques (1983), 'The Principle of Reason: The University in the Eyes of Its Pupils', *Diacritics*, 13: 3, pp. 3–20.

Kenner, Hugh (1973), *A Reader's Guide to Samuel Beckett*, Syracuse: Syracuse UP.

Laws, Catherine (2010), 'Beckett and Unheard Sound', in Daniela Casselli, ed., *Beckett and Nothing: Trying to Understand Beckett*, Manchester: Manchester UP, pp. 176–91.

McDonald, Rónán (2006), *The Cambridge Introduction to Samuel Beckett*, Cambridge: Cambridge UP.

Pilling, John (1998), 'Proust and Schopenhauer: Music and Shadows', in Bryden, ed., *Samuel Beckett and Music*, pp. 173–8.

Schopenhauer, Arthur [1818] (1966), *The World as Will and Representation*, trans. E. F. J. Payne, 2 vols, New York: Dover.

Worth, Katharine (1998), 'Words for Music Perhaps', in Bryden, ed., *Samuel Beckett and Music*, pp. 9–20.

Zilliacus, Clas (1976), *Beckett and Broadcasting: A Study of the Works of Samuel Beckett for and in Radio and Television*, Abo: Abo Akademi.

Embers: A Polyphonic Piece for Radio

Jürgen Siess

Abstract

This contribution starts with 'polyphony' as defined by the French linguist Oswald Ducrot. In Ducrot's view, polyphony is the superposition of several voices ('enunciators') as manifested in the utterance, and the *staging of these multiple voices by a speaker* [*locuteur*]. The linguist challenges the assumption that the utterance lets us hear a single voice, thus breaking the unity of the subject: the enunciator is not to be confused with the speaker. I want to show that in Beckett's 'piece for radio' polyphony as a well-organised discourse is undermined, that the author complexifies and problematises the polyphonic structure. In his text, multiple voices emerge, and in the soliloquy of the elderly man who is desperately looking for his lost interlocutors, one voice *among others* appears, although he seems to stage imaginary dialogues with absent addressees. Henry, the principal 'character' of *Embers*, has to deal with several competing speakers, these speakers do not recognise him as their master. At the same time, Henry's efforts to gain and maintain self-identity prove a failure. What is more, Beckett's text is supposed to imply the hearer who is confronted with a multiplicity of voices, to involve him in a play the rules of which are all but clear.

Polyphony is the inner structure of Beckett's *Embers*. Multiple voices emerge, and in the soliloquy of the elderly man who is desperately looking for his lost interlocutors, one voice among others appears, although he seems to stage imaginary dialogues with absent addressees.

Mikhail Bakhtin's concept of polyphony (several voices talking simultaneously in a text, none of them having the leading role) was adapted by Oswald Ducrot. Bakhtin explores the intertextual organization of whole texts; thus, he characterises Dostoevsky's novel as 'a plurality of independent and unmerged voices and consciousnesses, a genuine polyphony of fully valid voices' (Bakhtin, 1984, 6). However, Ducrot adapts this concept in a particular way: polyphony is the superposition of several voices ('enunciators') as manifested in the utterance, and *the staging of these multiple voices by a speaker* [*locuteur*]. The linguist challenges the assumption that 'the utterance lets us hear a single voice [*fait entendre une seule voix*]' (171; italics original), thus breaking the unity of the subject: the enunciator is not to be confused with the speaker (201). Using the theatre as a metaphor, Ducrot writes:

> the speaker, responsible for the utterance, gives through this utterance an existence to enunciators whose points of view and attitudes he organises. And his own position can be manifested either by his identifying with one of the enunciators [...] or simply because he has chosen to make him appear. (205, my translation)

Later in his essay, Ducrot adds that the speaker can distance himself from the enunciator when he refuses to take responsibility for an attitude expressed by him (208).

This conception allows for a detailed analysis of *Embers*. However, Ducrot's conception has to be modified in two points in order to account for Beckett's text: (1) Henry is not the only speaker — he has several competing speakers, voices popping up that cannot be controlled; (2) the enunciators invoked by him at certain moments do not recognise him as their master, and thus gain independence. This slightly modified conception allows to show that polyphony can be adopted for the analysis of a highly sophisticated fictional text, but also that Beckett complicates and problematises the polyphonic structure. He breaks up the unity of the subject in *Embers*; but, unlike Ducrot's theoretical text, Beckett's fictional text undermines the position of the speaker as such. I-Henry cannot hold the high rank the speaker is endowed with in Ducrot's 'hierarchy of speech'. In Marjorie Perloff's terms, Henry does not have 'control over the voices in the play' (Perloff, 107). He depends on other speakers and, to a certain extent, even on the very enunciators he pretends to give existence to.

As a result, Henry fails to master and orchestrate the voices invoked or springing up, so that an incoherent discourse is produced that does not allow for the constitution of a self-identity.[1] The appearance and disappearance of the different voices, the shifts between speaker and enunciator, sudden interruptions of Henry's discourse by other speakers have to be carefully noted in order to see to what extent a multiplicity of voices is generated, and to what extent coherence is sought.

The piece for radio starts with the sound of the sea, followed by the sound of somebody walking on the waterfront. Then, a voice comes out of the space suggested by those sounds, a space where water and earth touch one another, and are separated each time they do. The words 'On', 'On!', 'Stop', 'Stop!', 'Down', 'Down!' — 'That sound you hear is the sea' (Beckett, 253) let the listener of the

---

[1] I borrow my theoretical references mainly from French linguistics. I am here referring to François Flahault's 'identité du sujet' (58).

radio imagine a man under the spell of the sea and obsessed by its sound. He seems to experience the sea as despicable and attractive at the same time — 'I often hear it [...] and start talking, oh just enough to drown it' (254) — a sort of partner he cannot avoid meeting, a partner able to subdue him. It may be noted in advance that to a certain extent the voices the man appeals to appear as substitutes for — and as a protection against — the 'talking' sea he is obsessed with.[2]

The first addressee Henry (subsequently 'the speaker') is looking for is his father. The first enunciators he invokes are Holloway and Bolton, two old men, a doctor and his patient-friend; they appear in Henry's attempt to get an answer from the Father, who does not answer despite the speaker's sustained efforts (he has not even the function of enunciator at this stage). Henry slips from his assertion 'I usen't to need anyone, just [talking] to myself, stories, there was a great one' (254) to the story of the two old men he wants his father to listen to. He quotes a short exchange between them:

— My dear Bolton, it's now past midnight, if you would be good enough —
— Please! PLEASE! (255)

The two enunciators are introduced by the speaker who has the leading role. Once he has quoted them, Henry gets back to his third person narration, the term 'sound' is here repeated five times, with an emphasis on 'Shifting, lapsing, furtive like, dreadful sound'. The imperative that follows marks a new shift: 'Listen to it. [Pause.] Close your eyes and listen to it' — (indirect) address to the Father, followed by the question 'what would you think it was?' The speaker himself suggests an answer — '[Pause. Vehement.] A drip! A drip!' — it (drip) resumes the 'dreadful sound'; the suggestion is rejected immediately; 'No!' (255). Resuming his third person narration, the speaker tries to improve his story, but shortly after he states his failure. He then turns anew directly to the Father. He quotes a short exchange between young Henry and his father (the speaker, the man of the present time, imitating his voice):

— Are you coming for a dip?
— No.
— Come on, come on [...] A washout, that's all you are, a washout! (256)

---

2   Perloff goes further when she argues that 'the dominant voice is not Henry's but the voice of the sea. It is that voice that punctuates each of Henry's questions about his father'; in my view, however, the sound of the sea is rather the substitute of a voice or its counterpoint, and as such it can be placed on the same level as the different voices.

Evoking a second meaning of washout ('abortion') the speaker gets to his daughter Addie, here, too, he slips from the third person narration to a short exchange, the slippage allowing him to move to a new enunciator — in both cases he takes responsibility for the enunciation:

— Run along now, Addie, and look at the lambs.
— No, papa.
— Go on now, go on.
— No, papa.
— Go on with you when you're told and look at the lambs! (256)

New shift, from Addie to Ada, or from the daughter to the mother comes up; 'conversations with her [...] that's what hell will be like' (256). Despite this pejorative judgment he shortly afterwards addresses Ada (taking leave of the Father — 'Tired of talking to you'). Ada, his dead wife, is the fifth enunciator he invokes, after Holloway, Bolton, the younger father, and Addie.

However, as Ada accepts his wish to talk to him, she becomes a speaker of her own. Henry has not succeeded in his attempt at communication with his father. He seems to have more results with his wife, in constructing some kind of exchange. He talks with his wife about Addie's music master, jaegers and horses, laughing. Then he claims 'Listen to it! [Pause.] Lips and claws! [Pause.] Get away from it!' (258). He refers to the sound of the sea he is obsessed with; then he asks Ada to get up and go with him. Ada objects that they cannot go as long as Addie does not join them. Their exchange is crossed by independent voices popping up, interrupting the dialogue. The first intrusion in Henry's discourse begins with the sounds coming from a music room and a voice with a foreign accent:

[*Smart blow of cylindrical ruler on piano case. Unsteadily, ascending and descending, Addie plays scale of A Flat Major, hands first together, then reversed. Pause.*]
Music Master [Italian accent.]: Santa Cecilia!
Addie: Will I play my piece now please? (258)

Then the more the girl plays the more the teacher gets angry, making Addie cry. The master's discourse is reduced to monosyllables when he yells at the pupil — 'Fa', 'Qua', 'Eff'. The blows with the ruler on the piano case[3] become

---

3   The sound of the ruler can be considered as another substitute of a voice (like the sounds of the sea or the hooves).

more and more violent, the pedagogue misusing his position. The exchange ends with Music master's 'Eff! Eff! [*He hammers note.*] Eff! [*He hammers note.*] Eff! [*Hammered note, 'Eff!' and Addie's wail amplified to paroxysm, then suddenly cut off. Pause.*]' (259).

The hammered words seem to cut short also Henry and Ada, to put aside, together with the girl's timid questions and her cries, the dialogue of the couple. Nine replicas long the music master dominating the exchange with his pupil has the leading role at the expense of Henry who remains speechless. Ada, however, seeming less affected by the piano teacher's vehemence, tries to resume their exchange:

> — You are silent today.
> — It was not enough to drag her into the world, now she must play the piano.
> — She must learn. She shall learn. That — and riding.
> [*Hooves walking.*] (259)

Then, once more abruptly, another alien discourse interferes in the dialogue: the riding lesson. Not only does the teacher master the discourse, but the discourse is exclusively reserved to him. The girl has no articulated voice, and not a single word — 'Addie begins to wail', 'Addie's wail amplified to paroxysm'. The master's sentences are elliptic imperatives: 'Now Miss! Elbows in Miss! Hands down Miss!'. Here, once again, Henry remains silent, and once again Ada resumes the dialogue: 'What are you thinking of?' (259). We see that in both cases another speaker pops up and deprives Henry of the leading role. In the exchange that follows (it is, once more, resumed by Ada), another switch is operated:

> [*Boots on shingle, say ten steps. He halts at water's edge. Pause. Sea a little louder. Distant*] Don't wet your good boots. [*Pause*]
> Henry: Don't, don't... [*Sea suddenly rough*]
> Ada [*Twenty years earlier, imploring*]: Don't! Don't!
> Henry [*Ditto, urgent*]: Darling! (259–60)

The switch opens the seduction scene from the past; here man and woman appear as enunciators: the first speaker takes responsibility for the utterances of the couple. Thus Henry, for a moment, succeeds in retaking the leading role. Ada cries out, but after the switch to the present that follows, she takes over.

Ada is anxious about Henry's mental state; however as they memorise the past together, he seems to get some relief from his obsession. He tries to resume the role of the first speaker when suggesting to go for a row. His proposal is declined by Ada, who maintains the initiative, and also proves to have the better memory. Thus Ada claims the position of a speaker at least equal to Henry's. Finally she suggests to him that he should go on with his father and his stories. Henry claims he is not able any more to do so, and becoming anxious that Ada will end the conversation, he implores her to stay with him — 'Keep it going, Ada, every syllable is a second gained' (262), but all his efforts are in vain. She has activated in Henry something he clings to, but eventually she has some long replicas resembling a soliloquy and reminding of Henry's address to the father at the beginning. Ada not only emancipates herself, but her voice also gradually overpowers his. As a result, instead of helping Henry to constitute his identity, she actually contributes to constitute her own. Moreover, as Henry does not answer her self-ironic question — 'Is this rubbish a help to you, Henry?' — she announces that she abandons him, and thus maintains the leading role. Henry now will see no other solution than to return to what they tried to memorise together, and finally to his story.

Through his narration Henry tries to regain the position he has lost in his relationship with Ada. She has left him (thus confirming her independence), the Father is not willing to respond, and Henry himself recognises his failure, also in his expectation to improve the story, hence to get a reaction from the Father: 'No good'. The depreciation of his attempt to improve the Holloway-Bolton-story is followed by the exclamation 'Christ!', then by 'On' — the word that resumes the instruction to move that Henry addressed to himself at the very beginning ('On. [*Sea. Voice louder.*]. On! [*He moves on.*]' 253). Two times Henry is confronted once again with the obsessive sound: there are two occurrences of the direction 'Sea a little louder' (264).

Here he goes over the programme for the evening and for the next day — 'Little book', 'plumber', 'waste', 'words'. His last sentences are — after the particle 'nothing' several times repeated — 'All day all night nothing. [Pause.] Not a sound'. The last two sentences imply that there is nothing to do, nothing to be done, that there is not even the sound of another voice. However, in the original production (BBC, 1955) and in Beckett's translation into French, the sound of the sea recurs, and with this sound the play dies out. Thus, from the standpoint of this version, the voices Henry appeals to with the expectation that they will protect or at least distract him from the sound of the sea seem to function less as a substitute than as a counterpoint to the sound of the sea, which is likely to drown the voices out.

Moreover, Henry's attempts to obtain consistence, to build an identity, have failed. The speaker is about to be quite alone with his voice — as Ada has asserted (262). Henry, as we have seen, on the one hand fails in his attempt to get a response from his father, and has to fill in the gaps the other leaves with citations of unpleasant conversations they had in the past, of violent words the father threw at him. On the other hand, he eventually does not succeed in mastering the voices, whether he appeals to them (Father, Ada) or is confronted with them against his will (Addie's masters jumping into his space without taking any notice of him).

In linguistic terms, the first speaker supposed to organise and lead the voices cannot maintain his position. The principal enunciator he wants to involve does not respond to his expectation, he even remains absent. Other speakers are competing with the speaker who initiates the discourse. This competition does not allow for a coherent interplay of discourses, and not even for a coherent soliloquy. Thus, polyphony as a well-organised discourse is undermined, and no coherence obtained. It should be reminded that the first speaker also tries (in a more implicit mode) to constitute a self-identity. Identity-building (in Flahault's view) is the condition for assigning positions: the speaker is caught in a system of positions that involves his identity, and as far as he is able to assign the positions, he can gain or maintain self-identity. This is an unspoken goal of Henry's, and his prolonged efforts to achieve it, too, prove a failure.

The radio listener is confronted with a complex polyphonic discourse. After the first sentences uttered by the speaker, he gets aware that Henry's interlocutor is imaginary. He is but a disembodied voice evoked by the speaker, interwoven with Henry's own discourse. 'That sound you hear is the sea [...] You would never live this side of the bay' (253) — 'Listen to it! [...] Father!' (255) — 'a washout, that's the last I heard from you, a washout [...] Are you coming for a dip?' (256). By contrast, with Ada's first words — 'Yes' — 'Some little time' (257), another speaker enters the space; and, although invoked by Henry, Ada is getting more and more autonomy. Then a voice of a different kind, with a different function appears with the exclamation 'Santa Cecilia!' (258): the Music Master penetrates the space thwarting Henry's idea that he by himself could fill and organise it.

The polyphony seems in sharp contrast with the genre of the soliloquy in which the speaker is alone, has no other addressee than himself and is in full control of the discourses he invokes. In *Embers*, exterior voices eventually invade his space, his words being ignored by these voices. The radio offers a space where a multiplicity of disembodied voices can be displayed. One has only to think of the theatre play to become aware that the radio play, by contrast, allows for a polyphony of a particular kind: here no actor, no face or body (and no visible scenery) is present, the voices and the sounds alone constitute the 'characters', their relationships, and the surrounding world — as they are suggested by the media. We have seen that Beckett's piece for radio represents a particular case: the chosen media is problematised, but at the same time its specific potentialities are fully exploited as Julie Campbell argues:

> the listener hears Henry's thoughts, hears the one-sided conversation he has with his father, and hears both sides of the conversation he has with his wife, as well as the memories he summons up from the past, and the fictional story he is inventing. *Embers* is focused on exploiting the very effects that result from the listener experiencing a dramatic world through sound and silence alone. (25)

Embers exploits in a subtle way the potentialities of the genre, namely the radio play. The author works with voice and sound only, which is the generic characteristic that distinguishes the radio play from the dramatic and the narrative text. In this framework, the recipient has to imagine the actor/actress behind the voice, a face/body and the related movements. In the case of a narration, he/she has to project the voice upon the discourse. In a radio play, by contrast, the recipient has to try to produce a unity of the two sides of the audible and the imagined. Beckett, as for him, works on the specific situation of the hearer who is limited (in most cases) to an individual — or even solitary — experience. This distinguishes the radio play from the theatre play that allows for a collective experience. Moreover, it should be noted that the listener's situation can be viewed in parallel with that of the main speaker. Both are confronted with voices and sounds, and the hearer — as has been emphasised by Campbell — is exposed to a multiplicity of voices in which no coherence seems to be achieved. One may conclude that the hearer is supposed to continue the author's work, perceive the unity of the speaker and the building of identity as highly problematic.

Works Cited

Bakhtin, Mikhail (1984), *Problems of Dostoevsky's Poetics*, ed. and trans. C. Emerson, Minneapolis/London: U of Minnesota P.
Beckett, Samuel (1990), *The Complete Dramatic Works*, London: Faber and Faber.
Campbell, Julie (2013), 'Close Your Eyes: *Embers* and the Difficulties of Listening', in Peter Fifield and David Addyman, eds., *Samuel Beckett: Debts and Legacies*, London and New York: Bloomsbury Methuen Drama, pp. 133–52.
Ducrot, Oswald (1994), *Le dire et le dit*, Paris: Minuit.
Flahault, François (1978), *La parole intermédiaire*, Paris: Seuil.

Perloff, Marjorie (1998), 'The Silence That Is Not Silence: Acoustic Art in Samuel Beckett's *Embers*', in Lois Oppenheim, ed., *Samuel Beckett and the Arts: Music, Visual Arts, and Non-print Media*, New York: Garland.

PART 2

Voices of an Absent Other

∴

Samuel Beckett, Quickening the 'dead voices': From *Waiting for Godot* to *That Time*

Llewellyn Brown

Abstract

The Beckettian motif of the 'dead voices', in works of the 1940s and 1950s, testifies to the mortifying effect of language, which denies any experience or subjectivity. Later works however show how Beckett gives life to these impersonal acousmatic voices. The example of *That Time* shows voices — those of the visible Listener — coming from without, and which appear as a continuum marked by uncontrollable alternation and merging. The subject appears as one who cannot accept the events related as belonging to any experience that may be his. As an 'acephalous' being, he occupies the structural position of a 'flaw' or a 'hole' at the centre of the three voices that are 'braided' together. Beckett's use of equivocation points to the dynamic factor of Lacan's *'lalangue'* which, as grounded in the real, causes meaning to be irremediably incomplete.

If the question of the voice traverses Beckett's work in its entirety, the motif of 'dead voices' appears specifically in his work of the 1940s and 1950s — *Mercier et Camier*, *En attendant Godot* and *Textes pour rien* — where it expresses the prevalence of the mortifying quality of language, which denies life and subjectivity. To grasp its importance in the evolution of Beckett's work, we can compare a passage from *Waiting for Godot* with the treatment of the voice in *That Time*. We shall see that the status of the voice changes considerably: the 'dead voices' take on life, expressing a vivifying relationship to language.[1]

1 'Dead voices' in *Waiting for Godot*

En attendant Godot was composed from 9 October 1948 to 29 January 1949 — between *Malone meurt* and *L'Innommable* — and published in 1952. In this

---

1 The present text develops, in relation to a specific corpus, ideas expounded in previous articles, and in my book (Brown, 2016).

play, Vladimir and Estragon evoke the presence of what they call 'dead voices' (Beckett, 2006, 58). These voices express the effects of the mortification inflicted by language on the subject, to the point where, as Lacan points out, once the latter is postulated by the signifier, he 'can no longer destroy himself' and 'enters an unbearable chain' (Lacan, 2013, 114) where he encounters the 'eternalisation of his desire' (Lacan, 1966, 319). This is to be understood as the 'structuring, signifying necessity that forbids a subject to escape the concatenation of existence as it is determined by the nature of the signifier' (Lacan, 2013, 118). Here, for example, Hamlet's dilemma reveals that he is irremediably bound within the signifying chain (Lacan, 2013, 118), in an implacable binding where 'being remains identical to everything that he has articulated through the discourse of his life. There, there is no *To be or not to be* — whatever the circumstances, the *To be* remains eternal' (Lacan, 2013, 314). Hamlet has no guarantee that death will effectively bring an end to his existence.

For Beckett, such a condition leads to the encounter with the terrifying state of 'nightmare thingness' (Beckett, 1995, 69) and the threat of perpetual mortification, resulting from the lack of an original 'assent of the Other' (Lacan, 1991, 414) establishing the realm determined by the phallus: a breach inscribing a separation and a hierarchy of values and preferences. Indeed, defined as 'the signifier destined to signify as a whole the effects of the signified' (Lacan, 1966, 690), the phallus allows the composition of reality within a tableau, a 'limited whole'[2] that supports desire: the punctuation closing off a syntactical chain, thus allowing the invading voices to be stilled.

In *Waiting for Godot*, the passage describing dead voices is remarkable for its lyrical quality, which Beckett patterns somewhat on Paul Verlaine's poem 'Chanson d'automne' (Verlaine, 21–2). The link to melancholy is clear, particularly as Verlaine's poem is situated in the collection *Poèmes saturniens*, published in 1866. In a letter, he describes his condition as marked by: '*Cette chose molle, pénétrante, inconsistante comme le brouillard, comme un mauvais air [...] qui trouble le dessein, émousse la volonté [...], rend le cœur vague, la tête vide, la chair et le sang et les nerfs prépondérants sur l'esprit*' (Verlaine, 749).[3]

In order to deal with the apparently impervious and impersonal nature of these voices, Beckett seems to follow Verlaine, whose short poem is based on stanzas where two verses of four syllables are followed by one verse of three

---

2   I refer here to the developments of Jean-Claude Milner. See my article (Brown, 2013) or book (Brown, 2016, 68).
3   Trans.: 'This soft, penetrating thing that is as inconsistent as fog, as foul air [...] that troubles intention, dulls willpower [...], makes the heart vague, the head empty, flesh and blood and nerves preponderant over mind'.

syllables, thus producing an irregularity illustrative of the way the leaves are tossed around by the wind. The crucial stanza for Beckett is: *'Et je m'en vais / Au vent mauvais / Qui m'emporte / Deçà, delà, / Pareil à la / Feuille morte'.*[4] (Verlaine, 22). Beckett's composition is also broken up by pauses into 'stanzas': three of them evoke the sound of the voices by means of images, separated by two — of unequal length — using denotative language, attempting to define the nature and the status of these voices. We also find the alternation of long and short verses, as in Verlaine's poem. The lyrical quality is heightened by anaphors and successions of synonyms, gentle onomatopoeic sounds. In the context of a dramatic genre, these 'verses' are appropriate for a 'pseudocouple', since the 'dead voices' express the absence of any real dialogue:[5] the two characters collaborate to produce what appears as a form of interlude, by comparison with the exchanges that precede and follow this passage in the play.

The images used to describe the voices evoke the air (*leaves, rustle, wings, feathers*), soft sounds (*rustle, murmur, whisper*), while *ashes* and *sand* express the inanimate and terrestrial realm. The image of *ashes* returns in Hamm's description of the mad painter (Beckett, 2006, 113), while the sand — like the words describing sounds — suggests the impossibility of creating any structuring break: we can think of Democritus' 'impossible heap' evoked by Clov in *Endgame* (Beckett, 2006, 93), or the 'great alp of sand' (Beckett, 1953, 43) — 'in tiny packets of two or three millions the grains slip' — sliding so imperceptibly that Erskine is unable to objectively ascertain the reality of any change. These images thus show the voices to be limitless and impossible to order within syntactical sequences, causing a sensation like the unbearable 'sucking' of the sea heard by Henry in *Embers* (Beckett, 2006, 261). The sound Molloy hears is similar:

> But it is not a sound like other sounds, that you listen to, when you choose, and can sometimes silence, by going away or stopping your ears, no, but it is a sound which begins to rustle in your head, without your knowing how, or why. It's with your head you hear it, not your ears, you can't stop it, but it stops itself, when it chooses. (Beckett, 1965, 36)

If we refer the intertextual reference to Virginia Woolf's *Mrs Dalloway*, we can see how such a state can lead to suicide. Indeed, such is the fate of Septimus

---

4 Trans.: 'And I go away / In the bad wind / That bears me off / Here, there, / Just like a / Dead leaf'.

5 As is well known, the title of the play *Oh les beaux jours* refers to the poem 'Colloque sentimental' which, in contradiction to the title, illustrates the impossibility of any colloquy (Verlaine, 58).

Smith, the protagonist of this novel who, while wandering through Regent's Park, hears the voices of his comrades who died in the war (Van Hulle, 79–81).

This structural characteristic appears in the voices' incessant nature: 'To have lived is not enough for them. / They have to talk about it. / To be dead is not enough for them'. (Beckett, 2006, 58). The voices are not associated with any identifiable locutors: instead of being the expression of subjectivity, they are anonymous. They also testify to the existence of a past life, such as the one that Estragon says he cannot remember ever having in 'the Macon country' (Beckett, 2006, 57). If we understand the voice as being one form of Lacan's *objet a* — the part of language a subject cannot, for structural reasons, assume (Brown, 1998) — then the voices Vladimir and Estragon hear express the insistence of past lives that they have never been able to consider as theirs: the latter belong to their objective, biographical reality, but have never been 'experienced' by them. Since the voices will never be attached to any past subjective history, they can never cease. They simply express the senseless accumulation of memories endowed with no brilliance capable of conferring on them any significant meaning. The absence of any structuring punctuation is clear in the fact that these voices do not address anyone, or each other. They are excluded from any dialogue: 'They all speak together. / Each one to itself'. (Beckett, 2006, 58). They compose a myriad of singularities which are unable to be caught up in any signifying chain, and are therefore unable to mean anything for the subject.

We can thus better understand why Beckett resorts to this echo of a versified form. As the characters state: 'we are incapable of keeping silent. / You're right, we're inexhaustible. / It's so we won't think. / We have that excuse. / It's so we won't hear'. (Beckett, 2006, 58). If the invasive voices are never silent — as Lacan points out, the 'ears are in the field of the unconscious, the only orifice that cannot be closed' (Lacan, 1973, 178) — the only way to obtain some respite is to speak oneself. However, these characters' speech never attains a sufficient degree of enunciation — or *invocation* — to bring about a real silencing. They can only provisionally cover up the voices, imitating the latters' movement and elevating it to the status of an aesthetic object, which is in itself a triumph, but which Beckett's later work will find a more adequate structuring for. The versified form — establishing rhythm and stanzas — introduces a degree of closure that the dead voices deny.

However, Beckett succeeds in bringing about a crucial change in his creation, which radically changes the status of such voices. Éric Wessler (2017, 274–5) notes that as of 'From an Abandoned Work' (1954–5), Beckett's writing changed: his style became more contracted, centred on fixity, an orientation which enabled him to transform violence into poetry, in a context where the bodily image was dispersed by the gaze of the Other (intervening in the character of Balfe). Such a change would also seem to be related to his practice of the theatre, in which *En attendant Godot* represented an initial step, tearing away the material taken from *Mercier et Camier*, distancing himself from the perpetual metonymy of prose writing (Janvier, 15), and orienting his creation towards the *address* to spectators in a public performance. Whereas the latter crucial dimension was lacking in the anonymous speaking of the voices, it produces a vital subjective effect in the work for the theatre.

By way of contrast, we can note that Vladimir and Estragon *describe* the voices, but in no way make them heard, or allow them to speak: the voices are represented and evoked, but are not really dealt with. In the same way, we can observe that at this time — in *Dream of Fair to Middling Women, Le Monde et le pantalon*, the 1937 'German letter' to Axel Kaun — Beckett is able to describe or represent — by means of striking metaphors — stunning effects aiming to break up or fracture language, but has yet to discover the means to produce them in his creation.

2   *That Time*: A Counter-Example

That Time offers one example allowing us to observe how Beckett puts language to work to quicken the voices, to give them speech that will have an impact on the subject, in order to endow his existence with some consistency.

The play dates from about twenty years after *Godot*. Beckett started writing in Paris, on 8 June 1974, and completed it on 10 July 1974, but the final typewritten version is dated Paris, August 1975 (Pountney, 268). It shows the head of a man who intently listens to three voices — that are his own, coming back to him from without — recounting in the second person singular episodes of his life. The man's eyes are closed while the voices speak, then open when the voices stop: twice during the play, as well as at the beginning and the end.

At first glance, *That Time* may seem to represent a return to the incessant flux of voices that invade the space of the subject. Indeed, it would be possible to discern a form of continuity leading from *The Unnamable*, through *Not I*,[6] to *That Time*, in which the metonymical aspect of language is dominant. However, we shall attempt to show that the construction of the play as a theatrical whole succeeds in giving life back to the voices by means of intense framing and structuring, where visual and aural are central.

---

6   *The Unnamable* is seen as a source of *Not I* (Knowlson and Pilling, 197); cf. Knowlson, 590.

The setup of the play rests on the scission between seeing and saying: apparently incessant voices are emitted by loudspeakers; they are thus supported by electrical devices. The head, on the other hand, remains speechless: it is only visible. We could therefore ascribe this split to the absence of the founding 'unary trait' which, for Lacan, results from the 'assent of the Other' (Lacan, 1991, 414). By virtue of such an operation, the subject would be inscribed within the domain of a *limited whole*, and the voices would be both enclosed and their impact attenuated within a unified field of representation. To this situation, the theatrical device provides a response by means of its discursive structuring. That is to say: the absence of a separating *trait* (word expressing the inscription of a line) is put to use by Beckett to found his creation on the *objet a* (see Chattopadhyay), as the part excluded from the nameable. Indeed in the theatre, subject, stage and spectators form a tripartite configuration that is essential to his later dramatic pieces. Éric Wessler (2009) has studied in great detail — in relation to the evolution of modern literature — the role of self-reflexivity, which offers a subjective substitute throughout Beckett's work. Here the indispensable address to an Other affords such a structuring that was lacking in his earlier production. We could therefore describe the subjective setup of *That Time* as one where the subject/creator offers to the gaze of his Other a mute image or representation of himself as a detached head: while the latter is subjected to a spotlight that is in no way inert (as demonstrated by its regular variations in intensity), the spectator represents a collective Other whose gaze is captured by the gleaming source of reflected light. The gaze is thus not a persecuting one, but one that, marked by 'intentness' (Beckett, 2006, 329), can afford a sense of *percipi*. The head becomes the spectator's on-stage *delegate*. On the other hand, the subject makes his voices heard, silencing the audience's incessant babble: the voices thus take on form, their importance and their receivability being confirmed by the spectator.

3 Voices: Three Are One

The voices heard in this play come from without, and yet they belong to Listener: '*Voices* A B C *are his own coming to him from both sides and above*'. The three are one, just as Belaqua was 'trine' (Beckett, 1992, 120). The recourse to electric recording equipment is crucial, in conferring their full reality on the voices insofar as the latter represent the part of language the subject is structurally unable to assume as his own: they cannot be completely assimilated. This is particularly the case for Listener, who remains mute. For a theatrical representation, this setup also means that the spectator is equally subjected to the reality of the voices, which he cannot dismiss as being located 'in Listener's head'.

Three voices speak, each one endowed with its own specific identity: 'The B story has to do with the young man, the C story is the story of the old man and the A story that of the man in middle age' (Knowlson, 601), as Beckett explained. However, these identities are subordinated to their structural quality as *voice*. In other words, they are diverse in their expression — discrete insofar as they convey signifiers — but they all emanate from the part that the subject is incapable of experiencing as belonging to himself. They are therefore ceaseless manifestations caused by the part of his existence that is excluded from representation: the hole that underlies all attempts to name 'that time' or 'that subject'. To attain this ceaseless quality, Beckett worked on creating seamless connections between the different fragments, as Rosemary Pountney points out: 'the stories should, states Beckett, be "overlapping"' (269). She specifies: 'Beckett emphasizes the importance of continuity for each voice by underlining the first and last phrase in every paragraph'. (274).

This fundamental unity means that the voice manifests itself here as a continuum: Listener finds himself born along by incessant voices, instead of experiencing the signifying chain as marked by the open/close beating of the unconscious, as manifested, for example, in the intermittency of 'free association'. Indeed, usually, the subject only has sporadic access to the unconscious: the latter is never on open access.

For this reason also, Beckett insisted on making the tone of the voices both distinct and merged. The directions state: '*They modulate back and forth without any break in general flow except where silence indicated*' (Beckett, 2006, 388). The preliminary note stipulates: 'Moments of one and the same voice A B C relay one another without solution of continuity — apart from the two 10-second breaks. Yet the switch from one to another must be clearly faintly perceptible' (387). Any differences between the voices must be associated with merging. Beckett wrote to Alan Schneider:

> The chief difficulty, A B & C being the same voice, will be to make clear the modulation from one to another, as between attendant keys, without breaking the flow continuous except where silences indicated. I feel that dissimilar contexts and dislocation in space — one coming to him from left, a second from above, third from right — should be enough to do it. If not the effect will have to be assisted at level of recording. (Beckett, 1998, 328–9)

The musical metaphor and the different spatial locations show the way in which the voice intervenes as a quality distinct from the signifier, as imposing a difference that remains extremely difficult to qualify or pin down. In this way, the listener — on or off stage — is subjected to the voices, and unable to master them by rationalisation. Enoch Brater rightly observes the discomfort such a device produces: 'As in *Not I*, this piece, too, must work on the nerves of the audience, not its intellect' (Brater, 44). That is to say, the effect is not intended to be simply a form of imaginary representation.

4 Voices: Braiding the Three

The breaking up embodied in the signifiers of the voices is countered by the formal construction: the three voices alternate according to a strict pattern that binds them together. Their triplicity is expressive of their efforts to compose one identity for a subject… who is devoid of any: the latter is both all three, and none of them. The formal aspect takes on considerable importance, as in the first two 'acts', the voices follow an order which is disrupted before each pause. Antoni Libera explains: 'Each of the voices develops its own theme according to an order which, after three statements by each voice, undergoes a sudden disturbance, as if the form had outdistanced the story: something that ought not to have been said until later unexpectedly appears earlier' (Libera, 81). This brings into play what Libera calls 'flawed formalism'. The 'errors' at the end of the first two acts can be seen as preparing the final 'rectification'. They can appear as manifestations of a capricious Other, who finds himself unable to respect a logical order, and falters after noticing his mistake. They can also testify to the way Listener is able to act upon this Other, exerting an influence as 'editor'. We can see this form of rectification at work in Beckett's later play *What Where*.

It should also be pointed out that each sequence of three contains an 'error', since instead of starting by A B C, the voices follow the order A C B, thus reversing the second two letters. The following sequences maintain the latter two, placing them at the beginning: A C B becomes C B A. Thus, having instituted a flawed beginning — a form of *proton pseudos* — the sequences follow suit, leaving one element of the three out of place. This can perhaps be enlightened by another 'flaw' pointed out by Antoni Libera: 'the position reached (ABC) would have been the last in the collection of combinations which could have been formed from the three elements. Beckett's reason for not following the principle in part three was, we must assume, to avoid a closed globular construction' (Libera, 81). More precisely, what this points to is the presence of the subject as a hole; the latter being as much avoided — and called into being — as the problematic central point in *Quad*: 'E supposed a danger zone' (Beckett,

2006, 453). As can be noted in *How It Is* or *What Where*, the permutations that actually take place remain incomplete, pointing to the anamorphic structuring whereby the subject is irrecoverable by the signifying network, by representation. The subject is this void — which is not nothingness, as Lacan points out (Lacan, 2011, 53) — this radical absence or this defect in formal perfection, a quality which also proves its value when, at the end, the three voices rectify their sequence, thus provoking the conclusive smile of Listener.

The value of this is also apparent when considering Stanley Gontarski's observation concerning Beckett's progressive elaboration of the pattern: 'But clearly, after working with the content of the play over and over again, Beckett abandoned this means of organizing his narratives and established the final order formally, abstractly, musically' (Gontarski, 160). This corresponds to Beckett's words to Charles Juliet: *'Il faut être là — index pointé sur la table — et aussi — index levé vers le haut — à des millions d'années lumière. En même temps...'* (Juliet, 66–7).[7] This extreme gap describes the necessity both to be as close as possible to the irreducible materiality of words, and to order the literary composition with the most extreme detachment, as if from the point of view of Sirius (Beckett, 1995, 127). This 'abstract' or absolute organising — where content is considered as immaterial — leads to the most rigorous structuring of the play, by contrast with what seems to be the dispersion of any elements of narrative or identity. In this way, Beckett situates himself, as a subject, on the side of the values embodied by the spotlight that makes Listener's face glow. In the terms Beckett used in *Le Monde et le pantalon*: 'Espace et corps, achevés, inaltérables' (Beckett, 1990, 28).[8]

5   Voices: 'Lalangue'

The question that it is now necessary to address is in what way the dead voices are 'quickened' in this play. For this 'acephalous' subject, it is a matter of, retrospectively, being able to at last be present to what he has *lived* through without *experiencing* it: a past he can in no way recognise as belonging to him. Like the aim of the voice in *Company* — 'To have the hearer have a past and acknowledge it' (Beckett, 2009a, 22) — the ones in *That Time* — which address Listener by using the pronoun *you* — have to persuade him that the memories belong

---

7 Trans.: 'One must be there — index pointed at the table — and also — index raised — millions of light-years away. At the same time...'.
8 Trans.: 'Space and body, completed, inalterable'.

to him. It would seem important to take into account that in this 1974 text, Beckett is going over very old memories: ones that remain because they have never been symbolised, integrated into experience, endowed with meaning. If they had become experiences, they would have been relativised, caught up in the succession of larger and smaller events that bestrew a life. In *That Time*, they are therefore memories that insist, and that he is powerless to detach himself from. The question of the melancholic persists: what did he lose at *that time*?[9] Only the incessant voices will enable him, perhaps, to latch on to something of what happened or, at least, to relive the events; but in doing so, he is not only being lulled by them, he is attempting to find some support for his existence. The persistent question regarding 'that time' suggests the effort to attach the memories to a symbolic framework.

The treatment of language here can shed light on the way the voices endow the subject with a body, with an existence he cannot have by any other means. This entails the necessity of treating language not simply as meaning, communication or representation, but as having a real impact on the body. That also means not reducing the importance of the words to their continuity with the rest of Beckett's work. In speaking of *That Time*, Évelyne Grossman calls for a 'dynamic reading' of the text, stating 'there is, for me, no other way to read [Beckett] than to enter with him in this counter-depressive decomposition' (Grossman, 52). This, of course, is not an easy approach since a structural barrier exists. Behind every word, every expression, there are immeasurable intimate associations with precise events and the unspeakable impact words have had on the author. On the other hand, the spectator perceives an aesthetic object: one that takes on form by being addressed to the public. And never the twain shall meet, except in the realm of the aesthetic moment, which is also the place where the creator at last attains the symbolic inscription that was originally lacking. This mechanism is called 'sublimation':[10] the subject comes into being at this point, irrespective of what he may be or do in his biographical existence. Here, the texts that speak of 'failure' are thus a success:[11] ill seeing and ill saying are, at last for the subject, true seeing and saying,

---

9   In his founding study, Freud points out that the melancholic knows *whom* he has lost, but not *what* he has lost, in the way of a subjective function (Freud, 289).

10 Sublimation supposes a work of art addressed to a public, thus creating a ternary structure surrounding a hole that can never be assimilated. See Wajcman, 68. Erik Porge deals with the same ternary structuring, in the parallel between courtly love and Lacan's article on Marguerite Duras (Porge, 83).

11 But not in terms of mastery, as Isabelle Ost points out (124–5), contesting Bruno Clément's interpretation.

where the *letter* detaches signifier from signified. The creator lives what he was unable to live or experience at the time.

Lacan's later developments on *lalangue* can shed light on this question in *That Time*. Here language is not articulation — the unconscious 'structured like a language' by metaphor and metonymy — but resembles the lack of separation manifest in *lallation*. On a more existential level, it testifies to 'traces of what a subject has heard and registered. Things said [*Dits*] from his birth, that bear the mark of a saying [*dire*], of this saying that [...] supports all the said [*les dits*] that speech proffers' (Nguyên, 2010, 68). It is a matter of enunciation that strikes the body, leaving 'the indelible mark that sanctions for a subject his relation [*rapport*] to the real, that is to say nothing less than his style' (Nguyên, 2014, 149). This follows on from the way Lacan redefines the drives as 'the echo in the body of the fact that there is saying [*un dire*]' (Lacan, 2005, 17).

Conceptually, Jean-Claude Milner points out that *lalangue* 'prevents by incommensurability the construction of a class of languages that may include it; its most direct representation is in fact the mother tongue' (Milner, 21). It is what 'causes a language to be comparable to no other, in that precisely it has no other, in that also what makes it incomparable cannot be said' (Milner, 22). *Lalangue* is therefore perpetually situated outside of empiric utterances, being 'in any language, the register that destines it to *équivoque*', leading to a 'singular mode of creating *équivoque*' (Milner, 22), which we find in living tongues and, we should add, in creation. The word *équivoque* here engages the dimension of *non-sense* (or *hors sens*), not the simple copresence of competing meanings. By bringing this dimension of language to the fore, Lacan reveals the phallic dimension of enunciation in what he consequently calls the 'phunction of phonation' (Lacan, 2005, 127), which is capable of 'transmitting the function proper to the name' (Lacan, 2005, 76). Thus enunciation founded on *lalangue* is capable of ensuring the stabilising function that Lacan formerly ascribed to the Name-of-the-Father. What is also important for reading Beckett — with the 'acephalous' subject presented in the figure of Listener — is that 'something can be said, without any subject knowing it' (Lacan, 2001, 336): this enunciation brings into play knowing that cannot be assumed as knowledge transmissible by a subject. If there is no longer any Other — as a repository of knowing, as authority — language itself nonetheless contains this knowing which comes into being through saying and creating.

Thus phonation resounds against ultimate silence, retroactively transforming the 'acephalous' subject. Bruno Geneste describes this point as 'the silence said to be "of nature" or "of divinity" (*silere*), that is located on the fringes of the void and of which Echo, transformed into a large stone, is the fiction. It is a place where a hem is sewn between silence and voice, and to which subjective experience pushed to its limits can testify' (Geneste, 101–2). It is saying also that radically transforms the 'negative' images of the text, which are simply the latter's signified. That is to say that negation on the level of meaning takes on a completely different importance through *saying*: it is 'phallicised'. The words that describe destruction are clear: 'making it up now one voice now another till you were hoarse and they all sounded the same' (A4). The 'making it up' gives rise to the effective reality of the present representation born by the voice.

In *That Time*, we can see the use Beckett makes of *équivoque*. It is true that, in earlier works, he described such possibilities, when speaking of a 'blooming, buzzing confusion' (Beckett, 2009b, 4) or a 'Matrix of surds' (72), 'a cyclone of electrons' (Beckett, 1992, 113), or declaring: 'Everything divides into itself, I suppose' (Beckett, 1965, 176). However, these brilliant imaginary representations do not put such a use of language into practice: the persistence of dead voices testifies to this impasse. Beckett's extreme perspicacity was to find the words, ahead of time, pointing to the crucial procedures he would put to use in his later works.

If *lalangue* cannot be spoken, its effects are seen in the use of language (*langage*; Nguyên, 2014, 160), such as *équivoque*. Indeed, Beckett works on various levels to establish the breaking up of words, to give place to *lalangue*. On a macrostructural level, the single text Listener follows throughout the play manifests itself in the form of the three intertwined voices, and in the specific use of language they make. Their multiplicity leaves the spectator, along with Listener, in the uneasy position between 'pitches' or musical 'keys', without being able to locate himself in relation to a clear reference point.

Another form of fragmentation is the dissemination of elements throughout the text, moving from one context to another. Thus the 'muttering' is shared by the three voices. Voice C (old man) is 'muttering to yourself who else you'll never be the same after this' (C4): the absence of any interlocutor is accompanied by the denunciation of disappointed hopes for a decisive 'turning point' in life. The overlap between C5 and B5 (young man) produces 'or was that another time', followed by 'muttering that time altogether on the stone in the sun'. This brings a displacement from the bitter voice of C (expressed by the pejorative verb *mutter*) towards the idyllic scene of the young couple: the two are usually mute, but here the words they may have spoken are not amorous murmurs but mere mutterings, thus contaminated by Voice B. The invention of a life the subject may have had is immediately echoed in Voice B5 by 'making it up from there', a phrase which is also shared by the three voices. Later, voice A (middle age) picks up the same verb: 'muttering away now one voice now another' (A10), referring back to childhood efforts to people the emptiness by creating fictional interlocutors. In the same way, the 'marble slab' is a bench in the Portrait Gallery for Voice C1 or the mother's tombstone for Voice C2. But it also creates an echo with the two lovers' 'stone in the sun' (B3), or Voice A3's stone, where the child takes refuge in the ruins. These repetitions point to the insistence or the return 'at the same place' (Lacan, 1973, 49)[12] of the impossibility of dialogue, but for the auditor, they cause abrupt displacements that propel him from one point to another, as he attempts to latch on to shreds of meaning, to find which motif refers to what place, what time, and to determine what relationship there may be between the diverging occurrences. In these displacements, it is necessary to take into account the disturbing or anxiety-provoking aspect of the voices, whereby each segment of the sentence, each occurrence of a motif, produces a displacement, an overturning of *jouissance*, rather than witnessing a peaceful stroll among images; while at the same time admitting that the latter would be the 'phallicised' aspect of these voices.

Intensive use of antithetical echoes also serves to break down the use of language considered as determined by address and grammatical articulation. Thus in 'waiting with the nightbag till the truth began to dawn' (A5), the antinomy *night/dawn* injects a logic distinct from that of *waiting/arrival of truth* — the latter remaining suspended and unnamed — since the *night* also precedes the *dawn*. This antinomy breaks up the narrative succession or grammatical articulation, raising unanswered questions, such as: is there — or where is there — a narrative sequence composed of *night* and *dawn*? The saturation of prepositions serves to sap meanings in a similar way: 'dry off and on to hell out of there' (C2). Punctuating the phrase according to usual meaning would transcribe as 'to dry oneself', 'to continue', 'to go to hell', 'to evacuate a place'. However, the prepositions are so intensively used that *off* and *on* evoke quite a different and independent expression; *on to hell* implies progression, whereas in itself, *to hell*, is an interjection or expletive exclamation.

The reality of Malone's observation 'Everything divides into itself, I suppose' (Beckett, 1965, 176) is demonstrated in the intensive use of *équivoque* where words do not line up according to grammatical ordering, but irremediably interfere with each other on a microstructural level. This effect is achieved, among others, by absence of punctuation and by ellipsis, as we can see in the following short phrase, which evidences numerous possibilities: 'bit of a tower still standing all the rest rubble and nettles where did you sleep no friend all the homes gone' (A3). We can note:

---

12   This is one Lacanian definition of the *real*.

— *bit of*: a segment of 'Foley's Folly', referring to the words immediately preceding these
— *bit of a tower*: a phonetic echo — at a distance — of TOWpath
— *tower still*: epithet meaning 'immobile', 'calm', as in other texts of Beckett
— *still standing*: temporal adverb; the tower is upright even today
— *standing all*: all are erect
— *still standing all the rest*: everything is upright, except the tower
— *all the rest rubble and nettles*: on the contrary, everything has crumbled to ruins
— *rubble and nettles where*: interrogation, seeking to locate the ruins
— *did you sleep no*: question ('did you?') and answer ('no')
— *no friend*: friends do not exist
— *no friend*: address to another ('no, my friend')
— *no friend all homes*: friends do not exist, but there are houses all around
— *all homes gone*: the homes have disappeared

These variations in reading are in no way rationally justifiable, but they are distinctly what an auditor is forced to — fleetingly, without being necessarily able to recognise, and in a random manner — accept as part of one's own unconscious reception of words. What trumps meaning, for the auditor, is the *effect* produced: one reconstitutes fragments — images, scenes — each time differently. The auditor does not grasp all the acute divergences and subtleties that a reader can examine, but they are present, they are real, and one is aware of this reality. The effect is therefore a result of this precondition.

This means that practically each word produces an inescapable divergence[13] where actor and auditor remain in an indeterminate place. Isabelle Ost speaks, in relation to *Ohio Impromptu*, of the virtualising effect of the doubles, Reader and Listener, creating a paradoxical torsion whereby coexist 'the already-lived of the story consigned in the great book, the present of reading and the future of the multiple potential realisations' (Ost, 193). Here in *That Time*, *équivoque* does not point to a joyous plethora of meanings but to the ultimate absence of any meaning, to the *non-sense* that inhabits language in its entirety. It is here that each word produces an effect on the body, opening

---

13   Évelyne Grossman speaks of 'a syntax that leaves us as if undecided between retrospection [...] and prospection [...] In other words meaning — fragile, temporary — is only condensed for an instant and we have to grasp it as it flies past, between before and after, past and future, memory and invention' (Grossman, 64).

abysses, becoming an obstacle (*empêchement*, in Beckett's words), but also opens unsuspected perspectives that one can only explore at the risk of finding oneself faced with the same impasse with the following word. We could add that such divergences can involve meaning, intertexual and intratextual allusions, or references to other works by Beckett. However, it needs to be added that it is not simply a matter of creating uncertainty and confusion, since the effects of *équivoque* are only achieved insofar as the links of syntax and meaning remain strong and constraining.

The absence of punctuation — as signs, capitals, or breaks as in verse — contributes to reinforce these effects. When reading such texts however, one may have little difficulty in restoring meaning and finding one's bearings. The actor can choose to accentuate this aspect of the narrative, as does Niall Buggy in *Beckett on Film*, restoring punctuation by effective pauses. This raises the crucial question of the speed of delivery, which also concerns *Not I* or *Play*: we have a choice between appreciating the meaning and the poetic beauty of the text, or submitting the auditor to a profound musical impression that forever escapes him. This excludes, like for the psychoanalyst, any attempt at 'understanding'. Indeed Lacan denounces the latter: 'in the name of intelligence, there is simply elision of what must cause us to stop, and which is not comprehensible' (Lacan, 2015, 123). Here we find Albert Nguyên's note concerning the voice as a lost object in enunciation: 'The voice is lost as soon as it is emitted, as soon as it is silent, as soon as it structures silence. As soon as, once proffered, it detaches itself, it is lost' (Nguyên, 2014, 151). The auditor thus experiences this loss in an intensive manner. This means that in performance, it is necessary to find a position that lies between the clear breaking up according to syntactical logic, and the continual interference and confusion resulting from maximal speed. Such a position is in no way predetermined or strictly definable. The position that it is necessary to create is one that will cause the maximum of discomfort or uncertainty, which does not necessarily suppose (but does not exclude...) maximum speed. This position points towards the place of the subject: where the latter attempts desperately and ineffectively to latch on to meanings, but finds themselves caught up by the pure and ungraspable musicality. It may also be useful to point out that this discomfort is distinct from the way the cinema unburdens the subject, who allows themselves to be borne along and manipulated by the moving images. Here, by contrast, the subject is to be situated in the place of their ejection from signifiers.

Of course, according with the definitions of *lalangue*, such intensive and manifest formal use of *équivoque* does not constitute the only way to practise this dimension (or *dit-mention*) of language: all of Beckett's later creations represent different ways of approaching it, in what Albert Nguyên points to as *style*.[14]

Thus, in *Waiting for Godot*, the evocation of the 'dead voices' took the form of a calming and lyrical description, corresponding to the way Vladimir and Estragon seek to give themselves the impression they are alive (Beckett, 2006, 64). In *That Time*, the use of language actually endows Listener — and the creator-subject — with bodily consistency. This effect corresponds to Albert Nguyên's comment of Lacan's later definition of the drive, pointing out that the 'echo' Lacan speaks of is not determined by repetition but is 'an echo of separation, an echo that supposes that the voice has been incorporated' (Nguyên, 2014, 153). The notion of incorporation — which Lacan uses specifically with regard to the voice (Lacan, 2004, 318) — means that the voice creates a void in the subject, caused by the absence of any guarantee from the Other. Beckett succeeds in combining the breaking up of syntactic structure, with the rigorous structuring afforded by the point of view of Sirius.

Works Cited

Beckett, Samuel (1953), *Watt*, New York: Grove P.

Beckett, Samuel (1965), *Three Novels*, New York: Grove P.

Beckett, Samuel (1990), *Le Monde et le pantalon suivi de Peintres de l'empêchement*, Paris: Minuit.

Beckett, Samuel (1992), *Dream of Fair to Middling Women*, Dublin: The Black Cat P.

Beckett, Samuel (1995), *The Complete Short Prose: 1929–1989*, New York: Grove P.

Beckett, Samuel and Alan Schneider (1998), *No Author Better Served: The Correspondence of Samuel Beckett and Alan Schneider*, in Maurice Harmon, ed., Cambridge: Harvard UP.

Beckett, Samuel (2006), *The Complete Dramatic Works*, London: Faber and Faber.

Beckett, Samuel (2009a), *Company, Ill Seen Ill Said, Worstward Ho, Stirrings Still*, London: Faber and Faber.

Beckett, Samuel (2009b), *Murphy*, London: Faber and Faber.

Brater, Enoch (1987), *Beyond Minimalism: Beckett's Late Style in the Theater*, Oxford: Oxford UP.

Brown, Llewellyn (1998), 'La Voix, signe de l'impossible chez Samuel Beckett', *SBT/A*, 7: *Beckett Versus Beckett*, pp. 165–76.

---

14   The voice is one form of the *objet a* and, as Lacan states, parodying a phrase by Buffon: style is 'the man whom one addresses' (Lacan, 1966, 9). Addressed speech produces the *objet a* as encircled by its return to the speaker, which it thus divides.

Brown, Llewellyn (2013), 'Voix et illimité dans *L'Innommable*', SBT/A, 25: *Beckett in the Cultural Field/Beckett dans le champ culturel*, pp. 239–52.
Brown, Llewellyn (2016), *Beckett, Lacan and the Voice*, Stuttgart: Ibidem.
Chattopadhyay, Arka (2011), '"From inner to outer shadow": Reading the Obscure Object of Anxiety in the "Dramaticules" of Samuel Beckett', *Miranda*, 4, https://miranda.revues.org/1902, accessed 7 October 2015.
Freud, Sigmund (2006), *The Penguin Freud Reader*, ed. A. Phillips, Penguin Books, epub format.
Geneste, Bruno (2017), 'Samuel Beckett, l'"entre" vivifiant de lalangue et l'hiatus sinthomatique: contrer ces vérités du surmoi', in Brown, ed., *La Violence dans l'œuvre de Samuel Beckett: entre langage et corps*, Paris: Lettres modernes Minard, 'La Revue des Lettres modernes; Série Samuel Beckett' no. 4, pp. 89–116.
Gontarski, S. E. (1985), *The Intent of Undoing in Samuel Beckett's Dramatic Texts*, Bloomington: Indiana UP.
Grossman, Évelyne (2008), 'À la limite...: lecture de *Cette fois* de Samuel Beckett', SBT/A, 19: *Borderless Beckett/Beckett sans frontières: Tokyo 2006*, pp. 51–66.
Janvier, Ludovic (2012), 'Entretien réalisé par Martin Mégevand', *Littérature*, 167: '*Samuel Beckett*', September, 2012, pp. 7–22.
Juliet, Charles (2007), *Rencontres avec Samuel Beckett*, Paris: P.O.L.
Knowlson, James (1996), *Damned to Fame: The Life of Samuel Beckett*, London: Bloomsbury.
Knowlson, James and John Pilling (1979), *Frescoes of the Skull: The Later Prose and Drama of Samuel Beckett*, London: Calder.
Lacan, Jacques (1966), *Écrits*, Paris: Seuil.
Lacan, Jacques (1973), *Le Séminaire, Livre XI, Les Quatre concepts fondamentaux de la psychanalyse*, Paris: Seuil.
Lacan, Jacques (1991), *Le Séminaire, Livre VIII, Le Transfert*, Paris: Seuil.
Lacan, Jacques (2001), *Autres écrits*, Paris: Seuil.
Lacan, Jacques (2004), *Le Séminaire, Livre X, L'Angoisse*, Paris: Seuil.
Lacan, Jacques (2005), *Le Séminaire, Livre XXIII, Le Sinthome*, Paris: Seuil.
Lacan, Jacques (2011), *Le Séminaire, Livre XIX, ...ou pire*, Paris: Seuil.
Lacan, Jacques (2013), *Le Séminaire, Livre VI, Le Désir et son interprétation*, Paris: Seuil.
Lacan, Jacques [1978] (2015), *Le Séminaire, Livre II, Le Moi dans la théorie de Freud et dans la technique de la psychanalyse*, Paris: Seuil.
Libera, Antoni (1980), 'Structure and Pattern in *That Time*', JOBS, 6: Autumn, pp. 81–9.
Milner, Jean-Claude (1978), *L'Amour de la langue*, Paris: Seuil, 'Connexions du champ freudien'.
Nguyên, Albert (2010), 'Les Clefs de lalangue: Beckett, Cixoux, Joyce et... Lacan', *L'En-je lacanian*, 2:15: 'Rencontre et répétition', pp. 67–111.

Nguyên, Albert (2014), *Le Désir à l'heur du réel: Séminaire de Bordeaux 2013–2014*, École de psychanalyse des Forums du Champ lacanien.

Ost, Isabelle (2008), *Samuel Beckett et Gilles Deleuze: cartographie de deux parcours d'écriture*, Bruxelles: Facultés universitaires Saint-Louis.

Porge, Erik (2015), *Le Ravissement de Lacan: Marguerite Duras à la lettre*, Toulouse: Érès.

Pountney, Rosemary (1988), *Theatre of Shadows: Samuel Beckett's Drama, 1956–1976*, Gerrards Cross: Colin Smythe.

Van Hulle, Dirk (2010), 'En écrivant Godot: Beckett et la peine d'écrire', in Llewellyn Brown, ed., *Samuel Beckett 1: 'L'Ascèse du sujet'*, Caen: Lettres modernes Minard, 'La Revue des Lettres modernes', pp. 71–83.

Verlaine, Paul (2005), *Œuvres poétiques complètes*, Paris: Robert Laffont.

Wajcman, Gérard (1998), *L'Objet du siècle*, Lagrasse: Verdier.

Wessler, Éric (2009), *La Littérature face à elle-même: l'écriture spéculaire de Samuel Beckett*, Amsterdam: Rodopi.

Wessler, Éric (2017), 'La Violence comme métaphore de l'écriture dans l'œuvre de Beckett', in Llewellyn Brown, ed., *La Violence dans l'œuvre de Samuel Beckett: entre langage et corps*, Paris: Lettres modernes Minard, 'La Revue des Lettres modernes; Série Samuel Beckett', no. 4, pp. 263–81.

Scratching the Surface: The Dramaturgical Oxymoron in Beckett's Silences

Laurens De Vos

Abstract

Despite — or maybe because of — the insisting preoccupation with silence in Beckett's work, it is a state that seems hard to reach. Noise is continuously interfering in one way or another. Introducing the notion of the 'dramaturgical oxymoron' that opens up a gap between two different modes of narration, this essay will argue that Beckett's plays demonstrate the impossibility of ultimate silence, which lies outside the symbolic order. In this sense these background noises are similar to other disruptive signs, such as the scratch, which is a recurring motif in Beckett. What may seem a mere detail in *Krapp's Last Tape*, a scratch on the girl's thigh, inflicted by picking gooseberries, serves as a metaphor for the loss of completeness and one's alienation from the world. In the voice, finally, the character is disembodied, virtualised. Existing of nothing but thin air, in Mouth's 'own' words in *Not I*, the voice does not seem to belong to the body and gives rise to the alienating effect of what Derrida calls *s'entendre parler*. Although the French deconstructionist has never written on Beckett, his writings on the primacy of the voice and the opposing stance he distinguishes in Artaud probably say as much about Beckett.

1   The Metaphor of the Scratch

In her essay on Antonin Artaud, Susan Sontag argued that his attempt to put an end to all dualisms is bound to lead either to madness, suicide or silence (Sontag, liii). Obviously, Beckett's characters are no more capable of reaching silence than of killing themselves, as Estragon acknowledges: 'we are incapable of keeping silent', which may protect them from hearing '[a]ll the dead voices' (III, 54). Silence is a privilege that is not within reach of Beckett's protagonists. However, Krapp, for one, does seem to experience moments of absolute silence. These take place at instances of perfect balance. In the circular universe of Beckett, the epicentre or the exact middle is the only space of rest, peace and silence — the space where the organic body eventually turns into inorganic stone. The desire to occupy this middle can be associated, then, with Freud's death drive — it is a very persistent longing that Hamm in *Endgame* formulates most poignantly, demanding Clov push him 'right in the center' (III, 109). Beckett calls this stage in which all opposites are erased the wombtomb, a stage that amounts to a pre-oedipal, symbiotic state of existence. It bears the promise of the erasure of the lack of the subject, resulting from the sin of having been born. Therefore, the epiphany that Krapp experiences takes place during that 'memorable equinox' (III, 223), the moment when day and night are exactly equally long. Only then and there in the middle can life indeed turn to stone, to the inorganic stage of the unborn where nothing stirs and all is silent: 'Never knew such silence. The earth might be uninhabited' (III, 229).

Krapp's experience, obviously, is a fantasy, a narrated account of an ideal state of harmony that is as much complete as unobtainable. The idyllic scene of Krapp lying motionless in a punt with his face in his girlfriend's breasts is 'bruised' by a scratch he notices on her thigh. It all seemed too beautiful, too impossible, to be left unscathed; reminiscent of the scene in the prose-poem *Company*, in which the boy's repulsion by his mother is symbolised by his fall from the fir, afflicting bruises and scratches, the wound on Krapp's girlfriend's thigh equally represents a more existential affliction. She bears the scar of being (human), of being a castrated subject for whom the pre-oedipal state can only be dreamt of. Krapp's attempt and desire to attain an oedipal unity with his girlfriend as between mother and child by lying on her in an embryonic position cannot possibly be re-enacted. This is what the scratch on her thigh points at. A flawless unison is forever out of reach for whoever is born a human being. Birth was the death of him. In his essay on the drawings of Artaud, Derrida points out that '[t]he persecution of this *force* began the moment I was *born* [...] Deflection of force, theft, or *substitution* of the newly born, *imposture*, and insinuation of the *instrument*. I have been robbed, not of this or that, but myself robbed of myself, in the very stuff of myself' (Derrida, 1998, 93). Only with the introduction in the symbolic order and the concomitant manifestation of the human lack does the actual subject come into existence. The subject, then, is defined by a paradox that goes to the very core of his existence as a human being: the subject can only become a subject by giving up on himself, by appropriating and embodying the lack, the void of what Lacan calls the *extime*. It is a portmanteau word of the external and the intimate, with which the French psychoanalyst denotes the fundamentally alienated part of ourselves that in its absence structures the subject as a signifier in the symbolic world.

Moreover, in order to point out the self-alienation to which Krapp is subjected, the scratch is attributed to his girlfriend having picked gooseberries. Both the scratch itself and the seemingly facile explanation should raise our awareness for the metaphorical meanings behind the almost nonsensical nature of the anecdote as such. It brings to mind the expression 'playing gooseberry' which means 'to be with two people who are having a romantic relationship and who want to be alone together' (Longman). An intruder seems to come in between Krapp and his girlfriend. Their relationship Krapp dreams of as being a pre-oedipal, totalising symbiosis exhibits not so much literally but metaphorically a scratch, and it seems that paradoxically, it is his girlfriend who is the outsider in their own relationship. The merger cannot possibly be performed to the full; Krapp's desire to '[l]et me in' (III, 229) will always fall short and result in a never entirely satisfying union, as it is necessarily informed by the Lacanian lack. Because of the insatiability of desire and the impossibility of obtaining a flawless, 'scratchless' union that has not been subjected to the symbolic castration, Krapp 'thought it was hopeless and no good going on' (229). Not so much his so-called artistic aspirations have driven him towards giving up on his love, but the realisation of never reaching the terminus of the dynamics of desire. This is why the girl in the punt does not need to have a name; no woman can live up to the amniotic state of being Krapp craves. No matter how much she is engaged in their relationship, she will always also remain a bystander, forced to keep on playing gooseberry. She is, after all, a human being who is equally subjected to what Lacan calls the *demande-à-l'Autre*. Her desire oriented externally, Krapp can never fully complement her in his craving to undo his own lack by becoming *m'être-à-moi / maître-à-moi*. Not only will their mutual relationship always be marked by an intolerable lack, his girlfriend is also an outsider in Krapp's relationship with himself.

2   Beckett's Dramaturgical Oxymorons

Of course, it is all theatre. Elsewhere, I have argued that Krapp's accounts of his past are characterised by an embellishment of what is gone, and his regrets are primarily not focused on missed chances in life, but on the imaginary return to a past that never was (De Vos, 181). Krapp has not miscalculated in the past; he has never taken the wrong choice the consequences of which he still has to bear. On the contrary, his tragedy lies in the realisation that he never really had a choice, that, as Beckett acknowledged himself, 'whichever decision he might have taken, he would have failed' (qtd. in Lawley, 93). After all, there never was a decisive moment, as little as there was a paradisiacal situation of perfection in the punt with his former girlfriend. The symbiosis of Krapp and his girlfriend that he fantasises about is exactly this: a fantasy, an imaginary construction that cannot stand the test of reality. The play elaborately shows us the tricks that memory plays on us; the longer ago something happened, the more the past is idealised. Speaking about the realities that are closer to him in time shows the less embellished side of the idyll, as when he is commenting on his present relationship with Fanny, that '[b]ony old ghost of a whore' (III, 228).

There is, in other words, a lot of noise that prevents us and Krapp himself from seeing things the way they are. His vision is contorted and is always blurred by the *manque à être* and his own fantasies that continually shape and reshape his memories. Beckett manages to double the noise surrounding one's imagined authenticity on a metatheatrical level. The scratch that Krapp notices on his girlfriend's thigh and that represents the breakdown of the state of completeness finds itself reflected in the technology of the tape recorder. In a clumsy attempt to re-enact the desired harmony that he remembers to have experienced during the boat scene, Krapp 'suddenly bends over machine' (229), turning it into a 'maternal-erotic substitute' (Lawley, 93). Just as life itself is filled with noise, so are the accounts on the spools, with the incessant sound of the running tape recorder. Silence, then, is never really an option in this play either, as I mentioned in the beginning of this essay. Beckett closes his play with what we could describe as a 'dramaturgical oxymoron', a conflict of perception between the reader/spectator and the character: 'The tape runs on in silence' (230). As an audience we are watching and listening at the sound not of silence, but of recorded silence. All the dead voices come together in the murmuring noise of the running tape.

A similar trope can be found in *Embers*. Throughout the play there is a constant friction between the narration and the act of enunciaton. Whereas the narrated tale does not stop emphasising the dominant silence that marks the encounter between Bolton and Holloway ('no sound of any kind' 199), in order to render this dead silence Henry has no choice but to break it with his voice. The radio play's sound effects diverge from the voices. Some editions, such as the Faber and Faber one that includes both *Krapp's Last Tape* and *Embers* (2006b), stress this clash between the sound of the narration and the sound in the narration by very explicitly adding 'Sea' in the stage directions after Henry's last words: 'Not a sound' (III, 211). This addition is no more than an editorial detail, though, because in editions where this is omitted, the sound of the sea is equally present, as Beckett notes a few lines earlier: 'Sea a little louder' (210). Thus, in both cases the listener's attention is drawn to the medium of narration itself by the use of the dramaturgical oxymoron, as indeed in *Krapp's Last Tape*.

As the background noise conflicts with the narrative's content in a silence that is not so much as disturbed or interrupted but that can never take place, the ruthless passing of time becomes a heavily charged experience for the listener. 'Tape', Steven Connor argues, 'embodies not just the stopping of time, but the spreading and thickening of the present moment' (89). The audible continuation of time due to the running tape or other background noises paradoxically confronts us head-on with the human finitude. The absence of the subject is most poignantly manifested in the traces of a previous existence that he leaves behind. Connor points out that Krapp's appearances and disappearances reflect the recording, rewinding, winding forward and playback of the spools on the tape recorder. In addition, the rhythmic movement Krapp experiences in the punt on the lake (or the pool, Connor remarks, which is of course a palindrome of loop but also rhymes with spool) is analogous to the oscillations of the tape. To this observation I would add that this tableau is also an apt metaphor for the recorded silence itself; the immobility of silence finds its counterpoint in the continuous movement of the undercurrent, the waves of which will keep on rocking the boat endlessly after Krapp and his girlfriend have gone: 'We lay there without moving. But under us all moved, and moved us, gently, up and down, and from side to side' (III, 229). Similarly, the sea in *Embers* will continue to slosh amidst the silence of human absence. Despite the disappearance of the subject, time drags on. Despite his observation that due to the manipulations of tape recordings tape 'becomes an image of time susceptible of being looped' (90), Connor is adamant in his more recent findings that Beckett's work is more marked by finitude than generally believed. 'The sliding of the tape is a kind of decantation, with each passing inch a diminishment of the supply tape and an equivalent accumulation on the receiving spool. At the end of the play, as Krapp listens to his younger self arrogantly celebrating his freedom from his past, the tape runs on, and then, inevitably, exhausts the supply spool' (Connor, 95). The sting in the tail, however, is that although we may reasonably expect that eventually the spool will be entirely unwound, Beckett does not go that far, and ends the play before this final end, i.e. while the tape is still running. This is a crucial difference that we cannot easily dismiss. What is more, in line with Connor's previous comments on the repeatability of the loop, we may also assume that the end marks a return to the beginning. Krapp's life may come to an end, but the world, very much like the tape, keeps on spinning indifferent to who does or does not inhabit it. 'The earth might be uninhabited' (III, 229).

3   The Sound of Dying

Thus, what we are witnessing is not only a performance of self-alienation, but of an alienation from time too. Man cannot come to terms with his own finitude in relation to the everlasting continuity of the universe. Herein lie the alternative (or rather expanded) interpretations of the scratch on Krapp's girlfriend's thigh. In Beckett's universe the scratch is a heavily charged symbol. It is probably most prominently present in *Endgame*, with Hamm shouting in despair that 'humanity might start from there all over again!' (III, 115) when Clov starts scratching himself frantically, assuming a flea has bitten him. Hamm clarifies that a scratch takes us back to the beginning from where everything, indeed, starts from scratch. In this sense, the scratch draws our attention to the border where two times collide. A scratch, after all, just as a scar, is a trace of what is no longer present. It is a sign of an affliction that has once been. It points at both the cutting and the smoothness of the skin that must have preceded it, but that belongs to the unscathed perfection of life before birth. In laying bare this flaw it not only demonstrates the fall but also brings home to us the pre-oedipal harmony that is lost. In the scratch throbs the background of eternity against the itching of finitude in the foreground. The tape is bound to run on in an everlasting loop in which we as individuals can only momentarily participate. What is more, the almost organic merger of body and machine, well-documented by Lawley and Connor, finds its suture point in the image of the scratch. As scratching is also — as is well-known among DJs — moving back and forth a record, precisely in the way Krapp fumbles with his tapes, we may conclude that the metaphor of the scratch in the play also exemplifies the eternity *of* the finitude. What one does, after all, in manipulating 'the reproduction of a recorded signal' (Connor, 87) is scratching what has been scratched already.

Not only in *Krapp's Last Tape* do we encounter the existential, psychological lack come to the surface as background noise. Mouth's diarrhoea of words in *Not I* is constantly interrupted by a silent voice trying to push her in the direction of self-acknowledgement and self-awareness. In the stage directions Beckett himself associates the movements of Auditor downstage, dressed in a black djellaba, with Mouth's 'vehement refusal to relinquish third person' (III, 405). This figure, however, does not only remind Mouth of the fact that the person she is speaking about is she herself and that 'a voice she did not recognize ... at first ... [...] could be none other ... than her own' (408), Auditor also repeatedly points out to her the continued buzzing that disturbs the silence: 'all silent but for the buzzing [...] all dead still but for the buzzing' (408). In a remarkable repetition of the phraseology of *Embers* in *Not I* 'no sound of any kind' (408) can be heard. If we pursue this analogy, the buzzing fulfils a role similar to the fire in *Embers*, the sound of which is the only thing that disrupts the silence: 'no sound of any kind, only the fire' (199). Analogous to the sound of these embers, which is the 'sound of dying' (200), the buzzing in *Not I* that Mouth hears 'not in the ears at all' but that manifests itself as a 'dull roar in the skull' (407) comes from the process called dying. At the same time, though, and not contrary to this, it comes from the human machine in working modus. Once the body is set in motion, it is on its way to destruction and an inevitable death. Birth was the death of Mouth, too. Hence, the sound that is proof of the living being, unmistakably also bears the traces of death.

Noises are ubiquitous in Beckett's work. We have already referred to the dead voices Vladimir and Estragon hear that make a noise like wings. If Mouth hears a buzzing in her skull, Hamm in *Endgame* is tortured by the incessant sound of a heart dripping in his head. And also Winnie's head is full of cries. In Malone, all the noises of the world come together in 'one vast continuous buzzing' (II, 201). All these voices and noises, then, may be the sign of dying, yet they are not the sign of death. Silence itself is very explicitly associated with death in the text of *Not I*, as in 'all silent as the grave' or 'all dead still' (III, 408). But Beckett's protagonists are unable to assume a state of being that is ruled by utter silence. Only self-destruction might bring them there, but as long as they keep on going, they will have to bear the background noises of the world and life. On a more psychological level, ever since being born, they are cut loose from a pre-oedipal state of harmony and completeness, but the Real — as Lacan would have it — is a paradise lost once they have entered the symbolic order. Silence can only be found in the nothingness that lies beyond the symbolic.

Mouth refuses to acknowledge these noises and voices as her own. However much she has hung on to a life in complete silence, every now and then she cannot stop the words flushing from her mouth in an unstoppable stream. It is Auditor who reminds her of her self-alienation, both by focusing attention on the buzzing and by encouraging her to speak of herself in the first person. In other words, she declines the existence of the Other in order to deny her own position as a linguistic and hence divided subject. She tries to hold on to the illusion that the separation she speaks about concerns not her, but someone else. Although the appropriation of the voice would deprive her of her true self, implementing the lack into her being as a subject, it is inevitably also the only way to exist if she does not want to end it all, an act that is anathema to Beckett's protagonists. So whereas Mouth and other characters refuse to give in to the alienating voice that marks them as divided, they feel equally reluctant to return to the abysmal nothingness beyond the symbolic. They withdraw from both the voice and the void. Whether it is through recording and editing tapes, or through the narration of tales or the refusal to acknowledge one's own voice, the only way to have a taste of this flawless nirvana they long for is their fantasy. What Beckett's characters show us is the strength of imagination, and hence fiction, despite everything. Only through the imaginary order can we assemble a seemingly coherent picture of ourselves, as Lacan argued in his writings on the mirror stage.

At the same time, we are harshly confronted with the limits of fiction. All attempts to pursue ultimate silence and the liberation of the subject from the symbolic order are doomed to fail. Not coincidentally, it is through fictionalisation that the Unnamable seems on his way to attain total silence; Worm, the last invention of his imagination, has abandoned discourse yet he does not succeed in keeping silent altogether, as he mumbles: 'I have not ceased to hear his murmur, all the while the others discoursed' (II, 331). Despite his efforts to erase this external noise in order to obtain silence the Unnamable knows that it will be in vain: 'I'll hear it still, broken, faint, unintelligible, if I listen hard' (II, 386). The 'real silence' (II, 387), or the silence of the Real, will always remain out of reach. What Beckett offers us is 'the semblance of approaching the line between language and silence, since its journey will never take it across that threshold' (Watson, 1991, 34). In the game of life one is always playing gooseberry.

4   The Absent Presence of the Voice

To live is to die. Being a subject consists in coming to terms with the idea that the Real will be forever out of reach and that we borrow our identity from the symbolic order in which we act as a signifier. As linguistic beings we have no choice but to use the instrument of language that is inevitably an Other. In once more explaining this procedure, Žižek uses an interesting metaphor to describe this linguistic Other: 'the moment we enter the symbolic order, an unbridgeable gap separates forever a human body from "its" voice. The voice acquires a spectral autonomy, it never quite belongs to the body we see, so that even when we see a living person talking, there is always some degree of ventriloquism at work: it is as if the speaker's own voice hollows him out and in a sense speaks "by itself", through him' (Žižek, 92). Is the figure of Auditor in *Not I* not the Other behind the ventriloquist of Mouth, despite the absence of an abdomen? Although left out in many productions — for once with Beckett's approval — Auditor functions as her prompter. His presence does not mean that Mouth's role is restricted to a puppet on a string. After all, she is capable of rejecting his suggestions, much to Auditor's despair. At the same time, however, it is clear that she has to play the game within the limits that are set out for her. Although reluctant to appropriate the Other as herself, it is clear that Auditor offers her the only instrument that is at her disposal. Even the alternative of refusing it and thus keeping silent is doomed to fail; all of a sudden the words come flooding out. Despite her 'begging the mouth to stop' she 'can't stop the stream' (410). An alienated vehicle, the subject's speech never entirely belongs to himself. Referring to Derrida's notion of *s'entendre parler* — to hear oneself speak — Žižek confirms the effect of the voice as that 'which undermines most radically the subject's self-presence and self-transparence[.] I hear myself speaking, yet what I hear is never fully myself but a parasite, a foreign body in my very heart' (103). The Cartesian ontological certainty of a sovereign subject is deconstructed, as the subject evanesces as one comes into existence. Entering the symbolic order, one becomes a signifier in the web of language in which signification can only be reached in the perpetual reference to other signifiers. Whether it is the inner voice of thought or the external voice of speech does not detract from the self-alienation that is in place once the so-called symbolic castration has taken place with the entrance in the symbolic order. This makes Lacan rephrase Descartes' cogito to 'I think where I am not, therefore I am where I do not think' (Lacan, 2001, 183). What Lacan calls a *parlêtre*, the speaking subject is always absent from themselves; self-presence is nothing more than a far-away illusion. Lacan refutes Descartes' epistemology in that he does not 'make of the *I think* a mere point of fading' (Lacan, 1981, 224). Few other figures 'enact' this absence of the subject from themselves so pertinently as Mouth in *Not I*. The voice emerges out of nowhere yet simultaneously finds its source in the Other. What we see is nothing but a 'hole [...] no matter' (407); the empty and dark hole that the mouth consists of exemplifies the absence of the subject in the first place. Where her speech is, no I can be. For Mouth there is no alternative but to speak in the third person because she herself is not there. Mouth's inability for self-appropriation as a result of her inherent emptiness characterises, according to Lacan, the subject's struggle to find themselves. '*Alienation gives rise to a pure possibility of being*, a place where one might expect to find a subject, but which nevertheless remains empty. Alienation engenders, in a sense, a place in which it is clear that there is, as of yet, no subject: a place where something is conspicuously lacking. *The subject's first guise is this very lack*' (Fink, 52; emphasis in original). Hence, the subject is condemned to a state of being that is at the same time a state of non-being too. Likewise, the acknowledgement of the subject inevitably also implies the acknowledgement of the disappearance of the subject.

Whereas in *Krapp's Last Tape* it is the scratch that draws attention to the lack as the disruption of the idyllic scene, in *Not I* Mouth's peace and rest are disturbed by the continuous buzzing that does not allow the silence to set in. Both scratch and buzzing are phallic signifiers that denote the protagonists' functioning as symbolic beings, albeit that, as Žižek notes, 'the price to be paid is that we have to renounce the position of agent and consent to function as the medium through which the big Other acts and speaks' (109).

In his attack on the primacy of the voice at the cost of writing Derrida traces a firm belief in the metaphysics of the voice throughout Western thinking. The phonocentric idea consisted of the promise of a transparent self that does not need the external Other to claim authenticity and self-presence.

> The voice is *heard* (understood) — that undoubtedly is what is called conscience — closest to the self as the absolute effacement of the signifier: pure auto-affection that necessarily has the form of time and which does not borrow from outside of itself, in the world or in 'reality', any accessory signifier, any substance of expression foreign to its own spontaneity. It is the unique experience of the signified producing itself spontaneously, from within the self, and nevertheless, as signified concept, in the element of ideality or universality. The unworldly character of this substance of expression is constitutive of this ideality. This experience of the effacement of the signifier in the voice is not merely one illusion among many — since it is the condition of the very idea of truth — but [t]his illusion is the history of truth and it cannot be dissipated so quickly. (Derrida, 1976, 20)

Because of the illusory and elusive evocation of presence established by the voice that is considered to be able to retreat from the symbolic order, or even to predate the signifier, the voice has acquired an ontologically superior position that closes the phantasm of self-presence. As opposed to writing that lives on independent of one's being there, the resounding of the voice allegedly signifies the presence of the subject who speaks. In addition, Derrida's refutation of this metaphysics of presence was preceded by Lacan. Acknowledging the ambiguity of the voice as an inspiration that is intimate and interior yet ultimately Other at the same time, Lacan classifies the voice as *extime*, as part of the force that can only construct in the process of deconstructing.

This is what is at stake in one of Derrida's essays on Artaud too; in 'La Parole Soufflée' he explains the double connotation of the verb. On the one hand, all speech is stolen. With Artaud Derrida describes it with a similar scatological wording as in *Not I*: 'all speech fallen from the body, offering itself to understanding or reception, offering itself as a spectacle, immediately becomes stolen speech' (Derrida, 2001, 220). As writing, once spoken the voice no longer belongs to the speaker who equally has no control over its reception. On the other hand, Derrida interprets '*soufflé*' as inspired by a secondary source, by an external voice that disrupts the speaker of his presence to himself. The authenticity that is usually ascribed to the voice as the guarantee for bodily presence turns out to be no less secondary and borrowed than written language.

Derrida brings both these interpretations together in the claim that speech acts as an evocation of irresponsibility. Mouth's refusal to speak in her own name and take responsibility for what she says lays bare the alienating dichotomy that underlies every speech act, which does not come so much from the inner self but is prompted by an external Other.

> [T]he cyclonic breath [*souffle*] of a prompter [*souffleur*] who draws his breath in, and thereby robs me of that which he first allowed to approach me and which I believed I could say *in my own name*. The generosity of inspiration, the positive irruption of a speech which comes from I know not where, or about which I know [...] that I do not know where it comes from or who speaks it, the fecundity of the *other* breath [*souffle*] is unpower: not the absence but the radical irresponsibility as the power and the origin of speech. I am in relation to myself within the ether of a speech which is always spirited away [*soufflé*] from me, and which steals from me the very thing that it puts me in relation to. (Derrida, 2001, 221)

The staging of Auditor as well as the narrative itself seem to manifest Beckett's scepticism towards the phonocentric bias. Mouth's refusal to appropriate the voice points at the opposite as it tries to maintain a form of self-presence, similarly to Krapp's attempts to preserve his true self paradoxically by accumulating the spools that were the very means to do so. His autarkic project fails, as all his life he has done nothing else than excreting waste products; his spools are his excrements: 'Sour cud and the iron stool [*Pause.*] Revelled in the word spool. [*With relish.*] Spooool!' (228). Having piled up boxes full of spools, he indeed has defecated words. Not only his name but also the complaints about his unattainable laxation stress the analogy between language and excrements. Both Krapp and Mouth agree with Artaud in repulsing the scatological nature of words. However, their Artaudian quest for unity results in a multiplication of selves. If the voice is something which is *extime*, neither entirely internal nor external, it is this paradox which is ever-present in Beckett's work that follows a similar structure. The characters' ambitions are always flawed by the structure of the play. Hence, Beckett knows that he can impossibly live up to his own ambition that 'form *is* content, content *is* form' (IV, 503) which he infamously stated in his essay on Joyce, the impossibility of which is perpetually manifested in his plays.

Merging form and content, it seems, can only be performed not in the absence of sound, but in the presence of silence. But in view of the *perpetuum mobile* of the loop of the spool, what Beckett's dramaturgical oxymorons confront us with, is that this is not within reach for Krapp or any other of his characters.

Works Cited

Beckett, Samuel (2006a), *The Grove Centenary Edition*, ed. Paul Auster, 4 vols, New York: Grove P.
Beckett, Samuel (2006b), *Krapp's Last Tape* and *Embers*, London: Faber and Faber.
Connor, Steven (2014), *Beckett, Modernism and the Material Imagination*, Cambridge: Cambridge UP.
Derrida, Jacques (1976), *Of Grammatology*, Baltimore: Johns Hopkins UP.
Derrida, Jacques (1998), 'To Unsense the Subjectile', in Jacques Derrida and Paule Thévenin, eds., *The Secret Art of Antonin Artaud*, Cambridge (Massachusetts): MIT P, pp. 59–157.
Derrida, Jacques (2001), *Writing and Difference*, London: Routledge.
De Vos, Laurens (2011), *Cruelty and Desire in the Modern Theater: Antonin Artaud, Sarah Kane, and Samuel Beckett*, Madison: Fairleigh Dickinson UP.
Fink, Bruce (1995), *The Lacanian Subject: Between Language and Jouissance*, Princeton: Princeton UP.
Lacan, Jacques (1981), *The Seminar of Jacques Lacan: Book XI: The Four Fundamental Concepts of Psychoanalysis*, ed. Jacques-Alain Miller, New York: Norton.
Lacan, Jacques (2001), *Écrits: A Selection*, London: Routledge.
Lawley, Paul (1994), 'Stages of Identity: From *Krapp's Last Tape* to *Play*', in John Pilling, ed., *The Cambridge Companion to Beckett*, Cambridge: Cambridge UP, pp. 88–105.
Sontag, Susan (1988), 'Artaud', in Antonin Artaud, *Selected Writings*, Berkeley: U of California P, pp. xvii–lix.
Watson, David (1991), *Paradox and Desire in Samuel Beckett's Fiction*, New York: St. Martin's P.
Žižek, Slavoj (1996), '"I Hear You with My Eyes"; or, The Invisible Master', in Renata Salecl and Slavoj Žižek, eds., *Gaze and Voice as Love Objects*, Durham: Duke UP, pp. 90–126.

Why Is 'Listener' Named *'Souvenant'*? The Role of the Spectator in a Bilingual Reading of *That Time/Cette fois*

Kumiko Kiuchi

Abstract

This chapter seeks to elucidate a complex relationship between Beckett's self-translation and theatrical practice in *That Time/Cette fois* so as to illuminate a challenge Beckett set out in writing, staging and translating this piece. Treating Beckett's bilingual text as one literary work and his stage direction as part of his translation process for the evolution of the work, this bilingual reading pivots on two interlingual differences: 'that time' and '*cette fois*', and 'Listener' and '*Souvenant*' (one who remembers). These differences elicit the connection between this piece and the opening of Marcel Proust's novel *À la recherche du temps perdu*. Drawing on the use of tenses in the Proustian model of narrating the rhythm of sleep and waking as well as Beckett's comments on *That Time/Cette fois*, dictated by Walter Asmus in his Berlin-Werkstatt production, this essay explores the motives behind the change of name from Listener to *Souvenant* while elucidating the crucial role that the spectator is structurally required to play, inherent to this dramatic piece.

⋯

For Julie Campbell
De profundis clamavi ad te…
    ARVO PÄRT

∴

A published or staged text is usually seen as the closed and final state of a literary work. In this sense, *That Time* is a dramatic piece Beckett began writing in June 1974 and worked on intensively for the next three months (Knowlson, 531), then completed and sent in August 1975 to Donald McWhinnie who premiered in London in 1976 (Pilling, 197–8, 200). At the same time, Beckett always self-translated his texts. In his self-translation, the translated text does not merely replicate the content faithfully to the original but also evolves from it. Hence, it makes more sense to see the entity of his literary text as a process of changes from the original to the translation rather than the original as an entity, and the translated text as one that is subordinate to it. As Beckett began translating *That Time* into French on 14 November 1976 and *Cette fois* was published in 1978, there is at least the span of four years between 1974 and 1978 as part of the evolving process of *That Time/Cette fois*.

Furthermore, in that *That Time/Cette fois* is a dramatic piece, there is another level of 'translation' to his interlingual self-translation: his stage production. It is well known that Beckett alters his written text while directing. This also happened in directing the German version *Damals* with the assistant director Walter Asmus in the Berlin Theater-Werkstatt from 30 August to 22 September 1976 for the German premiere (Pilling, 200). The production diary Asmus kept provides valuable details on how Beckett changed his approach. In this respect, it can be assumed that Beckett's intersemiotic translation from text to stage likely nurtured his interlingual translation from English into French and that his stage production is part of the evolving process of this dramatic piece.

With this premise in mind, this essay rereads *That Time/Cette fois* by focusing on two puzzles in Beckett's self-translation and explores their connections with the evolution of this dramatic piece. The first puzzle is that 'that time', the title of the piece as well as the recurrent phrase in the text, is translated into 'cette fois' in French. While 'that time' refers to a distant moment in the past as opposed to the present, 'cette fois', a quasi-equivalent of 'this time' in English, articulates the present moment as opposed to the previous ones. In this dramatic piece where this phrase is followed by a scene in the past, it sounds as if 'that time' introduces a retrospective gaze harking back to the past; by contrast, 'cette fois' re-enacts past scenes as if summoning them in the present.

Though this may seem a minor difference, the second puzzle backs the assumption that the first puzzle should deserve careful attention: the name of the stage figure 'Listener' is translated into *Souvenant*, or one who remembers. For those who can easily swallow the understanding that Listener is *Souvenant* because he listens to his recorded voices recounting the past, even this difference may seem insignificant. However, careful spectators should notice and be confused by the fact that they cannot establish a clear connection between Listener and the voices during the play, as Listener does not respond to them in any obvious way. As another reference point, there are also listening figures, 'Auditor' in *Not I* (1972) and 'Listener' in *Ohio Impromptu* (1980) in Beckett's late dramatic pieces written before and after *That Time/Cette fois*. Both figures silently listen to a voice of someone else, the Mouth or the Reader without response, in which sense they are not much different from Listener in *That Time*. While these two are translated as 'Entendeur' and 'Auditeur' respectively, which convey the original meaning of 'listening', only Listener in *That Time* is curiously translated as *Souvenant*.

The name *Souvenant* invites the spectator to presuppose that the voices should be of the stage figure, as he is the subject of remembering and the owner of the recounted memories. In the genealogy of Beckett's work, the reader comes across several figures listening to both internal and external voices. The ultimate figure is the quasi-narrator in *The Unnamable*, where the unidentified narrator voices the speech of others without knowing who these others are or where their words are coming from. Yet, Beckett wished to deprive the stage figure in *That Time/Cette fois* of a speaking function altogether. In his letter to George Reavey of 1 September 1974, Beckett clarifies the importance of the name 'Listener' in *That Time* as opposed to the speaking function of Mouth in *Not I* (Ackerley and Gontarski, 568).

Those who read both Beckett and Proust cannot resist the temptation to associate *Souvenant* in *That Time* with *À la recherche du temps perdu* [hereafter abbreviated as *À la recherche*]. The association may appear quite arbitrary at first, but it can be justified not just for the essay Beckett wrote on Proust in 1930 but also for striking similarities between the beginning of *À la recherche* and *Cette fois*, which will be examined in this chapter. Biographical details are also favourable for this association: Beckett likely renewed contact with Proust's work in the early 1970s in at least two contexts. For one, in his letter to Barbara Bray of 1 June 1970, he mentioned a French translation of his aborted Proust essay which he 'read half a page then shuddered away' (Beckett, 2016, 234). The other concerns the film adaptation of *À la recherche* by Harold Pinter and Joseph Losey, for whom Bray worked as their assistant. Beckett advised on 22 February 1972 that they begin the script from *Le temps retrouvé* (Beckett, 2016, 284 n.2) and wrote on 5 March 1972 that he might 'have another go at it' after his holiday in El Jadida (288). He also wrote to Alan Schneider on 30 January 1972, mentioning Pinter's *Old Times* (1971) in comparison with Proust (Beckett and Schneider, 265). Inspired by Pinter, Beckett may have reread Proust around that time. Chronologically speaking, therefore, the Proustian *Souvenant* precedes the conception of the English 'Listener' in *That Time*. If Beckett initially opted for 'Listener' rather than the English translation of *Souvenant* to separate voices from listening, then the question is why Beckett later recuperated *Souvenant*. What does this change tell us about the creative process this dramatic piece went through?

The following section analyses *That Time/Cette fois* from three aspects: the interlingual translation of 'that time' and 'cette fois', the intertexual connections between this dramatic piece and the beginning of *À la recherche*, and the intersemiotic translation, i.e. the German production of *Damals*, which chronologically comes after Beckett wrote *That Time* and before translating into *Cette fois*. In order to accurately illustrate the gaps between the authorial intention written in the text (including stage instructions) and the actual staging of the piece, this analysis distinguishes two levels of reception: the reader and the spectator. The former has access to the written text, which includes notes and stage directions, and the latter sees the play only as a theatre production without reading stage directions.

1   Linguistic Difference of 'That Time' and 'Cette fois' in the Theatrical Setting

> Curtain. Stage in darkness. Fade up to LISTENER'S FACE about 10 feet above stage level midstage off centre.
> Old white face, long flaring white hair as if seen from above outspread. Voices A B C are his own coming to him from both sides and above. [...]
> Silence 7 seconds. LISTENER'S EYES are open. His breath audible, slow and regular. (Beckett, 2009, 99)

These are the stage instructions at the beginning of *That Time*. The stage is first imbued with darkness and gradually lit with a spotlight on Listener's face. The face with the closed eyes and the 'hair as if seen above outspread' elicits the intention to create an illusion that the spectator sees him lying down asleep from above, though they are actually looking up at him ('10 feet above stage level'). This distracts the spectator's spatial orientation. Although the stage instructions clarify the coordination of the eyes and the voices marked by light and darkness ('7 seconds'), the spectator has difficulty clearly identifying this coordination because Listener's face looks very distant and small on stage.

According to the stage instructions, Listener is surrounded by three loudspeakers from which the recorded voices A, B, C sound in turn. There are twelve sets of ABC divided into three parts (ACB–ACB–ACB–CAB, CBA–CBA–CBA–BCA, BAC–BAC–BAC–BAC).[1] All the voices are supposed to be

---

[1] All quotes from *That Time* in this chapter are from Beckett (2009), and *Cette fois* from Beckett (1986). Instead of page numbers, the passage numbers, used by Beckett in his notebook for Berlin production (1976) are used. A, B, C, refers to the three voices, and the numbers 1 to 12 indicate their passage number. For example, A1 is the first passage of voice A.

Listener's voices though they use the pronoun 'you', not 'I'. The reader of *That Time* can separate the three voices due to recurrent images that characterise each voice. To quote Beckett's own account of the voices, Voice A, 'a middle-aged man', Voice B, 'an emotional youth', and Voice C, 'a cynical old man' (Asmus, 92). Voice A recounts childhood aged ten to twelve (A4, A10), with recurrent images of the nettles, a night bag, the remains of the tramway, together with actions such as getting off a ferry, walking through the high street, sleeping over on the spot, talking to himself; Voice B has less repeated images, the rays of the sun, blue sky, wheat turning yellow and of course the lovers on the stone, the image of the 'shroud' (B4, B12); Voice C mentions specific locations: the Portrait Gallery (C1–3, C6), Public Library (C8, C11), and Post Office (C9), as well as the season and weather 'always winter always raining' (C1, C8, C9). Despite these characteristics, it is not easy for the spectators to differentiate the three voices of one person, let alone identify Listener as the owner of the three voices. The voices run seamlessly and the spectators never get to hear Listener's voice for he never speaks. Nor does Listener show any reaction that can be regarded as a response to the voices except for closing and opening his eyes. What is certain about Listener to the spectators is that he is somehow alive, for he is making breathing sounds.

In addition, the use of the pronoun 'you' of the voices creates a peculiar effect in the theatrical space of *That Time*. Despite the ambiguity of the relationship between Listener and the voices, the spectators assume that Listener is an addressee of the voices and try to make out their relationship. For this purpose, the spectator listens attentively, though without reacting to them. In this sense, the spectator is a listener 'overhearing' the voices. Curiously, this mirrors the attitude of Listener who may be listening but not responding to the voices. Here, the spectator is tempted to ask a question: Is this Listener an addressee of the voices or is he just overhearing as another spectator? Of course, the reader should dismiss this interpretation as the voices are instructed to be of Listener. An interesting point here is that the spectator may be counted as an inherent element of this dramatic piece, as I shall explain below. Besides, in that all the voices are pre-recorded, it is unlikely that the voices are to be directed to a definite listener or listeners, for the recorded voices cannot choose their listeners when they are recorded; it is their listeners who activate the recorded voices by playing them on some audio device.

As the play proceeds, the spectators are informed that the referent of 'that time' is unstable because all the voices come to question the certainty of 'that time' by asking 'when was that' (A1, C1, A2, B10) or 'was that the time or was it another time' (C5, C6, C8, C10) or saying 'another time that time' (C11, A12). Such questioning suggests that 'that time' which seems to pinpoint a specific moment in the past at the beginning in fact merely repeats 'old scenes old names' (A2). Nevertheless, there is one 'that time' or 'the time' that remains singular. C4 mentions 'the turning point': 'you could never be the same after crawling about year after year sunk in your lifelong mess', 'who else you'll never be the same after this you were never the same after that'. Such a singular moment is more clearly illustrated in B5: 'the first and last that time curled up worm in slime when they lugged you out and wiped you off and straightened you up'. This is an apparent reference to the moment of birth, circumscribing the referentiality of 'that time' to a lifetime, not beyond.

Now that the function of the English 'that time' is clear enough, let us compare the use of 'that time' and 'cette fois' in B5. To return to the expression 'that time' or 'cette fois', the act of 'making up' is a running theme in most of 'that time' and in the three voices after A4 (A4, B4, B5, C7, A7, B9, B11, A11).

> muttering *that time* altogether on the stone in the sun or *that time* together on the towpath or *that time* together in the sand *that time that time* making it up from there as best you could always together somewhere in the sun

> te marmonnant tes fables *cette fois* ensemble sur la pierre au soleil ou *cette fois* ensemble sur le halage ou *cette fois* ensemble dans les dunes *cette fois cette fois* et à partir de là du mieux que tu pouvais toujours ensemble quelque part au soleil (Beckett, 2009; my emphasis)

In this passage, 'that time' introduces the quick change of scenes from 'on the stone in the sun' to 'on the towpath' and to 'in the sand'. This almost sounds as an automatic enumeration of the already-mentioned scenes. Here, the use of 'cette fois' functions as a cue to a new scene or an abrupt cut inserted between scenes in a film. Its counterpart 'that time' also lacks a sense of temporal reference. Then, the reader is reminded that the recurrent scenes such as 'on the stone' repeated up to B4, and the scenes of 'in the sand' (B7 and B10) or of the 'towpath' (B9) are actually all 'made up'. Although there is not an exact equivalent of 'making up' in French, the phrase 'tes fables' indicates that these scenes are invented. In that all scenes are invented more or less, the temporal distance between the narrative present and the past is no longer an issue, and the linguistic difference between 'that time' and 'cette fois' here is almost annihilated.

Yet, to return to the beginning, the reader notices in A1 a decisive difference between 'that time' and 'cette fois'.

> that time you went back that last time to look was the ruin still there where you hid as a child when was that (A1)

> cette fois où tu es retourné cette dernière fois voir si elle était là toujours la ruine où enfant tu te cachais quand c'était (A1)

In English, 'that time' is followed by the past tense ('you went back', 'you hid as a child'), which indicates that the narrative present is disconnected from 'that time'. Furthermore, despite the temporal distance between the moment 'you went back' as an adult and 'you hid as a child', the simple past is used for both events as if spatialising them on the same past temporal plane. This contrasts the French 'cette fois' combined with the compound past and the imperfect. Compound past elicits the sense of continuation from or repercussion of the past action onto the narrative present, namely, the expression 'tu es retourné' insinuates the fact that the 'you' is 'here now' as a result of coming back. Despite the pre-recorded voices, the impact of the compound past combined with the pronoun 'you' is quite immediate: the spectators can feel the voices are present addressing to Listener. Yet, in the next instance, it moves on to imperfect tense to phase out of this immediacy. If Beckett wished to secure the temporal distance between the voices and Listener in the English text, he could have used the simple past in French. Yet, he did not do so. Why? It can be assumed that Beckett may have adopted in his dramatic piece the combination of the compound past and the imperfect which is said to be a narrative invention of the opening passage of *À la recherche*.

2 Proustian Connections: Grammar and Image

> Longtemps, je me suis couché de bonne heure. Parfois, à peine ma bougie éteinte, mes yeux se fermaient si vite que je n'avais pas le temps de me dire 'Je m'endors'. Et, une demi-heure après, la pensée qu'il était temps de chercher le sommeil m'éveillait... (Proust, 1987, 3)

> For a long time I would go to bed early. Sometimes, the candle barely out, my eyes closed so quickly that I did not have time to tell myself: 'I'm falling asleep'. And half an hour later the thought that it was time to look for sleep would awaken me... (Proust, 2005, 1)[2]

---

2 References from Proust will be abbreviated as below: F for the original French text (1987) and E for the English translation (2001).

The use of tenses here is identical to the first line of *Cette fois* in that it combines the compound past and the imperfect. The oddity is the combination of 'longtemps/for a long time', the adverb that indicates duration, and the compound past ('je me suis couché'), the tense used for a single action as well as a sudden transition from the singleness of the action to the habit in the imperfect. Among those who have addressed this puzzle, Gérard Genette's account provides a schematic account of the unconventional ways Proust uses tenses in *À la recherche*. Genette attributes it to 'the "singularism" of the spatial sensitivity and the "iteratism" of the temporal sensitivity' of the Proustian narrator (Genette, 124). To quote Genette, 'Proustian creature is as little sensitive to the individuality of moments as he is spontaneously sensitive to the individuality of places. Moments in Proust have a strong tendency to resemble and blend with each other' (Genette, 123–4). If that is the case, the use of the imperfect for what can be a single action ('mes yeux se fermaient [my eyes closed]', 'la pensée [...] m'éveillait [the thought would awake me]') suggests an iteratism of presumably his repeated action, whereas 'je me suis couché' refers to a singular connection to the place where he sleeps, a bedroom.

Misako Nemoto features bedrooms as key to understanding *À la recherche*. The Proustian narrator illustrates many unfamiliar bedrooms where he stays and is often unable to sleep. In the quote, the narrator should also be in a bedroom. In Nemoto's interpretation, the narrator in the narrative present is an insomniac who lost the habit of sleeping early, and the use of the compound past is not directly connected to the narrative present but an inducement to the narrator's dream time, a temporal limbo in his half-awake/sleep state (Nemoto, 29–30).

Interestingly, there are passages in the opening of the novel where the narrator's experience of an unfamiliar bedroom is narrated in the present tense, though in an indefinite third person 'he': 'The hour when an invalid, who has been obliged to set out on a journey and to sleep in a strange hotel' (Proust, F4, E2). The subject 'he' in the present tense continues to alternate the 'I' in the imperfect as if the two subjects were intermingling. Then, the subject 'he' appears again in the story of 'a man who is asleep' (Proust, F5, E3). In light of grammatical convention, the 'I' and the 'he' cannot refer to the same person; in the context of the novel, this indefinite 'he' should mirror the narrator himself or possibly the narrator's double, Charles Swann. Yet, the reader of the novel is more likely to believe that the 'he' is the 'I'. If the narrator 'I' in his dream can experience an instant and successive transformation of himself into the subjects of the book he was reading, 'a church, a quartet, the rivalry of François I and of Charles Quint' (Proust, F3, E1), he can also be a traveller or an insomniac in his drowsiness. The narrator's free incarnation ultimately leads to the antiquity and the origin of humanity, 'as Eve was created from a rib of Adam, a woman would be born during my sleep' (Proust, F4, E3). This curiously resonates Voice C in *That Time* where images of antiquity emerge from dirt and blot in paintings (C3) and then turn into 'Adam', and even 'Chinaman long before Christ born' (C6). In both *À la recherche* and *That Time*, the associations of images are much stronger than the order of chronological time, which challenges the temporal order marked by the use of tenses.

There are also similarities in the setting between *That Time* and *À la recherche*. Not to mention the fact that the figure is in an ambiguous sleeping posture by which it is not clear whether he is asleep or awake, an alternation of light and darkness in *That Time* resonates with the candlelight in the opening of *À la recherche* where the light repeatedly reveals a time lag between reality and the narrator's perception. One example is this: 'This impression would persist for some moments after I awoke; it did not offend my reason, but lay like scales upon my eyes and prevented them from registering the fact that the candle was no longer burning' (Proust, F3, E1). The narrator believed the candle was still lit, but it was already out. Another example is in the sequence where the narrator mistakes for sunlight a gleam from a candlelight coming through a gap underneath a door of a bedroom. Beckett may have incorporated this time lag in the coordination of the light and the eye movement of Listener/*Souvenant*: he closes and opens his eyes, not immediately after the voice begins and stops, giving a time lag of some seconds.

Beckett himself explains to Asmus this gap or 'silence' during his production of *Damals*:

> Beckett comments on the silence after each of the three parts: in these moments the man comes back to the present. While he was listening to his voice he was in the past [...] During the listening everything is closed. In the silence he is startled to find himself in the present, everything is open. (Asmus, 94)

Listener in the state of silence here resembles the dream time that the Proustian narrator experiences in darkness. The state of being 'closed' in the listening resonates with the moment of the narrator's free associations of memories and images.

Interestingly, some lines in the opening of *À la recherche* almost read as a commentary on the state where Listener/*Souvenant* is fixed in darkness. When the Proustian narrator wakes and 'would be astonished to find myself in a state of darkness', he finds it 'pleasant and restful' but at the same time 'incomprehensible, without a cause'. Here, the narrator, as if seeking a temporal index to orient himself, 'would ask myself what time it could be' (Proust, F3, E1). If this is the working of the voluntary memory, another example is involuntary. The narrator is so immersed in darkness that he is unable to even ask such a question when he wakes up: 'I had only the most rudimentary sense of existence, such as may lurk and flicker in the depths of an animal's consciousness; I was more destitute than the cave-dweller'. Here, he feels 'the memory [...] would come like a rope let down from heaven to draw me up out of the abyss of not-being [...] I would gradually piece together the original components of my ego' (Proust, F5, E4). It is the memory that descends upon him for rescue. This memory rope metaphor resonates a rhythmical repetition of the phrase 'that time/*cette fois*'. Although the utterance of this phrase mostly summons already clichéd images of the past, it nevertheless reintroduces the sense of time. As long as memory speaks to the present, time does still exist.

In discussing the difference between the two memories in *À la recherche*, Ernst Robert Curtius names the latter 'spontaneous souvenir' and differentiates it from the 'voluntary memory'. The former 'escapes the constraints of consciousness and reproduces the event with the fresh nuances of the original event', while the latter merely 'records dead materials' (37; my translation). Etymologically speaking, the word '*Souvenant*' is closer to the former; the verb form 'souvenir' was used in the eighteenth century to mean 'occurring to the mind' (OED); the prefix 'sous-' is 'sub-' in English and 'venir' is the verb 'to come'. Here, memory comes from below and happens to consciousness.[3] This contrasts the phrase expression 'se rappeler', literally meaning 'calling to myself'.

Based on Curtius's account, *Souvenant* does not solely suggest a superficial resemblance to the Proustian narrator but points to the possibility of reading their more fundamental connections: Beckett may have attempted to stage Proustian temporal dislocations and dream time in *That Time/Cette fois*. Of course, this also involves a decisive difference between the two works and writers. While Proust chose a novel and experimented with the ramifications of dream time in the past memories recounted in the first person, Beckett opted for theatre, keeping the voices separate from *Souvenant* as well as involving the spectator as a potential listener and overhearer by using the second person 'you'. As a result, Beckett almost loses the connection between the stage figure

---

3   The premise of Curtius's definition is Henri Bergson's influence on Proust. Proust explains his view of Bergson in his interview with Elie-Joseph Bois in the journal *Le Temps* no.12 (of 13 November 1913) that his novel is an attempt to distance himself from the philosophy of Bergson. 'My work would be part of the series of my "essay" ("attempt") of "Romans de l'Inconscient" (Novels of unconsciousness)'. See Proust, 1971, pp. 557–9.

and his memory but succeeds in visualising a 'destitute' state of the figure in the rhythm of opening and closing of the eyes instead of explaining it in words.

3   From 'Listener' to *'Souvenant'*

It was Beckett's conscious choice to dissociate the voices from the Listener/*Souvenant* figure. Nearing the completion of *That Time*, Beckett had already foreseen the difficulty in eliciting the relationship between the voices and Listener on stage. In his letter to Alan Schneider of 8 August 1975, Beckett wrote that he had reconciled himself with the uneasiness about the 'disproportion' between Listener's face and speech after trying to 'amplify' the image: 'I have now come to accept its remoteness & stillness — apart from certain precise eye movements, breath just audible in silence and final smile' (Beckett, 1998, 328). At this stage, his tone is not necessarily positive in 'accepting' this set-up. In the following year, in the process of his production, he sounds more approving of this 'disproportion': 'To the objection that visual component too small, out of all proportion with aural, answer: make it smaller, on the principle less is more' (Ackerley and Gontarski, 569).

What changed his mind is not very clear. In fact, he himself abstains from identifying a causality between the voices and the eye movement of Listener/*Souvenant*: 'It is not decided whether the voice stops and therefore he opens his eyes' (Asmus, 94). As mentioned earlier, this connection is the only potential clue for the spectator to identify Listener as the owner and addressee of the voices. If Beckett himself left this connection undecided and kept any dramatic effect that highlights the connection to the minimum, he was surely aware that the spectator would also face the same 'disproportion' that initially had concerned Beckett.

In fact, one of Beckett's comments on the play to Asmus helps explain a motive behind this 'disproportion'. Asmus's diary dictates Beckett's comment on A7 that Listener is 'depersonalized' (Asmus, 95). 'Depersonalisation' is a clinical state where one is unable to integrate one's past memories into one's present identity. If that is the case, Listener's lack of reaction cannot be interpreted just as a sign that he cannot hear or is not listening; it may be an indication that he just cannot relate himself to the content because, to his ears, the three voices were talking not of himself but of someone else. The effect created by this 'disproportion' can be compared to the relationship between radio and its listener. Radio waves are potentially there, but they are merely waves until a listener tunes in to listen. Once a listener begins to listen to them, waves can become a voice or voices addressing them, although the voice or voices would not know or even guess who their listeners are. Despite this disproportionate relationship, the listener is quickly captivated in an intimate relationship with the voices. In the set-up where the listening figure is 'depersonalised', the more likely candidate for the listener role for the recorded voices is the spectator, even though they can only act as overhearers. The change of name from Listener to *Souvenant* may reflect Beckett's acceptance of 'disproportion' during his German production. If the spectator is expected to be a potential 'Listener', the stage figure should have another name — *Souvenant* — that indicates that the memories are still his.

The theme of 'depersonalisation' could be further elaborated on by what Anne Atik dictated from her conversation with Beckett in her diary of 30 December 1976:

> *qui est qui* [who is who]. One would have to invent a new, a fourth person, then a fifth, a sixth — *to* talk about *je, tu, il*, never. *Qui est qui*. The logical thing to do would be to look out the window at the void. Mallarmé was near to it in the *livre blanc*. But one can't get over one's dream. (94–5)

Atik explains this is a comment on 'his new piece'. Considering the date, the piece is most likely to be *Verbatim/The Voice* begun on 16 January 1977, a blueprint of *Company* and *A Piece of Monologue*. This fragment consists of three elements, A (speech in the third person), B (overhearer of A), C (addressee of A), playing on the identification and differentiation between A, B and C. According to Beckett's notes on *Verbatim/The Voice*, the core lies in the change from 'recta' to 'obliqua', from the direct relationship between A and C to the indirect B as an overhearer of A. B hears that the voice is talking to him, but the content is of another listener (Beckett, 1993, 194). This makes him speculate upon the possible yet invisible presence of 'another' listener in the same darkness. It can be understood that this 'another' is the 'qui [who]', a silent presence deduced from the overhearer's subjective perception. The multiplication of 'another' is indeed explored in the narrative device in *Company* and *A Piece of Monologue*.[4]

The date of Atik's diary entry is soon after Beckett began the French translation of *That Time* in November the same year. The setting of *Verbatim/The Voice* is quite similar to *That Time*, except for the third person 'he' replacing the second person 'you', which is adopted in *A Piece of Monologue* that Beckett had already started writing in October. In this dramatic piece, a stage figure narrates the story of 'he' as Speaker, as if the story is not his but someone else's,

---

4   See Kiuchi (2005) for an analysis of the multiplication in *Company* and *A Piece of Monologue*.

though the stage setting clearly overlaps the content of the story, indicating Speaker is the 'he'. In *Company*, which Beckett was already struggling with in early 1977, the voice is split into two voices, one addressing in 'you' and the other narrating in 'he', as if combining *That Time* and *A Piece of Monologue* in prose. This suggests that *That Time* is not only a dramatic piece written in response to *Not I* but also a piece that prefigures and induces Beckett's writing in the late 1970s and the early 1980s.

This chapter began with the contention that Beckett's writing can be understood more in depth when it is considered as a process of his interlingual and intersemiotic translation. The above analysis demonstrated that this is valid at least in the case of *That Time/Cette fois*. Biographical details point to a possible connection between this dramatic piece and *À la recherche*. The intertexual reading also feeds into the bilingual reading of the piece. Two interlingual differences, 'that time/*cette fois*' and 'Listener/*Souvenant*' provided strong evidence to connect the two literary texts. The use of the compound past and the imperfect in French allows for the exploration of the experience of time in the two literary works to question the fluid borders between the past and the present and between dream time and reality. A reading of the beginning of *À la recherche* also confirms its influence on *That Time* in the use of images, and the free association of the mind. Finally, the intersemiotic approach elucidated how Beckett changed his take of the function of Listener in *That Time/Cette fois* during his German production and how this may have influenced the change of names from Listener to *Souvenant*. This essay argued that this change might result from the setting that the stage figure is 'depersonalised', so that in turn the spectator is expected to fulfil a listening function inherent to this dramatic piece. However, that the spectator can listen to a voice addressing in 'you' does not mean that they are the addressees of the voices. It may be that they are only overhearing it. The name *Souvenant* attests to Beckett's unchanged intention that the stage figure or his sign of life indicated by his breathing should be the owner of the voices and the memory spoken by them regardless of his silence and subtle movement.

Works Cited

Ackerley, C. J., and S. E. Gontarski (2004), *The Grove Companion to Samuel Beckett*, New York: Grove P.

Asmus, Walter D. (1977), 'Rehearsal Notes for the German Première of Beckett's *That Time* and *Footfalls* at the Schiller-Theater Werkstatt Berlin (directed by Beckett)', trans. Helen Watanabe, *JOBS* 2, pp. 82–95.

Atik, Anne (2001), *How It Was: A Memoir of Samuel Beckett*, London: Faber and Faber.

Beckett, Samuel (1986), *Cette fois* in Beckett, *Catastrophe et autres dramaticules*, Paris: Les Éditions de Minuit, pp. 7–25.

Beckett, Samuel (1993), *Samuel Beckett's Company/Compagnie and A Piece of Monologue/Solo: A Bilingual and Variorum Edition*, ed. Charles Krance, New York: Garland Reference Library of the Humanities.

Beckett, Samuel and Alan Schneider (1998), *No Author Better Served: The Correspondence of Samuel Beckett and Alan Schneider*, ed. Maurice Harmon, Cambridge: Harvard UP.

Beckett, Samuel (2009), *Krapp's Last Tape and Other Shorter Plays*, ed. S. E. Gontarski, London: Faber and Faber.

Beckett, Samuel (2016), *The Letters of Samuel Beckett*, Vol. IV, 1966–1989, ed. George Craig, Martha Dow Fehsenfeld, Dan Gunn and Lois More Overbeck, Cambridge: Cambridge UP.

Curtius, Ernst Robert (1928), *Marcel Proust*, Paris: Les Éditions de la Revue Nouvelle.

Genette, Gérard (1980), *Narrative Discourse: An Essay in Method*, trans. Jane E. Lewin, New York: Cornell UP.

Kiuchi, Kumiko (2005), 'Against Autobiography: Samuel Beckett's *Company/Compagnie* as an Autobiographical Writing of Another', *Interdisciplinary Cultural Studies* 8, pp. 143–160.

Knowlson, James (1996), *Damned to Fame: The Life of Samuel Beckett*, New York: Touchstone.

Nemoto, Misako (2004), *Nemuri to Bungaku* [*Sleep and Literature*]: *Proust, Kafka and Tanizaki*, Tokyo: Chuko-shinsho.

Oxford Dictionary of English (2005), Second Edition revised.

Pilling, John (2006), *A Samuel Beckett Chronology*, Basingstoke: Palgrave Macmillan.

Proust, Marcel (1971), *Contre Saint-Beuve précédé de Pastiches et mélanges et suivi d'Essais et articles*, ed. Pierre Clarac, Paris: Gallimard.

Proust, Marcel (1987), *À la recherche du temps perdu* t.1, eds. J.-Y. Tadié et al., Paris: Les Éditions Gallimard.

Proust, Marcel (2005), *In Search of Lost Time I: Swann's Way*, trans. C. K. Scott Moncrieff and T. Kilmartin, revised by D. J. Enright, London: Vintage Books.

Un-bodied Voices, the Thing Itself and Beckett's Neural Theatre

S. E. Gontarski

Abstract

Gilles Deleuze reminds us in his essay on Beckett's teleplays, 'The Exhausted', that the image is central to Beckett's art, neither representation nor thing but a process, a constant becoming, which is the ultimate impact of art, not only in cinema, but in other arts as well (Deleuze, 1995, 19). Such process, an emphasis on flow, becoming, and multiplicity, on mutability rather than stability, on partiality rather than wholeness, a perpetual betweenness — between text and image, between past and present, between sensation and matter, between embodiment and dis- or un-embodiment — suggests an incipient theory of theatre as well. Certainly such is the case in Beckett's later work, particularly his late work for theatre and media in which we find a preponderance of spectral figures, ghosts, absences, what Deleuze calls the 'ghostly dimension' (14). What appears on stage as a something, a material entity, a body, perhaps, or body part, is not always fully present, is thus something not quite wholly material, nor quite simply immaterial or ethereal either, something in between presence and absence, matter and image, between the real and surreal or trans-real, Beckett himself an artist in between, neither wholly of his time nor wholly of ours, fully neither, even as he is always, if partly, both. This essay explores the implications of such thought about art in Beckett's stage works, which are less simulations than events in and of themselves, and focuses attention on the voice and its untethering from body, its un-bodiness.

∙∙∙

> Pure perception is not the perception of something, it is the thing itself. It is in things that there is perception.
>
> Gilles Deleuze

1 In-Betweenness

In his assessment of French cineaste Jean-Luc Godard, Gilles Deleuze stresses the in-betweenness of Godard's work, between sound and sight, between television and cinema, between image and text, between perceiver and object, between consciousness and matter, between embodied and unbodied voice. This is Deleuze's critique of post-war cinema as a 'time image', as well, one which offers the perspective of a disinterested, bodiless perceiver, the camera, that (at its best) presents the pure flow of time as becoming. Such in-betweenness admittedly owes much to Henri Bergson's *durée* and multiplicity, whose formulation of the image Deleuze appropriates and reframes as something between matter and memory, between presence and absence, between perceiver and perceived, as much material object as immaterial consciousness, that is, immanence, or becoming, Deleuze's rendering of *durée* — matter spiritualised: the spirit materialised — the image both and wholly neither. The image, then, is matter *and* consciousness, material as well as construct of consciousness, as Deleuze uses it:

> In the early 1900's, Henri Bergson (1859–1941) developed the concepts of 'movement-image' and 'time-image' (in *Matière et memoire*), both of which anticipated the development of film theory. Bergson declares the image to be superior to the concept because the image is able to evoke thought content in a more fluent and less abstract fashion. In lectures held at the *Collège de France* between 1902–03, Bergson briefly refers to the possibility of 'comparing the mechanism of conceptual thought with that of the cinematograph' (now in *L'Évolution créatrice*, 1991, p. 725, note 1). Bergson's main philosophical theme is that temporality should be thought of as independent from concepts of spatiality. Bergson contrasts duration, as it is experienced by the human consciousness, with scientific definitions of time, the latter of which, in his view, tends to 'spatialize'. (2017)

Deleuze reminds us in his essay on Beckett's teleplays, 'The Exhausted', that the image is central to Beckett's art, neither representation nor thing, but a process, a constant becoming, which, as it generates affect, is the ultimate impact of art, not only in cinema, that is, but in other arts as well (Deleuze, 1995, 19). Such process, an emphasis on flow, becoming, and multiplicity, on mutability rather than stability, partiality rather than wholeness, a perpetual betweenness — between text and image, between past and present, between sensation and matter, between embodiment and dis- or un-embodiment —

suggests an incipient theory of theatre as well. Certainly, such is the case in Beckett's later work, particularly his late work for theatre and media in which we find a preponderance of spectral figures, ghosts, absences, what Deleuze calls the 'ghostly dimension' (14). What appears on stage as a something, a material entity, a body, perhaps, or body parts, is not always fully present, is thus something not quite wholly material, nor simply immaterial or ethereal either, something in between presence and absence, matter and image, between the actual and surreal or trans-real, Beckett himself an artist of the between, neither wholly of his time nor wholly of ours, say, fully neither, even as he is always, if partly or partially, both. The pacing May of *Footfalls* is a case in point: apparently a physical entity on stage, or at least we perceive a figure in motion, she may not be there at all, or not fully or materially there as the final short scene of the stage without her suggests. Spirit thus becomes light, perhaps a beam of light as the final image of the play suggests and as the assailing voice of *Eh Joe* would have it. Beckett's theatre is thus not about something, not a representation, the image or images of the artistic creation not images of something outside the work; they are 'that something itself', as he famously quipped in 1929 of James Joyce's then-titled 'Work in Progress'. Deleuze will call such experience or sensation an 'event', not a representation or simulacrum, not a copy of another realm: 'The identification of the immediate with the past experience, the recurrence of past action or reaction in the present, amounts to a participation between the ideal and the real, imagination and direct apprehension, symbol and substance' (55). Whether the voice we hear is connected to the body we perceive is not a given, as is the case with Voice in *Eh Joe*, identified only as Woman's Voice (202). Reading Beckett's *Texts for Nothing*, Michel Foucault reminds us, 'Beckett nicely formulates the theme with which I would like to begin: "What does it matter who is speaking;" someone said; "what does it matter who is speaking". In this indifference appears one of the fundamental ethical principles of contemporary writing [écriture]' (Foucault, 1969). In addition to asserting 'ethical' implications of Beckett's work, then, Foucault defines its theatricality or performability, voice foregrounded, the material body itself pixelated.

In *Ohio Impromptu* two figures, 'As alike in appearance as possible' (1986, 445), the text reminds us, sit at a table. At very least they look to be material, (nearly) identical entities, two physically present bodies, their materiality confirmed by knocks or raps on a table. And yet the narrative or memoir read by the figure functionally called Reader suggests otherwise, one a spiritual representative of an absent one, a former lover, apparently. If we assume some continuity, some congruence between the visual and the narrated images, a self-reflexivity to the performance or an embodiment of the narrative, that is, theatre as illustrative of a text pre-existing it, then one of the perceived figures on the stage, and perhaps the one apparently controlling the reading, the one called Listener, is a material presence, one an emissary, a shade, a spirit sent by an absent lover for something like consolation, an emissary or guide through Listener's travails, as Virgil sent by 'Bice', Dante's beloved Beatrice, 'to comfort you' (287). Our perception then may be faulty, the stage image 'ill seen', perhaps, since at least one of the figures may not be there — at least not as a material presence, Reader the extension of a text. Something of a dream is suggested here as well as indicated in the narrative by a third person, a 'he', 'in his dreams' (286), but reading the impromptu as dream does not necessarily solve the issues of presence and absence, the material and the immaterial. Moreover, the narrative further suggests something of the fluidity and mutability of being as the image of the Seine divided by the Isle of Swans is reunited on the far side of the Isle, and so finally after the division, 'its two arms conflowed and flowed united on' (286). Is this merging, this reunion, that of the lovers of the narrative, or of the two figures we believe we perceive on stage, one apparently material, one not, or the merger of dream and reality? But each of these possibilities is complicated as the narrative is both materialised and deterritorialised.

We might add that a third active entity is present in performance, the text itself, at least some forty pages long, on stage taking on a life as it speaks and shapes our response to the performance and so to the central, thematic, philosophical issues. Text itself, we might say, our third player in the performance, is a link, a bridge, between the lovers, between Reader and Listener, between the actual and the unreal, or the actual and the virtual, between materiality and imagination, or memory, thus linking past with present, which is what memory does, giving spirit or shade a material form and simultaneously questioning materiality itself since both figures may be dream images, or versions of the same figure as 'they grew to be as one', at which point, 'nothing is left to tell'. But such a phrase, the 'nothing' left 'to tell', is already written well before our hearing it, already scripted at the telling, and thus the reading, the performance already a repetition. Text, as text, has presumably been thought and read before, and will doubtless be read again even after the repeated 'Nothing is left to tell' (1984, 288), the imaginative image or memory (and they amount to the same) that we as audience perceive will be repeated, with difference, over and over again, the *Impromptu* not a telos but a loop, a repetition, always with difference, and a bridge between the material and the immaterial, between presence and absence, the engagement not between figure and figure but between figure and Other, between figure(s) and text, between material and immaterial, text already written.

Beckett's move into television re-emphasised the imagistic nature of performance with unbodied narrators' voices near or contrary to those images we see on the screen, the process offering further narrative dislocations, deterritorialisations. In Beckett's 1985 television version of the play *What Where*, a disembodied narrator tells us, for instance, that 'In the end Bom appears' (311); Bom as character is thus already an object Other than the narrating voice, who apparently is himself plural, already a multiplicity. 'We are the last five' (310), the Voice continues, the grammar eliding from singular, Bam, to the multiple, a voice that is a 'We'. At best, however, images of four characters are manifest, Bam, Bim, Bom, and Bem, the mysterious fifth, apparently 'Bum' if we follow the vowel sequence, only incipient or already dispatched, no longer part of our perceived actuality. 'In the present as were we still' (310), the voice intones, the subjunctive mood alerting us that this statement is contrary to fact. These are characters not there, finally, the pattern of images coming and going, moving to and fro, to an offstage fraught with possibility, to receive 'the works', Beckett already anticipating such in betweenness in his *Proust*: 'But he is not there because she does not know he is there. He is present at his own absence' (15).

Beckett's *...but the clouds...* offers another instance, and returns us to Foucault. The spirit of the teleplay (as of all of Beckett's teleplays, perhaps) is captured by Yeats's question from Part III of *The Tower*: 'Does the imagination dwell the most / Upon a woman won or woman lost?' *...but the clouds...* offers a variation on this recurrent, even obsessive Beckettian theme, love lost, in a medium that concretises the apparition but keeps it non-haptic, immaterial on the screen, the face of a woman, whom Beckett describes thus, 'The woman I see in her thirties. A haunting face, not necessarily beautiful' (Beckett, 2016, 445). She is lost *to him* because her only love was or is, apparently, poetry. The work thus mirrors or reverses *Krapp's Last Tape* in which Krapp bids 'Farewell to — [*he turns page*] — love' (Beckett, 1984, 57) for the benefit of his intellectual pursuits, we learn, themselves now failed dismally. In *Eh Joe*, Joe serially abandons female lovers, one of whom takes her own life in the aftermath. The image of a lost love in *...but the clouds...*, moreover, is not too unlike those manifest for an instant in a cloud in 'Enueg II' or in the ashes of an ingle in *Words and Music*. *...but the clouds...* features two images for the male figure: M hunched over, obscuring his desk, and M1, or 'M in the set' (257), either dressed for the road, in dark 'Hat and greatcoat', or for bed, in light 'robe and skullcap'. A voice, V, apparently but not necessarily M's even as Beckett tells us, 'M's voice', observes, records or directs M in set, imagining, revising, and repeating his ritualised daily comings and goings after which he conjures or 'begs' W, 'woman's face reduced as far as possible to eyes and mouth', to appear in the dead of night. V at first details the possibilities of her appearances: (1) she appears and instantly is gone; (2) she appears and lingers; and (3) she appears and utters the words of Yeats's poem. Yet the voice we hear is not hers but V's, V apparently ventriloquizing W, conjuring her visual image but not its auditory component, the inverse of *Eh Joe*. A fourth possibility exists as well, that she does not appear at all, whereupon M busies himself with mathematics, cube roots, awaiting dawn and the resumption of his aimless wanderings. But that fourth possibility is likewise not materialised.

Who or what is 'V', then, a multiple of M in the set, or another, an unbodied entity, pure voice? Approaching the work from the perspective of film and television theory (rather than the usual literary perspective), calling Beckett's teleplays 'essentially intermedial' and dubbing Beckett himself a 'media philosopher' (a phrase from which he would have doubtless recoiled), Atene Mendelyte comes close to defining the phenomenon of unbodied voice in televisual terms: 'the play in a self-reflexive positive gesture explores both the ontology of the television-image and the ontology of memory as a process of conjuration by presenting a successful emergence of the televisual Image-in-itself' (Mendelyte, 325). This, she suggests, further echoing Deleuze's terminology, is Beckett's intermediality, adapting the techniques of one medium to another. She cites (and translates) intermediality theorist Jürgen Müller: '"a medial product becomes intermedial, when it transfers the multimedial togetherness (*Nebeneinander*) of medial citations and elements to a conceptual cooperation (*Miteinander*)" (Müller, 83), that is to say, when the intertextual and intermedial references work together as a unified aesthetic and conceptual whole and become a singular structure, instead of tearing the structure apart by pointing back to their points of origin' (Mendelyte, 325). Such a de-emphasis on the allusive quality of the work is a refreshing re-emphasis. Beckett's images tend to overlay one another in something of a layered unity or strata, but different from or a variation on structure and certainly not 'singular structure'. 'Beckett's intermediality', she continues closer to the mark, now citing (and translating) Roloff, 'broadens the in-between spaces [*Zwischenraum, Interstitium*] between image and text' and 'makes visible the invisible and the eerie, the "other" space between the discourses, that Foucault qualified as heterotopy' (Roloff, 4). For Foucault these are 'real places — places that do exist and that are formed in the very founding of society — which are something like counter-sites, a kind of effectively enacted utopia in which the real sites, all the other real sites that can be found within the culture, are simultaneously represented, contested, and inverted. Places of this kind are outside of all places, even though it may be possible to indicate their location in reality. Because these places are absolutely different from all the sites that they reflect and speak about, I shall call them, by way of contrast to utopias, "heterotopias"' (Foucault, 1984, 3–4).

Asking how 'heterotopic' Beckett's spaces are suggests ways of engaging the texts and performances beyond the usual literary and performative constrictions that often wind up becoming struggles to simulate an actuality. Instead, heterotopically, the works become events in themselves without, necessarily, reference to an actual, familiar world, or if they are or suggest simulations they are simulations as simulations, opacities or translucencies rather than transparencies. Foucault's focus on space, for us stage space, suggests heterotopian, anti-utopian images with their narrative and visual disjunctions that disrupt expected continuity and are part of, or offer insight into, the pure flow of time as well, what Deleuze calls the Plane of Immanence, perceptions always on the verge of becoming, that is, becoming other, other than expected, something else, unsettling the received, that which we expect; they are thus a bridge that generates affect, an emotional response not always specified or specifiable. But planes are not strata. Planes are unstratified, or rather planes are time focused, strata space focused, but neither exclusively so. Beckett takes on these issues directly via the classical artist in his *Proust* treatise. The classical artist assumes an omnipotence and 'raises himself artificially out of Time in order to give relief to his chronology and [give] causality to his development', as Beckett notes (62). On the other hand, great art, minoritarian art, Deleuze would say, is the pure expression of pure feeling, or as Beckett noted in *Proust*, a 'non-logical statement of phenomena in the order and exactitude of their perception, before they have been distorted into intelligibility in order to be forced into a chain of cause and effect' (66). Such a non-logical statement of phenomena in a heterotopian space generating imminent becomings is difficult to achieve through language, however, language essentially a referential if not simulacric system, and Beckett recognised that deficiency: 'At that level you break up words to diminish shame. Painting and music have so much better a chance', he admitted to Lawrence Harvey in 1970 (249). Billie Whitelaw describes her performance in *Footfalls* thus: 'Sometimes I felt as if he were a sculptor and I a piece of clay. [...] Sometimes I felt as though I were modelling for a painter or working with a musician. The movements started to feel like dance' (Whitelaw, 1996, 144). Beckett's language thus is always a foreign tongue, Hiberno-English in his native land, minoritarian; an outsider's French in his adopted language, at times almost a non-language, pure sound, music, pauses. Speaking of his direction of *Fin de partie*, Beckett's French director Roger Blin noted:

> he had ideas about the play that made it a little difficult to act. At first, he looked on his play as a kind of musical score. When a word occurred or was repeated, when Hamm called Clov, Clov should always come in the same way every time, like a musical phrase coming from the same

instrument with the same volume. I thought that this idea was very much a product of the intellect and would result in an extraordinary rigor. He didn't see any drama or suspense in Clov's imminent departure. He would either leave or he wouldn't. (Blin qtd. in Gontarski, 172)

Beckett is thus, like Kafka, as Deleuze characterises him, always a foreigner in his own and in his adopted land, and so he is what Deleuze calls a minoritarian writer.

2 Neural Theatre

Such heterotopian worlds as Beckett creates are thus virtual worlds that include past and present, material figures, imagination, and memory; off stage or what appears to be empty space is thus a virtual whole, a nothing full of possibilities, including all possible actions and movements. In this regard Beckett's theatre runs contrary to that described by Peter Brook in his famous theatrical treatise *The Empty Space*, where theatre space is there to be filled; for Beckett the stage is never empty but always already full of the potentially possible. For Deleuze, 'Space enjoys potentialities as long as it makes the realization of events possible: it precedes realization, then, and potentiality itself belongs to the possible. But wasn't this equally the case for the image, which already proposed a specific means of exhausting the possible?' (1995, 11). That is, space too is an image and so as material as it is ethereal. The slight fourth scene of *Footfalls* features an apparently empty stage, but the space remains full of interpretive possibilities and opens the play to those possibilities. It is always replete, full of potential meanings and worlds, of all the possibilities that theatre has to offer since it includes the whole of the past as well as the full potential to create new worlds. The space then is always already full; in short, it contains the process of the virtual, part of what Deleuze will call the Plane of Immanence. Beckett's plays then do not represent or realise a world of actuality, a world outside itself, do not represent at all, but offer images that make us feel in their affect the movement of existence, its flow, becoming, *durée*. Possibilities are not closed off by separating inside from outside, matter from spirit, present from past.

What too often frustrates readers or spectators is precisely this resistance to representation that characterises Beckett's art, since most of us operate on the Plane of Transcendence that produces or alludes to an exterior to the artwork, the world we know and try to represent in art. This is the world of what Beckett calls the classical artist, a world from which he separated himself early on. For

Deleuze the perceiving mind of a doubting Cartesian subject is a piece of ribbon that separates inside from outside. The ribbon itself or a piece of paper, or as Beckett dubs it in *The Unnamable* a membrane or a tympanum vibrating, is in between, neither inside nor out but both in relation to the other, the vibration evading the Plane of Transcendence or a grounding of any sort; ultimate truths that we are driven to obey. The series of plateaus, perhaps 1,000, that Deleuze critiques in the book of that title, is an assault against such groundings, the stability of language included, as is Beckett's art. Transcendence is a human disease that Deleuze calls 'interpretosis', or what the director of *Catastrophe* in the process of creating an image calls 'This craze for explicitation. Every i dotted to death. Little gag. For God's sake!' (1984, 299). 'We're not beginning to... to... mean something', asks Hamm. 'Mean something!' responds Clov, 'You and I mean something? Ah, that's a good one' (1986, 108), and they share a communal laugh over the false promise of transcendence, that they might be part of a greater system, or a greater truth beyond images of themselves in process. The alternative to transcendence is to accept, even to love, simply what is; Deleuze's term like Foucault's is also an ethics, but, after Nietzsche in *The Gay Science*, an 'ethics of the *amor fati*', the love of not exactly fate but of what is. One anecdote that Hamm tells has often been cited but less than satisfactorily discussed. The 'madman' that Hamm visits in the asylum is shown the fecund beauty of the exterior, the corn, the herring fleet, from which the madman withdraws appalled (1986, 113–4). Hamm's conclusion is that 'He alone had been spared'. Critics may point out the likely reference here to the visionary poet William Blake, but what or how the 'madman' has been spared is seldom parsed. One possibility is that he has been spared preoccupation with a transcendent world, what Deleuze will call the illusion of transcendence that will close and explain experience. Hamm's 'madman' is thinking 'other', possible, alternative worlds. It may indeed be just those alternative worlds that Hamm keeps asking Clov to find beyond the shelter, but they are within as well. In Act II of *Waiting for Godot* the issue is put thus: '[*Aphoristic for once.*] We all are born mad.[1] Some remain so' (1986, 75). Perhaps those are the saved, the parallel to the saved thief on the cross beside Christ. Hamm's position is evidently to pull the madman back from the end of the world, a position that would resist or stop the flow of alternatives, becoming, *durée*. Later Hamm concludes the prayer scene with an overt statement about such transcendence, such 'ethics of knowledge'. Of a transcendental reality, God, he says, 'The bastard. He doesn't exist' (1986, 119). Perhaps Hamm too has (finally) been spared,

---

1 'All' and 'are' are reversed in the American edition.

saved. As a seated figure, Hamm is at a decided disadvantage, however. 'It is the most horrible position in which to await death', Deleuze tells us, 'sitting without the force either to rise or to lie down, watching for the signal [*coup*] that will make us draw ourselves up one last time and lie down forever. Seated, you can't recover, you can no longer stir even a memory' (1995, 6).

In his dramaticule of 1968 that Beckett designates as images of motion, *Come and Go*, we are denied access to information that would, if disclosed, shut down the process of thinking. Without that knowledge, the process of thinking, the generation of possibilities, alternatives, parallels the flow of movement on stage. Language is not so much devalued among the 128 (or so) words in this playlet since much of it is elegant and poetic, language as part of (and not apart from) an image of flow. Or at the end of Beckett's late masterwork, *Rockaby*, as the 'recorded voice' reveals another narrative thread, 'and rocked / rocked / saying to herself / no / done with that', we might ask, 'Done with what' or 'saying [what] to herself' (Beckett, 1986, 442)? What is resisted in such interruption is knowledge that would still such movement and freeze it, and end a process that Deleuze calls philosophy. When the American actress Jessica Tandy complained, first to director Alan Schneider and then, bypassing him, directly to Samuel Beckett, that *Not I*'s suggested running time of twenty-three minutes rendered the work unintelligible to audiences,[2] Beckett telegraphed back his now famous but oft misconstrued injunction, 'I'm not unduly concerned with intelligibility. I hope the piece may work on the nerves of the audience, not its intellect' (Brater, 200). If we take Beckett at his word and do not simply treat this comment as a one off, as a dismissal of the actress or an admonition that she listen to her director, through whom, he told her, he would henceforth communicate, then he is suggesting a theoretical position,

---

2   Of late, performances of *Not I* have taken on as much the character of athletic competitions as theatre events, actresses performing not only for a personal best but for a world record as well. In May 2013, forty years after the landmark 1973 Billie Whitelaw world premiere under Samuel Beckett's direction, *Not I* returned to the Royal Court Theatre with a performance by anointed Billie Whitelaw successor, Lisa Dwan, who was 'tutored in the role by Billie Whitelaw', as the Royal Court's press release and the post production video interview with Whitelaw (from 2009) inform us. Dwan's iteration was first performed at BAC in 2005, at the Southbank Centre in 2009, and the inaugural International Festival of Beckett in Enniskillen in 2012. The running time for Dwan's performance is an astonishing nine minutes, but still at a £20 ticket price, we might add, although on the night I saw the performance, 25 May, critic Michael Coveney proudly announced in the post production chat-up, the talk back to fill out the scant programme, that the nine-minute barrier had been broken. The evening's first question from the audience was whether or not Ms Dwan had a back story for the monologue. She admitted that she had as an *aide-mémoire*, but, mercifully, for the integrity of the performance, that is, she did not disclose it.

a theory of theatre. Evidence for the latter may be found in his attitude about *Play*, which similarly should be staged at incomprehensible speed, language become sound, music even, a pace which, admittedly, many a director, Alan Schneider among them, has resisted. Beckett's instructions to Schneider were that '*Play* was to be played through twice without interruption and at a very fast pace, each time taking no longer than nine minutes', that is, eighteen minutes overall. The producers of the New York premiere, Richard Barr, Clinton Wilder, and, of all people, Edward Albee, threatened to drop the play from the programme if Schneider heeded Beckett's pacing. Schneider capitulated, and wrote to Beckett for permission to slow the pace and eliminate the *da capo*: 'For the first and last time in my long relationship with Sam, I did something I despised myself for doing. I wrote to him, asking if we could try having his text spoken only once, more slowly. Instead of telling me to blast off, Sam offered us his reluctant permission' (Schneider, 341).

What then are we to make of so neural a theatre, one that seems to put the emphasis on what Deleuze, writing *after* Beckett, will call 'pure affect'? We can resist Beckett here, as Schneider's producers and, finally, Schneider himself did, or take him at his word; that is, this is how theatre works, not by creating simulacra, nor by dealing with transcendent truths, but by constructing images of process and change, life as immanence, even as it is materially rooted in pure perception. 'Make sense who may', Beckett concluded in his valedictory work for the theatre, *What Where*. In these shorter plays, then, Beckett's most radical artistic vision, his most revolutionary theories of theatre, emerge in images one might deem heterotopic. This brings us, moreover, to one of the most vexing and contentious questions in Beckett studies, the degree to which Beckett's work is representational at all, or, on the contrary, whether its persistent preoccupation is with resisting representation, or rather to focus on how slippery and artificial representations are as they are played amid the Plane of Immanence, the perpetual flow of being. That is, Beckett's art on stage or page is not a stand-in for or simulation of another reality; it is an event itself, that reality more often than not 'virtual' in the Deleuzian sense of that term. Beckett's theatre is always a theatre of becoming, of deterritorialisation, a decomposition moving towards re-composition, itself decomposing. It is a theatre of perpetual movement or flow, all comings and goings, a pulse that expands and contracts creating affect. Even as it often appears stationary or static, even amid the Beckettian pauses, images move, flow, become other, not representing a world that we know, but perpetually creating new worlds. Bergson would call this *durée*, Deleuze 'becoming'; Beckett would simply call it art. It is a heterotopic theatre struggling to resist the world we know, with voices unembodied but which retain their own materiality, theatre struggling to resist conceptualising our world and the condition of being since those are mere snapshots and not the process, the flowing, becoming.

Works Cited

Beckett, Samuel (1957), *Proust*, New York: Grove P.
Beckett, Samuel (1984), *The Collected Shorter Plays of Samuel Beckett*, New York: Grove P.
Beckett, Samuel (1986), *The Complete Dramatic Works*, London: Faber and Faber.
Beckett, Samuel (2016), *The Letters of Samuel Beckett*, Vol. IV, 1966–1989, eds. George Craig, Martha Dow Fehsenfeld, Dan Gunn and Lois More Overbeck, Cambridge: Cambridge UP.
Brater, Enoch (1974), 'The "I" in Beckett's *Not I*' *Twentieth Century Literature*, 20: 3, pp. 189–200.
Deleuze, Gilles (1986), *Cinema 1: The Movement Image*, trans. Hugh Tomlinson and Barbara Habberjam, Minneapolis: U of Minnesota P.
Deleuze, Gilles (1995), 'The Exhausted', trans. Anthony Uhlmann, *SubStance* 24: 3, pp. 3–28.
Deleuze, Gilles (2017), *The Movement-Image: Bergsonian Lessons on Cinema*: Lecture 4, 1 December 1981, Purdue University Research Repository, doi:10.4231/R7319T3M, available online at: https://purr.purdue.edu/publications/2734/1.
Foucault, Michel (1969), 'What is an Author?', available online at: http://www.generation-online.org/p/fp_foucault12.htm.
Foucault, Michel (1984), 'Of Other Spaces: Utopias and Heterotopias', trans. by Jay Miskowiec. *Architecture/Mouvement/Continuité*. October (originally 'Des Espaces Autres', March 1967), available online at: http://web.mit.edu/allanmc/www/foucault1.pdf.
Gontarski, S. E. (1986), *On Beckett: Essays and Criticism*, New York: Grove P.
Harvey, Lawrence (1970), *Samuel Beckett: Poet and Critic*, Princeton: Princeton UP.
Mendelyte, Atene (2015), 'The Image of a Mind-Skull: Samuel Beckett's *...but the clouds...* and Television-Philosophy', *Film-Philosophy Journal*, 19, pp. 325–43.
Müller, Jürgen (1996), *Intermedialität. Formen moderner kultureller Kommunikation*, Münster: Nodus Publikationen.
Roloff, Volker (1994), 'Einleitung: Buñuels reflektierte Intermedialität', in Ursula Link-Heer and Volker Roloff, eds., *Luis Buñuel: Film, Literatur, Intermedialität*. Darmstadt: Wissenschaftliche Buchgesellschaft, pp. 1–12.
Schneider, Alan (1986), *Entrances: An American Director's Journey*, New York: Viking P.
Whitelaw, Billie (1996), *Billie Whitelaw ... Who He?*, New York: St. Martin's P.

Zourabichvili, François (2012), *Deleuze: A Philosophy of the Event: Together with The Vocabulary of Deleuze*, trans. Kieran Aarons, Gregg Lambert, and Daniel W. Smith, Edinburgh: Edinburgh UP.

PART 3

Voices of the Vulnerable

∴

Pacing as Repressed Memory of Embodiment and Enactment in *Footfalls*

Svetlana Antropova

Abstract

The image of a lonely woman grasping her body, as though in grief, and walking incessantly becomes form and content in *Footfalls*. As the hierarchy of image and the movement of pacing over the text was explicitly highlighted by Beckett, this chapter attempts to shed light on the understanding of this movement through the binary lens of psychology and psychoanalysis. Pacing is discussed in this chapter as the container of May's life-story and as a memory trigger. The lack of self-identification, obscure life turning points together with the ambiguous language of the play full of repetitions, fragmentations, alienation, overlapping of past and present, lead us into the field of repressed memory. On her solitary journey, May's steps trigger the echoes of her memories and evoke her Mother's Voice from her 'deep sleep'. The spectator is presented to a pseudo-fusion between the daughter and her mother; albeit two different entities, they are intertwined through their memories and through their craving for unity. Thus, the trauma of birth is inscribed in this play through the movement of pacing. Incessantly walking nine steps back and forth along a lit path, May's 'destination' is to reach the security of her mother's womb, and/or to return to the state of non-existence.

Footfalls (1976) is one of the most mysterious plays of Samuel Beckett. No consensus has been reached so far on its meaning. Knowlson and Pilling write about the general state of bewilderment after its premiere (221). The image engraved in the audience's mind is of a woman 'grasping her shoulders in a gesture of isolation and distress' (221) relentlessly pacing the stage. The hierarchy of this image and the movement of pacing over the text was explicitly noted by Beckett: 'This was [my] basic conception…', Beckett commented, 'the text, the words were only built up around this picture' (221). He writes in a letter to Billie Whitelaw: 'The pacing is the essence of the matter, to be dramatized to the utmost. The text what pharmacists call excipient' (Beckett, 2016, 424). Furthermore, the playwright was precise about the theatrical image and especially movement in this play. The only character onstage, May, dressed in 'worn grey wrap' (Beckett, 1986, 399) with her shoulders bent and her arms wrapped around her slim body, is rhythmically pacing the stage as if in a hypnotic trance: nine steps to the left — wheel — nine steps to the right.

In the performance of the play *Tritte* (in Germany), directed by Beckett, Hildegard Schmahl had problems with acting due to her total loss in the understanding of the play. Beckett insisted on her emphasising her footsteps: 'Her most significant leap with the role coincided with her decision to make the primary ground for her performance physical and not psychic' (Kalb, 64). The actress's taut stiff body affected her articulation and opened her psyche 'through calculated physical behavior' (Kalb, 64). Thus, it is the movement which becomes the engine of *Footfalls*, as May's pacing gives birth to words and preconditions her speed of utterance. Pacing can be considered both form and content of this play.

In this chapter we attempt to discuss the movement of pacing in relation to memory evocation through the binary lens of psychology and psychoanalysis. The relation of this play to psychology was pointed out by Knowlson: "*Footfalls* grew out of Beckett's long-standing interest in abnormal psychology. May's solitary pacing seems like the externalization of some inner anguish" (544). The origins of the play may be found not only in the case of a young woman from Tavistock Clinic, of whom it was said that she had never been born, but also in Lucia Joyce, whom Beckett visited in the hospital at Ivry in 1939 (544). Beckett's interest in psychology and psychoanalysis is well documented,[1] as

> Beckett studied both Freud and his disciples with a keenness bred of his own personal neuroses. And only two years before writing *Footfalls*, he had also met the daughter of an old friend, who described to him graphically her own depression, distress, and extreme agoraphobia, telling him how, unable to face the world, she used to pace relentlessly up and down in her apartment. (544)

Therefore, the recent research in the field of psychology carried out by Daniel Casasanto and Katinka Dijkstra can shed new light on the importance of movement and its connection to memory and emotion. These authors state that bodily movements and postures not only influence the retrieval of emotional memories and the speed of recall (179), but also that memories can be encoded in our brain through kinesthetic, spatial, and affective aspects, which

---

[1] Beckett's reading in the fields of psychology and psychoanalysis was extensive. After his death, his notes on psychology were discovered in a trunk in his cellar, which detail his interest in the writings of Rank, Adler, Freud, etc. (Knowlson, 172).

form part of our original experience. In their previous research, Dijkstra et al. write that:

> ... the memory trace of an experience includes the body posture in which the experience was acquired. The facilitation of a compatible body position with the content of the stimuli materials to be processed or remembered could be the result of a greater availability of processing resources. (141)

Hence, assuming the congruent body posture and recreating the sensorimotor environment in which a past experience was stored facilitates retrieval of autobiographic memories. In the same vein, May's posture and movement can be interpreted in the light of memory storage and its further retrieval. As May's life-story is represented in the movement of pacing, it can be discussed both as memory *per se* and as a memory-trigger. Furthermore, as the language of the play is full of repetitions, fragmentations, false starts, alienation, overlapping of past and present tenses, we can relate this play to the repressed memory narration. In the discussion of post-modern theatre agendas, Jeanette Malkin gives special importance to staging of repressed memory:

> Memory theatre might be doubly defined as a theatre that imitates conflicted and sometimes repressed or erased memories of a shared past, and as a theatre that initiates processes of remembrance through practices of repetition, conflation, regression, through recurrent scenes, involuntary voice, echoing, overlap, and simultaneity. (8)

May's pacing represents her past and her present and can provide a clue to the understanding of this character in relation to memory and trauma. This chapter analyses the movement of pacing according to its main characteristics and relates it to repressed memory, in particular the trauma of birth and its enactment in *Footfalls*. The criteria selected for this phenomenological analysis are already present in Beckett's stage directions: lighting, acoustic quality, rhythm, the number of steps and rotation, and textual echoes of footfalls.

1   Lighting as Body and Memory Fragmentator

As far as lighting is concerned, Beckett's directions are the following: '*Lighting: dim, strongest at floor level, less on body, least on head* [...] *Fade up to dim on strip. Rest in darkness*' (1986, 399). Malkin stresses the importance of lighting in memory-thetare, since it is a powerful technical device able to conjure up images from the past, to deconstruct the body, and to create memory spaces (21). Likewise, in *Footfalls*, lighting performs multiple roles. Firstly, emphasising May's steps 'strongest floor level', it directs the audience's attention towards pacing, making it the central image of the play. Secondly, by directing stronger light on feet, Beckett achieves the deconstruction of the theatrical body. Whilst May's feet are firmly grounded and brightly lit, the head and the body in semidarkness have an ephemeral quality. This lighting of the onstage image may be interpreted in the light of Bergson's eternal duel between materiality and spirituality. According to Bergson, our material body is time-and space-bound, while our spirit as well as our memory is free, thus mobile (60). Consequently, the deconstruction of the performative body by the light may be an attempt to free the memory from the cell of the body and make it a present experience. The overlapping of past and present in the play as well as body fragmentation directs our further discourse into the field of repressed memories. Malkin stresses that 'Bodily repetition that evokes a sense of timelessness, and thus of pastness incorporated in the present, is a theatrical device found in much postmodern theatre' (63).

The lighting directed towards May's feet contributes to the creation of two zones in *Footfalls*: the zone of light and the one of semidarkness/darkness. The latter can be related to the staging of the subconscious and the repressed. Enveloping May's head, darkness becomes the space of her remembering and the dominium of a bodiless voice of her mother. Like Henry in *Embers*, May evokes her Mother's Voice from the darkness: the voice of a presumably dead mother, which keeps her company in her solitary walking. By the evocation of this voice, May reshapes the theatrical reality, as another character enters the play and instead of a monologue, a dialogue is established between the two women.

Thirdly, the lighting limits the space of May's movements and traps her inside the lit path. We may interpret her pacing as of one imprisoned in an invisible cell, doomed to walk to and fro. Rehearsing for the Schiller Theatre production, Beckett revealed to Hildegard Schmahl that the whole play was centred in 'life-long stretches of walking' (Knowlson, 554); thus, the lit path may be interpreted as May's life journey based on continuous repetitions of nine steps to and fro.

And finally, lighting manages to achieve a ghostly quality of the performance: 'like moon through passing rack' (Beckett, 1986, 402). May herself is dressed in a 'tattered grey' long dress, and already looks like an apparition onstage. Ruby Cohn writes that 'The play's power lies in the tattered gray tangle, where places, times and words are fused in a stage presence that revolves around absence' (337). Dim lighting manages to create another reality onstage, with May on the threshold between two worlds: the living and the dead, her inner and outer selves, her past and her present. In the letter to Morton Feldman, Beckett includes a poem, which can serve as a powerful metaphor for May's ghostly walking:

> NEITHER
> to and fro in shadow from inner to outer shadow
> from impenetrable self to impenetrable unself
> by way of neither (Beckett, 2016, 436)

Katharine Worth also outlines this ghostly quality, claiming that the whole impression is that 'a ghost calls up a ghost' (106). This ghostly performance places this play in the rank of memory-plays, as May is a simple entity onstage: her present identity is absent, and her past identity is shrouded in continuous repetitions around several memory traces.

Furthermore, there are four fade-outs in the performance, which not only signal the end of the scene but also add an effect of memory blank-out or 'shudder of mind' (Beckett, 1986, 402), and thus signal the shift to another piece of memory. Moreover, the light is gradually dimming in the run of the performance. Worth writes, 'Beckett often dwells on the fading, making it a thing of unearthly sadness and beauty' (47). Besides adding a poetic quality to the performance, this fading light also creates a linear direction of the play towards May's total absence.

May's pacing together with the moments of her onstage immobility and fade-outs create the dramatic tension of presence/absence, which is mirrored in the text by May's affirming her not being there. Fade-outs interrupt the perception of May's pacing the stage four times during the play. Apart from shifting time, they prepare the audience for the end of the play, or for May's definite absence.

2 Acoustic Quality and Rhythm

Acoustic quality is another characteristic of May's pacing. The steps are faintly audible and together with the dragging of a long garment, they constitute the soundscape of the play. During the London premiere, to make the steps conspicuous, Billie Whitelaw wore ballet shoes with sandpaper attached to the soles (Knowlson, 624), thus amplifying the sound.

May is aware of the sound she makes and insists on it being heard, since 'the motion alone is not enough' (Beckett, 1986, 401). 'This strip of floor, once was carpeted' (401), informs the offstage voice, but May urged to take the carpet away: 'I must hear the feet, however faint they fall' (401). Here the question of self-perception may be raised. The fall of the steps on the bare floor reaffirms May's existence, since she perceives herself through this sound, and becomes the aural representation of May. While the footfalls reverberate in the theatrical present, she is still there walking her solitary road. According to Bergson, reality is mobility (27), ergo the footfalls may be considered as May's symbol of life. Like a metronome, walking the same lit passage in circles, she does not know whether she began and whether she will end. With obscure past and indefinite present, May becomes pure motion. The echoes of her steps prove her existence to the audience, chaining her to the present moment; she is not a ghost yet.

May has been pacing all her life; consequently, all her memories are intertwined with the sound of the steps, which can be interpreted as the soundscape of her memories. According to Bergson, 'there comes a moment when memory reduced in such a way is embedded so finely in our current perception that it is impossible to distinguish where such a perception ends and memory begins' (66; my translation). Thus, the sound of the steps may physically represent the stream of May's memory in the present stage moment.

The rhythm of May's pacing dictates her speed of uttering, her breathing, repetitions in speech, therefore, her whole onstage existence. The slow and 'clearly audible' (Beckett, 1985, 399) movement influences the pace of the performance: the voices are both 'low and slow throughout' (399). The rhythm of this pacing marks May's words, making their utterance a physical experience.

3   Number Nine

Enoch Brater compares the image of May to 'Dante's damned' (52). And the solitary onstage figure has Dante's heritage not only in its visuality, but also in the obsession with numbers. Number 'nine' gains symbolic meaning in this play: 'One two three four five six seven eight nine wheel one two three four five six seven eight nine wheel' (Beckett, 1986, 400), says the Voice at the very beginning of the play, making number nine prominent, as though the physical representation of this number is not enough. These nine steps in their essence make the 'revolving' of the main action and the theme of the play acquire an obsessional quality. Nevertheless, these nine steps may have other interpretations. Like the horse hooves in *Embers*, these steps may serve to mark the time, as concrete time references are absent in *Footfalls*. With every step May takes, she is one step closer to the end. Hence, every step, like a grain of sand trickling through the hourglass, is one moment gone into the abyss of the past. Here, a certain parallelism with Bergson's quantity–quality complex can be drawn. The quantity of steps makes 'time in essence materialised, time becomes quantity as it develops in space' (16; own translation). Moreover, the steps create a metronome, the image suggested by Beckett (Worth, 54), and like the spools in *Krapp's Last Tape*, they make the present time reverse into past.

Time *per se* is forgotten by the entities onstage: there are only oblique references to time, such as 'once', 'one night', 'one autumn Sunday evening', etc.: both women are even not sure about each other's age:

> M: What age am I now?
> V: And I? [*Pause. No louder.*] And I?
> M: Ninety.
> V: So much?
> M: Eighty-nine, ninety. (400)

Mother's age 'ninety' and 'eighty-nine', again draws our attention to the number of steps. So what could be the meaning of 'nine' in this play? Several hypotheses could be formed. With the ghostly eerie figure of May pacing the stage up and down, nine may refer to nine circles of Dante's Hell.[2] Dante's Hell has certain environmental characteristics that make the suffering more intense, some of them present in *Footfalls*: the condition of being trapped, extreme temperatures (cold or hot), bodily discomfort and seemed time immobility. Thus, May can be making her private circular journey in hell. Her bodily posture, arms wrapped around her fragile body, speaks about her physical and psychological discomfort. Deprived of sleep, her relentless rotating becomes a physical torture. Beckett stated that in *Footfalls* 'everything is frost and night' (Brater, 61), and as initially 'south door' was stated in the script of *Footfalls*, he replaced it for 'north', as it seemed colder: 'North door is colder. You feel cold — the whole time, in the way you hold your body too' (Beckett, 1992, 339). As a result, the dim lighting together with the image of May embracing herself creates the effect of coldness. Moreover, this posture

---

2 It is well known that Beckett was an arduous reader, and Dante's *Divina Commedia* was among his favourite books, which he used to read in the original. Beckett learnt Italian during his university years with the help of Bianca Esposito, who was his private tutor of Italian (1923–26). And 'acccording to Beckett, it was Esposito, not his Trinity College Italian Professors, who nurtured his love for Dante's *Inferno* and *Purgatorio* [...] For his love of Dante remained with Beckett until the end of his life and deeply influenced his own writing at several different points of his career' (Knowlson, 52).

can be associated with sufferings and distress, as by embracing ourselves we want to give us warmth and comfort and shield us from the outer world threatening us.

The medieval *locus* of Hell may give another meaning to the rotation movement at the end of each nine-step stretch. The 'wheel' as such has many symbolic meanings, but in relation to memory the revolving wheels were made prominent in Ramon Llull's system of memory. The latter was based on the concept of the figures of Art of God's dignity (nine in total)[3] that were moving. Francis A. Yates explains that 'One of the figures consists of concentric circles, marked with the letter notation standing for the concepts, and when these wheels revolve, combinations of concepts are obtained' (176). These were revolutionary devices to represent the movement of the psyche, since all nine Divine Dignities influence Man and help him to reach the understanding of his Ego. Furthermore, Knowlson equates May's pacing to a 'mythic status', as 'harking back to Ixion on his wheel, Tantalus tortured by hunger and thirst, or Sisyphus pushing his stone forever uphill. May's own eternal chore, however, is an inner compulsion rather than a preordained punishment' (544). Thus, May condemns her own self to walk these nine steps along the lit path, unable to understand what happened to her. The existential question, 'Will you never have done... revolving it all?' (Beckett, 1986, 400), makes her halt as though in surprise. Captivated by the ambiguity of 'it', May's only answer is to resume pacing. The impersonal pronoun 'it' may refer to many things in *Footfalls*: life, beginning, pacing, memory, grief, etc. Nevertheless, this question, taking into consideration May's onstage movement, is absurd, since it is 'revolving' that she has been physically re-enacting all her life; it is the revolving movement which becomes the core of her existence. Instead of constituting meaning in her life, May is obsessed with the acoustic traces of her bodily existence. When the words fail, physicality of movement gives evidence of her presence and urges her to continue her journey.

On the other hand, 'nine' may lead us to the type of trauma that kept May prisoner all her life: the trauma of birth. A pregnancy, or the physical unity between mother and child, lasts nine months. Matthew Feldman states that 'Beckett's notes on Rank are both more complete than on Adler and Stekel, and are more immediately associated with a longstanding interest in the caul' (107). Therefore, we can suggest that, metaphorically, May may be pacing her

---

3 'The Divine Dignities form into triadic structures, reflected from them down through the whole creation; as causes they inform the whole creation through its elemental structure. An art based on them constructs a method by which ascent can be made on the ladder of creation to the Trinity as apex [...] Divine Dignities: Deus, Angelus, Coelum, Homo, Imaginativa, Sensitiva, Vegetativa, Elementativa, Instrumentativa'. (Yates, 179)

intrauterine time; consequently, the mother's voice coming out of darkness points to their physiological unity or symbiosis. As a result, the whole stage may be taken as a womb. Although, paradoxically, it is the mother, who hears May in her 'deep sleep' (Beckett, 1986, 399). There is a certain shift of roles here: a daughter should be peacefully asleep inside the womb instead of a mother. Nevertheless, in this play it is May who cannot 'snatch' a bit of sleep. And sleepwalking may point to the troubled psyche of the character and her non-acceptance of the present situation: May is already out in this world, separated from her mother and grieving her enormous loss. This suggests that in losing her mother, she has lost her own self.

Severed from her loved one, May is not complete. Hence, she seems not to accept her mother's absence and by the evocation of her mother's voice, who may be interpreted as her second half, May tries to prolong her mother's existence. While her mother's voice is still heard, she is not wholly dead to May.

Therefore, May's nine steps can be understood as a means of recreation of those nine pleasurable months when she was still one with her mother, when she had not been halved yet. Once May began as a separate being, her suffering started. Ergo, these nine steps may be also seen as Freudian 'return-to-mother' desire; the steps visually and acoustically link May to the womb memories. May wants to reunite with her dead mother reversing the time to the womb, her beginning, and by this, to forget her feeling of loss. Paradoxically, time is irreversible in this play — with the dimming effect of the light and narrowing of the paces, it takes May to the tomb instead of the womb, and the death-birth circle is embodied in May's rigid posture with the expression of grief and pain. Thus, the Voice's words pleading for forgiveness in the play may be understood in relation to the trauma of birth/death, as forgiveness for having brought May into the world and forgiveness for having abandoned her in death. Beckett writes in *Psychology Notes*:

> Primal anxiety-effect at birth, which remains operative through life, right up to the final separation from the outer world (gradually become a second mother) at death, is from the very beginning not merely an expression of the new-born child's physiological injuries [...] but in consequences of the change from a highly pleasurable situation to an extremely painful one, acquires a psychical quality of feeling. (TCD MS 10971/8/36, qtd. in Feldman, 111)

The discussion of the trauma of birth leads us to daughter/mother relations. Twice May calls 'Mother' in the beginning of the play, awakening her from her 'deep sleep'. Immediately, we are presented to a very close bonding between the two. 'There is no sleep so deep I would not hear you there' (Beckett, 1986, 399), informs the voice. This 'deep sleep' gives another perspective to the whole play: it looks as though May calls her from the dead. Consequently, the following dialogue may signify a reawakening of memories. It was May who took care of her dying mother: injecting her, positioning her, straightening her pillows, passing her bedpan, etc. The mutual dependence is stressed in this dialogue; the entities are interlinked and cannot survive one without the other. Likewise, their memories are mutually dependent: the Voice reconstructs May's memories, and May reconstructs the Voice's memory. As has already been stated, there is a definite confusion of roles throughout the play. For instance, in the second part,[4] the Voice at first starts speaking in the first person singular: 'I walk here now' (401). As the result of this confusion in self-identification, which is based in the instability of pronouns, the theatrical effect achieved is of one body, which becomes the container of two voices — two consciousnesses.

The physical mother-child bond is always present in the first years of childhood: small children physically depend on their mothers, who satisfy their children's primal physical needs for food, hygiene, and sleep. Furthermore, the mother is the major referent for the child during his/her infancy. The British psychoanalyst Wilfred Bion theorized about how mother's 'thinking ability' ('alpha elements'), 'could contain and process the raw material, the so called "beta elements", the undirected anxieties and sensations of the infant, and hand them back translated into manageable feelings to the baby' (Mitchell, 96). Thus, mothers become the symbol of security and life; mothers know it all and remember it all, so later in life they become keepers of our childhood memories. Nevertheless, the Voice's memories of May's childhood are scarce and imprecise, rotating around the origins of May's pacing:

> V: She has not been out since girlhood. [*Pause.*] Not out since girlhood. [*Pause.*] Where is she, it may be asked. [*Pause.*] Why, in the old home, the same where she — [*Pause.*] Where it began.[5] [*Pause.*] It all began. [*Pause.*] But this, this, when did this begin? [*Pause.*] When other girls of

---

4 As far as the construction of the play is concerned, Ruby Cohn comments that Beckett divided the play into four main scenes: (1) Dying Mother; (2) Mother back; (3) Epilogue [changed to Appendix]; (4) Empty strip (Cohn, 335). All the scenes are marked by fade-outs and successively dimmer lights and fainter chimes.
5 Mother's reluctance to say 'born' has its origins in Carl Jung's lecture at the Tavistock Clinic in London, which Beckett attended in 1935 (Beckett, 1992, 284). This may be the reason for the pauses after the word 'began' in the text.

her age were out at... lacrosse she was already here. [*Pause.*] [...] I say the floor here, now bare, this strip of floor, once was carpeted, a deep pile. Till one night, while still little more than a child, she called her mother and said, Mother, this is not enough. The mother: Not enough? May — the child's given name — May: Not enough. (Beckett, 1986, 401)

The narration is very fragmented, full of repetitions and omissions of time of events. No age is mentioned here, and we hear only vague 'once', 'more than a child' and it is the use of the past tense which signals the past event. This memory is very inaccurate, and there is dissociation in the narration. The Voice does not admit her relation to the little girl, and the whole memory is told from a witness's perspective, which points to a kind of repressed memory. Furthermore, the monologue is full of pauses, false starts, and repetitions, which can be interpreted in the light of repressed memory narration. The Voice is desperately trying to reconstruct the true story of May's life, trying to find the right and precise words. Nevertheless, as repressed memories are not recorded linguistically, the words do not come easily, and the narration goes in circles, starting with 'I walk here now' and finishing with 'It all' and the physicality of May's continuous pacing till the second fade-out.

Both characters agree on the time of the day when it all began — night. The motif of night runs throughout the whole play and is made prominent by the stage darkness, which may be viewed as a theatrical device to recreate the subconscious or internal reality. The way that perception influences the shaping of reality and the subconscious *per se* captivated Beckett (Feldman, 84). In his *Psychology Notes*, the notes he kept during the interwar years (1932–36) Beckett defines its essence:

> The unconscious, therefore, according to psychoanalysis, may be summed up as a region of mind the content of which is characterized by being (1) Repressed (2) Cognitive (3) Instinctive (4) Infantile (5) Unreasoning (6) Predominantly Sexual. (Feldman, 98)

Some of the features of the unconscious, as repressed and infantile, are made visible in *Footfalls*. All May's repressed memories have to do with her childhood memories, as though she has not grown up at all, the rest of her life has been incessant pacing since her girlhood. Therefore, sexuality (womanhood) is totally excluded. This infantile being is present in all the memories, as though the umbilical cord between herself and her mother is still uncut. May seems to be in a desperate need of her mother's womb for security. Mothers give birth to daughters, and a daughter to other daughters, and since life is considered as suffering in Beckett's world, the mothers are responsible for 'it all'. This is a probable reason why May has sacrificed her sexual maturity, choosing pacing as her physical shield. Adler writes:

> In girls, the longing for security is as a rule more pronounced analogy to the relation to the father [...] The 'uterine fantasy' which is placed in the foreground by G. Grüner, I have also found employed by neurotics only when they wish to express that peace can be found only with the mother [...] that is, the wish to return to the same state in which they were before birth. (The hermaphroditic progression backward.) (148)

Consequently, we may propose that May's relentless pacing represents her attempt to reach the final fusion with her mother. This pseudo-fusion is achieved not only through pacing but also through language. May's speech mirrors her mother's in a narrative tone, dissociation, images, repetitions, and the choice of vocabulary. Beckett stressed the importance of 'parallelisms' between the mother and the daughter (Knowlson, 554), which can be found in the language of this play, represented by textual echoes.

4 Footfalls Echo in the Memory[6]

While May is pacing the floor, her steps produce a faint echo. The cadence of her footfalls goes beyond the acoustics, like the ripples of a pebble on the water, the steps reverberate in the text of the play. The whole play is abundant in repetitions and repetitions-permutations, which have an echo quality. The steps trigger the retrieval of memories: mother and daughter try to reconstruct the same stories from their past with slight differences. These traces of memories are very unstable, first paralleling the actual stage image; they serve as 'mirrors' or, better say, 'shattered mirrors', since the remembering is not complete. Here Lacan's idea of infant's mirror-stage may be brought into view:

> For Lacan, the unconscious developed as a language; the infant learning how to speak, came to see itself as a linguistic sign, and came to deal with itself as a social construction independent of its original self. (qtd. in Pattie, 175)

A child should recognise him/herself in the mirror as a separate being, and this is a crucial stage in any infant's development. This suggests that May is

---

6 T. S. Eliot, *Burnt Norton*, 13.

still in the mirror-stage: she has not matured into a woman. As a child in the mirror-stage imitates her mother, so do May's construction of sentences and choice of vocabulary echo her Mother's utterances:

> V: Will you never have done? [*Pause.*] Will you never have done... revolving it all? (Beckett, 1986, 400)
> M: Will you never have done... revolving it all? (403)
> V: In your poor mind. (400)
> M: [...] His poor arm. (402)

Just as Clov uses Hamm's words in *Endgame*, saying 'I use the words you taught me' (113), the same happens with May: her speech imitates her mother's. Furthermore, May is failing to recognise herself as the one who is pacing the stage. Both mother and daughter describe the physical stage image, creating the cadence of textual mirror images. Although while the mother's voice only describes the actual physical movement, May shapes a poetic description of herself as a brief reflection in a mirror:

> V: But let us watch her move, in silence. [*M paces. Towards end of second length.*] Watch how feat she wheels. [*M turns, paces. Synchronous with steps third length.*] Seven, eight, nine, wheel. (401)
> M: The semblance. Faint, though by no means visible, in a certain light. [*Pause.*] Grey rather than white, a pale shade of grey. [*Pause.*] Tattered. [*Pause.*] A tangle of tatters. [*Pause.*] Watch it pass — [*Pause.*] — watch her pass before the candelabrum, how its flames, their light ... like moon through passing rack. [*Pause.*] Soon then after she was gone, as though never been there, began to walk, up and down, up and down, that poor arm. [*Pause.*] (402)

The mother's voice wants to attract the attention of the invisible audience towards May's pacing, as though taking pride in her daughter's movement. And while it is only Mother's voice that counts May's steps, May in turn seems to be oblivious of her nine steps, since it is an unconscious movement for her. She simply describes it as 'pass' (402).

May's speech, quoted above, may be interpreted in the light of Lacan's mirror-stage, as May does not recognise her own self. Her self-description is extremely fragmented: 'a tangle of tatters' and the passing movement in the light of the candles are the central textual image. Failure of personalisation together with the instability of the pronouns, 'it' and 'she', creates confusion: May cannot decide whether it is a woman or a thing that she is describing. It seems that she has never seen her real self: May is not sure of what she is and what happened to her; therefore, even her present self may be considered as her hypothetic self, a stranger.

We may interpret this lack of self-identification in the light of the psychological theory of the construction of autobiographic memory. The psychologists Skowronski, Walker, and Benz discuss the importance of assimilating certain important events and integrating them into our life-story in the formation of autobiographic memory (ABM), ergo, in forging the unique identity. These landmarks are the periods of transition, which place our identity in time and provide a unity: 'Temporal landmarks tend to form when events are both experienced in time and have personal significance' (Skowronski et al., 201). May's temporal landmarks are scarce, and her memories are very uncertain and discontinuous. There are three episodes from the past recreated in the play: taking care of her dying mother, an attempt to remember her origins and the church story. Paradoxically, May's origins are related to her movement of pacing, hence, it is not the place or the date of birth which becomes the landmark of May's existence.

The Voice and May remember the origins of *locus* of pacing differently. For the mother's voice, 'revolving it all' started in 'the old home' (Beckett, 1986, 401), and May gives us another version of its origins: 'little church' (402), albeit both confirm that it was at 'nightfall' (401, 402). 'When' and 'where' form part of an episodic memory, and time and location are cornerstones of ABM. The fact that May recreates an episode of her memory, different from her mother's story, points to a possibility of her past identity. Obviously, it is a small piece of her consciousness, the one that she narrates in the third person singular, but it can prove her separate existence at least for a small amount of time. The location of this memory is a little church, where she entered by 'the north door' (402) at nightfall.

The church as a memory *locus* brings us to medieval times. The chimes throughout the whole play give evidence of the truthfulness of May's memory, and even recreate the *locus* of a church. The bells in church normally chime for God's worship or for a funeral service. Both events have references in the text: the church service in May's story and May's mourning for her mother. Moreover, the image of a church awakens Biblical allusions in the text, developed further in May's narration with reference to the church service in Evensong. Knowlson and Pilling compare May's walking in relation to Christian symbolism in her narration ('His poor arm',[7] 'lacrosse' 401) and to Christ's Calvary. It

---

[7] Roman Catholic churches are built in the form of a cross, thus 'His poor arm' image deals with May walking along the north gallery of the church. Katharine Worth also states that in the north transept there is a bank of candles to light praying for the dead (Worth, 68).

seems that May has her personal Calvary: 'Beckett developed the figure of May as a tormented soul, in the world but not of it, suffering every day from some 'shudder of the mind' (Knowlson and Pilling, 228).

Although physically present, May still tries to reject her past existence: 'A little later, when as though she had never been, it never been, she began to walk' (Beckett, 1986, 402). Obviously, the spectator knows that the origin of this play was a strange mental case exposed by Jung in the lecture that Beckett attended. Carl Jung explained the case of a girl who thought that she had never been born (Knowlson and Pilling, 222). May affirms and denies her existence at the same time. Her strange negation that 'she was not there' (403) at the church service together with the reference to the 'Holy Ghost' (403) rejects her past existence, albeit it is the sound of her footfalls that proves that May is still physically present, therefore alive. While May negates her existence, the footfalls are used as affirmation technique throughout the whole play. Pacing forms the real origins of her identity; thus, pacing makes her unique and separates her from her mother. While May is moving, total fusion is impossible to accomplish: May belongs to the world of the living and her Mother to the dead. Footfalls constitute a feeble pulse of her ephemeral being. And though all her being is craving for non-existence and the final union with her mother, May is unable to cease to be.

The final stage tableau is impressive in its imagery: against the acoustic landscape of fading echoes of chimes, the last remnants of May's presence, the strip of light is devoured by stage darkness. Hence, the last thing that disappears from the stage is May's path, or her memory traces. However, the theatre is still impregnated with the echoes of her steps and the final chimes, which may be understood as a toll for her final absence. Her wish to be gone is granted, and her voice most probably has joined the darkness, achieving the complete unity with her mother. Although many spectators, who saw this play, affirm that even in her absence May is still present onstage. After three fade-outs, our eyes are prepared to see May again, and our imagination conjures up an image of her still there onstage.

Works Cited

Adler, Alfred (1921), *The Neurotic Constitution (Outlines of a Comparative Individualistic Psychology and Psychotherapy)*, New York: Moffat, Yard and Company.

Beckett, Samuel (1986), *The Complete Dramatic Works*, London: Faber and Faber.

Beckett, Samuel (1992) *Theatrical Notebooks of Samuel Beckett*, Vol. III, ed. James Knowlson. London: Faber & Faber.

Beckett, Samuel (2016), *The Letters of Samuel Beckett*, Vol. IV, 1966–1989, ed. George Craig, Martha Dow Fehsenfeld, Dan Gunn, Lois More Overbeck, Cambridge: Cambridge UP.

Bergson, Henri (2004), *Memoria y Vida*, Madrid: Alianza Editorial.

Brater, Enoch (1987), *Beyond Minimalism: Beckett's Late Style in the Theatre*, New York: Oxford UP.

Casasanto, Daniel and Katinka Dijkstra (2010), 'Motor Action and Emotional Memory', *Cognition*, 115, pp. 179–85.

Cohn, Ruby (2001), *A Beckett Canon*, Ann Arbor: U of Michigan P.

Dijkstra, Katinka, Michael P. Kaschak and Rolf A. Zwaan (2007), 'Body Postures Facilitates Retrieval of Autobiographic Memories', *Cognition*, 102, pp. 139–49.

Eliot, T. S. (1971), *Four Quartets*, Orlando: Harcourt Inc.

Feldman, Matthew (2006), *Beckett's Books: A Cultural History of Samuel Beckett's 'Interwar Notes'*, London: Continuum.

Kalb, Jonathan (1989), *Beckett in Performance*, Cambridge: Cambridge UP.

Knowlson, James (1996), *Damned to Fame: The Life of Samuel Beckett*, London: Bloomsbury.

Knowlson, James and Pilling, John (1979), *Frescoes of the Skull: The Later Prose and Drama of Samuel Beckett*, London: John Calder.

Malkin, Jeanette R. (1999), *Memory-Theatre and Postmodern Drama*, Ann Arbor: U of Michigan P.

Mitchell, Juliet (1998), 'Trauma, Recognition, and the place of Language', *Diacritics* 28:4, pp. 121–33.

Pattie, David (2000), *The Complete Critical Guide to Samuel Beckett*, King's Lynn: Biddles.

Skowronski, John J., Richard W. Walker, and Andrew L. Benz (2004), 'Who Was I When That Happened? The Timekeeping Self in Autobiographical Memory', in Denise R. Beike, Jmaes M. Lampinen, and Douglas A. Behrend, eds., *The Self and Memory*, New York: Hove Psychology P, pp. 183–207.

Worth, Katharine (1999), *Samuel Beckett's Theatre: Life Journeys*, Oxford: Clarendon P.

Yates A., Francis (1966), *The Art of Memory*, London: Routledge.

'Rock her off': The Paradoxical Tension of the Split Voice in *Rockaby*

Teresa Rosell Nicolás

Abstract

References in classic literature associate the rocking chair with an image of tradition such as motherly comfort and hospitality. Also, the movement of rocking creates a fundamental rhythm and a disposition to recall old rhymes, songs, and popular tales. The question that arises in Beckett's *Rockaby* is in what way this traditional homely image is reversed into a more perplexing, disturbing one. In this play, the only character, W, a woman in a rocking chair, does not have control of communication as we can only listen to a recorded voice, which is apparently hers. This only character on the stage cannot dominate the rocking movement either, as the power that keeps the chair moving back and forth comes, paradoxically, from outside her. This maternal symbol, related to the lullabies that babies hear in cradles, is used by Beckett as the rhythm of the passing of time — perhaps the woman's heartbeats until they cease — and to show the strong presence of doubled voices in a play where W cannot control her own representation, being 'played' by the chair.

What is the relation between the voice that speaks the story of a woman who gradually withdraws from the exterior world and W, who rocks in the chair? According to Anna McMullan, in much of Beckett's late drama, a 'struggle emerges through the interaction between the performative subject who repeatedly attempts to articulate his/her experience and the symbolized fragments of his/her existence' and which focuses on the 'destabilization of the textual and visual frames used to figure the subject and [his/her] history' (McMullan, 46); that is, the voice constructs the stage image and a tension between the static image and the narrative voice is created. As Charles Lyons argues, Beckett's last plays, which mostly depict the image of solitary women, remind us 'that the objects observed have no existence outside of the language of identifying or describing statements' (Lyons, 1990, 151). In this sense, McMullan states that the only access to history or memory in Beckett's characters is through language (McMullan, 50). This chapter will study the importance of the image of the rocking chair from a comparative approach in order to analyse this split subject that is depicted in a compressed, but also subtle, poetic image.

∙ ∙ ∙

A writer like Beckett invents or creates a metaphor, an image for the human condition, and the way in which you experience it is that you are riveted by an image that you don't quite grasp intellectually, but that image is so powerful as a metaphorical statement that it'll probably remain with you for the rest of your life and you can go back to it over and over again. This is the miracle of all the great art, that it comprises an enormous number of levels of statements into the most concise and transportable, quotable and memorable form. I think this is what it really is all about.

MARTIN ESSLIN[1]

∵

1 The Artistic Image

It is well known that Samuel Beckett always showed a great interest in fine art and that he had very good knowledge of it. He frequently visited museums and art galleries, where he often scrutinised a single piece of art for more than an hour, and collected art catalogues. He wrote essays on art criticism. He was a close friend of contemporary artists, like Giacometti (see Arikha; Cavecchi) who collaborated in the set of his plays. Martin Esslin stated that 'his directing is a form of painting' (qtd. in Cavecchi, 123). For the last decades Beckett scholars have paid special attention to Beckett's use of images taken from the visual arts (Oppenheim; Ben-Zvi, 2003; Brater, 1987) and to the artistic references that invade his later plays. James Knowlson details how he made use of images from paintings which had impacted him and that he subsequently rearranged when he developed the visual images that predominate in his drama,[2] especially in the powerful images in later works:

---

1 Martin Esslin in *Rockaby, a play by Samuel Beckett* (film) directed by D. A. Pennebaker and Chris Hegedus (1982), New York: Pennebaker-Hegedus Associates, 37:50–38:44.
2 'The American theatre scholar and friend of Beckett, Ruby Cohn, said that it was in 1975, while she was in Berlin for rehearsals of *Waiting for Godot*, that, together with Beckett, she saw the Berlin Caspar Friedrich paintings in the famous collection of German Romantics. As they were looking at Friedrich's painting, *Mann und Frau den Mond betrachtend* (*Man and Woman Observing the Moon*) of 1824, Beckett announced unequivocally: "This was the source of *Waiting for Godot*, you know"' (Knowlson, 1996, 378).

> We know that Beckett was steeped in the visual imagery of these paintings and that, over a period of years, he could compare different paintings by the same artist in some of their most intricate visual details, the parallels or echoes become at the very least highly intriguing [...] But is the technique of what we might call 'imaginative blending', that is, borrowing and transforming many different elements from different areas of his experience into a new creation, one that came naturally to Beckett? (Haynes and Knowlson, 71)

Apart from this 'imaginative blending' technique, Knowlson also uses the expression 'visual abstinence' to define Beckett's late works, as he often employed only a single or double image, illuminated and surrounded by dark, empty spaces (Haynes and Knowlson, 44). When Beckett started to assist in rehearsals and work in a practical way in the theatre, he became fascinated by the effects of light and shade that stage lighting could produce: 'faces emerged starkly out of the darkness in *That Time*, *Rockaby* and *Catastrophe*; shadows fell on the ghostly figure of May in *Footfalls*' (Haynes and Knowlson, 80).

As Anthony Uhlmann states, 'the Beckettian image, then, appears, vanishes, yet lingers. It is also extracted from surrounding contexts; it is "an autonomous mental image" like that Deleuze identifies in Bacon' (Uhlmann, 62). So, the striking quality of Beckett's images asks to be interpreted but, at the same time, they resist it and, consequently, it is difficult to establish a sense in a straight way as the powerful, yet hermetic character of these late plays lies in the poetic concentration of an image.

After the premiere of Marcel Mihalovici's opera of *Krapp's Last Tape* in the Städtische Bühnen in February 1961, Beckett said to some students:

> For me, the theatre is not a moral institution in Schiller's sense. I want neither to instruct nor to improve nor to keep people from getting bored. I want to bring poetry into drama, a poetry which has been through the void and makes a new start in a new room-space. I think in new dimensions and basically I am not very worried about whether I can be followed. I couldn't give the answers which were hoped for. There are no easy solutions. (Knowlson, 477)

This difficulty often lies in ambiguities and tensions which are confronted by strong dualities. In this sense, the image of the woman rocking herself into death in *Rockaby* looks like 'a fascinating fusion of ancient and modern' (Haynes and Knowlson, 69) and Knowlson links the impacting visual image of this play with all-time great paintings:

> One thinks perhaps first of Rembrandt's "Margaretha Trip (de Geer)" that Beckett knew well from the National Gallery in London, and of the flashes of light and colour from the jet sequins on the dress of the woman in *Rockaby* that perhaps echo the magnificent Giorgione self-portrait that so captivated Beckett in Brunswick in 1937. Perhaps memories of "Whistler's Mother" in Whistler's painting or Madame Roulin in Vincent van Gogh's "La Berçeuse" [sic] are also evoked within the image. Certainly the closing moments of Beckett's play have something of the ambiguity of Jack Yeats' painting "Sleep", in which an old woman sits by the window, her head drooping low onto her chest in sleep or in death. (Haynes and Knowlson, 69–71)

The question we have to think of is how Beckett adapts elements from these paintings and, especially, in what sense he uses tradition to subvert it. As Castagnino notes,[3] if we think of the painting *Whistler's Mother*, the image is striking for the contrast between the straight lines that make up the background and the curved lines of the seated figure. It is important to note the presence of pictures on the wall of the painting. These pictures in white with black frames may work as outside windows and they establish a relation with the black dress and white bonnet and cuffs that 'frame' the woman — the object of representation. The shades in black and grey unify the background of the painting, including the woman's body. So the cuffs and the white bonnet bring light and stress her hands and especially her abstracted face expression. There are also some flashes of light from a dark curtain that add movement to the sense of stillness of the painting. Van Gogh's *Berceuse* operates in a completely different way. Here the background as well as the woman are very colourful. The chair's curving lines seem to be totally adapted to the rounded figure of the woman. Again, the painting highlights the woman's severe face

---

3 In *Whistler's Mother* there is a possible 'degree of metareflection of the pictorial representation given by the presence of paintings inside the painting, with their black frames and white rims that find an echo in the black dress and the white cap and cuffs that "frame" the woman — object of representation. The black and grey shades unify the background of the painting, which includes the woman's body, practically "erased" [...] and thus the white cap and cuffs highlight the only elements of a more vivid color: the hands and, mainly, the abstracted expression on her face. There are, however, flashes of light in the dark curtain [...] Van Gogh's "La Berceuse" operates almost in opposition to Whistler's painting: here the background and even the lower half of the figure are very colorful, and it is the black outfit [...] that delineates the figure and makes the head stand out, again with an abstracted face expression and her expressive gnarled hands on her lap' (Castagnino, 6; my translation).

and hands on her lap. In Rembrandt's *Margaretha de Geer*, we are confronted by a frontal portrait of a woman that is looking straight at us. We can observe the same play of light and shade as in *Whistler's Mother*, but what centres our attention is, again, the woman's hands: one of them holds a white handkerchief, the other grasps the arm of the chair strongly.

These paintings express an intimate look, that of seated older women in a contemplative, introspective attitude. Stage directions describing the woman in *Rockaby* share some features with them: 'W: Prematurely old. Unkempt grey hair. Huge eyes in white expressionless face. White hands holding ends of armrests' (Beckett, 1990, 433). And directions on the costume also echo those of Rembrandt and Whistler's portraits: 'Costume: Black lacy high-necked evening gown. Long sleeves. Jet sequins to glitter when rocking. Incongruous flimsy head-dress set askew with extravagant trimming to catch light when rocking' (433). The black and white that frame head and hands in both paintings are provided by the use of lights and shadows: 'Light: Subdued on chair. Rest of stage dark. Subdued spot on face constant throughout, unaffected by successive fades. Either wide enough to include narrow limits of rock or concentrated on face when still or at mid-rock. Then throughout speech face slightly swaying in and out of light' (433).

As we can observe, the importance of light in these celebrated paintings is also present in the restrained but glittering visual image created by Beckett in *Rockaby*. These 'ordinary' women and mothers, portrayed in the atmosphere of their daily life, are illuminated lovingly by the painters as well as by Beckett. In fact, in *Rockaby* the light enhances the ambivalence of the play. The alternate use of light, in and out, is closely related to the rocking movement of the play. The text is also doubled: the woman doubles some lines from the voice — apparently hers — which could work as the representation of the women's consciousness in the paintings.

Words spoken by characters have almost disappeared in Beckett's later plays, but his stage directions are very precise and detailed. The rocking chair in *Rockaby* must be extremely simple: 'pale wood highly polished to gleam when rocking', with 'footrest. Vertical back. Rounded inward curving arms to suggest embrace' (433). In fact, it plays a very active role in this play, as it moves 'without assistance from W' (434). We also know that the woman is not the subject in the rocking action but the object, as her feet are visible on the footrest — as in Whistler's painting. So the rocking chair creates its own movement independently of the woman sitting on it. The aspect of the chair is rigorous — like the woman's appearance — but, at the same time, it has motherly features, such as the arms 'rounded inward [...] to suggest embrace' (433), also present in Van Gogh's portrait *La Berceuse*.

However, the probable connection between *Rockaby* and the above-mentioned paintings is not so simple and direct, as personal memories are also involved. As Knowlson states:

> In creating this unusual stage image, Beckett drew on a store of personal memories. There was the frail figure of his maternal grandmother, 'little Granny', Annie Roe, dressed in 'her best black', sitting in a rocking chair at the window of Cooldrinagh, where she lived out the final years of her life. The woman in the play gazes out at other windows for 'another living soul', as Beckett himself sat, often for hours on end, staring at the rows of cell windows on the grey Santé prison. One biographical starting point shades almost imperceptibly into another, as the creative imagination shapes, develops and transforms its sources. (1996, 662)

One can tell that chairs are important sets on Beckett's bare stages, from the 'folding stool' used by the wanderers in *Waiting for Godot* to the, according to the stage directions, 'little visible' rocking chair. If Winnie could show and enjoy a collection of objects that were the last remains of life — 'in the old style' — that was never to return, all these items were removed to the essentiality of a chair, the only thing which may allow the character to rest.

In fact, the 'armchair on castors' in *Endgame* as well as the rocking chair in *Rockaby* point out a principal question: the tension between the immobility which implies the fact of being seated and the possibility of movement. This tension, as Beckett said, is the leitmotif of *Endgame*, and he defined Hamm as 'a king in this chess match lost-from-the-start', 'a poor player [...] trying to postpone the unavoidable end' (Cavecchi, 129).[4] The circularity and repetition of their movements — doing and undoing — show a different time: not the linear, measurable, chronological, time of History but a time when the modern subject gets stuck and when only 'passing time', without a well-defined goal, is possible. Time, then, is especially visible when the characters look back and recall their memories, even if these are fragile, fleeting and unreliable.

Therefore, all these mobile/static elements on stage — 'folding stool', 'chair on castors', 'bicycle wheels' and 'rocking chairs' — reflect the paradoxical state of these characters that desperately try to move but whose movements only undo the previous one, going 'to and fro', 'high and low'. In this sense, the

---

4 As Cavecchi points out, among the remaining objects, no longer available, there are bicycle wheels, which Hamm would like to use, instead of the castors, and Nagg and Nell lost their 'shanks' in an accident with their tandem.

rocking chair presents contradictory impulses: it calms and relaxes but it also works as a mechanical engine that permits to continue an action, a narrative. However, the narrative actions disappear in *Rockaby* in favour of a paradoxical form of poetics. In the play there is a pattern of movement and stasis: the voice and the rocking chair seem to soothe W even though she urges on 'more'.

2   The Philosophical Image

As we have seen above, Beckett borrowed images from paintings and reused them in his plays, but, as Uhlmann inquires accordingly, might the same be claimed for Beckett's use of philosophy? That is, did he borrow images used by philosophers? (Uhlmann, 1). According to Uhlmann, the question must be answered affirmatively, and he justifies that the rocking chair, a recurring image in Beckett's works, might be traced to Geulincx, and he discusses how this idea is developed in *Murphy*, *Film* and *Rockaby*.

The image of the cradle is used by Geulincx to explain the relation of our will to the will of God, as this philosopher denies that human beings have any real power over their actions. We seem to act and think we act, he says, but this is an illusion brought about by our ignorance (Uhlmann, 79). As Uhlmann explains:

> Geulincx argues, we will recognise that we do not understand how even the simplest movement of our own body is accomplished. Furthermore, even if we do have some kind of knowledge of certain aspects of this — a scientific knowledge of the nature of the circulation of blood, for example — this knowledge is not what causes our blood to circulate. In fact, Geulincx argues, we have a completely inadequate understanding of how our bodies function. He then ties this realisation to a proposition which he uses to buttress his philosophical system again and again: if you do not know how to do something, if you do not have full control over it, you cannot in fact be said to do that thing. I do not know how my body works, so I cannot be said to work it. From here, Geulincx goes on to argue that it is God who possesses this knowledge and therefore it is God who really controls my actions. I am merely a spectator of the machine which is my body. Yet, if I do not have any physical freedom, I do, for Geulincx, have complete freedom of will. I can desire to do whatever I please. Such desires, however, will often only reflect my ignorance and my true powerlessness. (79)

Geulincx shows the problematic connection between free will and physical powerlessness in relation to suicide using a strange image: a newborn baby. We think we start the engine that creates the cause-effect relationship, but in fact something else makes it happen, and he compares this to a newborn baby — the paradigm of powerlessness: 'The baby cries because it wants the cradle in which it lies to be rocked. And the cradle is rocked, but not by the baby; rather, it is rocked by the hand of the mother or the nurse, who in turn rocks the cradle because she thinks the baby wants the cradle to be rocked. To the baby it might seem that there is a direct relation between the desire and the action, but the action is in fact brought about by another' (Uhlmann, 80).

The image of the cradle, like the rocking chair seen above, suggests ease and love, but it is unusual that Geulincx uses it to depict suicide. Also, to illustrate true powerlessness, in spite of being a comforting image, it is an image of desire, the desire to be calmed, soothed, at peace. So, as Uhlmann suggests:

> Yet because it is an image of a desire, which we know can never properly be fulfilled, it is harrowing rather than comforting. Strangely, then, rather than reconciling us to our impotence, it brings to our attention how awful such an impotence is. The cradle is a striking image: at once it brings with it a sense of comfort and being comforted and a sense of our utter powerlessness to realise our desires (the most cherished of them along with the rest). (81)

Beckett read this actual passage, which appears in his forty pages of notes to the *Ethics*,[5] and therefore it is not surprising that the cradle and the rocking chair are strongly associated in his works, even though it reveals more ostensibly in *Rockaby*. This word, which we associate with the rocking chair in the play, clearly also refers to cradle songs or lullabies and to one such lullaby in particular:

> Rock a bye baby, on the tree top,
> When the wind blows the cradle will rock.
> When the bough breaks the cradle will fall,
> And down will come baby, cradle and all.
> Rock a bye baby, gently you swing,

---

5 Beckett, 1936 typescript, 'Notes to Arnold Geulincx', 26. Geulincx mentions the mother or nurse rocking the cradle on three occasions throughout the entire *Ethics*, and Beckett copies elements of these passages on each occasion (Uhlmann, 166).

> Over the cradle, Mother will sing,
> Sweet is the lullaby over your nest
> That tenderly sings my baby to rest.

Like in most lullabies, the sound contrasts sharply with the lyrics. If a nursery rhyme's aim is to relax the baby, the lyrics — the same thing happens in versions in different languages — show death: 'the cradle will fall / And down will come the baby, cradle and all' in the first stanza and, implicitly, the 'rest' in the second one. So the tension between birth and death comes together in the lullaby: Rock-a-bye.

Surprisingly, this tension in also shown in *Rockaby*. The woman is rocked to death accompanied by the marked rhythm of the voice. According to Knowlson, Beckett told Billie Whitelaw that *Rockaby* should have 'the quality of a lullaby' (Haynes and Knowlson, 129). Furthermore, W, the woman who rocks, seems like a baby for several reasons that can be inferred from the play: firstly, the play text tells us that the rock is 'controlled mechanically without assistance from W' (434), so W does not impulse the rocking, but the strength to move it comes from outside; secondly, the chair has 'rounded inward curving arms to suggest an embrace' (433); thirdly, W listens to a voice reciting a narration that calms her, as if it were a lullaby, and at the end of it, when the voice is silent, she asks for 'More', so she practically only speaks in demanding, like babies. Moreover, as M. A. Doll points out, Billie Whitelaw pronounced it more like 'Maw' to suggest the idea of being fed (Doll, 1988, 46) and even 'Ma' (Doll, 1989, 116). We can still find another element which emphasises the connection: the title of the French version of *Rockaby* is *Berceuse*. The French word 'berceuse' has different acceptations, and it is associated with lullaby, cradle song and nurse who rocks the baby and the rocking chair. In fact, the word derives from 'bercer', the French word for 'cradle'.

Nevertheless, in spite of asking for more, W's live voice in *Rockaby* gets softer and softer, and she also wants to stop. This is clear in the repetition of her desire in this passage, which connects the woman/baby, the rocker/cradle and birth/suicide/drive-to-death/death, very much like Geulincx's image:

> so in the end
> close of a long day
> went down
> let down the blind and down
> right down
> into the old rocker
> and rocked

> rocked
> saying to herself
> no
> done with that
> the rocker
> those arms at last
> saying to the rocker
> rock her off
> stop her eyes
> fuck life
> stop her eyes
> rock her off
> rock her off
> (Together: echo of 'rock her off', coming to rest of rock, slow fade out.)
> (441–2)

W finally speaks to 'the rocker' asking to 'rock her off'. She understands that she does not have control over her own life or the capacity to end it, so that 'it is the rocker (the chair, or the unseen power which causes it to move) that is implored in the end, the rocker that is asked to intercede on her behalf' (Uhlmann, 82).

Rockaby contains four narrative sections, and in each of them we are told about new — past — activities, like W's decision to stop 'going to and fro' in the outside world in search of 'another like herself'; sitting at her upstairs window, searching the windows opposite to see another: 'one other living soul'; her watch to a search for a raised blind that would suggest the presence of another creature; and W's movement downstairs to sit in her mother's rocking chair where she will wait for death, introducing the audience to the time of the present moment (Lyons, 1983, 178). In fact, as Charles Lyons suggests, the object of each section is not to explain what is new — as it happens when actions are developed in a traditional plot — but to 'emphasise the series of endings, each of which marks a reduction in the objective of her search' (178).

As it has already been mentioned, the image of the rocking chair is first used in *Murphy*. When Murphy sits in his rocking chair, naked — like a baby — and tied — powerless — he desires to achieve a complete separation from the outer world as the chair soothes his body and frees his mind from his body, in fact the chain in which he will die. As in *Rockaby*, or Geulincx's cradle, the chair is related to the paradox of being at ease and impotent at the same time (cfr. Uhlmann, 82–3). In the same way, O, the protagonist of *Film*, sits in the rocking chair, after having covered over or eliminated all the eyes in the room that were watching him, and he destroys all his own photographs going back in time, ripping the last one when he was a baby in the cradle. In a way, in *Rockaby*, W also lowers the blind and she ceases to be seen from the outside, being extracted from the world.[6]

In these three works, Beckett presents an image of isolation from those who rock and who want to be removed from exteriority and descend into their deeper conscience. Action is reduced to the limit as it is based on 'undoing' in this continuous, rhythmic 'to and fro' movement.

3   The Mythical Image

We could certainly find a long list of classical heroes in which the dramatic scheme corresponds to the identification of the protagonist with a parent: Orestes, Oedipus, Hamlet, Oswald in Ibsen's *Ghosts*, Phèdre, etc. In each of these cases, the protagonist's identification of any sort with the parent implies his or her destruction and 'they feel inside them a familiar and yet alien presence' (Lyons, 1983, 181). In *Rockaby* Beckett develops this tension through a minimum of contextual reference: 'W's attempt to seek "another like herself" forms the opposite of her mother's solipsistic retreat [...] A model she elects to re-enact or a restrictive limitation in which she is caught' (182).

Mary Doll states that in his last plays, Beckett subverted the dominant philosophical Aristotelian requirements of Western drama to meet some qualities that are characteristic of mythic drama: 'not plot, but image; not action, but rhythm; not character, but ghosts. These three negatives clear the way for Beckett's new drama' (1989, 110). For Doll, the myth that allows to represent these qualities is that of Demeter.

In Greek mythology, Demeter is the goddess of agriculture and fertility, the divinity of the cycle of life and death, the protector of marriage and the sacred law; she is worshipped as the bearer of the seasons. Together with her daughter Persephone, who had to marry Hades and became the goddess of the underworld, they used to be invoked as *to theo*, or the two goddesses. When Persephone was young, she was called Kore, meaning 'maiden'. Hades, god of the underworld, kidnapped her to make her his wife. When Demeter realised her daughter had disappeared, she began to look for her around the world for nine days and nine nights, but she did not find her. Eventually, she asked Zeus,

---

6   In *Krapp's Last Tape*, Krapp knows that his mother is dead when the blinds in her room are lowered and he can see it from outside.

Persephone's father, for help. He told her that Kore was no longer a maiden but the wife of Hades. This made Demeter very angry and, being the goddess of fertility, she forbade plants to grow, and soon the whole world became a desert. In the end Zeus ordered Hades to give Persephone back to her mother, but that was not possible, because while Persephone was in the underworld she had eaten six grains of pomegranate, and anyone who tasted the food of the dead could not leave that world. However, as Persephone had only eaten six grains, she was allowed to spend six months in the world of the living and the other half of the year in the world of the dead. She is usually represented as a young girl with a bouquet of daffodils in hand — the flowers she was picking when she was kidnapped — or sitting on a wooden throne — similar to a rocking chair — as the Queen of the Dead.

This myth is often cited to explain natural processes, related to the rise and descent of the goddess bringing about the change of season, because when Demeter and her daughter were together, the Earth flourished with vegetation. So both mother and daughter know and represent the superior and inferior world. According to Doll,

> The myth that explores the dynamic between mother and daughter is also the myth that explores the dynamic between body and soul, ground and under-surface, seen and unseen. [...] Significantly, although the central event of the myth is Persephone's abduction, the central impact of the abduction is on the mother, Demeter. [...] Demeter had always been oriented to earth and its bounty. Suddenly this orientation shifts with the disappearance of her daughter. She becomes consumed by absence. At the core of the myth is a mystery of this shift, for it is Demeter — not Persephone — who is led away (abducted). Consciousness, not flesh, is abducted. [...] The mother feels her daughter's absence not intellectually, abstractly, but sensually, concretely. [...] When her daughter is returned to her, there is no reunion, for a pattern has been set of everpresent absence. (1989, 110)

This ritualistic image is also presented by Anna McMullan: 'Ritual is concerned with the reconciliation of difference, with bringing to an end to the continual reproduction of the cycles of self and other, the desire and its object, thus enabling the restless dynamic of desire to be laid to rest. [...] The evocation of a ritualised movement of contraction and descent seems to reflect a return to the womb' (104).

This is not the first time that the Demeter-Kore myth is employed to interpret Beckett's works. Rosette Lamonte reads *Eh Joe* with the use of this myth as a decoding device:

> Both Joe and the viewers receive enlightenment from Voice's tale of two women, herself and the other. In mythic terms, the older and younger women [...] assume the Demeter/Kore archetypal situation. [...] The matriarchal oneness of the two females annulled the male incursion into the group. Because Demeter and Kore are the two poles of the Eternal Feminine, the mystery of their fusion celebrates a renewal independent of male sexuality. (Lamont, 233)

In *Rockaby*, W is isolated and inaccessible, that is, 'the character is self-enclosed within the routine of her movement' (Lyons, 1990, 158). She listens to a narration, the narration of her own story, going back and fro in time[7] but still on that chair, practically 'not there', being rhythmically rocked in a ceaseless movement strongly marked by the repetitive, monotonous voice. This narration gradually narrows to the only sound of the rhythm of the rocking chair. According to Mircea Eliade, these elements conform ritualised actions and 'can have the effect of making sacred that which is profane' (qtd. in Doll, 1988, 47). So, ritual, made up of rhythm and repetition, makes the occasion a special one — she is in 'her best black' — through this 'dramatised poem', as Enoch Brater names it, like a litany or a mantra. The rhythm of the narration, accentuated by the rocking of the chair, is expressed through a 'nonchronological, repetitious, spiralling, cumulative language' (Hale, 138). Through a perpetual descent into her inner self, W's consciousness is represented through the recitation of a poem which comes from outside, being played by someone/something else but which is, paradoxically, inside her.

As McMullan states, these later plays are 'directly concerned with responding to loss through the formation of words. Words both displace the other and produce an other; loss is [...] resolved through the figural or literal restoration of the other. [...] The absence or loss of a desired object during the protagonist's life is countered by the (magical) presence of an other voice/body — the "another like herself" sought by the subject in Rockaby. The restored other [...] is the lost object of original desire, the Mother' (92). The proximity between the search for one other — 'like herself' — and 'mother' is evident. So the play displays this split subject and the desire to be finally one in this final embrace — 'those arms at last' — (442) in spite of the presence of the third person singular: 'saying to the rocker / rock her off' (442). In the documentary *Rockaby, a play by Samuel Beckett*, filmed by D. A. Pennebaker and Chris Hegedus, which shows the process of creation of *Rockaby* on stage with the

---

[7] Beckett told Danny Labeille 'The woman in no way initiates the rock; the memory initiates the rock' (qtd. in Brater, 1987, 173).

actress Billie Whitelaw, the American director Alan Schneider, and the producer Daniel C. Labeille, Schneider considers that *Rockaby* implies 'a kind of acceptance, a coming down'; that 'the play is not about dying, not about coming to die; it's about accepting death [...] It's a coming to terms with mother, mother rocker, mother earth, mother death' (Pennebaker).

In Beckett's later plays, visual and textual levels run concurrently. As Brater says, sound structures sight as sight structures sound (1987, 169) in an image which becomes a poem in a 'diminuendo of everything until stillness is achieved', as Beckett admitted (174). Interviewed by Linda Ben-Zvi about how she prepared the character of W, Billie Whitelaw answered: 'I wrote on the margin of my copy of the play the words *solitary, monotonous, lullaby*. She is again a disembodied voice. There I was working for a certain inflexion, a certain pitch in order to get that "no colour". Different shades of grey' (Ben-Zvi, 1990, 8). When arranging the production of *Rockaby*'s premiere in 1981, Daniel C. Labeille asked where the voice was coming from and Beckett answered: 'I don't know that. It's a lullaby'.

Works Cited

Arikha, Avigdor (2006), 'Avigdor Arihka on Beckett and Art', in James and Elizabeth Knowlson, eds., *Beckett Remembering/Remembering Beckett: Uncollected Interviews with Samuel Beckett & Memories of Those Who Knew Him*, London: Bloomsbury, pp. 143–5.

Beckett, Samuel (1990), 'Rockaby', in *The Complete Dramatic Works*, London: Faber and Faber, pp. 431–42.

Ben-Zvi, Linda, ed. (1990), *Women in Beckett: Performance and Critical Perspectives*, Urbana and Chicago: U of Illinois P.

Ben-Zvi, Linda, ed. (2003), *Drawing on Beckett: Portraits, Performances, and Cultural Contexts*, Tel Aviv: Assaph Books.

Brater, Enoch (1987), *Beyond Minimalism: Beckett's Late Style in the Theater*, Oxford: Oxford UP.

Brater, Enoch (2010), 'The Seated Figure on Beckett's Stage', in S. E. Gontarski, ed., *A Companion to Samuel Beckett*, Chichester: Wiley-Blackwell, pp. 346–57.

Castagnino, María Inés (2012), 'El espejo de dos caras: relaciones entre algunas piezas teatrales de Samuel Beckett y las artes pictóricas', in *VIII Congreso Internacional de Teoría y Crítica Literaria Orbis Tertius*, Centro de Estudios de Teoría y Crítica Literaria — IdIHCS/CONICET Facultad de Humanidades y Ciencias de la Educación Universidad Nacional de La Plata, http://citclot.fahce.unlp.edu.ar/viii-congres, accessed June 2015.

Cavecchi, Mariacristina (2009), 'Samuel Beckett, Visual Artist', in D. Guardamagna and R. Sebellin, eds., *The Tragic Comedy of Samuel Beckett: 'Beckett in Rome' 17–19 April 2008*, Rome: Università degli Studi di Roma «Tor Vergata» — Gius. Laterza & Figli, pp. 122–42.

Davis, Robin J. and Lance St J. Butler (1988), *'Make Sense Who May': Essays on Samuel Beckett's Later Works*, Gerrards Cross: Colin Smythe.

Doll, Mary A. (1989), 'The Demeter Myth in Beckett', *JoBS*, 11/12, pp. 109–22.

Doll, Mary A. (1988), 'Walking and Rocking: Ritual Acts in *Footfalls* and *Rockaby*', in R. J. Davis and L. St J. Butler, eds., *'Make Sense Who May': Essays on Samuel Beckett's Later Works*, Gerrards Cross: Colin Smythe, pp. 46–55.

Hale, Jane (1987), *The Broken Window: Beckett's Dramatic Perspective*, Indiana: Purdue UP.

Haynes, John and James Knowlson (2003), *Images of Beckett*, Cambridge: Cambridge UP.

Knowlson, James (1996), *Damned to Fame: The Life of Samuel Beckett*, London: Bloomsbury.

Lamont, Rosette (1990), 'Beckett's *Eh Joe*: Lending an Ear to the Anima', in L. Ben-Zvi, ed., *Women in Beckett: Performance and Critical Perspectives*, Urbana and Chicago: U of Illinois P, pp. 228–35.

Lyons, Charles R. (1983), *Samuel Beckett*, London: Macmillan Education.

Lyons, Charles R. (1990), 'Male or Female Voice: The Significance of the Gender of the Speaker in Beckett's Late Fiction and Drama', in L. Ben-Zvi, ed., *Women in Beckett: Performance and Critical Perspectives*, Urbana and Chicago: U of Illinois P, pp. 150–61.

McMullan, Anna (1993), *Theatre on Trial: Samuel Beckett's Later Drama*, London: Routledge.

Oppenheim, Lois (2000), *The Painted Word: Samuel Beckett's Dialogue with Art*, Ann Arbor: U of Michigan P.

Pennebaker, D. A. and C. Hegedus (1982), *Rockaby, a play by Samuel Beckett* (film), New York: Pennebaker Associates.

Uhlmann, Anthony (2006), *Samuel Beckett and the Philosophical Image*, Cambridge: Cambridge UP.

Technology and the Voices of the More than Human in Beckett's *All That Fall*

Anna McMullan

Abstract

Though to date the radio play *All That Fall* has remained somewhat tangential to Beckett ecocriticism, it is an important text in relation to what Mary Bryden has termed Beckett's critique of 'species hierarchy', where the human occupies a privileged place in the order of creation and indeed, the biosphere. Rather, Beckett's texts foreground mutual inter-species vulnerability, especially in *All That Fall*, through their encounters with increasingly technologised machines that threaten their existence. Creating a dialogue between discussions of Beckett's radio plays by, for example, Julie Campbell, Everett Frost, Catherine Laws, Ulrika Maude, and Emilie Morin, and selected ecological readings of Beckett by Paul Davies, Greg Garrard, and Carl Lavery, the essay argues that *All That Fall* exploits the technologies of radio in a parody of both divine and human models of creation, inviting the listener to attend to the voices of the more than human, however mediated. From that perspective, the essay reflects on the decision to represent the animal sounds by electronically modified human voices in the BBC Third Programme premiere of the play in 1957, directed by Donald McWhinnie.

> Beckett shows us what might emerge if we accept that the worst has already happened and that there is no solution to the ecological crisis. In this moment of ontological weakness and lameness, this acceptance that everything is already exhausted, a different kind of knowledge emerges. Here the *oikos* is no longer pushed away, forgotten, dispelled; it is admitted, allowed to exist, given a space to appear. (Lavery, 2018, 24–5)

> MRS ROONEY: Oh, the pretty little woolly lamb, crying to suck its mother! Theirs has not changed, since Arcady. (Beckett, 1984, 34)

During the 1950s and early 1960s, Beckett experimented across a wide range of media or genres, exploring their different processes and possibilities of world-making, embodiment and voice.[1] Several preoccupations can be traced throughout his work at this time, including the depiction of highly regulated spatial or spatio-temporal systems which subject the human bodies that inhabit them to repeated cycles of activity (as in *How It Is* and some of the mimes, for example),[2] or a devastated world, inhospitable to human life, where only the hardiest species, such as fleas or ants, still procreate, as in *Endgame* and *Happy Days*. Mary Bryden refers to Beckett's 'species consciousness' (2013, 3),[3] and she and other scholars have explored the ways in which Beckett often 'animalises' his human creatures (see Weller, 2008 and 2013) eroding the ontological distinctions between the human and the more than human,[4] or reorients attention from the human towards a range of other species from horses to fleas that co-habit the narrative worlds of his texts. Scholars have also focused on the elements that constitute the biosphere in which his creatures exist, including the atmosphere (Connor, 2003) and the weather (Davies, 2008). Beckett's radio play *All That Fall* is a particularly apt example of Beckett's refocusing of his listeners' attention from the interior thoughts and experiences of his main protagonist, Maddy Rooney, towards what is, for Beckett, a remarkably rich and diverse world of flora and fauna, and the weather conditions that change from the bright sunlight of Maddy's setting out on her journey to the local railway station, to the 'shrouding' of the day on her return, as the wind rises and rain begins to fall.

However, the ways in which worlds and creatures are invoked in Beckett's texts are medium-specific, reflecting on the conditions and conventions of prose narration, theatrical performance, or radiophonic technologies. *All That Fall* is pivotal to a second transmedia concern of Beckett's texts written in the late 1950s: the dissociation of the voice from the body of the speaker —

---

1 Beckett completed *Fin de Partie* (*Endgame*) in 1955, the radio drama *All That Fall* in 1956 followed by his other radio plays and silent mimes over the next few years, *Krapp's Last Tape* in 1958, the novel *Comment c'est* (*How It Is*) between 1958 and 1960, and *Happy Days* in 1961.
2 See, for example, *Act Without Words II* (1958/9) and the prose texts *Imagination morte imaginez* (*Imagination Dead Imagine*) and *Le Dépeupleur* (*The Lost Ones*) from the mid-1960s. McMullan 2010, 57–66, analyses a number of abandoned mimes and dramatic fragments from this era which 'present non-individualized human figures (A, B, the players) in a series of confining situations where the body is subject to an implacable system' (64).
3 *How It Is* makes several references to 'loss of species' (Beckett, 1984, 29) or having 'clung on to the species' (52).
4 The term 'more-than-human', sometimes though not always hyphenated, was coined by David Abram in *The Spell of the Sensuous: Perception and Language in a More-than-human World* (1996) and is now frequently used in ecological discourses to refer to the species, elements and systems (such as weather) in the earth's biosphere.

whether the voice of the individual speaker is mediated through recording technologies as in *Krapp's Last Tape*, or whether, as in *How It Is*,[5] there is a more impersonal sense of the voice as transcorporeal utterance expressed through, though not necessarily originating in, the body of the speaker. In the stage and radio dramas, the recording of the voice heightens both the dispersal of an individual's identity across time, and the transitoriness of human bodily existence in contrast to the technology that allows the voice to live on beyond the moment of its recording and indeed the life of the speaker. The medium of radio, of course, depends entirely on acousmatic sound[6] which accounts for its ability to 'soar beyond time and space and unite actual happenings with thoughts and forms independent of anything corporeal' (Arnheim, 1936, 15).[7] As Julie Campbell has argued, radio can therefore 'present extensive movement both effectively and economically', freed from the solid contours of the visually perceived body (147), but yet retains an inherent 'ghostliness' due to its incorporeality, and because the sonic world of radio can be extinguished in a second by switching off, for example.

All That Fall specifically exploits these radiophonic qualities to evoke the laborious journey of its elderly and ailing protagonist, Maddy Rooney, through the rural environs of the village of Boghill as far as the railway station to meet her husband Dan from the city train, and their walk back together. The play also self-consciously focuses on technology as, on the one hand, the very medium through which the sound world of the radio play is created and transmitted, and, on the other, a destructive force threatening the web of living creatures evoked in the narrative. Building on discussions of the voice in the radio plays by, for example, Julie Campbell, Everett Frost, Catherine Laws, Ulrika Maude, and Emilie Morin, and selected ecological readings of Beckett by Paul Davies, Greg Garrard, and Carl Lavery, this essay will analyse Beckett's use of the acousmatic medium of radio in *All That Fall* to place the human in a framework of technological intervention on the one hand, and, on the other,

---

5   In his study of the voice in Beckett's work, Lewellyn Brown notes 'the impersonal dimension of language in that the latter pre-exists the subject' (8). The *Texts for Nothing* and *How It Is* refer to 'scribes' who are noting the coerced utterances of the narrated bodies, and the narrator in *How It Is* insists that the narrative originates in an 'ancient' voice once outside but now within him: the phrase 'I say it as I hear it' recurs throughout the novel.

6   The term 'acousmatic' to refer to the separation of a sound from its original source, was coined by *musique concrète composer*, Pierre Shaeffer (Morin, 1).

7   Several scholars writing on *All That Fall* note that Beckett had read Rudolf Arnheim's *Film as Art* which includes a chapter on radio drama and indeed that McWhinnie drew on Arnheim's theories on radio in his own *The Art of Radio*: see Frost, 1991, Hartel, 2010 and Laws, 2017, 108.

to direct attention to the more than human voices in the play. However, before placing these discourses in dialogue with each other, I want briefly to explore some of the ecological approaches to Beckett's work that have emerged over the last decade or so.

1 De-centering the Human *Oikos*

Ecological readings of Beckett's texts in the twenty-first century tend to focus on what Paul Davies has called 'the condition of human alienation from the biosphere'(74), or on the interrelationships between the human and other inhabitants of the planet and how Beckett refigures those relationships in his work.[8] While Greg Garrard (2012) and Joe Kelleher (2015) acknowledge the overt references to a historically devastated environment in *Endgame* and *Happy Days* respectively, which may be linked to the fear of nuclear catastrophe following the United States attacks on Hiroshima and Nagasaki in 1945 and the post-World War II Cold War,[9] they, along with Davies, argue that an ecological reading needs to go beyond the literal level of representation or content. Beckett was evidently not an eco-activist concerned with saving the planet, indeed salvation of any kind is always a myth in Beckett's work, but his texts might be aligned with what Timothy Morton has called the ecological way of thinking (Morton, 2010), which decentres the place of the human in the time and space of the planet. Garrard cites Morton's concept of 'kinship in mutual

---

8   In general, ecocriticism is concerned with resisting the positing of humans as masters of the earth's resources, but rather positions them as a species that shares the biosphere with other species, but which has become so dominant, especially since the technological advances of the Industrial Age, that they have caused major impact upon and indeed damage to the earth's environment. The effect that humans have had on the environment is reflected in debates about whether we are now entering, or in, a new age — that of the Anthropocene, rather than the Holocene age which has been ongoing for the last few thousand years: 'The International Union of Geological Sciences are currently debating the relevant scientific merits of the so-called Anthropocene Epoch, which would allow the organization to recognize a diachronic rift separating the epoch of the Holocene — since the last Ice Age receded almost twelve millennia ago — from our current "human epoch"' (David and Turpin, 2015, 4).
9   See, for example, Gibson, 2010, 133: 'From the mid-1950s onwards, there is a strain in Beckett's art which seems less abstract than global. The works in question are fraught with the recognition that something has happened to history itself. They clearly respond to a historical condition, that of the Cold War — or, at least, to particular phases of it — which seemed all-encompassing as none had before'. Seán Kennedy has added other specific layers to these historical traces in Beckett's work in his reading of *All That Fall* and other texts as evoking the declining Anglo-Irish social milieu of the 1930s Irish Free State (2004).

vulnerability as well as struggle for survival' (394) that connects the human with the more than human in a refusal of what Bryden terms 'species hierarchy'. Rather, Bryden argues, in Beckett's work: 'those conceptions of difference may give way to perceptions of some kind of shared subjection' (3). I will explore that 'shared subjection' or 'kinship in mutual vulnerability' between the human and more than human in relation to *All That Fall* below.

In his 2018 essay, Carl Lavery offers a detailed assessment of Beckett's approach to the medium of the theatre as an enclosed space cut off from the 'chaos of everyday life', not to 'eject or deny the world in an act of spurious aesthetic autonomy, but to find another way of engaging with it' (17), which is attentive to the expanded experience of both time and species that Beckett's work offers: 'In Beckett's hands, theatre is no longer a space where the essence of the human appears; on the contrary, it is a site where the human dis-appears, subjected, as it is, to a series of "more than human" flows and processes that challenge its much-vaunted exceptionalism and apparent omniscience' (11). Drawing on Jean-François Lyotard's discussion of the *oikos* (1993), a term whose original meaning evokes the domestic or interior home and foyer of human life, Lavery places the obsession with or search for home or homecomings throughout human culture with the *oikos* (from which the English word ecology derives) as the life world beyond the human individual or species:

> Instead then of an ecology that surreptitiously seeks to master the earth, I want to argue for an *oikolog*y that undoes the human subject by placing it — *the anthropos* — in an immanent world that it is unable to dominate. From this perspective, homecoming, the search for the *oikos*, would be a paradoxical process, something that is doomed, in advance, to failure, a realisation that human being, *contra* its designated place in western metaphysics, is always a deferred or impossible being. In ecological terms — and this is why Beckett's work is so important — there might be more to be learnt in accepting our absence than in clinging to our presence. (12)

Lavery identifies Beckett's treatment of time as essential to how his theatre functions and works on the spectator: his drama 'slows perception down to the point where things and experiences that ordinarily go unnoticed are allowed to impress themselves upon us' (19), and where we feel ourselves subject to 'the passage of time in our bodies' (23) that we might ordinarily seek to master or ignore. Therefore, he argues: 'theatre's ecological significance resides in the material charge of the theatrical medium itself, in the way in which an affective dramaturgical sculpting of time and space has the potential to disorder and reorder perception to the point where we are able to welcome in the troublesome guest, the *oikos*' (14). He suggests that Beckett's theatre in performance 'recalibrates our vision' and our experience of temporality by his 'sculpting of time', creating an environment where, as in the quotation which serves as epigraph to this essay, 'the *oikos* is no longer pushed away, forgotten, dispelled; it is admitted, allowed to exist, given a space to appear' (25). I will argue that *All That Fall* activates such a recalibration of our aural perceptual faculties by suggesting a shared species kinship in the mutual vulnerability of life to both ecological and human forces of destruction, and by shifting the listener's perspective from sharing Maddy Rooney's experience of time (both that of the listening present and that of humanly regulated time in the railway station clocks), as she anxiously labours to meet the twelve thirty train, to glimpses of a temporality in which the human appears as an aberration, if a largely destructive one. The acousmatic medium of radio is integral to this placing of the human voice in relation to heightened and self-conscious technological mediations of sound in the play, on the one hand, and, on the other, the sonic evocation of non- and more-than-human sounds and temporalities.

2   *All That Fall* and Acousmatic Technologies

In his foundational study of Beckett's radio plays, Clas Zilliacus notes that the period of the 1950s, when Beckett began writing for radio and was working with the BBC radio drama team including Donald McWhinnie, Barbara Bray and Desmond Briscoe,[10] was one of intense experimentation in the radio medium. This climate of innovation was influenced by developments in French radio pioneered by *musique concrète* composer Pierre Schaeffer which, as Morin notes, the BBC was keen to emulate (2). Zilliacus also cites Irving Wardle who referred to a simultaneous trend towards the 'interiorization' of radio drama (14). Wardle described this trend, which he saw as particularly dominant in West German radio drama, as 'the emergence of individual consciousness as the only certain reality' (15). The tension between, on the one

---

10   Donald McWhinnie was appointed Assistant Head of Drama at the BBC Third Programme in 1953, with Barbara Bray as Drama Script Editor (Zilliacus, 13). Desmond Briscoe was a drama studio manager at the BBC in the 1950s and worked on the sound effects of the BBC's 1957 *All That Fall*, subsequently co-founding the BBC Radiophonic Workshop.

hand, the ability of radio to 'locate the drama inside the head of the protagonist' (Frost, 2009, ix), and on the other, to exploit abstract radiophonic sound effects which draw attention to the constructedness of the sound world of a radio play, is epitomised in Beckett's *All That Fall*, broadcast on the BBC Third Programme on January 13, 1957.[11]

In his book *The Art of Radio* Donald McWhinnie, the director of the BBC's 1957 premiere of *All That Fall*, affirms the power of radio 'to communicate secret states of mind, the inner world and private vision of the speaker. [...] The very intimacy of radio [...] means that we may have acutely the sense of sharing his thoughts and experiences as though they are our own' (57). Everett Frost has argued that listeners to Beckett's first radio play 'experience the action and perceptions of the play as originating entirely and exclusively from within the mind of Maddy Rooney' (1997, 194). The use of what McWhinnie called 'close focus', the aural equivalent of filmic close-up (57), by placing the microphone closer to the actor playing Maddy Rooney than anyone else, intensifies the sense of sharing Maddy's interior processes of perception and consciousness: 'the effect we want is of an unspoken thought, magically overheard [...] Magnified by the microphone, it draws us into the mind of the character, it is almost as though it had been spoken in our own head' (134–5). These moments of aural intimacy are contrasted with Maddy's vocal level when she is addressing the inhabitants of Boghill that she meets, which is louder and has a different relationship to the microphone. The proximity effect of Maddy's internal reflections establishes Maddy's inner consciousness as the most 'real' layer of the play.

However, the psychoacoustic qualities of *All That Fall*, where the listener creates the world of the play as it is evoked through Maddy's spoken thoughts, dialogue and the sound effects of a rural landscape and then village train station, are juxtaposed with many self-conscious references to the medium, as when the opening animal sounds are denaturalised through being treated as choric or musical elements, appearing singly on cue and then together (as Beckett would do with human speech later in *Play*) or self-conscious references to the conventions of radio drama where only that which is heard exists.

---

11   The history of Beckett's involvement with the BBC, the invitation to write a play specifically for radio by John Morris, Controller of the Third Programme in 1956, its subsequent development, and the context of BBC radio at that time have been discussed in detail by such scholars as Zilliacus (1976), Frost (1997), Morin (2011), and the edited collection *Samuel Beckett and the BBC: A Reassessment* (Addyman et al, 2017), which includes a detailed and fascinating analysis of the creative collaborations and resulting sound world of the BBC's *All That Fall* by Catherine Laws.

Donald McWhinnie and his team immediately saw that Beckett's script would enable them to experiment with exactly the kinds of denaturalisation and formalisation of sound that they wished to explore. According to Catherine Laws, the 1957 broadcast was concerned with 'exploiting the dramatic tensions of manipulated concrete sound within a more abstractly conceived formal, musical structure' (Laws, 124). This led to the decision to realise the animal voices at the beginning and throughout the play by technologically modified human impersonations. McWhinnie argues that the opening of the play 'demands a strict rhythmic composition; a mere miscellany of animal sounds will not achieve the effect' and that 'the way to deal with the problem seemed to be by complete stylization of each sound, that is to say, by having human beings to impersonate the exact sound required. This enabled us to construct an exact rhythmic pattern' (133). So, for example, the hoof-beats of Christy's horse were 'made by recording the sound of an actor's mouth playing tunes on the roof of his mouth' which McWhinnie compares to 'drum-strokes [...] in a formal rhythm' (136). Even the sounds of the weather were replaced by human-produced sounds: the wind 'was human breath, technically treated, used on this, and subsequent, occasions as a purely formal device with the barest pretense at realism' (144).[12]

Undoubtedly, both Beckett's script and, to an even greater extent, McWhinnie and his team's broadcast interpretation of it, foreground what Laws refers to as 'the composedness' of the world of the play: 'composed by Maddy herself, as her words and sounds guide us, but the radiophonic mediation points beyond this, reflexively, to other agencies: the author, the production team [...] and ultimately ourselves, as we piece together the ambiguous soundscape' (107). In this sense, technology enables and mediates the creative labour of the play and its realisation. I will explore this focus on composition or creation in more detail below, and will return to some of the stylised choices of the BBC production in the light of that argument. However, the narrative of *All That Fall* incorporates an awareness of the destructive consequences of the human will to make or create (*techne*) on the life-world. I am interested in how

---

12 The 1957 BBC *All That Fall* also musicalised the sounds of Maddy's and Dan's corporeal efforts of walking; unassisted by mechanical means of transport, the dragging feet and panting become formalised into precisely rhythmic, percussive sounds which only gradually become interpretable as human footsteps. The one exception, as McWhinnie notes, was the sequence where Maddy is hoisted into Mr Slocum's car, as 'the one scene in the play which may be handled realistically, since its farcical detail is so extravagant and unreal in itself' (141).

the play combines parodic references to the divine creation of the world with a historical sense of the human invention of ever more powerful machines.

3   Technological Interventions and the Parody of Creation in *All That Fall*

The opening of the text of *All That Fall* introduces the listener to the sound of four animals: a sheep, bird, cow and cockerel '*severally, then together*' (Beckett, 1984, 12). This stylisation may suggest that we are hearing the animal voices through a human consciousness which we shortly understand to be Maddy's, or, as Laws suggests above, that this is an entirely sonically constructed and rhythmically composed world from the outset, where all the creatures and the sounds they make are subject to the creative and technical processes of the author, director and technical team. However, the opening of *All That Fall* follows the order of creation in the book of Genesis: animals *before* humans, and, as many scholars have noted, there are several ironic references to the Bible, most emphatic and savage in the eponymous reference to the Lord upholding all that fall, subjected to 'wild laughter' by Dan and Maddy (38). When Maddy also questions the Biblical passage which values one human life as equivalent to many sparrows, Dan asks: 'Does that put our price up?'(37). Their irony towards the assumption that human life is of greatest value in the order of creation suggests what Mary Bryden has termed wider 'antipathy' in Beckett's work to 'the notion of a species hierarchy in which God presides over an order of creation which descends through human beings down to the 'lower' order of flies and minute pond life' (Bryden, 3).

Such self-awareness of the act of artistic creation as invoking (ironically) the divine creation of the world recurs throughout Beckett's work and particularly in some of the work written in the 1950s: Charles Lyons notes the recurrence of anti-creation motifs in *Endgame*, linked to an attack on genesis and generation (1964), and *How It Is* takes place in a post-Judgement cosmology which consists exclusively of an *infernal* mudscape with occasional glimpses of a life 'above in the light'.[13] Beckett contracts and expands time, drawing attention to the phenomenological moment of listening, but also placing that moment of the ever receding now in the context of a temporality that goes beyond the human. In *All That Fall*, Maddy's evocation of the 'dust [that] will not settle in our time'

---

13   As Daniela Caselli among others has demonstrated, the muddy cosmology of *How It Is* is modelled on Dante's *Inferno* (Caselli, 2005, 148–82).

(16), suggests both the moment in her journey when she and Mr Tyler have been nearly run over by Connolly's van, and the dust to which human bodies must return, and perhaps the universe as well.

Several critics have noted that Maddy is conceived as a creator figure, or 'ironic earth mother' (Frost, 1997, 198) as she conjures the world of flora — 'there is that lovely laburnum again' (14, 36), and especially the world of animals, from the 'pretty little woolly lamb' (34) to the cooing ringdoves, or the feeding animal world at the end of the day: 'The cows — [*Brief moo.*] — and sheep — [*Brief baa.*] — ruminate in silence' (32). Sarah Bryant Bertail notes Maddy's calling of the animals into being in an ironic echo of Adam's act of naming the animals in Genesis: Maddy is 'the mouth that produces the landscape, the matrix through which creation *takes place*' (1995, 10), though she invokes them as they are subsiding into silence (and therefore radiophonic non-being), leaving Dan and Maddy 'Alone. There is no-one to ask' (32). If Maddy is a creator or 'orchestrator' figure, as Katarzyna Ojrzyenska calls her (49), her ability to compose the voices of other species falters, as Ojrzyenska notes: Maddy becomes increasingly exhausted, feeling, 'very cold and faint' (34) on the walk back from the station in the final part of the play. This may be echoed in the fading of the more than human voices she invokes in the extract cited above — the animals are not heard directly in the sound world of the play after this moment.

Moreover, Maddy contrasts the voices of the animals to her own human speech, which seems to her increasingly bizarre, anachronistic and on the edge of extinction: Dan complains that Maddy sounds as if she is 'struggling with a dead language', and Maddy replies: 'Well, you know, it will be dead in time, just like our own poor dear Gaelic' (34). The language of the animals, however, 'has not changed since Arcady'. Everett Frost argues that the animal sounds in the text 'are not sound effects at all. They are other voices in the text, speaking a language that [...] survives unchanged from pre-lapsarian times, and unintelligible to human ears closed to Arcady by the fall' (Frost, 1997, 198). Therefore, while Maddy's attention to the more than human world around her allows their voices into the sound world of the play, she has no omniscient authority over them. Instead, she shares with them a 'kinship in mutual vulnerability' faced with the increasingly threatening and invasive technological machines that threaten both human and other living creatures.

Maddy encounters layers of human technology and intervention during her journey which enact a history of the Anthropocene from the invention of the bicycle, to the horse driven cart, the motor car and finally the monstrous train associated with modernity and the Industrial Revolution. The text stresses the 'exaggerated station sounds' that should herald the arrival of the train with 'great hissing of steam and clashing of couplings' (27).[14] However, each of these incrementally more powerful machines proves increasingly disastrous for the animal species and even the human species, since the reason for the delay of the twelve thirty train is that a child was killed by falling under its wheels (the reason for the child's fall is never confirmed). There is also a gendered perspective on this destruction — the bicycle, horse and car are driven by men (though the train seems to be pure machine) while the victims are mostly female, from the hinny that Christy wallops, to the hen run over by Mr Slocum's car. Indeed, Maddy shares a cross-species experience of endangered female reproduction. Most of the female animals in *All That Fall* are either sterile, like the hinny harnessed to Christy's cart, or beyond reproduction,[15] like Maddy herself — even her daughter, 'little Minnie', had she survived, would be 'girding up her lovely little loins, getting ready for the change' (16). Although the published text refers to a genderless 'little child' (39) who fell under the wheels of the train, in a letter to Kay Boyle in 1961, responding to her request for clarification about Willie's motives in *Happy Days*, Beckett replied that that is 'like the question in *All That Fall* as to whether Mr Rooney threw the little girl out of the railway carriage or not. And the answer is the same in both cases — we don't know, at least I don't. (Beckett, 2014, 435): Beckett here, whether consciously or not, seems to conceive of the child as also female, like the other victims of technology in the play.

In addition to the physical effort of the journey, and the threatening world of machines that Maddy has to negotiate to get to the station, she encounters increasingly unsympathetic and indeed violent human beings. Although Christy and Mr Tyler are friendly enough, Mr Slocum regrets offering Maddy a lift in his motor car, and Miss Fitt has to be shamed into lending Maddy a helping arm in order to ascend the steep path leading to the station: 'Your arm! Any arm! A helping hand! For five seconds! Christ what a planet! [...] Pismires do it for one another. [*Pause*] I have seen slugs do it' (23). In addition to the attempts of everyone else on the platform to ignore or get away from Maddy, there are acts of human on human violence: in a sound cue that might

---

14 McWhinnie interpreted this sonic evocation of the train in psychological and affective terms as communicating the significance of the arrival of the train for the humans awaiting their delayed 'nearest and dearest': 'The sound-complex in its grotesque fantasy must fulfil the wildest expectations and fears of the people who have been biting their nails on the platform; we should hear it as the nightmare realization of their own heightened anxiety' (147).

15 See Stewart who refers to Beckett's 'horror of female reproduction' (133).

be overlooked (see Frost, 1997, 217–8), Mr Barrell delivers a 'back-handed blow' to young Tommy the station porter after several earlier threats, for which he is reprimanded by Mr Tyler (24), and, on their journey from the station, Maddy and Dan hear the cries of Mrs Tully whose husband 'is in constant pain and beats her unmercifully' (33). In general, the human comes across as a species which destroys other species and the environment and is unlikely to come to the aid of its fellow beings unless compelled to. Their attitude to animals is entirely instrumental and indeed cruelly indifferent. Only Maddy is tuned to the voices of the more than human and opens a space in the technologised soundscape of *All That Fall* for them to be heard.

4 Human and More than Human Voicings in *All That Fall*

In contrast to all of the other humans in the play, Maddy is extremely alert to the world of flora and fauna, noticing the 'lovely laburnum', and listening to the doves, the lambs and other creatures. This can be read as confirming Maddy's privileged perspective: we access the voices of the more than human via her perception. Yet she does not speak for them, acknowledging that they are a species apart with their own distinct language. Though Maddy at times speaks of the flowers and animals around her as inhabiting an innocent, unspoiled Edenic or Arcadian world from which humans have been outcast, at other times, she acknowledges that they have their own 'troubles' and embodied forms of suffering: from the 'cleg-tormented eyes' (13) of the hinny harnessed to Christy's cart, and coerced into moving on its owner's demand, to the hen run over by Mr Slocum's car: 'What a death! One minute picking happy at the dung, on the road, in the sun, with now and then a dust bath, and then — bang — all her troubles over. [*Pause*]. All the laying and hatching' (19). As Christy gives his hinny 'a good welt on the rump', Maddy muses: 'If someone should do that for me, I should not dally' (13). Maddy positions herself alongside these fellow creatures, rather than as their master, recognising that she and they share a 'kinship in mutual vulnerability'. She identifies with their subjected status, refusing hierarchies which are otherwise embedded within the human and technological world of the play.

This de-centring of the human in relation to a greater web of species in *All That Fall* sheds some further light on Beckett's disagreement with McWhinnie on the use of human actors to impersonate the animal sounds in the play. Beckett was very pleased with many of the elements of the BBC 1957 production, as he wrote to McWhinnie, including 'The double walk sound [of Dan and Maddy] in the second half' and 'their wild laugh (marvellous)' (Beckett, 2014,

12), as well as the performances of Dan (James Gerard Devlin), Miss Fitt (Shiela Ward), and especially Maddy (Mary O'Farrell).[16] However, in the same letter, he notes 'I didn't think the animals were right'. Beckett does not articulate his reasons for this in detail, though he had expressed concern about McWhinnie's approach to the animal sounds in an earlier letter on 18 December 1956, during the production process: 'I do not see why the animal utterances by mere humans' (687), the adjective 'mere' suggesting a rather cynical view of humans as privileged inhabitants of the planet. Beckett continues: 'Perhaps your idea is to give them the unreal quality of the other sounds. But this, we agreed, should develop from a realistic nucleus. I think the absurd apropos with which they occur, and their briefness, are enough to denaturalise them. And if not could they not be distorted by some technical means?' (688).[17]

Beckett was therefore in sympathy with McWhinnie's desire to foreground the constructed nature of the radiophonic world evoked in the play. However, while the replacement of recorded, even technologically mediated 'real' animal sounds enhances the technological interventions on human and more than human life in the play, as well as its author's and director's strategies of radiophonic composition, it focuses exclusively on human agency and entirely erases any sonic echo of the *oikos*. Frost emphasises that in the Voices International production for American public radio in 1986, 'it seemed essential to use real animal sounds — so that there be no possibility of confusing the Arcadian animal language with something human and fallen. The animals make a wonderful music of their own that conveys on radio a context that is rural but not real' (200). Maddy may orchestrate these voices, as do the author and technical production team, but she does not simulate or impersonate them, rather she continually invites them into the listener's perceptual consciousness, and draws attention to their vulnerability to the man-made environment she shares with them.

In the light of the argument above, Beckett's desire to retain a denaturalised version of real animal sounds can be interpreted as wishing to retain the play's invocation of a life world and biosphere which is not just the home and property of humans. Though Maddy longs to be back at home — returned 'safe to haven' (34) — that *oikos* is 'offstage' in *All That Fall*, and 'being at home' is defined earlier in the play as 'a lingering dissolution' (15). Dan would prefer to

---

16 See Zilliacus, 65–8 for a more detailed discussion of the actors in the 1957 BBC *All That Fall*, which included Patrick Magee as Mr Slocum, and Jack MacGowran as Tommy.

17 Catherine Laws has carried out detailed research into the production process of *All That Fall* at the BBC, and explains that what Beckett was recommending would in fact have been very difficult to achieve with the technology available to the BBC in 1956 (Laws, 111).

avoid 'the horrors of home life' (33) and dreams 'of another home, another — [*He hesitates.*] — another home' (32). *All That Fall* (along with much of Beckett's other work) portrays the human species as attempting to control or create a world, but also displaces or exiles the human in a temporality and web of life in which they are transitory, inconsequential visitors. The abandonment of the human by divine indifference and their subjection to a biosphere that they cannot control is emphasised by the ending of the play. As the act of creation is mimicked in the opening of the play, the ending evokes a 'tempest of wind and rain' (39) that subsumes the entire sonically evoked world, including Maddy and Dan, in a soundscape that suggests a Flood-like apocalypse, interweaving technological, biblical, and ecological versions of extinction.

5 Conclusion: 'We're Talking of the Species the Human'[18]

All That Fall is one of Beckett's most overt portrayals of the negative impact of human technological agency on the *oikos*, even while it uses radiophonic technologies to creatively realise that agency. Beckett's next radio play, *Embers* (1959) is set even more specifically in the mind of its protagonist Henry: though we hear his bodily movements, those of his wife Ada are silent, suggesting that she is a ghostly presence he has conjured. Henry invokes sounds such as horses' hooves which are abstracted and formally structured, appearing and disappearing on command as if we are indeed inside Henry's head. Yet, the play is set on a strand, between land and sea, and the rhythms of the sea counterpoint the imagined or produced sounds and stories with which Henry attempts to 'drown' out the sucking sound of the shingle which is associated with death, specifically the disappearance of his father who has apparently drowned, and, like the tempest of wind and rain at the end of *All That Fall*, with a non-anthropomorphic force oblivious and indifferent to human existence. The inner and outer spheres are not collapsed into a pathetic fallacy, rather the *oikos* retains its opacity, its resistance to human interpretation.

In most of Beckett's subsequent radio plays, the focus is as much on the efforts of composition (verbal and musical) as on the narrative of the play. However, these efforts of creation are strangely impersonal, as words and music are conceived as separate sound streams, embodied as characters in *Words and Music* but simply 'opened' and 'closed' in *Pochade radiophonique* and *Cascando*. In some of the prose work of the mid 1960s including *Imagination Dead Imagine* and *The Lost Ones*, though the animal world is absent, the

---

18   Beckett, 1964, 52.

enclosed spaces in which the human bodies are located with no apparent exit resemble self-regulating biospheres, with references to their changing climates and temperatures. In these texts, the imaginative or generative faculties of the creator or deviser can produce only almost extinguished worlds in which the human animals are rigorously subjected to the seemingly arbitrary rules and systems of their constructed biosphere.

In relation to Beckett's later work, therefore, *All That Fall* seems both exceptional and pivotal. On the one hand, Mrs Rooney, as the first female protagonist in Beckett's work whose consciousness and perception is the gateway to the world of the play, is remarkably attuned to the living world around her, and, in terms of Beckett's radio work and indeed his oeuvre, the vivid if satirical evocation of the thinly disguised world of Beckett's boyhood in Foxrock in both its social milieu and its landscape is also exceptional.[19] However, on the other hand *All That Fall* clearly shaped Beckett's experiments with sound and the dissociation of voice from body across the different media of his subsequent work. From an ecological point of view, *All That Fall* is an important text in an investigation of Beckett's 'species consciousness': as Lavery has argued in relation to Beckett's theatre worlds, *All That Fall* 'recalibrates' our perceptual apparatus, creating an aural space for the voices of the *oikos* to be heard, and inviting the listener to question the 'species hierarchy' between the 'mere' human and the more than human, foregrounding rather their interdependence and mutual vulnerability.

Works Cited

Abram, David (1996), *The Spell of the Sensuous: Perception and Language in a More-than-Human World*, London: Vintage Books.

Addyman, David, Matthew Feldman and Erik Tonning, eds. (2017), *Samuel Beckett and BBC Radio: A Reassessment*, Basingstoke: Palgrave Macmillan.

Arnheim, Rudolf (1936), *Radio*, trans. M. Ludwig and H. Read, London: Faber and Faber.

Beckett, Samuel (1964), *How It Is*, London: John Calder.

Beckett, Samuel (1984), *The Collected Shorter Prose*, London: Faber and Faber.

Beckett, Samuel (2011), *The Letters of Samuel Beckett*, Vol. I: 1929–1940, ed. George Craig, Martha Dow Fehsenfeld, Dan Gunn and Lois More Overbeck, Cambridge: Cambridge UP.

---

19 Scholars have linked the writing of *All That Fall* in English to Beckett's return to his early memories of Ireland. See Kim, 2010, pp. 80–1.

Beckett, Samuel (2014), *The Letters of Samuel Beckett*, Vol. II: 1941–1956, ed. George Craig, Martha Dow Fehsenfeld, Dan Gunn and Lois More Overbeck, Cambridge: Cambridge UP.

Briscoe, Donald and Roy Curtis-Bramwell (1983), *The BBC Radiophonic Workshop: The First Twenty-Five Years*, London: The British Broadcasting Corporation.

Bryant-Bertail, S. (1995), 'The True-Real Woman: Maddy Rooney as Picara in *All That Fall*', Assaph: Studies in the Theatre, 11, pp. 1–17.

Bryden, Mary, ed. (2013), *Beckett and Animals*, Cambridge: Cambridge UP.

Campbell, Julie (2009), '"A Voice Comes to One in the Dark. Imagine": Radio, the Listener, and the Dark Comedy of *All That Fall*', in Steven Barfield, Matthew Feldman and Philip Tew, eds., *Beckett and Death*, London: Continuum, pp. 147–68.

Caselli, Daniela (2005), *Beckett's Dantes: Intertextuality in the Fiction and Criticism*, Manchester: Manchester UP.

Connor, Steven (2003), 'Beckett's Atmospheres', a paper given at the 'After Beckett/ Après Beckett' conference in Sydney, January 2003, available online at: http://stevenconnor.com/atmospheres-2.html, accessed 11 March 2018.

David, Heather and Étienne Turpin (2015), *Art in the Anthropocene: Encounters Among Aesthetics, Politics, Environments and Epistemologies*, London: Open Humanities P.

Davies, Paul (2006), 'Strange Weather: Beckett from the Perspective of Ecocriticism', in S. E. Gontarski and Anthony Uhlmann, eds. *Beckett after Beckett*, Gainesville: UP of Florida.

Frost, Everett (1991), 'Fundamental Sounds: Recording Beckett's Radio Plays', *Theatre Journal*, 43: 3, pp. 361–76.

Frost, Everett (1997), 'A "Fresh Go" for the Skull: Directing *All That Fall*, Samuel Beckett's Play for Radio', in Lois Oppenheim, ed. *Directing Beckett*, Ann Arbor: U of Michigan P, pp. 186–219.

Frost, Everett (2009), 'Preface', Samuel Beckett, *All That Fall and Other Plays for Radio and Screen*, ed. Everett Frost, London: Faber and Faber, pp. vii–xxiii.

Garrard, Greg (2012), '*Endgame*: Beckett's Ecological Thought', *SBT/A*, 23: *Filiations & Connexions/Filiations & Connecting Lines*, pp. 383–97.

Gibson, Andrew (2010), *Samuel Beckett*, London: Reaktion Books.

Hartel, Gaby (2010), 'Emerging out of a Silent Void: Reverberations of Rudolf Arnheim's Radio Theory on Beckett's Radio Pieces', *JOBS*, 19: 2, pp. 218–27.

Kelleher, Joe (2015), 'Recycling Beckett', in Clair Finburgh and Carl Lavery, eds., *Rethinking the Theatre of the Absurd: Ecology, the Environment and the Greening of the Modern Stage*, London: Bloomsbury, pp. 127–46.

Kennedy, Seán (2004), '"A Lingering Dissolution": *All That Fall* and Protestant Fears of Engulfment in the Irish Free State', in Linda Ben-Zvi, ed., *Drawing on Beckett: Portraits, Performances, and Cultural Contexts*, Tel Aviv: Assaph Book Series, pp. 247–61.

Kim, Rina (2010), *Women and Ireland as Beckett's Lost Others*, Basingstoke: Palgrave Macmillan.

Lavery, Carl (2018), 'Ecology in Beckett's Theatre Garden: Ways to Cultivate the *Oikos*', *Contemporary Theatre Review*, 28: 1, pp. 10–26: a special issue on Staging Beckett and Contemporary Theatre and Performance Cultures, ed. Anna McMullan and Graham Saunders.

Laws, Catherine (2017), 'Imagining Radio Sound: Interference and Collaboration in the BBC Radio Production of Beckett's *All That Fall*', in Addyman et al. eds., pp. 103–38.

Lyons, Charles (1964), 'Beckett's *Endgame*: An Anti-myth of Creation', *Modern Drama*, 7: 2, pp. 204–9.

Lyotard, Jean-François (1993), 'Oikos' in *Political Writings*, trans. Bill Readings and Kevin Paul Geiman, London: UCL P., pp. 96–107.

Maude, Ulrika (2009), *Beckett, Technology and the Body*, Cambridge: Cambridge UP.

McMullan, Anna (2010), *Performing Embodiment in Samuel Beckett's Drama*, London: Routledge.

McWhinnie, Donald (1959), *The Art of Radio*, London: Faber and Faber.

Morin, Emilie (2014), 'Beckett's Speaking Machines: Sound, Radiophonics and Acousmatics', *Modernism/modernity*, 21: 1, pp. 1–24.

Morton, Timothy (2010), *The Ecological Thought*, Cambridge, MA: Harvard UP.

Nicholson, Simon, and Sikina Jinnah (2016), *New Earth Politics: Essays from the Anthropocene*, Cambridge, MA: MIT P.

Ojrzyenska, Katarzyna (2014), 'Music and Metamusic in Beckett's Early Plays for Radio', in Sarah Bailes and Nicholas Till, eds., *Beckett and Musicality*, London: Routledge, pp. 47–62.

Stewart, Paul (2011), *Sex and Aesthetics in Samuel Beckett's Work*, Basingstoke: Palgrave Macmillan.

Wardle, Irving (1968), *New English Dramatists 12: Radio Plays*, Harmondsworth: Penguin Books.

Weller, Shane (2008), 'Not Rightly Human: Beckett and Animality', *SBT/A*, 19: *Borderless Beckett/Beckett sans frontières: Tokyo 2006*, pp. 211–21.

Weller, Shane (2013), 'Forms of Weakness: Animalisation in Kafka and Beckett', in Bryden, pp. 13–26.

Zilliacus, Clas (1976), *Beckett and Broadcasting: A Study of the Works of Samuel Beckett for and in Radio and Television*, Abo: Abo Akademi.

A Creamy Work: Schiller and Beckett

Arthur Rose

Abstract

This chapter considers the aesthetic judgement implied in three reflections on the German playwright and philosopher Friedrich Schiller attributed to Samuel Beckett from, variously, 1937, 1961, and 1985. Rather than test the veracity of their attribution, which has been the subject to some debate in Beckett studies, it suggests they might provide a starting point for a more speculative discussion about aesthetic principles expressed by Schiller and Beckett, and how these principles might be brought into a creative, 'proximate' alignment. Drawing on Beckett's critical engagement with Schiller's *Maria Stuart* (1800) in his German Diary (1936–7), the chapter offers a reading of Beckett's critical assessment of Schiller's drama that, it will transpire, accords with Schiller's own aesthetic theory. This synthetic aesthetic effort will provide a useful structure for approaching Beckett's late drama. By reading Schiller via Beckett and, reciprocally, Beckett via Schiller, the chapter offers a polyphonous response to 'all the dead voices' offered by, and in dialogue with, these playwrights. Moreover, it replicates this response in its methodology, by using only the quoted accounts of another scholar to render references by Beckett to Schiller necessarily speculative.

∴

> Why can't the living spirit manifest itself to the spirit?
> If the soul *speaks*, alas, it is no longer the *soul* that speaks.
> FRIEDRICH SCHILLER, *Sprache*

∵

This chapter considers the speculative aesthetic judgement implied in Samuel Beckett's three invocations of Friedrich Schiller. In 1937, Beckett diagnoses Schiller's *Maria Stuart* as a 'creamy work' (qtd. in Nixon, 2011, 77), an indictment we find echoed in Theodor Adorno's *Minima Moralia*. For Adorno, Schiller's theatrical work turns action into 'a harmonious, logically consistent context of meaning' (153). The failure of Schiller's work for both Beckett and Adorno lies in its aesthetic 'smoothness': it does not prove itself lumpy enough for their critical interest. Early Beckett disparagingly remarks of Schiller's style that it is 'machine writing' (Nixon, 2011, 204), recalling his reference to Balzac's determinism as a 'snowball act' (Burrows, 6). And yet, it is towards 'machine writing' that late Beckett seems to be grasping in his prose and his drama. By contrast, Schiller is referred to in organic terms: he is 'alive to me', Beckett writes in 1985 (qtd. in Büttner, 46). In 1961 Beckett will classify Schiller's moral theatre as a device to inform or teach, in opposition to his own work, 'which has been through the void' (qtd. in Knowlson, 477). Beckett's ventriloquism of Schiller's aesthetics consistently places the German Romanticist as his theoretical antithesis. Placing the comments from 1937, 1961, and 1985 alongside each other demonstrates a historical progression, the clearer for their historical remoteness. But Schiller functions as more than a mere placeholder for Beckett's dialectical contrariness. Schiller's own aesthetic theory, as articulated in his *Letters upon the Aesthetic Education of Man*, advocates a dialectical method of aesthetic understanding that does not simply seek to smooth over historical discrepancy. This essay will argue Beckett's response to Schiller realises a historical version of Schiller's own theory that serves as a corrective to the more homogenous readings of the *Letters*. It then turns, briefly, to Beckett's final play, *Quoi Où*, to consider Beckett's tendency towards Schillerian hypostasis in his own 'machine writing'.

Prior to the publication of Mark Nixon's *Samuel Beckett's German Diaries*, Beckett's most explicit reference to Schiller had seemed to come from a discussion with 6th form students in a Bielefeld bookshop in 1961, when he offered the following explanation of his view on the theatre:

> For me, the theatre is not a moral institution in Schiller's sense. I want neither to instruct nor to improve nor to keep people from getting bored. I want to bring poetry into drama, a poetry which has been through the void and makes a new start in a new room-space. I think in new dimensions and basically am not very worried about whether I can be followed. I couldn't give the answers, which were hoped for. There are no easy solutions. (Knowlson, 477)

These lines, published by the *Spectakulum* in 1963, are apocryphal. According to Beckett in a letter to Gottfried Büttner, dated 3 January 1985, 'I did not write the lines quoted by *Spektakulum*. They sound like a write-up of disconnected indiscretions' (Büttner, 46). In the same letter Beckett goes on to add that 'Schiller's Theatre is quite alive to me' (46). Büttner glosses Beckett's reference to Schiller's Theatre: 'Theatre as a "moral institution"? An unexpected statement by the great man. There is no key that will unlock every problem thrown up by Beckett's work' (46). Büttner's gloss implicitly attributes the reference to Schiller's 'Die Schaubuhne als eine moralische Anstalt betracht [The Stage/Theatre as a Moral Institution]'. But, as shown in both the German Diaries and the first volume of *The Letters*, we know that Beckett watched a production of Schiller's *Maria Stuart* in Berlin's Schauspielhaus on the evening of 8 January 1937, after reading a copy, bought on the 5th, over the previous three days (Nixon, 2010, 258–9). Is it possible, then, that Beckett means Schiller's *theatre* rather than his 'Theatre'?

In reconstructing the history of this inquiry, we may observe in his notes on German Literature (TCD MS 10971/1) that Beckett read about Schiller in John G. Robertson's *A History of German Literature* (1902) and, though he skipped the chapter on Schiller, about Schiller's relationship with Goethe in G. P. Gooch's *Germany and the French Revolution* (1920). In preparing his Philosophy Notes, he would also have come across several pages dedicated to Schiller and Goethe in Wilhelm Windelband's *A History of Philosophy* (1901). This contact might, in part, account for the significant effort he made to go to the houses of both Schiller and Goethe when he was in Weimar, as well as explaining the detailed notes he took there. But by this time, he had also already read *Maria Stuart* and seen the performance, which, as we shall see, he described in less than glowing terms.

Maria Stuart is a five-act play that traces the final three days of the life of Mary Queen of Scots. Its focus is her relationship with her cousin, Elizabeth I, which Beckett clearly knew when he noted in the German Diary that the climax of the play, the argument between the cousins, was an aesthetic failure. There is some evidence of further reading in this diary entry, dated the evening of the performance (8th), since he notes that the final act was written somewhat later than the previous four, after Schiller had completed his translation of *Hamlet* (it was, in fact, *Macbeth*), facts mentioned in neither Robertson nor Gooch.[1] There is also some discrepancy in his account of the performance. He claims the last act was cut, but then refers to the strength of the Mary actress's performance in delivering her Act 5 remark about France: 'Alas, I was ever there' (Schiller, V, viii). But this historical lumpiness is perhaps not as interesting as the philosophical synthesis Beckett gives for the play:

> Altogether a very *creamy* work, 'homogénéisé', with the Euripidean intentions insufficiently immediate. The Oedipan Destiny, whose implements

---

[1] I have not been able to confirm whether this is mentioned in Charles Simond's *Schiller 1759–1805* (1907), a copy of which is listed in Beckett's library.

are every act of evasion, is made petty by such rationalistic comment as Marys [sic] in the last act, when she tacks the penalty for a crime she has not committed on to a crime she has committed (Darnley's murder). So that the play does not end in a last act of understanding, as in Racine, but in self-solace. (Nixon, 2011, 77)

Beckett repeats the complaint in a letter to Thomas MacGreevy, dated 9 January 1937, when he again refers to the play as 'creamy' (2009, 421).[2] Beckett's assessment of the work's creaminess is no commentary on its dramatic action, since a key character, Mortimer, commits suicide onstage.[3] Moreover, accusations of the 'creaminess' of Mary's confession are somewhat anachronistic, since it was precisely the confession scene that Goethe advised Schiller to cut. The scene provoked enough offence that it was adapted or censored, which caused Schiller to make the following shocking statement: 'I am going to write a play in which a woman is raped — and they *have* to watch' (Sharpe, 1991, 254). The 'uncreamy' extremities of action and historical reception suggest, then, that Beckett's comment is a formal complaint about the play's rationalist treatment of tragedy. The comparison with Racine, a recurrent feature of Rachel Burrows's lecture notes from Beckett's classes at Trinity in 1931/32, suggests that Schiller's 'self-solace' recapitulates problems Beckett previously diagnosed in Corneille (he shows people 'as they are meant to be', where Racine shows them as they are), or, perhaps more compellingly, Balzac ('Racine, occasional absence of character gives glimpse of background. Balzac, the protagonist is devoured, annexed by his background') (qtd. in Burrows, 6). Tragedy, for Beckett, requires clarity, not, what is presented, 'serene obscurity' (Nixon, 2011, 77). Paradoxically, this serene obscurity stems not from Schiller's unclear intentions, since of that Beckett expresses little doubt. Rather, Beckett echoes, in his response to Schiller, Friedrich Nietzsche's criticism of 'Euripidean intentions'. Nietzsche accuses Euripides of replacing tragedy with the dramatised epic: 'to excise that original and all-powerful Dionysian element from tragedy and to rebuild tragedy purely on the basis of an un-Dionysian art,

---

2   Rereading this essay in January 2021, more than eight years after presenting it in draft form, I am reminded of Julie's suggestion that I make more of the double entendre implicit in Beckett's reference to creaminess. If, ultimately, the seriousness of the topic made me resist the suggestion, this, I now think, was a missed opportunity to play a little more. So the voices of the dead come to one in the dark. Imagine.

3   In 2008, Daniel Hoevels accidentally slit his own throat while playing Mortimer in Maria Stuart, when the crew failed to blunt the prop knife properly. Damien Pearce, 'Actor slits his own throat as knife switch turns fiction into reality' in *The Guardian*, 11 December 2008, http://www.guardian.co.uk/world/2008/dec/11/actor-slits-throat, accessed 25 February 2016.

morality and world-view' (68). Beckett's observations on Schiller's 'creaminess' might be an extension of Nietzsche's critique of Euripides's aesthetic rationality, but they do not originate in Nietzsche, since Beckett does not identify it as a problem for Euripides himself. More likely, Beckett follows Racine's favourable opinion of Euripides, since it is Schiller whose work is 'insufficiently immediate' to its Euripidean intentions. Beckett is making an implicit judgement on Schiller's stated intention (in a letter to Goethe dated 26 April 1799) to write *Maria Stuart* in the Euripidean method. At this point, the reader might be excused for wondering whose Euripides is under scrutiny. Schiller, who aspires to a Euripidean method, is scathing of Racine's Euripides, particularly with his inclusion of a love story between Achilles and Iphigenia: 'diese kleine, eigennützige Leidenschaft würde sich mit dem hohen Ernst und dem wichtigen Interesse des griechischen Stücks nicht vertragen [this small, selfish passion would not be tolerated within the loftiness and important interests of the Greek play]'.[4] Schiller's emphasis on the Greek play suggests that Schiller's Euripides develops an aesthetic critique of political ideology, while Racine's is more concerned with interpersonal relationships.

In the play, the individual (Mary) is overcome by the machinations of a political system (represented by Davison, the incompetent bureaucrat, who allows the signed death warrant to be taken by Burleigh, the schemer, who uses it to ensure Mary's death when Elizabeth vacillates about her sentence) the final authority of that system (Elizabeth) seems unable to control. Mary's confession is itself an 'Oedipal evasion': she, like Elizabeth, cannot face the political necessity of her death (there can be only one Queen) and resorts to rationalising it through the trope of personal guilt and sin. This is apparently Beckett's problem with the play — the personal rationalisation prevents Mary from understanding her fate. It was certainly an objection Adorno made of Schiller's theatre, in which 'the connection of alienated history to the human heart was already [...] a pretext for justifying the inhumanity of history as humanly comprehensible' (143). There is a crucial moment, following Mary's confession, after Beckett's 'homogénéisé' of rationalism and confession (Nixon, 2011, 77), where she encounters Leicester as she is being led to the scaffold. Leicester, who had promised to help her escape only to betray her, catches her as she faints. She responds with cutting solicitude:

---

4   Qtd. in Lamport 266. Lamport also notes that, for all Schiller's criticism of Racine (for making Achilles and Iphigenia lovers) in his *Anmerkungen* to *Iphigenia in Aulis*, Leicester in *Maria Stuart* also departs from historical record to become a failed suitor: 'All Schiller's tragedies contain a love-story, whether as a principal or as a subsidiary focus of interest, and this need not necessarily be a sign of French influence' (266).

> You keep your word, my Lord of Leicester: for
> You promised me your arm to lead me forth
> From prison, and you lend it to me now.
> [...] Farewell, my lord; and, if you can, be happy!
> To woo two queens has been your daring aim;
> You have disdained a tender, loving heart,
> Betrayed it in the hope to win a proud one:
> Kneel at the feet of Queen Elizabeth! (v, xi)

The double significance Mary gives to freedom (as both liberation and death) in the action, 'to lead me forth/from prison', points to her 'final act of understanding': it is through the betrayal of her supporters that she is undone. The bitter irony invested in her exchange with Leicester, however, demonstrates Mary's failure to understand the inhuman political dynamic of her situation (for Adorno, 'a social and political reality already incommensurable [...], no longer comprehensible in terms of human motivations' [143]). Understanding Leicester's actions in affective terms ('woo'; 'disdained'; 'betrayed'), she does not see that she has been overwhelmed by a necessity of political structure: one cannot 'woo' two sovereigns at the same time. Her recriminations come, and deal with, the personal betrayal she feels at Leicester's political expediency, not the structural principles that underpin this expediency.

Schiller's Euripidean intention is to create a tragedy in which Mary martyrs herself for the stability of the state, a decision which must appear excessively rational to the understanding of tragedy as a genre implemented by 'every act of evasion'. But, for Beckett, her martyrdom is all the more bitter for being unnecessary to the tragedy: it sets up an obscure dialectic between Mary's 'tender, loving heart' and Elizabeth's 'proud one'. This dialectic is, for Adorno, precisely the problem of 'false humanisation'. The obscurity is not simply a matter of historical inaccuracy. Beckett ends his comments on the play by noting *'neither queen was that kind of person'*, but qualifies this as 'another story altogether'. This recalls Robertson, who thought *Maria Stuart* a 'bürgerliche tragödie', historically inaccurate and with 'virtually no political background' (389). Critically, Robertson makes a similar judgment on its theatrical failure:

> The long, final act, in which she receives the consolations of her religion and takes farewell of her women, is harrowing rather than tragic; for the reader has the feeling, and this is in spite of the poet's accentuation of Mary's early sins, that she has no guilt upon her soul to expiate; her death is, in the economy of the drama, an accident, not a necessity. (390)

Mary's confession, the rationalistic comment that renders the 'Oedipan Destiny' 'petty', is, for Robertson, 'harrowing rather than tragic' because it attempts to expiate an absent guilt. Since she is innocent, it is not 'a necessity' that she die. Her death, 'in the economy of the drama, an accident', fails to justify itself as such. Both Beckett and Robertson interpret the political dimensions of the play in terms of individual affect; Schiller, on the other hand, understands the personal wholly in terms of its inevitable, uncomprehending, defeat by political necessity.

Beckett's aesthetics are often articulated in antithesis to such literary determinism (also evident in his criticisms of Balzac's snowball act), particularly in his pursuit of moments of 'liminal consciousness' (Burrows, 6). He naturally favours Racine's emphasis on the interpersonal over the importance Schiller gives to the political. Moreover, he generally stands against celebratory nationalist politics (as evidenced, for instance, by his infamous '¡UPTHEREPUBLIC!' response of the same period [Cronin, 187]). His distrust of Schiller's rationalism matches his disaffection with Schiller's nationalist proclivities, whose co-option by Nazism is comprehensively demonstrated by the 10,600 performances of his work that took place in Germany between 1933 and 1945. It would appear, then, that little is left to tell. Indicted by Adorno's accusations of false humanism, Schiller can remain a footnote to Beckett's more protracted argument with Balzac. But the danger in this neatness of identification is that it excludes two rather lumpy features of Beckett's account: the role of religious aestheticism represented by Schiller in both his thought and his plays, and the mysterious remainder in Schiller's dramatic work that manages to remain 'alive' from 1937 to 1985.

Beckett's frustration with Schiller's religious aestheticism is evident when he condemns Mortimer's conversion speech, which 'could only have come from the miserable Protestant idea of Roman Catholicism as a welter of the fine arts' (Nixon, 2011, 77). After his conversion to Catholicism, Mortimer, the nephew of the jailor, dedicates himself to freeing Mary. The conversion is spoken of as,

> [...] the sublime
> Creative spirit held my soul a prisoner
> In the fair world of wonders it had framed.
> I ne'er had felt the power of art till now.
> The church that reared me hates the charms of sense;
> It tolerates no image, it adores
> But the unseen, the incorporeal word. (I, vi)

Mortimer's prime mover is the power of art, but his disenchantment is with Protestant aesthetics, an aesthetics of the 'incorporeal word'. The concept raises inevitable resonances with Beckett's letter to Axel Kaun from 9 July 1937, and his desire for 'a literature of the non-word' and for 'word-storming in the name of beauty' (2009, 520). Beckett's criticism, surprisingly, does not strike against the logocentrism of Schiller's incorporeal word. Given Beckett's development towards 'logoclasm' later that year, the absolute idealism of Mortimer's disembodied word, together with his equally idealistic assumption of the 'image' ('the fair world of wonders it had framed' [I, vi]), would have frustrated him, beyond his accusation of 'a welter of fine arts'. In other words, behind Beckett's criticism of Schiller's vulgar Protestant/Catholic dialectic, we might advance a more fruitful debate about Schiller's religious aestheticism.

Schiller's aesthetics, and their religious connotations, are generally understood to be a little 'creamy'. This creaminess is in no small way related to the assumption that Schiller's terms are as creamy as they sound. So, the 'Theatre' is often understood to be an actual 'moral' (didactic) institution and the synthetic harmonisation of the various drives is often understood as the attempt to dissimulate the Kantian duality of *noumena* and *phenomena*. These assumptions need to be challenged before Schiller's work, philosophical and theatrical, can be brought into dialogue with Beckett's.

The prospect of synthesising Schiller's aesthetic philosophy, while responding to Beckett's remarks with this synthetic reading, is sufficiently daunting to limit me to a few brief remarks. These are not intended to do justice to the complexity of Schiller's thinking on aesthetics. Rather, they are intended to respond to certain common misconceptions about the shifting significance the moral has for the aesthetic in Schiller's 'The Stage as a Moral Institution' and *Letters on the Aesthetic Education of Man*. Instead of the pure didactic theatre implied by the titles, both works lay out the synthetic role aesthetics plays in uniting the opposing drives of Form [*Formtrieb*] and Sensation [*Stofftrieb*] via the Play drive [*Spieltrieb*]. Lesley Sharpe denies the moral principle, espoused by Beckett and his sources, that Schiller created characters meant to edify the audience: 'The freedom experienced by the spectator must therefore be clearly distinguished from any moral victories won over self by the characters within the play' (1991, 128). An apprehension of freedom — accessible via the aesthetic for Schiller in his foundational concept of beauty as 'Freiheit in der Erscheinung' (freedom in appearance), later reformulated as 'lebende Gestalt' (living form) — is not conveyed through the moral injunctions given in the content of art. Rather, it is the self-determining or autonomous quality of the beautiful object that is 'detached from the compulsion that normally governs objects in the phenomenal world' (Schiller,

1967, 2). While this provides a moral *Form* of autonomy similar to that of Kant, it departs from Kantian dualism by not separating the object from causality *within* the phenomenal world. Thus the beautiful, for Schiller, harmonises the moral (*Form*) with the sensible (*Stoff*) through the Play drive (*Spieltrieb*), defined as 'everything that is neither subjectively nor objectively contingent, and yet imposes no kind of constraint either from within or from without' (Sharpe, 1991, 158). The Play drive brings together *Formtrieb* and *Stofftrieb* and keeps them together in a dynamic tension that, unlike Kantian ethics, does not imply a constraint of sensation by law or rely on the apprehension of the object by a transcendental subject. Sharpe's argument has been formative in dispersing what Frederick Beiser has called 'the myths or legends' of past and present scholarship (10). Beiser, in his elucidation of these myths, notes that it has been popular in 'Marxist and post-modernist circles' (we can assume he includes Adorno), to accuse Schiller of 'aestheticism because he makes beauty into a motive for moral action and a justification of the state' (12). Schiller replies to this charge, Beiser argues, by 'insisting that aesthetic value can never be a reason for moral action' (12). The relationship between the sensible, the moral, and the aesthetic in Schiller's aesthetics is therefore demonstrably more sophisticated than is evident when aesthetic is interpreted as a means for the moral to overcome the sensible. Aesthetics, for Schiller, is not meant to 'instruct, improve or keep people from being bored' (12). The reading that Schiller's aesthetics did imply a manifest didacticism in artworks, though not necessarily germane to Beckett, is evident in Robertson's understanding of Schiller in *History of German Literature*. Sharpe, in her review of the critical reception of Schiller's aesthetics from 1795 to 1995, observes that Robertson's prejudices led him to be hostile to Schiller's *a priori* approach to aesthetics, dismiss Schiller's 'harmony-loving mind', and conclude that 'Schiller the philosopher [...] looks backwards rather than forwards [...] he endeavoured to reconcile the critical philosophy with the rationalism that had preceded it' (Sharpe, 1995, 37–8). Robertson's view was that Schiller had attempted to 'reconcile' Kantian 'severity' with 'a life of beauty and dignity, which has risen, through obedience to the law, to a perfect moral freedom' (364). This interpretation, as Breiser demonstrates, is flawed. Not only does it fail to appreciate Schiller's conscious political aims in his oblique responses to the republican tradition of Machiavelli, Montesquieu, Rousseau, and Ferguson, it also underestimates the significance of Schiller's attempt to extend Kant's account of aesthetic judgment to an objective aesthetic. Schiller's problem with the *Kritik der Urteilskraft* (1791) was that it failed to square the claim that the aesthetic experience, as a feeling of pleasure, 'designates nothing whatsoever in the object', with the requirement that aesthetic judgment demands universal assent (Beiser, 49). In his attempt to secure an objective aesthetic, Schiller postulates that 'aesthetic judgments must refer to some sensible properties of the object itself' (55). Although Schiller was ultimately unsuccessful in his attempt to secure the argument for hypostasis outside of an appeal to Kantian understanding (for Schiller, 'Reason'), what his attempt gestures towards is something Schiller would later call the reciprocal subordination of both *Formtrieb* and *Stofftrieb* in a footnote to the Thirteenth Letter of *Aesthetic Education*:

> For even though it is true that limitation can never be the source of the Absolute, and hence freedom can never be dependent upon time, it is no less certain that the Absolute can of itself never be the source of limitation, or a condition in time be dependent upon freedom [...] without form no matter, and without matter no form. (1967, 85)

Robertson's 'reconciliation' is exactly the 'subordination of the sensuous drive to the rational' that Schiller dismisses in this footnote (85). This is particularly interesting in Beckett's aesthetics of exhaustion in the later texts, so ably commented upon by Gilles Deleuze, since 'exhaustion' requires 'the indefinite exchange of mathematical formulations and the pursuit of the formless or the unformulated' (154). The exhaustion of the combinations of the forms, taken to aesthetic extremes, leads back to a sensible exhaustion of the body. If anything, Beckett's 'exhaustion' eliminates the possibility of Schiller's aesthetics because it makes limitation itself the end-product of the absolute: 'the exhausted person exhausts the whole of the possible' (152). It is by taking reason to its illogical extremes that it gives way to sensuous failure. This, however, is perversely a proof of Schiller's intimations about aesthetics *against* his arguments for this aesthetics. The only manner in which Beckett's 'exhausted' texts can be said to have 'coherence' in Adorno's sense of the word is if their exhaustion of the rational makes beauty from the abstraction of the tragic and the disintegration of its 'symbolic' elements. This makes Beckett's work the dialectical opposite of Schiller's aesthetics, and yet precisely the 'living form' to which his aesthetics aspires. There is an element of this exhaustion in the manner that Mary makes her farewell to Leicester: having exhausted her possibilities, she appeals to Catholic communion as a political act of defiance, only to give way to her emotions when faced with the character who disappoints her most. This failure to end in self-understanding is eclipsed by more political questions of systemic violence and scapegoating, less as humanist critique than as marker for the arbitrariness of sovereignty as such, which would preoccupy the politically sensitive Beckett throughout his career, and would lead, ultimately, to his own 'machine writing'.

Evidently the play maintained a certain hold on Beckett until this ending. His letter to Mary Manning Howe from 18 January remarks that 'it stays alive for 4 acts without betraying how it continues to do so' (2009, 423). He says much the same thing in another letter to MacGreevy of the same day: 'The Schiller remains alive till the last act without betraying the secret of how it contrives to do so' (2009, 432). If Schiller's play should be so mysteriously 'alive' for Beckett in 1937, then there is an obvious parallel with his comment to Büttner in 1985, which suggests that, in both instances, Beckett refers to Schiller as a playwright rather than as a thinker, but also a playwright whose successes and failures are curiously co-determined. This may be why Beckett refers to *Maria Stuart* as 'machine writing'. The phrase occurs in opposition, Mark Nixon notes in *Samuel Beckett's German Diaries 1936–1937*, to the more 'human' style of Goethe (204). Machine writing might also be a derivative of the aforementioned snowball act, Beckett's description of Balzac's literary determinism. But Beckett's equivocal critique of *Maria Stuart* belies the complexity of Schiller's mature aesthetics on the question of moral instruction and the potentially illustrative power it has in considering aesthetic-political implications of Beckett's late play, *Quoi Où* (1983), and its English and German incarnations, *What Where* (1983) and *Was Wo* (1985). Indeed, the increased mechanisation of characters in the play's revision for television makes of the work 'machine writing', in some superficial sense. However, as Ulrika Maude, Anna McMullan and Steven Connor have argued, it is precisely the elimination of the human that provides *Quoi où* with its dramatic aesthetic. Anna McMullan, in *Performing Embodiment*, notes:

> In the television version, the bodies have disappeared, leaving only shadowy faces that are blurred and insubstantial, as if in the process of vanishing [...] The faces [...] are inscrutable — we do not read there any signs of individual subjectivity, but perhaps rather the '*sub specie aeternitatas* vision' that seemed to the young Beckett of 1936, writing to Thomas MacGreevy, 'the only excuse for remaining alive'. (102)

The *sub specie aeternitatas* vision, 'under the aspect of eternity', replaces the vicissitudes of the individual with a constant unchanging *Form*. Beckett once said, apropos of Joyce, 'I take away all the accidentals because I want to come down to the bedrock of the essentials, the archetypal' (Esslin, 47–8). Whether they are 'gimmicks' or 'accidentals', the drives, or what Beckett once described as 'the two needs', seek to eliminate these things to reach a kind of pure *Form* or archetype. It seems, in a philosophical understanding of aesthetics, to be a subordination of sensibility by form via the mediation of a transcendental subject (the *sub specie aeternitatas* vision).[5] This subordination is even implied in the transformation of the play from a theatre play (with a live, present, and therefore unpredictable audience) to 'much more a television play' (with an absent, implied and relatively passive audience), who 'Make sense who may' (Beckett, 2006, 504). However, the process is more complicated than that, as becomes evident when formal 'elimination' is juxtaposed with historical 'restorations' as *Quoi Où* is translated into *What Where* and later to *Was Wo*. For, Gontarski continues his gloss on 'Process of elimination' (a most succinct summary) as follows:

> The play's mime (lines 34–54), the initial enactment of the play's pattern of appearance and disappearance (that is, another form of coming and going), was cut in the French text and performance, *QO* (PC), and initially in the English text, *WW* (SEG). Subsequently Beckett felt that he overcut the French text and so restored the mime for the American première of the revised text. (450)

Beckett's resistance to his own formal aesthetics of elimination is particularly interesting in this case. In a rational process of elimination, it would make sense to cut the words first. This would result in something similar to *Quad I* and *II*. However, cutting the words would also cut the heart out of the play, since the play turns around a dialectic between Bam's Voice (V) and Bam as a figure (P). If anything, the formal significance of this relationship is visually emphasised by the decision to represent the Voice with a distorted reflection of Bam's face in the television version. This relationship is necessarily of two different spaces. Steven Connor writes, 'we cannot be sure whether the voice inhabits the same dimension as the four performers or, as seems likely, the physical stage space is being used to designate the non-localized places of dreaming or imagination' (146). The play requires a tension between Voice and Performers, and that tension can only be maintained if the Voice has something to say.

The mime, then, appears to be the more superfluous, hence Beckett's initial decision to cut it. However, as Connor puts it, 'what is even more surprising in Beckett's theatre is the giving over of the stage not to action, but to the

---

[5] This perception of art *sub specie aeternitatas* resonates with something written by Wittgenstein in *Notebooks 1914–1916*: 'The work of art is the object seen sub specie aeternitatis; and the good life is the world seen *sub specie aeternitatis*. This is the connection between art and ethics'. This was written in October 1916. Later in the same month, he borrows a line from Schiller, 'Life is serious, Art is gay' (Tilghman, 46).

preparation for or preliminary to action' (147). The mime has a satiric role to play. By pre-empting or 'preparing' the action, it undermines the urgency of Bam's 'enlightened' need to know the 'it', the 'what' and the 'where', with the repetitious quality of the interrogations and their formal arrangements. The teleology of this enlightenment has always already been exhausted by the repetitious quality of its approach. The form of the play — a mime opening followed by a series of interrogations and dismissals — reflects on its content — the search for the ipseity and the location of an essential 'it' — which in turn reflects on its editorial process — the search for a particular form for the play, for an ideal measure of cuts and restorations. The inclusion of dialectics appears to frustrate the play's 'creaminess', since the ideal *Form* of elimination necessarily gives way to entrenched relationships between the Voice and the Performers, the mime and the interrogations and a shift from indeterminate figures to 'Faces only. / Full face throughout / As alike as possible' (Gontarski, 427). While this final change 'eliminates' the movement and the body, it also restores a priority to the face, which, though 'as alike as possible', must still allow for the distinction between a distorted Bam (the 'Voice'), Bam and the others. Thus, while Anna McMullan is convincing when she argues that, 'Beckett's two television adaptations from the stage, *Not I* and *What Where*, constitute the most radical denaturalization and fragmentation of the body in his entire oeuvre', there is an important 'sensibility' to this denaturalisation and fragmentation (102). McMullan suggests as much when she writes, 'It is as if these traces of extreme sentient experience from across the ages have remained sedimented in the excorporated flesh of the visible' (102). This incorporeal aesthetic is therefore one which has not entirely lost its flesh. Although, following Ulrika Maude, 'the bodies in the late prose pieces and the TV versions of *What Where* lack agency and seem to perform their permutations as on a computer loop' (288), there is still the need for bodies, whether they be 'faces' or 'figures'. Beauty needs to take its shape in visible form, or in 'living form'. The harmony of this 'compulsion', despite its apparent 'creaminess', always comes from the difficult negotiation between the rendering things down to their 'essentials' and the restoration of inevitably essential 'accidentals'.

In closing, I would like to make three parenthetical remarks to bring these diverse observations together. The first is to note the references to freedom in *Quoi Où*, *What Where* and *Was Wo*, when Bam asks the various interrogators, 'Are you free?' The question seems to be about availability: 'Are you free [to give him the works]?'. However, we may regard it as an ontological question, about condition, as much as a mundane question about occupation or disposition. We should recall that if Schiller saw a single meta-didactic purpose in the theatre, and in art, it was in giving freedom visual form. The beautiful, autonomous and itself free from contingency, allows the observer, moved by it, to recognise their own freedom. Of course, the answer Bom, Bim and Bem give, 'yes', is true ontologically — they are free subjects — but not true intentionally — they are ruled by the will of Bam (and behind Bam, Bam's Voice, and behind Bam's Voice, Beckett). The irony of their collective 'yes' is a moment in which the collision of form (when the yes is true) and sensibility (when the yes is not true) create something equable with Schiller's play drive.

The second is the mutual anxiety felt by Beckett and Schiller in associating their thoughts on aesthetics with their actual works. This association, by no means peculiar to these two writers, is nevertheless an interesting aside when considering the weight of scholarship that has invested in the conflation of the aesthetics with the work. Schiller, in a letter to Wilhelm von Humboldt, remarked on how little *pure* concepts helped in the writing process:

> You must not be surprised, dear friend, if I think of science and art as being farther apart and more opposed than I was inclined to do a few years ago. I have just directed all of my efforts to practical work, and it is my daily experience how little the poet is advanced in practice by *general, pure* concepts; in this mood I would occasionally be unphilosophical enough to sacrifice everything I and others know of the elements of aesthetics for a single empirical advantage, for one trick of the trade. (Sharpe, 1991, 121–2)

Beckett's famous declaration to Gabriel D'Aubarède, in 1961, when asked whether the existentialists provided the key to his writing is similar: 'There's no key or problem. I wouldn't have had any reason to write my novels if I could have expressed their subject in philosophic terms' (Graver and Federman, 217). Beckett's responses on this occasion are germane to the discussion, not simply because they resonate with Schiller's scepticism about the applicability of his aesthetics to his practice, but because they also relate to feeling. In response to the question, 'what was your reason?' Beckett replied: 'I haven't the slightest idea. I'm no intellectual. All I am is feeling. Molloy and the others came to me the day I became aware of my own folly. Only then did I being to write the things I feel' (Graver and Federman, 217). The 'feeling' of the piece, alongside Beckett's disavowed intellectualism, manages to capture a sense of Schiller's play drive — the reciprocal subordination of feeling to rationalism and rationalism to feeling.

Finally, even as the apparent creaminess of Beckett's later formalism seems to give way to a tension between *Form* and *Stoff*, the later work of Schiller also proves to be less creamy than the Beckett of 1937 thought. It remains debatable whether it was this Schiller or the other that was living for Beckett in 1985. What we can say, however, is that the weight of Beckett's purported remarks in 1961 — that he did not agree with the idea of theatre as moral institution — leads us to reconsider our assumptions about Schiller's wider aesthetics and how his aesthetics subvert these assumptions, affecting how it is when we read or watch Beckett today.

Works Cited

Adorno, Theodor (2005), *Minima Moralia: Reflections on a Damaged Life*, trans. E. F. N. Jephcott [1974], London: Verso.

Beckett, Samuel (2009), *The Letters of Samuel Beckett*, Vol. I, 1929–1940, eds. Martha Dow Fehsenfeld and Lois More Overbeck, Cambridge: Cambridge UP.

Beckett, Samuel (2006), 'What Where' in Paul Auster, ed., *The Grove Centenary Edition Volume 3: Dramatic Works*, New York: Grove P.

Beiser, Frederick C. (2008), *Schiller as Philosopher*, Oxford: Oxford UP.

Burrows, Rachel (1989), 'Interview with Rachel Burrows', with S. E. Gontarski, Dougald McMillan and Martha Fehsenfeld, *JOBS*, 11–12, pp. 1–15.

Büttner, Gottfried (1999), 'Samuel Beckett as a Modern Initiate' in Bruce Stewart, ed., *Beckett and Beyond*, Gerrards Cross: Colin Smythe, pp. 42–52.

Connor, Steven (1988), *Samuel Beckett: Repetition, Theory and Text*, Oxford: Basil Blackwell.

Cronin, Anthony (1996), *Samuel Beckett: The Last Modernist*, New York: Harper Collins.

Deleuze, Gilles (1998), 'The Exhausted' in *Essays Critical and Clinical*, trans. Anthony Uhlmann, London: Verso, pp. 152–74.

Esslin, Martin (2006), 'On his debt to Joyce' in James and Elizabeth Knowlson, eds., *Beckett Remembering/Remembering Beckett: A Centenary Celebration*, New York: Arcade Publishing, pp. 47–9.

Graver, Lawrence, and Raymond Federman, eds. (1997), *Samuel Beckett: The Critical Heritage*, London: Routledge and Kegan Ltd.

Knowlson, James (1996), *Damned to Fame: The Life of Samuel Beckett*, New York: Grove P.

Lamport, Francis (2005), 'Schiller and Euripides: The Translations of 1788 and Schiller's Later Plays', *German Life and Letters*, 58: 3, pp. 247–70.

Maude, Ulrika (2008), '"Hint of Jugular and Cords": Beckett and Modern Medicine', *SBT/A*, 19: *Borderless Beckett/Beckett sans frontières: Tokyo 2006*, pp. 281–91.

McMullan, Anna (2010), *Performing Embodiment in Samuel Beckett's Drama*, New York: Routledge.

Nietzsche, Friedrich (1967), *The Birth of Tragedy and the Case of Wagner*, trans. Walter Kaufmann, New York: Vintage.

Nixon, Mark (2010), 'Chronology of Beckett's Journey to Germany 1936–37', *JOBS*, 19: 2, pp. 245–72.

Nixon, Mark (2011), *Beckett's German Diaries 1936–1937*, London: Continuum.

Pearce, Damien (2008), 'Actor slits his own throat as knife switch turns fiction into reality' in *The Guardian*, 11 December 2008. http://www.guardian.co.uk/world/2008/dec/11/actor-slits-throat, accessed 25 February 2016.

Robertson, John G. (1902), *A History of German Literature*, New York: G. P. Putnam's Sons.

Schiller, Friedrich (2006), *Mary Stuart*, trans. Joseph Mellish, *Project Gutenberg*, 26 October, 2006, available online at: http://www.gutenberg.org/files/6791/6791-h/6791-h.htm.

Schiller, Friedrich (1967), *On the Aesthetic Education of Man in a Series of Letters*, trans. Elizabeth A. Wilkinson and L. A. Willoughby, Oxford: Clarendon P.

Sharpe, Lesley (1995), *Schiller's Aesthetic Essays: Two Centuries of Criticism*, Columbia, SC: Camden House.

Sharpe, Lesley (1991), *Schiller: Drama, Thought and Politics*, Oxford: Oxford UP.

Tilghman, Benjamin R. (1991), *Wittgenstein, Ethics and Aesthetics: The View from Eternity*, Albany, NY: SUNY P.

PART 4

Cinematic Voices

Filmic Perspectives in Speaker's Narrative of *A Piece of Monologue*

Mariko Hori Tanaka

Abstract

A Piece of Monologue is a short play by Beckett, which vocalises the filmic gaze through Speaker's narrating voice, as if the camera eye structured the account of an old man resembling him. The story begins with long shots and medium shots that give us an objective observation of the old man's room and his actions, but as the play unfolds, we perceive close-ups of the old man's body parts that would make us lose our sense of wholeness, remain suspended and feel dislocated. Beckett utilises close-ups to infuse the spectator with a sense of the uncanny through the bodiless, ghostly protagonist. He also employs unusual camera angles and framings to convey the protagonist's inner torment. This essay aims to explore how early film theories and camera techniques are reflected in the filmic perspectives in Speaker's narrative of *A Piece of Monologue*, effectively structuring a dramatic text by illustrating the 'profounds of mind' (Beckett, 448) of the old man.

A Piece of Monologue is a monodrama in the sense that an actor standing still on stage gives a long monologue; however, this is more of a set of stage directions for his action, as Kristin Morrison claims that the narration 'sound[s] like the stage directions of a play' (351). Nevertheless, no action narrated in 'the stage directions' takes place on stage, even though Speaker, the onstage character, resembles the protagonist depicted in his narrative.[1] If what looks like stage direction is not meant for an actual theatre performance, what is it aimed for? Considering that it is vocalised by Speaker who faces the audience,

---

1 Morrison says that 'the speaker tells a "story" of a man so much like himself that it is clear he is simply speaking of himself in the third person' (349), adding in her note that '[t]his similarity between speaker and subject is sharply emphasized in actual production' (354). C. J. Ackerley and S. E. Gontarski, however, warn us not to simply accept the parallel of the narrator and the figure in the narrative: 'To confuse the stage image, the present theatrical moment, with the narrative or fragments of memory is to miss the point' (437). Jane Alison Hale lists up multiple roles of Speaker as 'not only the chronicler, but also the actor, director, and spectator of the character he presents to our eyes, ears, and imagination' (114).

it is directed to them: it is the audience members who listen to him, follow his directions and create the images he describes.

Indeed, Speaker's narrative resembles more a film or a television script than the stage direction of a play, as has been pointed out by many critics. Rosemary Pountney, for example, finds 'a set for television, seen through a camera lens' in such a description as '[w]hite foot of pallet edge of frame stage left' (214), while Anna McMullan remarks that funeral scenes in the narrative are 'short film sequences' (2010, 112). Sarah West goes further by arguing that 'this short play aspires to being screened rather than staged' (177). West even emphasises how Speaker's monologue is close to film or television as 'Speaker's elliptical descriptions often sound like written stage directions read aloud, and his use of terms associated with film or television further distance [sic] the audience from a theatrical experience' (177).

Like the description in a film script, every 'direction' Speaker gives vocally is a photographic or filmic image as if shot by the camera, working as a set of instructions for the creation of a film. Every action portraying the old man — the protagonist in Speaker's narrative — is seen through the camera eye. Thus, every line spoken by Speaker projects filmic images with various movements, as if intended to be part of a film script, and each vocalised image is transmitted to the spectators' minds. Particularly, Speaker's language projects scenic images onto their 'mental screens'.

Thus, the spectators, listening to Speaker's narration, create images in their minds from his words and feel as if watching filmed and edited scenes full of movements, despite the onstage figure standing still and speaking in a monotone. The sensation is not only created by the way the narrative manoeuvres spectators into film viewers, but also comes from the way Speaker stands immobile in front of them, as if playing the role of a projector — a machine that projects filmic images.

With the immobility of Speaker, who resembles the subject in his narrative, the spectators concentrate on his narration and follow the movements of the visual images embedded in it. The play thus requires the audience's concentration as they listen to Speaker's voice, simultaneously projecting his narration in their minds.

Utilising the camera eye in Speaker's narrative, which functions as a tool to evoke mental images in the spectators, Beckett, who challenged the limit of language, must have found a way to depict something difficult to describe with words, as he was aware of the effects of what Béla Balázs calls 'poetic montage':

> Very deep subconscious idea-associations can emerge or be touched off by such editing [poetic montage]. [...] Such effects are certainly not 'liter-

ary', for no words can convey this non-rational correlation of shapes and images which take place in our subconscious mind. (1931, 126)

What Beckett does in this piece of work is to depict such 'shapes and images' — perhaps personal trauma[2] — within human subconsciousness through the filmic perspective of the camerawork.

This work thus demonstrates Beckett's understanding of the camera as a tool to investigate the mind and of the camera lens perspective to show its depth, that is, what he calls 'profounds of mind' in *Ohio Impromptu* (Beckett, 448). His understanding of how it works derives from his readings of early film theories on black and white silent films. Indeed, the images evoked in the viewers' minds will be black and white, which are referred to on and off in the play with their variation — the colour of grey. The contrast of light and darkness mentioned in the play also reminds its spectators of silent film.

This essay aims to explore how early film theories and camera techniques are effectively utilised in the descriptions of Speaker's narrative in *A Piece of Monologue*, which voices its protagonist's inner torment and affects the theatre audience who, like film viewers, visualise it in their minds through film-like images that a camera lens would create.

1 The Audience as Film Viewers

Although the filmic perspectives detected in Speaker's narrative of *A Piece of Monologue* remind us of the early film theories and camera techniques that Beckett was familiar with, the narrative does not consist of mere 'stage directions' or 'film text'; instead, this is a poetic stage piece that is meant for the theatre audience to listen to with the hope that the narrated images of a ghost — an old man in limbo — will appear in their minds. In that sense, the play is the 'doubling of media' (Connor, 148), 'surpassing theatre's boundaries' (West, 177).

The audience watching this play are manipulated as film viewers through the focus on Speaker's poetic language, as well as Figure, who stands still on

---

2 *A Piece of Monologue* is a play describing personal trauma of the protagonist in Speaker's narrative, grasped from such descriptions as the surprise at a funeral scene and the enigmatic 'rip word' (Beckett, 429). Morrison explains that the 'rip word' 'reveals what is hidden, the unpleasant or discreditable truth which may be disguised or submerged but never completely evaded' (349). The protagonist has suffered from 'the birth trauma and the pain' (Feldman, 112) and is now suffering from 'the fear of dying' (Homan, 217).

stage. Unlike a usual theatre piece, no action occurs on stage; the only movement glimpsed is his mouth spewing words as Mouth does in *Not I*, though, unlike Mouth, the audience are able to see his still body and whole face with his cheeks and eyes moving on and off. Nothing else moves; it is almost like watching a tableau, although we hear an actor's deep voice narrating fragmented stories of an old man. Stories are not narrated in an ordinary sense, but rather as sequences of photographic images.

What Speaker illustrates here is an old man, who is dying in the room where he was born, repeating the routine he has followed in the last segments of his life; he is leaning towards the windowpane beyond which the darkness spreads, standing in the room, lighting an oil lamp with matches, facing a wall, remembering the day he was born or when the wall had many family pictures that he had later torn to shreds and thrown onto the floor, and imagining someone's funeral scene. Since nothing is acted on stage, an attentive audience is expected to follow Speaker's words and imagine what is going on in the narrative, i.e. what the old man is doing and contemplating. This ideally happens not via the will of the spectator but via the vocal power of the narrative. The ideal spectator ought to feel as if they were hearing the narration against their will.

Although almost nothing moves on stage, the content of the narrative is full of filmic movements. As if filmed by a camera, it shifts from a long shot to a medium shot or to a close-up, or from a fade-in to a fade-out. The audience keeps busy listening to Speaker's voice and following the narrated images as they are evoked in their minds. The static onstage figure not only helps the audience imagine what is going on in the narrative, but also 'prints' the old man's image onto their minds even after he is gone at the end of the play. This approach echoes nineteenth-century photography in which subjects had to be still for a long time without stirring. The onstage standing figure, then, resembles an object of a camera, and one could only imagine how torturous it must be for them to be it, sensing an unseen camera's voyeuristic and controlling power and consequently feel discomfort upon looking at them.

Thus, as in many other Beckett plays, both the actor and the viewers share the pain of being an object, and it is this pain that the actor conveys in *A Piece of Monologue* by playing the role of an old man who, like the figure in the narrative, stands facing the wall of his room (which is also the fourth wall, allowing him to face the audience), and giving fragmented episodes of the man. Nevertheless, the actor does not use the first person 'I' but the third person 'he'. Just like Mouth in *Not I*, Speaker objectifies the story of the old man, sometimes assuming the perspectives of both the film director and the playwright. Moreover, like Mouth, he resembles a machine that spews words, helping generate filmic images in the minds of the spectators as if he were a film projector. The filmic images of the old man in the narration are then projected by Speaker, a character played by an actor, who conveys them to the audience.

2 Close-ups and Fading Effects

The narrative of Speaker in *A Piece of Monologue* may seem to be repetitive at first sight, but it has variations and changes. The narrative begins with the story of 'he', the third person, whose every action is narrated in the way he is performing it with his will at first, that is, in the way he is a subject in the narrative.[3]

The story opens humourously with the image of a man whose life was a 'fiasco' from the beginning, being tossed 'from mammy to nanny and back' (Beckett, 425) and who, 'ghastly grinning' (425), waits for 'the lid [of his coffin] to come' (425). The opening key sentence, 'Birth was the death of him' (425), suggests that Speaker narrates it derisively, distancing his own life by using the third person.[4]

The sentence gets shortened next when we hear the same comment again: 'Birth the death of him' (Beckett, 427). Then, only 'Birth' is repeated a couple of times later, but accompanied the description of how the word is spewed from his mouth: 'Waits for first word always the same. It gathers in his mouth. Parts lips and thrusts tongue forward. Birth' (428); or 'Stands there staring beyond waiting for first word. It gathers in his mouth. Birth. Parts lips and thrusts tongue between them. Tip of tongue. Feel soft touch of tongue on lips. Of lips on tongue' (428). It is as if a camera is shooting a mouth of the old man in close-up. It is, however, a very unusual close-up, that is used in silent films: 'the lips are no longer word-forming physical organs but a means of visual expression — the distortion of an excited mouth or the fast chatter of lips are not mere by-products of talking' (Arnheim, 1957, 110). Dialogue in silent films

---

3   The third person subject, however, is eliminated in most of the sentence, so that, from the beginning of the play, Beckett 'succeeds in reducing linguistic representation to a minimum when the individual is cut off from social reality and allowing other forms of representation to become more manifest, such as gesture and lighting' (Besbes, 138).

4   The phrase 'be the death of' (Cohn says it is 'an Irish cliché of casual conversation', 356) is often used hyperbolically or humorously when something or someone makes someone laugh to death, so that not only his birth was the beginning of his death — the recurrent theme of Beckett — but the protagonist 'he' cannot believe that he was born and alive up until his death.

does not have to be shown by the real movement of lips. It does not have to coordinate with 'the proper pronunciation of sounds', because 'the actor in the silent film spoke in a way intelligible to the eyes, not the ears. He could do this precisely because he had no need to speak in a manner intelligible to the ear' (Balázs, 1931, 68–9). Therefore, the close-up of the movement of a mouth in *A Piece of Monologue* may look grotesque on the viewer's imagined screen.

Another silent film technique regarding the expression of a sound Beckett employs is the depiction of a cry. There are cries mentioned by Speaker in the course of the play; for example, 'Faint cry in his ear. Mouth agape. Closed with hiss of breath. Lips joined. Feel soft touch of lip on lip. Lip lipping lip. Then parted by cry as before' (428). A cry is not represented as a sound but rather recognised from the shape of mouth. Such description of the cry reveals the 'painful process of birth' and 'the anguish of perceivedness' (Hale, 125).

The emotional pain of the man is conveyed by another magic dimension of Beckett. That is, the 'cry' is announced before the mouth movement is recounted. It is as if we are watching a silent film in which titles are projected before their speaking images are shown. While emphasising the difficulty of inserting captions in silent films, Balázs praises 'a particularly subtle technique [...] of using titles to frame images of particular significance': 'Scenes focusing on facial expressions are emphasized *and named* by titles, much like particular stanzas in a poem or chapter headings in a novel. They are memorable and provide emphasis, like a succinct quotation from a poem' (2010, 75; italics original). The 'cry' can be emphasised by being 'named' before the actual mouth movement and thus gives an effect of 'a poem'. Through such poetic emphasis of a cry, the spectator may feel that he hears the old man's moan of pain.

Now, let us return to other descriptions of the old man in *A Piece of Monologue*, in which the camera lens moves from a long shot to a close-up. Let us observe his actions in the room:

> Gropes to window and stares out. Stands there staring out. [...] Gropes back in the end to where the lamp is standing. Was standing. When last went out. Loose matches in right-hand pocket. Strikes one on his buttock the way his father taught him. Takes off milk white globe and sets it down. Match goes out. Strikes a second as before. Takes off chimney. Smoke-clouded. Holds it in left hand. Match goes out. Strikes a third as before and sets it to wick. Puts back chimney. Match goes out. Puts back globe. (425–6)

The action of the man standing by the window and lighting an oil lamp is illustrated objectively so that the spectators may imagine him doing his routine work in a kind of long shot that 'includes the whole of everything that is relevant to the particular total situation' (Arnheim, 1957, 77). As the narration goes on, however, the same action loses 'the whole of everything'. His whole movement is explained by a series of close-up shots on each part of his body:

> Eyes to the small pane gaze at that first night. Turn from it in the end to face the darkened room. There in the end slowly a faint hand. Holding aloft a lighted spill. In the light of spill faintly the hand and milkwhite globe. Then second hand. In light of spill. Takes off globe and disappears. Reappears empty. Takes off chimney. Two hands and chimney in light of spill. Spill to wick. Chimney back on. Hand with spill disappears. Second hand disappears. Chimney alone in gloom. Hand reappears with globe. Globe back on. (427)

Here the man's body is split as parts — 'eyes', 'hand' and 'second hand' — and shot separately. Although the spectators can surmise the man's whole routine action from the earlier portrayal, they lose their desire for unity when the sense of wholeness is gone. The role of the close-up is to '[help] the artist give an enlargement of something which would not be obvious as a mere detail of a long shot [...] but it also takes some characteristic feature out of the whole' (Arnheim, 1957, 79). The close-up is a snippet cut out of the whole, so that if the sense of wholeness is gone, the feeling of inequilibrium can arise in the viewers. 'Parts may represent the whole', continues Rudolf Arnheim, 'suspense may be created by leaving what is important or remarkable out of the picture' (81). Thus the viewers will be suspended and feel dislocated in watching close-up scenes. In the scene above, the spectators may even sense the power of a camera controlling its objects — human body parts. Human will power is thereby diminished. 'Eyes', 'hand' and 'second hand' are turned into objects as are other things such as 'globe' and 'chimney'.

Moreover, the same action the old man does later has simplified descriptions: 'Eyes glued to pane. As if looking his last. Turns away at last and gropes through faint unaccountable light to unseen lamp. White gown moving through that gloom. Once white' (428). Here we get an impression of his body being lost. Only 'white gown' is moving through darkness. The impression of his bodilessness becomes stronger when his attire is explained as 'White hair catching light. White gown. White socks' (429). He thus becomes bodiless as the play unfolds, but his head is somehow not lost. His head 'almost touching wall' (429) is mentioned even if his body is lost: 'Stock still head haught staring beyond' (429). His head and his eyes 'staring beyond' being prominent, we get the feeling that his mind is working while his body is gone.

The audience here may be convinced that this man is dying or almost dead. We acknowledge that his body is lost and his senses are lost, too. He sees 'none from window' (425) and hears 'none' (426), though he questions that nothing is seen and heard by saying 'no such thing as none' (425, 426) and 'No such thing as no light' (427). Now that he is in limbo, he sees and hears nothing, but he thinks he is still alive in the room. He strives to see and hear something as every living human being does.

He is also eager to see beyond the wall. Beyond the wall, however, would be hell, as Hamm mockingly says 'Old wall! Beyond is the... other hell' in *Endgame* (104). In *A Piece of Monologue*, Speaker reveals that nothing but ghosts stirs beyond the wall: 'Nothing stirring. Faintly stirring. Thirty thousand nights of ghosts beyond. Beyond that black beyond. Ghost light. Ghost nights. Ghost rooms. Ghost graves. Ghost' (429). And beyond the wall (the fourth wall) in front of Speaker sit the audience. Thus, the audience members become ghosts. The old man's fate of death is generalised as the destiny of all human beings. The play ends with 'the globe alone' (429) twice said, though even 'alone' is 'gone' (429) with a blackout. Only the 'globe', the earth, inhabited by no one, might be suggested here, a chilly ending of the human species.[5]

At the end of the play, the man, the ghost, who is 'staring beyond' in complete darkness, does not notice the light going with the word. He loses all of his senses in the deepening of darkness. The darkness in the play deepens as a camera reduces the aperture or lighting fades out in the theatre. Speaker onstage, however, 'remains "barely visible in diffuse light", but still there. [...] Now he stresses its continued presence in the room, and the figure of Speaker is seen by the audience still to be there within it. This seems to make the close of the play a continuum rather than an ending' (Pountney, 217). Speaker will continue to narrate the story of an old man dying and going as far as the theatre, the Shakespearean 'globe', exists. Human species might be extinct from this merciless world, but their ghosts hover in limbo. In film, 'by the fades and dissolves projected on to the screen the camera in fact shows us invisible things' (Balázs, 1931, 144–5). Beckett makes use of 'the fades and dissolves' fully at the end of the play. As mentioned in the previous section, the static onstage figure can 'print' the old man's image on the audience's

---

5 'The earth inhabited by no one' is referred to in Beckett's work as a metaphor or its background. *Endgame* and *Happy Days* are set in a world where no human being survives other than the characters on the stage. In *Krapp's Last Tape*, the phrase 'The earth might be uninhabited' (221, 223) reverberates from the tape, figuratively describing the silence at midnight.

minds even after he is gone, helping them to imagine that the man is really a ghost.⁶

Shadow and darkness in film symbolise something 'uncanny, dangerous, and evil' (Arnheim, 1997, 59). Something 'uncanny' hidden behind ordinary life would be death. Shadow and darkness are often symbolically used in Beckett. Cathal Quinn, director of Mouth on Fire, a Dublin-based theatre company, made huge silhouettes of Speaker and arranged the lamp to stand out sharply on the stage's back wall in his direction of *A Piece of Monologue*.⁷ In his Tokyo production, the silhouettes reflected on the wall were so large, almost touching the ceiling, that the actor standing downstage almost looked as if he had been swallowed by his own shadow. Shadows had an overpowering presence while live objects — both the old man and the lamp — lost their presence. Thus, the audience was led to sense the shadowy presence of Speaker more than ever. In this production, the afterimage of the silhouetted Speaker, rather than that of Speaker onstage, was left in the audience's mind in the last fade-out so that the body reflected on the wall as a shadow strengthened the absence of the man, the bodiless ghost in the play.

3 Film Montage

Although the narrative of *A Piece of Monologue* evokes many visual images of the close-up, it also utilises the merits of long and medium shots. The atmosphere of the room is conveyed from the illustration of how an old man stands on the sets and in which direction he faces in every action he does. We are informed that the room has a window, a wall, a bed, as well as a lamp with the same height as Speaker.

All those sets are not just a backdrop of the stage figure. Each set claims its presence, as in Japanese woodblock print. Sergei Eisenstein stresses that the film montage is composed similarly to Japanese woodblock print:

> You have a branch of a cherry tree or a landscape with a sailing boat. From this whole the pupil cuts out compositional units: a square, a circle, a rectangle. He creates a shot! [...] The other method, used by the

---

6 A second image that is not clear on television is called 'ghost' or 'ghosting' which happens when an image is displayed for a long time on CRT (cathode-ray tube) display. Beckett might have expected the spectators to have such a 'ghosting' effect.

7 Mouth on Fire's *A Piece of Monologue* was performed in Samuel Beckett Working Group meeting in Southampton in 2012 and at Theater X(Cai) in Tokyo in 2014.

Japanese, is that of 'capturing' with the camera, using it to organise. Cutting out a fragment of reality by means of the lens. (147–8)

A camera usually shoots everything clearly and in detail. Japanese woodblock print is composed of an assemblage of fragmented parts painted in detail and merges square canvases together in one picture. This account by Eisenstein must have intrigued Beckett, who was deeply interested in geometry.[8] In his television play *Ghost Trio*, he had the camera take every square set — a window, a door, a bed, and a wall — and then exposed them within a square television screen. Again in *A Piece of Monologue*, its narrative voice calls our attention to square sets: the window, the wall, and the bed, though their contours are not clear in this play. The window loses its frame in the darkness while only the white foot of pallet bed is visible. The wall the old man faces is also frameless; he stares beyond it as if he can go through it. The square pictures that used to be on the wall are all gone to pieces, thus emphasising the framelessness.

If the actor speaking the narrative on stage overlaps with the protagonist in his speech, the stage sets can be the sets referred to in the narration. However, what we see on stage are an actor who looks like a protagonist, an electric (not an oil) lamp, and the foot of the pallet bed. There are no square sets: no window, no bed as a whole, and no wall (apart from Cathal Quinn's directorial piece, the back wall of the stage is usually unseen in darkness). Therefore, no frame of them is seen on stage.

Moreover, Speaker 'stands well off centre downstage audience left' and the lamp with the 'same level, same height' stands 'two metres to his left', off centre as well, while the white foot of pallet bed is 'visible extreme right' (425). Nothing is in the centre and there is no focal point. Even the human figure is in parallel with a lamp as if the lamp is his double, as McMullan rightly says: 'The objectification of the body is accentuated through the direct parallel with the inanimate lamp which is of the same height and size as the speaker and whose globe is compared to a skull' (1993, 62).

This kind of objectification of the body is often seen in silent film. Balázs comments that in silent film, objects have the same quality as human beings:

> [O]bjects are not degraded or diminished [...] but *share with human beings a quality of silence* that makes the two almost homogenous, and

---

8 Eisenstein calls the photographic nature of a Japanese woodblock print as 'the *framelessness* of a Japanese impressionistic drawing' (211; emphasis added), which he thinks is ideal for cinema.

hence enhances the mute object's vitality and significance. Since it does not speak less than human beings, it says just as much. (2010, 23: italics original)

It might be suggested that Beckett learned his precise arrangement of objects and bodies through silent film. This is again a characteristic of a Japanese woodblock print, which has no central focal point.

Beckett also creates the visual difference of speed and tempo by using fragmented sentences and unique arrangements of words, as tempo is added in arrangements of words in poetry. When sentences are shortened in the play as the body of the man gets fragmented, they give us an impression of speedy successions of edited cuts of a film that accelerates our pulses. Balázs calls our attention to the inner expression that the rhythm of montage provides: 'Close-up shots of the scene may [...] be speeded up, rushed along in a galloping tempo in order that the external rhythm of the picture movement may convey to us the internal storms, the quiverings of internal tension' (1931, 130–1).

In the next section, let us discuss how 'the internal storms', in other words, inner conflicts within the old man in *A Piece of Monologue*, are portrayed in the use of uncommon filmic shots.

4 Unusual Camera Angles and Framings

The inner conflicts of the old man in *A Piece of Monologue* are shown when his most traumatic memory comes back. It returns as a flashback scene, and film is the most suitable media to depict it. Beckett, aware of that, makes the best use of film techniques, particularly unusual camera angles and framings, to render the old man's inner conflicts.

Although things are frameless in the dark room in this play (as is discussed above) and even the family pictures that used to be 'pinned to wall' were 'unframed' (426), the images in the eyes of the old man's mind that Speaker narrates and conveys to the audience are framed as photographs or filmed shots. As if reminding us of the existence of a camera, he refers to the frame of a shot: 'Foot of pallet just visible edge of frame' (427) and 'Coffin out of frame' (428). The latter coffin, however, comes into view when the same scene is mentioned next: a coffin, which is 'out of frame' in the former scene, is seen moving 'on its way' (429) within a frame.

The character in *A Piece of Monologue* sees in his mind framed images of a funeral scene. Underlining this is the author's artistic desire to frame it but at the same time to create the whole, which, however, both the author Beckett and his character find difficult. It is almost impossible to provide a sense of wholeness, especially with regard to the traumatic event represented as a funeral. Shots of a funeral are incomplete, and non-unified parts are framed as filmed shots. The character's shock and surprise are conveyed from the unusual angle of their viewpoints as well as from the utterance of Speaker: 'Which loved one('s)?' 'He?' (428, 429).

The funeral scene is first viewed as 'Seen from above' (428), but next as 'Seen from on high' (429). The former scene is presented as if taken as a close-up while the latter scene as a medium or long shot, but both are taken from above. It is an unusual camera angle. As Balázs emphasises, '[t]he angle is what gives all things their shape' (1931, 47), it is a very important element in film. 'A sudden change of angle', says Balázs, 'renders the most commonplace thing strange. This feels like an unmasking, suggesting the eye's ability to sense the invisible' (2010, 118). Especially '[a]n unusual camera angle', which not only can 'characteriz[e] the object in a particular sense', but also 'introduc[e] an attractive element of surprise by the unexpected shapes which a familiar object can assume' (Arnheim, 1957, 42).

An unusual camera angle suggested in the funeral scene thus corresponds with the sudden shock of the old man who encounters it, sensing 'the invisible'. His surprise is emphasised by the strange camera angle. From Speaker's depiction quoted above, it is uncertain whose funeral it is.[9] Whoever it is to be buried in the empty grave, the old man's response to the scene clearly has a tone of surprise or shock. When the scene is gone, he sees the 'dark whole' (428, 429). He then repeats, 'No. No such thing as whole' (428, 429). Wholeness is something that he cannot accept, just as he does not accept his situation of being surrounded by no sound and nothing in view, that is, in deep darkness. 'Whole' is also the homonym of 'hole'. The old man in darkness sees an empty hole in the ground of the funeral scene, but he does not conceive of it as his own grave, though it might be, as some critics surmise (See footnote 9). Adhering to his belief that he is not dead, he is not willing to sacrifice his life just to comprehend the world around him. The (w)hole is an unknown darkness

---

9 There is a great amount of debate about whose funeral it is. H. Porter Abbott writes, 'the funeral scene three times' corresponds with 'the three individuals who have been specified as gone or going: father, mother, speaker' (153–4). It may be appropriate to presume that the funeral of a beloved would be his mother's if we think of Beckett's feeling of guilt towards her and being born. But assuming that it resembles Hamlet's encounter with Ophelia's funeral, the model of the loved one could be Beckett's former sweetheart, Peggy Sinclair, whose death must have been his lifelong trauma (See Hori). It is quite possible to surmise from the way the old man is surprised that it might be his own funeral in the near future as Morrison (352–3) and McMullan (1993, 69) suggest.

that a dead man enters after he dies. His 'fear of dying' (Homan, 217) shuns his acceptance of the 'whole', which is also the world for the dead 'beyond the wall'. He as a ghost clings to the 'faint diffuse light' (Beckett, 425) sustaining the last bits of life in him, the 'profounds of mind', perhaps as long as the 'globe' exists.

From early film theories, the notion of the 'whole' is a central issue in film making. While framing 'is the art of choosing the parts of all kinds which became part of a set' (Deleuze, 22), montage, the 'assemblage of movement-images as constituting an indirect image of time' (34), is 'the determination of the whole by means of continuities, cutting and false continuities' (33). Beckett, linking his quest for an artistic unity with film making, might have attempted to frame the images in his narrative and to assemble them and determine the whole, though he, like the protagonist, finds it an impossible attempt. As Gilles Deleuze calls it 'false continuities', contending that only a camera lens can frame the environment and mould the 'whole'.

The author's unfulfilled attempt to frame the whole is thus metaphorically manifested in the old man's denial of the (w)hole and the impossibility to see the dead 'beyond the wall'.

5 Conclusion

Beckett thus used silent film theories and camera techniques in Speaker's narration in *A Piece of Monologue* to express the protagonist's indescribable inner torment, helping theatre audience film viewers grasp it. While the close-ups on a body part make it possible to create a grotesque shot where the sense of the whole body is absent, the protagonist's inner shock or surprise emerges from framing and unique camera angles. As Balázs writes, '[i]n the film, every occurrence [...] is made interesting and exciting by close-ups of detail and rhythm of cutting' (1931, 131), what makes the static play 'interesting and exciting' is the filmic camera movements, particularly the 'close-ups of detail and rhythm of cutting' in the narrative.

When Speaker, reminding us of the key terms used in early film theories, says 'No such thing as whole' (428, 429), 'No such thing as none' (425, 426), or 'No such thing as no light' (427), he is claiming that the protagonist is not dead yet. But, at the same time, these derisive comments might be the author's critical comment on film. Film is an art that projects illusions on the screen. It seeks the whole yet cuts out a part of it by using framing. At least in early silent film, there is no sound and a slice of life is projected onto the screen, which is white and 'none', that is, zero. Although Beckett uses language through Speaker's voice, it functions as 'poetic montage' in film, projecting scenic images on the white 'screen' of the spectators' minds.

Works Cited

Abbott, H. Porter (1996), *Beckett Writing Beckett: The Author in the Autograph*, Ithaca, New York: Cornell UP.
Ackerley, C. J. and Gontarski, S. E. eds. (2006), *The Faber Companion to Samuel Beckett*, London: Faber and Faber.
Arnheim, Rudolf (1957), *Film as Art*, Berkeley: U of California P.
Arnheim, Rudolf (1997), *Film Essays and Criticism*, trans. Brenda Benthien, Madison: U of Wisconsin P.
Balázs, Béla (1931), *Theory of the Film*, trans. Edith Bone, London: Dennis Dobson.
Balázs, Béla (2010), *Early Film Theory: Visible Man and the Spirit of Film*, ed. Erica Carter, trans. Rodney Livingstone, New York: Berghahn Books.
Beckett, Samuel (1986), *The Complete Dramatic Works*, London: Faber and Faber.
Besbes, Khaled (2007), *The Semiotics of Beckett's Theatre: A Semiotic Study of the Complete Dramatic Works of Samuel Beckett*, Boca Raton, Florida: Universal Publishers.
Cohn, Ruby (2001), *A Beckett Canon*, Ann Arbor: U of Michigan P.
Connor, Steven (1988), *Samuel Beckett: Repetition, Theory and Text*, Oxford: Basil Blackwell.
Deleuze, Gilles (2013), *Cinema I: The Movement-Image*, trans. Hugh Tomlinson and Barbara Habberjam, London: Bloomsbury.
Eisenstein, Sergei (1988), *S. M. Eisenstein Selected Works, Vol. I: Writings, 1922–1934*, ed. and trans. Richard Taylor, London: BFI Publishing.
Feldman, Matthew (2006), *Beckett's Books: A Cultural History of Samuel Beckett's 'Interwar Notes'*, London: Continuum.
Hale, Jane Alison (1987), *The Broken Window: Beckett's Dramatic Perspective*, West Lafayette, Indiana: Purdue UP.
Homan, Sidney (1984), *Beckett's Theaters: Interpretations for Performance*, Lewisburg: Bucknell UP.
Hori, Mariko (2014), 'Beckett's Struggle with His Traumatic Memories', *The Economic Review*, 6, Institute of Economic Research, Aoyama Gakuin University, pp. 1–20.
McMullan, Anna (1993), *Theatre on Trial: Samuel Beckett's Later Drama*, London: Routledge.
McMullan, Anna (2010), *Performing Embodiment in Samuel Beckett's Drama*, London: Routledge.
Morrison, Kristin (1982), 'The Rip Word in *A Piece of Monologue*', *Modern Drama*, 1:1, pp. 349–54.

Pountney, Rosemary (1988), *Theatre of Shadows: Samuel Beckett's Drama 1956–1976*, Gerrards Cross: Colin Smythe.

West, Sarah (2010), *Say It: The Performative Voice in the Dramatic Works of Samuel Beckett*, Amsterdam: Rodopi.

Cinematic Adaptations of Beckett's *Breath*

Anna Sigg

Abstract

Beckett's *Breath*, which focuses on bodily sounds and amplified recordings of breaths and screams, gives up plot and language to represent traumatic pain. The birth cry, in particular, has been interpreted in various different ways, and it has often been associated with the trauma of birth, which may instigate a secondary cycle of ongoing trauma — the trauma of existence. The original primary trauma, which *Breath* seems to articulate, may remain inaccessible and unknowable. However, if 'held breath' in the cinematic adaptations can bring about an engaged silence emanating from the listener, the potential trauma, which that silence represents, can arguably also be temporarily 'held' and contained. I compare four productions of the play available on video, a production by the National Theatre School Canada from 2008, an Arsonist Production from 2007, the 'Beckett on Film' version directed by Damien Hirst, and a German performance directed by Gerd Conradt from 2009. The most politically engaged performance is the Brechtian production directed by Conradt. Although it is a misinterpretation of the play in that it does not closely follow the text's script, it asks the spectator to get involved by articulating a 'countervoice' of refusal. Instead of having an actual actor perform the play, the director asks the audience to perform the *objet a* voice of trauma (the breaths and cries) themselves. By making the collective 'body' of the audience the 'actor' in the play, the trauma appears less isolating, and through its synchronisation and repetition, the countervoice conveys agency.

1 Introduction

How does Beckett articulate and respond to pain, pain that cannot be expressed through language? In his short plays, he uses the body as a voice in order to speak back to pain, suffering, and arguably also trauma — even if the origin of that trauma may remain inaccessible. In *Breath*, the most minimalist of his plays, Beckett completely gives up plot and language as a means to represent pain. Instead, the 'unspeakable' is conveyed through various layers of mediation that provide the necessary distance to access and process pain. On the page, the stage, and the screen, *Breath* relies almost exclusively on amplified, dramatised breaths and screams to represent the traces of meaning that remain. I will compare four cinematic adaptations of the play to the dramatic text itself, a filmed production by the National Theatre School Canada from 2008,[1] an Arsonist Production from 2007,[2] the 'Beckett on Film' version directed by Damien Hirst, starring the voice of Keith Allen,[3] and a German production directed by Gerd Conradt from 2009.[4]

It seems that the body on stage and screen both literally and figuratively 'screams back' to pain by emitting an engaged countervoice of agency that is shared with the audience. The audience and viewers take on the performative role of the silent — and sometimes not so silent — therapist, while the body, too, stares back at the audience in much the same way a trauma therapist stares back at their patient in silence. Depending on the performance and cinematic adaptation, the spectators and viewers can thus assume the role of the therapist or end up traumatised and 'contaminated' themselves. In both cases, resolving or releasing the pain is attempted through the broken, fragmented voice of the body. In other words, the body does not simply 'perform' audible symptoms of pain; in fact, the voice it emits on screen exerts a kind of resistance: a countervoice articulating a sound of agency. Mladen Dolar states that 'the voice is elusive, always changing, becoming, elapsing, with unclear contours, as opposed to the relative permanence, solidity, durability of the seen' (2006, 79). Indeed, the voice of traumatic pain in Beckett's minimalist short plays does not seem to emerge as a response to a specific event or entity; it is often inaccessible, porous and in a constant process of becoming.

Various post-traumatic symptoms and bodily articulations conveyed through these cinematic adaptations enable a response with distance on the part of the audience — and distance may lead to release, recovery, and agency. In other words, through these bodily countervoices, the mind accepts not only the sounds of its own bodily object voice, but also the avatar of the trauma of the real. This acceptance is certainly an alienating process because it reminds the subject of its own mortality. The act of witnessing oneself 'freeze', breathe, bleed, and live, or hearing sounds that only exist in one's head, is inherently disturbing and traumatic. It may be a reflection of the repressed 'original' trauma in a form of acoustic displacement, but this shift can turn into a positive form of release on both the stage and the screen and render trauma less

---

1 Beckett, Samuel (2007), 'Breath', Online video clip, *YouTube*, http://video.google.com/videoplay?docid=-8915465772259371796#, accessed 21 January, 2021.
2 Beckett, Samuel (2008), 'Breath', Online video clip, *YouTube*, http://www.youtube.com/watch?v=1rZ8xParVmE&feature=player_embedded#at=77, accessed 21 January, 2021.
3 Beckett, Samuel (2007), 'Breath', Online video clip, *YouTube*, http://www.youtube.com/watch?v=vw6HWwPEQm8, accessed 21 January, 2021.
4 Beckett, Samuel (2010), 'Breath', Online video clip, *YouTube*, http://www.youtube.com/watch?v=S2K9LAof064, accessed 21 January 2021.

overwhelming. Hence, this phenomenon allows the audience and video viewers to enter into a conversation with the traumatic pain Beckett articulates. Through the filter and mediation of the screen, Beckett's viewers can possibly 'contain', grasp and release the voice of trauma from the somewhat detached and safe distance of observer figures.

An analysis of the minimalist short plays, and *Breath* in particular, is most successful if examined in combination with Beckett's ideas on sound, the voice, silence and the role of acoustics. Beckett explains, in his letter to Axel Kaun dated 9 July 1937, that the means to speak back to traumatic pain must lie within the 'voice' of silence:

> more and more my own language appears to me like a veil that must be torn apart in order to get at the things [...] behind it. [...] Is there any reason why that terrible materiality of the word surface should not be capable of being dissolved, like for example the sound surface, torn by enormous pauses, of Beethoven's Seventh Symphony, so that through whole pages we can perceive nothing but a path of sounds suspended in giddy heights, linking unfathomable abysses of silence? [...] At first it can only be a matter of somehow finding a method by which we can represent this mocking attitude towards the word, through words. In this dissonance between the means and their use it will perhaps become possible to feel a whisper of that final music or that silence that underlies All. (1983b, 171–2)

The following quote by Walter Benjamin aptly explains what Beckett might have meant by 'this mocking attitude towards the word, through words'. Benjamin states: 'Was it not noticeable at the end of the war, that men returned from the battlefield grown silent — not richer but poorer in communicable experience?' (84). Of course, Benjamin most of all refers to the general breakdown of meaning and communication inherent in modern experience, but he also links it implicitly to the sonic traumas of war by invoking the concrete image of the battlefield. Indeed, the sonic traumas of the constant bombings that one experiences on a battlefield often lead to a person 'grown silent' — to hearing loss, tinnitus, and a form of 'muteness' to express the trauma through the realm of language. Traumatic pain can thus not be heard by listening to the words, as the traumatised subject's language often becomes alienating and foreign. However, the suffering can arguably be perceived by listening to the body. In fact, the more language fails to communicate trauma, the more one must listen to the bodily whispers behind the words to understand Beckett's oeuvre. It may be through this voice of silence, the body's own physical countervoice of silence, such as the simple sound of human breath, broken laughter, cries or disturbances of the voice, that Beckett attempts to both represent and transcend traumatic pain.

It seems that the visceral breaths and amplified primal cries of suffering — when mediated through a filter that the distance of the screen and cinematic adaptations provide — transform into a powerful, visceral countervoice of what can be understood as Lacan's *objet a*. Often referred to as 'object-cause of desire' (Žižek, 1989, 53), *objet a* is described as a leftover or placeholder, which also carries elements of wholeness. Žižek argues that it is 'objectively nothing, though, viewed from a certain perspective, it assumes the shape of something' (1991, 12). Lacan argues that '*objet a* is something from which the subject, in order to constitute itself, has separated itself off as organ' (1977, 103). More specifically, he relates *objet a* to the drives, such as 'the anal level (the faeces)' (103–4), and the invocatory drive (the ears and the voice). Due to its chameleon-like characteristics, it always remains somewhat distant and inaccessible. Despite its elusiveness, it is the avatar of traumatic pain and suffering, which is exactly why it appears so disturbing. It represents a confrontation with unspeakable pain, and the limits of its own representation.

In conjunction with Lacan's theory of *objet a*, Dolar's theory of the object voice will serve as a foundation for Beckett's various countervoices in *Breath*. This countervoice, more specifically, emanates from the body on stage through the filter of the screen as the viewer watches the cinematic adaptations. Dolar points out that

> silent inner voices, but also acoustic sounds that are not human [...] can take the place of the 'objet a'. In order to conceive the voice as the object of the drive, we must divorce it from the empirical voices that can be heard. Inside the heard voices is an unheard voice, an aphonic voice, as it were. For what Lacan called objet petit a [...] does not coincide with any existing thing, although it is always evoked only by bits of materiality, attached to them as an invisible, inaudible appendage, yet not amalgamated with them: it is both evoked and covered [...] the voice is not somewhere else. (2006, 73–4)

Due to its incomprehensibility and overwhelming nature, *objet a* voice remains foreign and strange. Trauma can never become one with the subject, and voice can never become one with its body. Dolar argues that the object voice is a 'voice whose origin cannot be identified, in search of a body, but even when it finds its body, it turns out that this doesn't quite work, the voice doesn't stick to the body, it is an excrescence which doesn't match the body' (2006, 60–1). Dolar also calls this object voice the acousmatic voice. It is disembodied and resounds from 'elsewhere'. Žižek describes the alienation, which the object voice generates as adding a soundtrack to a silent movie. Dolar states: '"Acousmatic" describes "the noise which we hear without seeing what is causing it" [...] The voice whose source cannot be seen, because it cannot be located, seems to emanate from anywhere, everywhere; it gains omnipotence' (2006, 61–2).

Similar to trauma, which is not an event, but a condition 'constructed retroactively' (Žižek, 1989, 56), the object voice can be defined solely by its delayed secondary effects. Dolar suggests that 'to attach the voice to the body and to endow it with materiality involves all kinds of obstacles — one is ultimately faced with an unbridgeable gap, since the trouble is that the object never fits the body' (1996, 10). Dolar further points out that there is a 'time-lag between perception and understanding [...] the object voice is always understood nachträglich, subsequently, retroactively' (2006, 136). Indeed, the object voices in some cinematic adaptations of *Breath* seem foreign and strange.

2   *Breath*: The Dramatic Text

Breath is one of Beckett's least studied plays, perhaps because it features no dialogue. James Knowlson and John Pilling see the play as a strange, brief 'mixture of the comic and the serious' (127). Other critics have read it as a representation of mortality. Ulrika Maude, for example, views it as a representation of a 'blurred boundary between life and death' (109), and Alfred Alvarez sees in *Breath* 'that last gasp' (134), after which nothing survives. However, hope can be located within the breath itself, since it not only represents a confrontation with mortality and the brevity of life, but also life within, after, and through trauma. Bob Mayberry aptly points out that the 'inhalation lasts ten seconds and the light becomes brighter during these ten seconds [...] [t]his implies that as the unseen someone breathes and lives, the world grows brighter' (31). The breath appears to be the locus of hope in the play.

The bodily sounds in these various adaptations of *Breath* are not simple physical markers of trauma, which victimise the characters and intensify their trauma through constant sonic or physical recollection. They also may have the potential to 'compose' a countervoice of agency, which releases, re-directs or distracts from the trauma, makes symbolisation possible, and empowers the subject. Just as trauma can be grasped and partially counteracted through the usually hidden post-traumatic echoes, 'one must be careful [...] not to miss the tension, the antagonism, between a silent scream and a vibrant tone, that is, the moment when a silent scream resounds' (Žižek and Salecl, 93). Dolar suggests that an object voice is a 'sound with meaning' (2006, 23), and the voices of the body, filtered through the screen, are not just sounds, but also object voices — they are sounds with meaning in that they articulate the importance of remembrance and memorialising trauma. The silent resounding screams Žižek mentions manifest themselves through a form of bodily release, a countervoice that attempts to 'resound', drown out, and counteract the voice of the 'original' trauma. This voice also contaminates and engages the viewer affectively, proclaiming the refusal to forget suffering. Through the acoustic distance of this bodily countervoice, both the audience and the characters on stage can possibly grasp, contain, and enter into a meaningful conversation with the trauma that was originally overwhelming. When trauma is experienced directly, it is overpowering and confronts the subject with the larger implications of his or her own mortality. Yet, trauma expressed through dramatic texts lacks immediacy and is rendered metaphysical. However, when the traumatic silent scream resounds through the body on stage and the screen, it manifests itself as a meaningful countervoice to the original trauma and is perceived as a sound of agency.

The body's recorded 'voice' of breath in the cinematic adaptations of *Breath* to be explored can potentially purge the pain so that the 'fullness' and affective intensity of the traumatic suffering reaches out to the spectator while also creating the necessary distance and safety from which to process the pain. When the viewer watches a cinematic adaptation of a performance of *Breath*, the release happens through equal amounts of closeness and distance with regard to the representation and processing of the painful experience. In other words, the liminality of the screen generates a sense of detachment, which enables the viewer to turn into both therapist and observer without being too overwhelmed. The doubled space of the screen filtered through the voice acts as a safe window from which to observe traumatic events.

As many critics have suggested, pain, in *Breath*, may be closely linked to the birth cry or the 'trauma' of birth. However, it is important to understand that the question of trauma, in Beckett, generally tends to remain somewhat incomprehensible and inaccessible. Cathy Caruth explains that 'the historical power of the trauma is not just that the experience is repeated after its forgetting but that it is only in and through its inherent forgetting that it is first experienced at all' (1995, 8). Trauma can never be fully grasped; the traumatised individual simultaneously gets close to and tries to escape from his or her trauma. Yet, in *Breath*, through a moment of silence, the traumatic pain can possibly be controlled and temporarily stopped — albeit only for five seconds — by holding the breath. Absolute silence, for Beckett, is essentially the utopian ideal of suicide, which would promise a relief from suffering, but which one can never commit successfully. It is linked to the experience of trauma in that trauma, too, cannot be fully healed or overcome. I argue that if breath and 'held breath' on the screen have the power to control and bring about silence — even if only for a brief moment — trauma, which that silence represents, can potentially also be temporarily 'held', contained and controlled. The play's plot can be quickly summarised: a moment of 'recorded vagitus' (Beckett, 2006, 401), a birth-cry, precedes an 'amplified recording' (401) of an invisible body's sounds of inhaling. Silence is 'held' (401) for five seconds and the sound of exhalation again precedes five seconds of silence. The intensity of the light changes. Finally, the birth cry is repeated, silence is held for another five seconds, and the play ends. Beckett makes clear in his stage directions that the stage must not include any verticals within the fallen world of 'miscellaneous rubbish' (401), decay, and death dramatised on stage.

The play's 'action' is driven forward exclusively through the avatar of trauma, *objet a*: the sound of breath. Beckett's stage directions insist that light and breath are to be 'strictly synchronized' (401), which conveys a sense of unity and harmony between external and internal trauma. In other words, through the synchronisation of the body and its environment, Beckett allows for a possible resolution to trauma. Life persists through the sound of the body, and pain can possibly be grasped, controlled and contained through the voice of 'held breath'. Although some scholars, such as Benedict Nightingale, have read the imagery of the play as suggestive of the historical events of the mid-twentieth century, critics have not explicitly considered it an example of trauma literature. However, the setting of *Breath* may, indeed, resemble a setting of World War II trauma. The stage directions suggest the traumatising experience of living in a bombed World War II city: the empty, disembodied stage is 'littered with miscellaneous rubbish' (401) and no 'verticals' (401), an image, which, through its absence, not only suggests the destruction of metaphysics, but also the destruction of hope. The scene recalls Adorno's insightful point about *Endgame*: 'Without realizing it, humankind continues to vegetate, creeping along after events that even the survivors cannot really survive, on a rubbishheap that has made even reflection on one's own damaged state useless' (244). It also evokes the Beckett comment concerning his work for an Irish Hospital in St.-Lô, which had been bombed: 'St.-Lô is just a heap of rubble, la Capitale des Ruines as they call it in France. Of 2600 buildings 2000 completely wiped out' (Knowlson, 313). Indeed, the setting of *Breath* is a bombed stage of destruction and decay, recalling the post-World War II traumatic events. The body as a functioning entity has disappeared; instead, the strange, disembodied, recorded breaths and cries of a foreign sound body emerge, mourning human existence. The two cries at the beginning and the end of the play may be avatars of historical trauma, *objets a*, and define life, according to Nightingale, 'as two faint cries and the world as a rubbish-heap' (390). Most of all, they are cries for help, which signal deep suffering, pain and loss. While the cries are simply a reflection or representation of trauma, the breath suggests a possibility to counteract or drown out trauma. Agency can be located within the breath, because it controls the play's rhythm. Due to the minimalist setting and the lack of characters, it is the breath, which generates the musical rhythm of the play and defines its actions. This rhythm of inhaling and exhaling creates a sense of structure, which renders it easier to grasp the disturbing effects of traumatic suffering. The breath leads to, and in fact, literally contains and captures a moment of silence, since the five seconds occur between the sounds of inhaling and exhaling. The end of pain, which silence on this littered cinematic stage of rubbish represents, can possibly be achieved through the bodily rhythm itself — albeit only for five seconds.

Despite the insistence on recording and remembering trauma, the act of amplifying the cry renders it an *objet a*, an avatar of trauma. This allows for the possibility to cope with trauma, because of the acoustic and temporal distance the recording creates. It makes the cry 'faint' (401); it literally renders it an avatar, as noted in the script, and thus less frightening and overwhelming, which again recalls Dolar's and Žižek's ideas of the silent screams that resound. Beckett insisted that both the cry and the breath, both so central to the play, be recorded rather than live. The recording acts as a mediating filter and generates distance. Beckett also demanded that the breaths and cries be amplified. The alienating effects of the amplified breaths can convey a helpful acoustic distance, which the live breath cannot.

3   *Breath*: Four Cinematic Adaptations

The National Theatre Production, which is shown from two angles, follows the text closely. The rubbish consists of old, rusted furniture. The recordings of the breaths and the baby's cries are well timed and the five seconds of silence have an uncanny, visceral effect, appealing to the audience, which now hears its own breaths amplified through the sudden silence. Through repetition, it seems that the breaths and screams 'fail again, fail better' (Beckett, 1983a, 7) into the extended moment of silence. The production recalls a line from Beckett's *Text 8* in *Text for Nothing*, where the narrator describes a similar phenomenon: 'But it will end, a dehiscence will come, or the breath fail better still, I'll be silence, I'll know I'm silence, no, in the silence you can't know'

(2006, 132). By portraying an endpoint in human existence, a blank moment of silence after trauma, the production conveys an opening, a dehiscence — a possibility for uncertainty. This can be either liberating or terrifying, depending on how the audience decides to fill it.

The uncanny filmed performance by Arsonist Productions places less responsibility onto the audience. The added unscripted sound effects at the beginning render the traumatic pain quite overwhelming. The fact that the 'miscellaneous rubbish' consists of unbroken, functional instruments seems somewhat unfitting and ignores the political elements inherent in the play. The performance of the breath, however, is not simply a weak gasping for air, but appears determined and amplified as scripted, through which the broken, traumatised body regains some of its agency. Also, due to the good timing of the cry and breath and the fact that they speak to each other rhythmically, they seem to be in conversation with each other, which suggests that there is a hint of agency to be found in the performance of the breaths and cries. However, the added sound effects distract from hearing the cry of agency that would speak back to trauma and its containment through the breath. Suffering, as represented in this production through the sound effects, leaves its listeners terrified, helpless, and unable to cope with the secondary trauma, which they just witnessed.

Hirst's bleak production for the 'Beckett on Film' project leaves even less room for interpretation. It is successful in that it recognises the political potential of the play, but by omitting the birth cry from the performance, it fails to represent the suffering and the visceral, horrifying effects of the birth trauma Beckett conveys. More specifically, it removes the means through which the body's cries for help can be heard. The performance puts the trauma in a very concrete context: the rubbish consists of hospital and medical waste and cigarette butts, which form swastikas. The image of the swastika, a symbol of suffering, murder, and gas chambers, undoubtedly hints at the trauma of World War II. Derval Tubridy argues that this directorial choice evokes Adorno's concern about the possibility of representation after Auschwitz:

> Remembering the statement [...] — 'No symbols where none intended' — we are jolted from the a-historical microcosm of Beckett's play which exists between the inhalation and exhalation of any breath, into the historically specific macrocosm of death as genocide with the political, social and religious contexts that are necessarily implied. (118)

Although I agree that putting the trauma articulated in the script in the concrete context of science and medicine might be somewhat limiting, it acknowledges and confronts the political elements of the script. In fact, it recalls Beckett's own traumatising experience working in an Irish hospital. Gordon Burn explains:

> [Hirst's] disinhabited dumb boxes speak of modern death in tiled hospital rooms, and silent technologised removal. They speak [...] of how the technological media, which enormously reinforce and heighten the illusion that death happens only to others, have put a distance between us and our own dying. (10)

The specific type of trauma that the production intends to convey is thus certainly appropriate. However, from an acoustic point of view, it is the bleakest performance among the productions to be analysed, because the suffering is silenced and cannot be clearly perceived.

The most successful, politically responsible, and hopeful performance seems to be the unconventional Brechtian German production directed by Gerd Conradt. Although the production is most certainly a misinterpretation of Beckett's play in that it does not closely follow the text's script (for example, it does not display the miscellaneous rubbish), it asks both the spectator in the audience and the spectator in front of the screen to get involved by articulating an engaged, communal voice of refusal. Instead of having an actual actor perform the play, the director chose to have the audience perform the breaths and cries themselves. The minimalist black and white production films the audience's repeated synchronised breaths and cries. Listening to the breaths performed by the audience, a loud, energetic, and determined countervoice of refusal seems to emerge. Due to the communal performance, trauma may appear less isolating, and through its synchronisation and repetition, the breaths seem determined to drown out the 'original' trauma.

4   Conclusion

Due to its emphasis on suffering, and the amplification and recording of the body sounds, *Breath* has the potential to engage and indirectly involve the audience watching the play in front of the screen. William Hutchings points out:

> relying exclusively on sensory perceptions (i.e., sight and hearing) and lacking any spoken words to be apprehended and considered by reason, *Breath* achieves a goal that Beckett expressed to Jessica Tandy about

> *Not I*: it is a work designed so that, first and foremost, it will 'work on the nerves of the audience, not its intellect'. (87)

In other words, the play's cries and screams may be cries for help, which appeal to the audience and video viewers in an immediate, bodily manner. Moreover, the recording of the body sounds renders the breaths and screams uncannily present and real, generating an immediate visceral confrontation with mortality, which can be traumatising. However, they also become faint, distant avatars of trauma, *objets a*, which make trauma more approachable. The performances demonstrate through the recording and amplification of the breaths and screams that they are not simply accidental and automatic, but conscious and deliberate voices with a purpose and direction: *objets a*. The breaths and cries become controlled and deliberate, which appeal to the listener's conscience. They appear as reflective, immortal cries for help, which, through the act of recording, the distance, and the layer of mediation that the cinematic recording provides, convey a powerful, visceral, and politically engaged refusal to forget the traumatic history of the mid-twentieth century.

Thus, Beckett's minimalist short plays seem to reveal an almost obsessive need to perform traumatic pain through the often very physical noises surrounding moments of silence. Carla Locatelli suggests that Beckett's silence is an 'engaged silence' (29). This engaged and persistent countervoice of silence becomes an audible manifestation of traumatic experience and the distressing unheard sounds of body itself: the silent yet audible threats to the wounded self. Listening to silence and the sounds generated through and around moments of silence are essential aspects of trauma theory. Lacan, for example, distinguished, 'in one of his unpublished seminars [...] between *sileo*, a simple absence of voice and sound, and *taceo*, which entails an act' (Fonteneau, 126). Beckett wants his audience and viewers to hear silence and the bodily countervoice that originates from it, a paradoxical gesture that promises both to resolve and to perpetuate trauma. However, this visceral countervoice also perpetuates another form of trauma: both the character and the listener of the trauma are forced to listen continuously to the body's self-generated sounds of survival. The hyperaware bodily sounds, such as amplified sounds of hearing oneself bleed and breathe, confront the subject with his or her own mortality in the most visceral, traumatising way. The resounding voices of Beckett's characters' bodies may be seen as countervoices to and expressions of individual and collective trauma. Beckett's dramatisation of the voice not only recognises and echoes traumatic history, but it also speaks back to it by appealing to the audience's conscience and capacity for empathy. In an interview with Jessica Tandy, Beckett made an important statement about the unique, visceral meaning that can only truly emerge in performance. He conceived of his play *Not I* as 'a work designed so that, first and foremost, it will 'work on the nerves of the audience, not its intellect' (Hutchings, 87). In fact, many of the performances and cinematic adaptations of *Breath* discussed above seem to have a similar goal: to work on the audience's nerves, but through the 'safe' distance and filter of a screen. In answer to Dolar's question as to whether 'hiccups [can] be a philosophical statement' (2006, 25), depending on the performance, they might not always be a philosophical statement, but in most performances, they certainly are psychological statements proclaiming the importance of remembrance and resistance. It is the resounding countervoices of the traumatised individual's silent screams, and the body's self-generated voice of silence, where hope can possibly be located. However, some of these bodily echoes also contaminate their listeners, which generates another cycle of secondary traumas. The characters' perception of their own bodily sounds is comparable to the characters' reaction to an immediate encounter with traumatic experience. When trauma is approached too closely, it is perceived as a horrifying auditory hell, but when the scream resounds around moments of silence (for example, through a mediating cinematic filter), manifesting itself as a meaningful echo voice of the original trauma, the characters, spectators, and viewers perceive trauma as a countervoice of agency and oneness, which renders symbolisation achievable.

Works Cited

Adorno, Theodor (1991), 'Trying to Understand Endgame', *Notes to Literature*, ed. and trans. Shierry Weber Nicholson, New York: Columbia UP, pp. 241–75.

Alvarez, Alfred (1992), *Samuel Beckett*, London: Fontana.

Beckett, Samuel (2007), 'Breath', Online video clip, *YouTube*, http://video.google.com/videoplay?docid=-8915465772259371796#, accessed 21 January 2021.

Beckett, Samuel (2007), 'Breath', Online video clip, *YouTube*, http://www.youtube.com/watch?v=vw6HWwPEQm8, accessed 21 January 2021.

Beckett, Samuel (2008), 'Breath', Online video clip, *YouTube*, http://www.youtube.com/watch?v=1rZ8xParVmE&feature=player_embedded#at=77, accessed 21 January 2021.

Beckett, Samuel (2010), 'Breath', Online video clip, *YouTube*, http://www.youtube.com/watch?v=S2K9LAof064, accessed 21 January 2021.

Beckett, Samuel (1983a), *Worstward Ho*, London: Calder.

Beckett, Samuel (1983b), 'Letter to Axel Kaun, 9 July 1937', in Ruby Cohn, ed., *Disjecta: Miscellaneous Writings and a Dramatic Fragment*, London: John Calder, pp. 171–2.

Beckett, Samuel (2006), *Dramatic Works*, Vol. 3, New York: Grove P.
Benjamin, Walter (1969), 'The Storyteller', in Hannah Arendt, ed., *Illuminations*, New York: Schocken, pp. 83–110.
Burn, Gordon, George Poste and Damien Hirst (2000), *Theories, Models, Methods, Approaches, Assumptions, Results and Findings*, New York: Gagosian Gallery.
Cage, John (1961), *Silence: Lectures and Writings*, Middletown, CT: Wesleyan UP.
Caruth, Cathy (1995), *Trauma: Explorations in Memory*, Baltimore: Johns Hopkins UP.
Caruth, Cathy (1996), *Unclaimed Experience: Trauma, Narrative, and History*, Baltimore: Johns Hopkins UP.
Dolar, Mladen (1996), 'The Object Voice', in Renata Salecl and Slavoj Žižek, eds., *Gaze and Voice as Love Objects*, Durham: Duke UP, pp. 10–31.
Dolar, Mladen (2006), *A Voice and Nothing More*, Cambridge, MA: MIT P.
Fonteneau, Françoise (1999), *L'éthique du Silence: Wittgenstein et Lacan*, Paris: Seuil.
Hutchings, Williams (1986), 'Abated Drama: Samuel Beckett's Unbated *Breath*', *Ariel*, 17: 1, pp. 85–94.
Knowlson, James (1996), *Damned to Fame: The Life of Samuel Beckett*, London: Bloomsbury.
Lacan, Jacques (1977), *Seminar XI: The Four Fundamental Concepts of Psychoanalysis*, New York: W. W. Norton & Co.
Locatelli, Carla (2000), 'Unwording beyond Negation, Erasures and Reticentia: Beckett's Committed Silence', in Henry Sussman and Christopher Devenney, eds., *Engagement and Indifference: Beckett and the Political*, Albany: SUNY P, pp. 19–42.
Maude, Ulrika (2009), *Beckett, Technology, and the Body*, Cambridge: Cambridge UP.
Mayberry, Bob (1989), *Theatre of Discord: Dissonance in Beckett, Albee, and Pinter*, Rutherford: Fairleigh Dickinson UP.
Nightingale, Benedict (1997), 'Benedict Nightingale in New Stateman', in Lawrence Graver and Raymond Federman, eds., *Samuel Beckett: The Critical Heritage*, London: Taylor and Francis, pp. 370–5.
Tubridy, Derval (2010), 'Beckett's Spectral Silence: *Breath* and the Sublime', *Limit(e) Beckett*, 1, pp. 102–22.
Žižek, Slavoj and Renata Salecl, eds. (1996), *Gaze and Voice as Love Objects*, Durham: Duke UP.
Žižek, Slavoj (1989), *The Sublime Object of Ideology*, London: Verso.
Žižek, Slavoj (1991), *Looking Awry: An Introduction to Jacques Lacan through Popular Culture*, Cambridge, MA: MIT P.

Translating Silence: Ashish Avikunthak's Cinematographic Version of *Come and Go*

Thirthankar Chakraborty

Abstract

In *Proust*, Samuel Beckett writes, 'There is no communication because there are no vehicles of communication' (Beckett, 2006a, 539). And yet, Beckett's oeuvre has travelled not only in Europe but also across continents, perhaps not so much because of the words he has left behind as because of the underlying silence in between the words. This chapter considers Beckett as a figure of world literature, and, as a case study, it examines an Indian cinematographic adaptation and translation of his dramaticule *Come and Go*, entitled *Antaral* (*Endnote*). The cinematographer Ashish Avikunthak recreates the moments of silence in an Indian context in this short film where he also relocates the trialogue translated into Hindi, adding Bengali nursery rhymes. Using concepts that are central to the *Cinema of Prayōga*, Avikunthak mirrors reflections on time, memory, and habit addressed in Beckett's *Proust* and dramatised in the play. Repetition and camera techniques are employed to explore the lives of the three female characters, while also delving into the darkness and the absurd that surround Beckett's stage. As conclusion, the paper asserts that the translation, adaptation, and recreation of Beckett's works give them a new meaning and significance in the world, and are crucial to Beckettian scholarship.

1   Beckett as a Figure of World Literature

Literary works travel across national, cultural, religious, and linguistic borders, and help us better understand the nature of the world. Classics today live not just as original pieces, but frequently through translations, adaptations, and recreations that reflect the coexistence of diverse cultural and artistic values. A major part of the debate about World Literature begins when an author like Samuel Beckett is refracted globally in various ways, to the extent that the works take on new meaning and significance. Inevitably, ethical and aesthetic questions arise concerning misunderstanding and untranslatability, often disputing the free flow of ideas, highlighting the hegemony of certain ideologies over others, and revealing the prevalent differences below surface similarities. These questions call for a better understanding of the original source, often based on the increasing accessibility to biographical, archival, and historical data. They also lead to a better knowledge of the readers and audiences, especially writers and international artists who adapt and recreate from the original. Beckett's late modernist works are thus not only 're-visioned' in new contexts, but also redefined by 'circulation' drawing from 'the collision of differences and the resultant hybridization through processes of cultural mimesis' (Friedman, 2012).

Amongst the recent theories of World Literature, the idea of a peaceful globalisation in the literary field has been variously and vigorously disputed. When discussing Beckett in light of world literature, for instance, Pascale Casanova places him at the centre of a literary revolution: starting with his rejection of an Irish inheritance in favour of exile, then relying on his ability to write 'in neither French nor English', Beckett spearheaded 'the first truly autonomous literary revolution' (347). Culminating in verbal aporia, Beckett composed a literature formed of broken syntax and paratactic phrases, an epanorthosis towards the impossibility of communicating in language a world exempt from verbal significance. Casanova's primary concern in *The World Republic of Letters* is to explain the creation of this autonomous space as a result of Beckett's position in her so-called 'Greenwich meridian of literature' (95), relating Beckett's world with the avant-garde Parisian centre of the early twentieth century (see Chakraborty). As Roland Barthes observes, however, Beckett's works did not remain for long with the intellectuals and snobs, but crossed national boundaries into wider and wider circles (Barthes, 2002, 497). If Beckett's preoccupation was with the 'unword' ever since relinquishing Joyce's influence and rejecting the 'excesses of language' (Beckett, 2006b, 111), one could argue that it is this very undertaking that makes him overcome national, socio-political and cultural restraints. He creates a new form, conveying more than words in one language or another.

Beckett's drive towards the vanishing point of language, which works as a perfect analogy, can consequently be viewed from numerous perspectives, added to the fact that the original works are also encountered across genres and media: book, stage, radio and film. Furthermore, Beckett creates this vanishing point of language through a paradigmatic shift that constantly refers back to 'Ever tried. Ever Failed. No matter. Try again. Fail again. Fail better' (Beckett, 2006b, 471). Faced with an ontological impasse, the works can only gain (or fail still better) through further translations as they resort to Berkeley's '*Esse est percipi*', which Beckett refers to at the start of *Film* (Beckett, 2006c, 323). Or, as the narrator in *Malone Dies* states: 'The search for myself is ended. I am buried in the world, I knew I would find my place there one day, the old world cloisters me, victorious' (Beckett, 2006b, 193). In other words, translations of Beckett's works, worldwide productions, interpretations, relocations, and inspirations drawn from his work regenerate the Beckettian world, increasingly unrestricted by the established 'meridians' that Casanova locates in Paris, or even in London, Dublin, New York, and Berlin. This opens Beckett's world to ever expanding literary spaces with varying symbolic power that interact with each other in innumerable ways.

In the Indian context, Beckett has been translated into several languages, including Bengali, Hindi, Assamese, Marathi, and Tamil. His best-known works are familiar not just in academia, but amongst a much wider populace and are circulated in various intercultural functions, at times in forms other than the written word or stage enactments. One way of addressing this widespread circulation is through Moretti's contentious model of 'distant reading', with its focus on 'units that are much smaller or much larger than the text: devices, themes, tropes — or genres and systems' (2000, 56). When considering Beckett in India, however, the preliminary results of a Google search can only scratch the surface of a much deeper association, which remains hard to map electronically, as Moretti (1994) attempts with canonical works of literature. Hence, instead of the traditional normative approach, the picture plane must be balanced between the original texts and the receiving cultures and languages. In conjunction with what Itamar Even-Zohar and Gideon Toury have identified as the 'descriptive perspective' following Bourdieu's *field theory* (Heilbron, 430), this picture plane contains the Beckettian vanishing point as the source of universality and shifts depending on the perspective. Amongst its constituents are silence revealed through words, darkness accentuated by light, habit contained in ritualistic repetition or minimal movement, and memories couched in movement and stillness: perspectives on these universal attributes vary, depending on clusters of cultural, social, political, and other factors.

2   The Cinema of Prayōga

Amrit Gangar first coined the expression 'Cinema of *Prayōga*' in 2005 as an alternative to the avant-garde experimental film in the West (Butler and Mirza, 10). In a lecture presented in 2010, Ashish Avikunthak, an Indian film artist, elaborates:

> [...] Cinema of *Prayōga* provides an interpretative framework that does not discard the critical tradition of Western philosophy but provides a discursive edge to it by summoning Indian epistemic traditions to grasp

complex texts of postcolonial cinematic modernity that not only challenge the hegemony of prevailing modes of representation but are radical enough to create a new mode of postcolonial cinematic modernity. (Avikunthak, 2013a, 36)

Besides combining Indian thought with Western phenomenology, the Sanskrit term *prayōga* may be loosely translated as 'experiment', with connotations of 'device', 'practice' and 'representation', so that the Cinema of Prayōga may be regarded as an experimental practice that extends across continents (Butler and Mirza, 24). Moreover, 'the term *prayōga* suggests the eternal quest, a continuing process in time and space', and it can be traced back to the works of the earliest pioneer of Indian cinema Debasaheb Phalke (Butler and Mirza, 11). For Avikunthak, more particularly, *prayōga* is 'a theory of experimentation that is not just limited to aesthetics but also the production aspect of cinema', which is one of its major distinctions from Bollywood or other forms of popular cinema produced in the vernacular languages (Butler and Mirza, 25). Regarding this association more closely, whilst Beckett has been frequently advertised to the mass for matters he never supported, as Stanley Gontarski points out and the media frequently exemplifies (2006, 1–10), the case with Ashish Avikunthak's short film *Antaral (Endnote)* is quite different. The cinema artist works independently of the profit-driven capitalist world (Mason, 2015, and Avikunthak, 2013, 32). His films are non-commercial, screened in art theatres, festivals and academic events, and they aim for what Bourdieu calls 'the long run' in production cycles. Being self-sponsored, they may or may not 'rise to the status of cultural objects', much like the conjecturing and risk-factor involved during the publication of *En attendant Godot* by Éditions de Minuit, which Bourdieu uses as an example (1993, 97–8). The avant-garde nature of these works lies partly in this aspect of production, as instead of catering to pre-existent demand for established forms that return immediate economic profit or loss, they raise the stakes for future cultural value and recognition through their non-self-exegetic forms.

Regarding *Antaral*, Avikunthak writes: 'I wanted to push the polysemic narrative intrinsic to the play to further its disenchantment' (2013b). Since its first production, the three characters from Beckett's *Come and Go* have been compared to the three witches at the start of *Macbeth*, the protagonists of Chekhov's *Three Sisters*, and the Three Graces, while according to Gay McAuley, the final tableau 'suggests one of those Hindu statues of several bodies in complicated jutaposition [sic] which are supposed to represent certain universal and eternal qualities' (440). Similar to the numerous ways that Godot can be interpreted, the whispers on stage between the three women permit their stories to remain open. The difference between a stage whisper and these unheard whispers is crucial, since it rejects fixed Aristotelian conventions, leaving the audience in the dark to ruminate about all that unfolds and their own thought processes. Avikunthak's production, likewise, resists any decisive interpretation and also avoids explaining its own construal. The whispers are not directly addressed, but retain their element of mystery. Instead, an array of disparate scenes fill the moments of silence, and although they contain an element of foreboding, there is no clear identification of the whisperings or the appalled looks that greet them. Could it be that the women relate to the tantric procession of '*dandi khata*' (Chattopadhyay, 2015)? Are they trapped like the fish in the bowl? Do they await a carnivorous end trapped in patriarchal society, dreaming of love? These questions and more are raised but remain unanswered.

Borrowing Andrei Tarkovsky's concept of filmmaking as 'sculpting in time', Ashish Avikunthak's film is 'an attempt at invoking *kaal* (Sanskrit for time) as a metaphysical entity, rather than *kaal* as a temporal category' (Buter and Mirza, 73). The idea of time and memory, as discussed by Avikunthak and represented in his film, resonates with what Beckett writes in *Proust*: 'Yesterday is not a milestone that has been passed, but a daystone on the beaten track of the years, and irremediably part of us, within us, heavy and dangerous' (2006a, 512). Moreover, the artist, in Beckett's words on Proust and voluntary memory, 'cannot *remember* yesterday any more than he can remember to-morrow. He can contemplate yesterday hung out to dry with the wettest August bank holiday on record a little further down the clothes-line' (521). This understanding of time is one way of approaching Avikunthak's translated adaptation of *Come and Go*: it is a pastiche of disjointed memories captured through the moving images of a camera, a Beckettian form intricately explored in a localised setting.

3   Staging *Come and Go* and Filming *Antaral*

The title of the short film *Antaral (Endnote)* is helpful when interpreting the format of Avikunthak's cinematographic adaptation. Beckett's *Come and Go* is the endnote to the film so that the entire dramaticule is re-enacted in the final four and a half minutes of the eighteen-minute production, while the rest of the film is an interlude (*antaral* in Sanskrit) formed of an amalgamated rendition of the brief verbal exchanges extracted from Beckett's trialogue. The first conversation is from the point just after Flo re-enters the scene, while the second exchange is from slightly earlier when Vi enters, and the next one is from the end of the drama. The ritualistic movement of coming and going in the dramaticule, which is reminiscent of some of Beckett's earliest motifs and characterisations, is thus mirrored by Avikunthak's handling of the narrative form, as scenes shift to and fro. Unlike the French and German versions of the play that reveal the characters' names right at the start, the film adheres more to the English edition of the text and discloses their names only towards the end of the first three minutes (Gontarski, 1995, 197). The visual narrative does not unfold in a chronological order or stable setting, but is held together through disjointed scenes that last no more than a few seconds each. In black and white, sepia, and colour, these scenes expose the filmic fabric, and are highly reminiscent of Beckett's self-reflexive prose. The indeterminate space in which the three characters are seated in Beckett's play becomes at the end a courtyard cramped by towering walls with windows that evoke a voyeuristic gaze into the drama that unfolds between the three, although hermeneutically shut off from the rest of the world.

Instead of using professional actors, the artist films his wife, her sister and a cousin, and sets the film at his own house in Kolkata where he spent eighteen years of his life. He calls this 'an ossified memory space', which intimately connects the artist to the work (Butler and Mirza, 72). Apart from the sarees, which add a strong sense of materiality or specificity to the characters, the first few minutes of the filmic representation transform the three into nameless ghosts — they become the memories rather than those who engage in acts of memory. In a way, this echoes the German director Walter Asmus' note to himself regarding the start of the play: 'The freeze at the beginning should surpass speechlessness and insecurity'.[1]

According to Beckett's direction, the ages of the three female characters are indeterminable, and they have been variously staged as being young adults, middle-aged or old. This leaves ample scope for Ashish Avikunthak to select his actors: three middle-aged women who are renamed as Kuheli (Flo), Ashwini (Vi), and Aditi (Ru). It is worth noting that Beckett too changed the characters' names for the German production of the play, *Kommen und Gehen*, performed at the Schiller Theater in 1978, where the costumes were also revised, as indicated in Beckett's Production Notebook. On the final page of the production script, Beckett notes:

> Hats: flimsy, broad brimmed, beflowered — ribboned — feathered, to stir in draught.

---

1 'Die Erstarrung Anfang in Tonlosigkeit + Unsicherheit übersteigen' (Beckett, 1999, 237).

Dress: Loose, light, for same effect
shoes: genre ballerina, exits silent. (Beckett, 1999, 233)

Regarding these costumes, moreover, Gontarski adds that the 'diaphanous quality of the costumes and the silent movement suggests something ethereal, other-worldly, ghostly' (Beckett, 1999, 233). This is clearly similar to Avikunthak's representation of the women, although instead of wearing dresses or full-length coats as in the English and French versions of the dramaticule, the three characters are wrapped in sarees with dull violet, yellow, red and green borders. Although the sarees do not conform with the name-specific dress colours — Aditi (Ru) keeps to violet while the other two interchange their colours — unlike the other-worldly German version, they add a cultural specificity and relocate the characters in an Indian context. Rather than disappearing into darkness or behind unseen drapes as per Beckett's stage directions, the three are seen in and out of focus behind metallic fences or mossy boundary walls throughout the short film, making the suppressed trauma behind the spoken words all the more graphic and realistic, yet only suggestive. Moreover, the position of the hands in the final tableau, which Beckett illustrates in his stage directions, is adapted to the way the three women hold hands while playing a game of gyrating in circles. Instead of holding their hands out straight, as in the original, they cross their hands when holding their neighbours'. These criss-crossed hands add to the feeling of entrapment and hint at the closed circular world that they inhabit, especially when related to their game, which re-enacts the circular movement of the three on stage surrounded by darkness.

The film begins in bright white light, reminiscent of a blank page, out of which there appears a window. The opening of this window at the start of the video (not unlike the turning of the first page in a book) works as an invitation to step into the cinematographic world or the artistic space of *Antaral*, which could at first be regarded as being incompatible with the minimalistic Beckettian scenario denuded of location. However, through an over-exposure of the camera lens together with the black and white or sepia film, the artist subtracts realistic elements from the setting, creating instead an uncanny house haunted by memories. Following several shots of windows and other parts inside and outside the house's compounds, Avikunthak reverses the camera on three indistinct figures standing silhouetted outside the fenced walls darkened by the glaring light. Re-imaginations of the faces shadowed by their hats' rims, these figures suggest that the three women within the house appear subjected to their own gaze, creating an uncanny scenario that is reminiscent of Beckett's *Film*.

Moreover, the colourful streets of Kolkata on the outside that can be glimpsed fractionally in fast-forward bring out a stark contrast to the house. Regarding this Indian city, in the foreword to Tapu Biswas's book on Indian interpretations of *Waiting for Godot*, Robert Emmet Meagher writes: 'From my admittedly limited experience of India, its streets and its people, [...] one might well stumble on Beckett's characters in Kolkata much as one would in Dublin' (ii); and whilst *Come and Go* was also performed in French and German shortly after it was written, relocating its obscure setting to the house and the streets of Kolkata is not in fact entirely farfetched. Avikunthak's film thus adapts the darkness that surrounds the stage in *Come and Go*, transforming it into a unique cultural backdrop, whilst the three characters are seen recollecting indistinct memories that lie within and around the compounds of the illuminated house.

4   Translating Silence and the Absurd

Similar to the way that the light on stage is recast onto a bungalow set in Kolkata, the moments of silence in between the short phrases that are translated into Hindi are deconstructed into flashbacks of those who inhabit the house. The film performs a psychological excavation, digging into the moments of silence to reveal the dormant crow calls, flashes of vivid blood colouring the fish sold in the market, the drum sounds during rituals, all of which, as elaborated by the filmmaker, divulge neither fond nor terrible memories (Butler and Mirza, 72). Thus, towards the start of the film, after Kuheli remarks in Hindi 'Dreaming of ... love', the next scene is of her sitting on the ground with her aunt combing her hair, while she appears to be daydreaming and lost in her thoughts. Kuheli initially translates Miss Wade's playground as just a garden, although this is later specified as being Miss Wade's garden, and Aditi remembers about them sitting together on a swing rather than a log, so that the next scene is a fragment of the three playing a game of skipping within the house's corridor. Moreover, when Ashwini asks: 'May we not speak of the old days? Of what came after?' the following scene depicts the three women behind the compound's railing watching a *dandi-khata* procession where women wrapped in sarees and towels repeatedly lie prostrate on the streets after every few steps. Although the English script specifies that 'No rings are apparent', in the Production Notebook Beckett comments: 'But why last words given to Lo [Flo]? Because she touches both left hands (wedding rings)' (Beckett, 1999, 228). Although the three do not appear to be wearing any rings throughout the film, Kuheli (Flo) wears bangles around her wrist and twirls a chain around her neck when she utters not just the final lines of the play, but also the words 'Dreaming of ... love'. However, the bangles and chain appear indistinct in the final re-enactment of the trialogue. Moreover, Avikunthak's Hindi translation of the last line is not literal, but adds a figurative meaning to the words: 'I can touch those feelings', Kuheli says, translating 'feel' as a tactile function and 'the rings' as a metaphor for feelings, of maybe love. Likewise, there are various other scenes that are woven into the narrative, for instance, when the three visit the fish market, and when they play various games and sing classical Indian ragas.

What is noteworthy about these fragmented scenes is the repetition that is depicted in diverse ways. For instance, the trio repeat the *sargams* or music scales, the ragas and the nursery rhymes numerous times; when they enter the fish market, the fishmonger repeatedly shouts 'Ilish! Ilish!', a delicacy in West Bengal; the women performing their ritual lie prostrate on the road after every few steps; even the background music of the film is a set of notes monotonously repeated over and over again. Regarding music, Breon Mitchell suggests: 'Musical analogies seem particularly appropriate in the case of *Come and Go*'; for, 'Like music, the play offers an aesthetic experience accessible in and of itself' (248). Correspondingly, Avikunthak's film 'invokes the elliptical non-linearity of Indian classical music', similar to other films that have been associated with *Prayōga* (Avikunthak, 2013a, 34). Caught in this endless self-referential circle of sound and moving image, the film reflects gyrating motions accompanying the musical repetitions. For example, the women are seen skipping, holding hands and spinning in circles, while towards the start of the video, the camera pedestals up to reveal a spiral staircase. These movements and repetitions are disseminations of what Avikunthak calls the haunting cyclical nature of Beckett's script translated into a filmic medium (Butler and Mirza, 75).

Furthermore, the movements exemplify various manifestations of habit, which, according to Beckett in *Proust*, 'is a compromise effected between the individual and his environment, or between the individual and his own organic eccentricities, the guarantee of a dull inviolability, the lightning-conductor of his existence. Habit is the ballast that chains the dog to his vomit' (2006a, 515). The role of habit as depicted through repetition is portrayed throughout a number of Beckett's works. In *Act Without Words II*, for instance, A constantly broods more out of habit than out of any genuine concern, while B repeatedly checks his watch after each of his actions. Similar to *Waiting for Godot*, where almost identical events take place over the two acts of the drama, the ending of *Act Without Words II*, with A repeating exactly what he does at the start of the mime, also suggests that A and B will presumably re-enact mechanically their roles of waking up, brooding, checking the watch, praying, taking pills, exercising, wearing clothes, and so on, over and over again. Beckett develops this cyclical nature of habit with almost mathematical precision in *Come and Go*, so much so that his inscription 'mathematically desirable' when sketching the three characters' positions in the German Production Notebook is hardly surprising, since the play requires another full circle to have Flo and Ru back in their original places (1999, 229).

Through the many repetitions and gyrations, there is also the element of the absurd that pervades much of *Antaral*, particularly highlighted in the two Bengali nursery rhymes that are made up of paratactic phrases, yet recited in a matter-of-fact way. The following is a loose translation of one of the rhymes sung by the three characters:

> Indi, Bindi, Shindi were peeping through the trees on Saturday. One day they heard a nasal song, hearing which Indi Bindi got spooked. Indi Bindi then got hungry and came down from the tree and started crying for *khichdi*. Mother came and scolded them and did not give them food and out of anger Indi Bindi went to sleep. (my translation)

Whilst reminiscent of Sukumar Ray's *Abol Tabol*, a collection of nonsensical poems first published in 1923, or Lewis Carroll's 'Jabberwocky' (1871), these rhymes have been passed down orally through generations and are intrinsically part of Bengali culture. They create a penchant for the absurd from early childhood. Consequently, the ritualistic act of prostrating oneself on the road every few steps as adults and all the other repetitive habits that are depicted in the film are performed without question.

By producing a film that depicts 'temporal inconsistency' (Butler and Mirza, 75), the artist destabilises the past, present and future (the latter as evinced through the gnarled fingers of Kuheli's aunt, for instance, when compared with the three women's hands, and the *sindur* she puts on her hair, which is customarily worn after marriage), and re-evokes experiences of a non-sequential world. The scene at the fish market and the bloodied hands of the fishmonger incorporate a grim significance when juxtaposed with the cursory glimpse of the pet goldfish in a bowl towards the end. Likewise, the significance of the procession of women on the street is elaborated when Ashwini, Aditi, and Kuheli witness a group of young girls following suit. And most strikingly, although the three seem to be recollecting past experiences, the past is re-enacted by the same three and not their younger selves. This suggests metaphorically that the present is formed through inflections of the past and future, while the past and future are shaped by the cinematographic present, constantly interacting with one another, emphasising the fluidity of time that eliminates fixed temporal divisions.

5   Beckett in the World

Ashish Avikunthak writes about another of his films entitled *Dancing Othello* that, in combining *Kathakali* performance with Shakespearean dramaturgy, he is attempting 'to grapple with the irony of the postcolonial situation, which cultural theorists such as Homi Bhabha and Gayatri Chakravorty Spivak have tried to enunciate in their scholarly works' (Butler and Mirza, 76). Despite dealing with an English text while adapting Beckett's *Come and Go*, Avikunthak does not feel the need to tackle the same postcolonial situation or even to stick to Beckett's English script, although he does translate it into Hindi and relocate it in the urban capital of West Bengal. Perhaps this is because, as Patrick Bixby writes, 'Beckett's celebrated formal experimentation fragments the developmental narratives associated with both imperialism and nationalism and thus refuses to reterritorialize or reauthenticate the dislocated identities of postcolonial subjects' (8). Thus, although Avikunthak's entire short film is based on a translated, relocated and restructured version of Beckett's *Come and Go*, the highly minimalistic and fragmented dramaticule leads to no identity clash when recreated in Hindi and placed within the Bengali cultural backdrop. The dramaticule's 'glocalisation', to use one of David Damrosch's terms (Damrosch, 109), finds redemption in its muffled silences couched between words, in the darkness through which the characters appear and disappear, and the absurd movements that embody the workings of habit. So much so that all Ashish Avikunthak is left to do is disclose in the opening credits '*Endnote (Antaral)* , a film by Ashish Avikunthak, based on the play *Come and Go* by Samuel Beckett'.

By resisting traditional forms and conventions of Western literature, a major portion of Beckett's oeuvre fits well in the postcolonial era, since, like Beckett's writings, it also reflects a disintegrated Zeitgeist with a growing number of exilic and diasporic writers and artists constantly re-questioning ideas of nation and nationality. Unlike in *Dancing Othello*, where Avikunthak has to 'subvert and destabilize (his) own authorial legitimacy' (Butler and Mirza, 76), he already finds in Beckett a 'glocal' text that can be bodily shifted into an Indian context, where even 'the playground at Miss Wade's' finds its place (Beckett, 2006c, 354). Additionally, since Beckett's characters are frequently tramps or characters without any fixed nationalities and with minimal background information, his works are well received by the twenty-first-century avant-garde artists within their own cultures and diaspora. To elaborate this point, Patrick Bixby writes:

> The deterritorializing thrust of this narrative project reconfigures the politics of nationalism towards postnationalism, homeland towards diaspora, possession towards dispossession, sameness towards diversity, speaking to a world ever more deterritoralized by the expansion of mass media, capital flows, and postcolonial migrations. Beckett, the dispossessed Irishman, is finally a writer between territories, between cultures, between languages, who is thus able to recognize that both home and identity can become prisons insofar as they are defined by rigid boundaries. (203–4)

Come and Go not only constitutes a model to represent Beckett's place in world literature, but also reveals how universality is figured even in this minimalist dramaticule, which is barely two pages on paper and a few minutes on stage. In his frequently cited German letter to Axel Kaun, Beckett writes: 'To bore one hole after another in it [the veil of language], until what lurks behind it — be it something or nothing — begins to seep through; I cannot imagine a higher goal for a writer today' (1984, 172). Supposing this is Beckett's intention throughout his later works, it could be said that he develops a body of work that surpasses nationalistic values in favour of a world that is entirely its own, but which also reflects today's world heritage.

To conclude, when considering translations, adaptations, and recreations of Beckett's works into various languages and different media, one must bear in mind that Beckett translated his own texts from French to English and from English to French and also helped directors to stage his plays in other languages. Regarding Beckett's self-translations, numerous critics have remarked that it is impractical to decipher which comes first, and *Come and Go* is just one example where 'simultaneous translations' have resulted as 'textual variants' (Gontarski, 1995, 197). Consequently, the question arises whether Beckett wields an authorial power and takes liberties with his own translations, or whether in naming the unnameable the theatre and prose retain an element beyond verbal formulation that other languages and other forms can only attempt to capture through their own unique set of expressions, devices, techniques, and cultural associations, rather than a literal translation. Artists and writers often discover a sense of freedom in Beckett's works, and Ashish Avikunthak reveals just how adaptable the Beckettian space is in his cinematographic creation. He uses this space not only 'as a metaphor for the existential predicament', but in *Antaral* 'the spatiality becomes an implicit way of exploring space between relationship' so that 'spaces become memory spaces, as metaphors for an inconceivable loss' (Butler and Mirza, 75). Thus, Beckett conveys a significance that lies within the multi-layered nature of his work, communicating through silence, repetition, indistinguishable whispers, and unseen spaces, couched in the words, actions, and directions on stage.

Works Cited

Avikunthak, Ashish (2010), *Ashish Avikunthak, 1995–2010*, DVD, Calcutta: Ashish Avikunthak Productions.
Avikunthak, Ashish (2013a), 'In Search of a Genealogy: Experimental, Avant-Garde or Prayōga?' *Deep Focus*, 1: 4, pp. 32–36.
Avikunthak, Ashish (2013b), 'East by Northwest', Interview by Michael Guarneri, *Débordements*, 31 March, 2013.
Barthes, Roland (2002), *Oeuvres Complètes*, Tome I, ed. Éric Marty, Paris: Éditions du Seuil.
Beckett, Samuel (1984), *Disjecta: Miscellaneous Writings and a Dramatic Fragment*, ed. Ruby Cohn, New York: Grove P.
Beckett, Samuel (1999), *The Theatrical Notebooks of Samuel Beckett: The Shorter Plays*, ed. S. E. Gontarski, New York: Grove P.
Beckett, Samuel (2006a), *The Grove Centenary Edition: Volume IV, Poems, Short Fiction, Criticism*, ed. Paul Auster, New York: Grove P.
Beckett, Samuel (2006b), *The Grove Centenary Edition, Volume II, Novels*, ed. P. Auster, New York: Grove P.
Beckett, Samuel (2006c), *The Complete Dramatic Works*, London: Faber and Faber.
Biswas, Tapu (2006), *Samuel Beckett's* Waiting for Godot: *Indian Interpretations through Critical and Analytical Studies, Translations and Stage Productions*, Kolkata: Avantgarde.
Bixby, Patrick (2009), *Samuel Beckett and the Postcolonial Novel*, New York: Cambridge UP.
Bourdieu, Pierre (1993), *The Field of Cultural Production: Essays on Art and Literature*, ed. Randal Johnson, New York: Columbia UP.
Butler, Brad, and Karen Mirza (2006), *Cinema of Prayōga: Indian Experimental Film & Video, 1913–2006*, London: No.w.here.
Casanova, Pascale (2004), *The World Republic of Letters*, Cambridge: Harvard UP.
Chakraborty, Thirthankar (2020), 'Samuel Beckett and the World Republic of Letters', *Journal of World Literature* 5:2, pp. 222–39.
Chattopadhyay, Arka (2015), 'The Politics of Non-Arrival: Avikunthak Waiting for Kalki', available online at: www.avikunthak.com.

Damrosch, David (2009), *How to Read World Literature*, Chichester: Wiley–Blackwell.

Derrida, Jacques (2001), 'What Is a "Relevant" Translation?', trans. Laurence Venuti, *Critical Inquiry*, 27: 2, pp. 174–200.

Friedman, Susan Stanford (2012), 'World Modernisms, World Literature, and Comparativity', in Mark Wollaeger and Matt Eatough, eds., *The Oxford Handbook of Global Modernisms*, Oxford: Oxford Handbooks Online.

Gontarski, S. E. (1995), 'Editing Beckett', *Twentieth Century Literature*, 41: 2, pp. 190–207.

Gontarski, S. E. (2006), 'Viva, Sam Beckett, or Flogging the Avant-Garde', *JOBS*, 16: 1, pp. 1–10.

Heilbron, Johan (1999), 'Towards a Sociology of Translation: Book Translations as a Cultural World-System', *European Journal of Social Theory*, 2: 4, pp. 429–44.

Mason, Bruce (2015), 'Death *is not* an End: It is just another way of dealing with life', in Melissa McCarthy, ed., *Momentum: Research and Innovation*, U of Rhode Island, pp. 50–5.

McAuley, Gay (1966), 'Samuel Beckett's *Come and Go*', *Educational Theatre Journal*, 18: 4, pp. 439–42.

Mitchell, Breon (1976), 'Art in Microcosm: The Manuscript Stages of Beckett's *Come and Go*', *Modern Drama*, 19: 3, pp. 245–54.

Moretti, Franco (1994), 'Modern European Literature: A Geographical Sketch', *New Left Review*, 1: 206, pp. 86–109.

Moretti, Franco (2000), 'Conjectures on World Literature', *New Left Review*, 1, pp. 54–68.

PART 5

Enacted Voices in Performance and Media

∴

Without Colour: Beckett and the Stage Voice

A dialogue by Nicholas E. Johnson and Cathal Quinn

Abstract

Though widely cited in scholarship and criticism, Samuel Beckett's admonitions to actors across several of his plays to perform in a 'toneless' manner or 'without colour' (see Germoni and Sardin, 2012) belies some of the complexity involved in actually *voicing* Beckett in performance. There are also numerous testimonies that point in the opposite direction from 'toneless', since Beckett as a director also emphasised musicality, rhythm, depth, timbre, range, breath, and specificity in relation to actors' voices. Drawing on a consciously 'vocal' form — the philosophical dialogue — this contribution collects the insights gained by two Dublin-based practitioners. They reflect on how their experiences of studio practice, actor training, and theatre directing might point towards a more complex reading of the Beckett 'voice' in performance.

Nicholas E. Johnson (NJ): As we both come from the background of practice, I suppose we ought to start with our general considerations about Beckett and the voice. Beyond the wealth of published material that has been written about Beckett's theatre, we have the chance to consider it from the perspective of training — from a perspective of getting actors ready to go on stage and do it, or of going on stage and doing it ourselves. What are your initial thoughts and ideas about the voice, when you start work on a Beckett text?

Cathal Quinn (CQ): For any heightened texts, I would apply similar exercises, but I'll then try to make them specific to the texts themselves. So first of all, I have to get them grounded, or myself grounded. The exercises I would use for that, if you wanted to go into the practical things first, would start with the hips: the Bartenieff exercises, Feldenkrais for the whole body, but really working on those hips. If they are having to stand or kneel for a long time, you have to get their breath support there. You *ground* them first of all, so lots of stretches and yoga, for the hamstrings, the abs, the adductors, the calves etc. They have Alexander in the place I teach now, in the Lir, for two years once a week, and they have an extra class in third year, which is great.[1]

---

[1] Techniques referenced include those developed by Irmgard Bartenieff (1900–81) and Moshé Feldenkrais (1904–84), as well as the Alexander Technique originated by F. Matthias

NJ: Can I pause you there, Cathal, because I think that for readers who have no theatre background, or readers who are coming exclusively from literature, they might not necessarily think of the voice and the hamstrings as being connected in some fundamental way. I'd love if you could explain as you might to the non-expert in voice: why does the body matter in relation to voice?

CQ: The body must matter, because you can't get your breath out unless your body is grounded. You have to work on the breath support muscles, and you have to ground the body for them to be free. If you're grounded, if you find that you have a relationship with the floor, suddenly you are allowed to breathe deeper. And when you breathe deeper, you have more choices for how you deliver the text, because your support is behind what you say. That is fundamental for me. I have about seven areas — basics about different parts of the voice — that we would use and apply not only to Beckett, but to everybody. I also do *Qigong* with them, which is a great way of grounding that lower body.[2] So, for instance if you are doing something like *A Piece of Monologue*, which I have done — not myself, but I have done an excerpt from it, and trained an actor with it as well — you know, he's standing there for at least half an hour, he never moves. To get into that sense of stillness with only his eye and his head moving occasionally, he needs to do an awful lot of grounding first, and to have a relationship between himself and the fourth wall, the invisible fourth wall that he is looking at. After a while it gets easy, but certainly for our younger students, or less trained actors, it's very difficult to be that still.

NJ: I see the same difficulty sometimes in my students as well: the feeling that 'acting' means doing, so they always want to be *doing* something. It's hard to get the power of rootedness and stillness into people, unless it's a situation that actively constrains the body, which a lot of Beckett's theatre does. That's one of the reasons I've found Beckett's work useful within actor training.

CQ: I've always found that resistance exercises are great. I've heard that from the Royal Shakespeare Company as well, from their voice teachers, who use

---

Alexander (1869–1955); see Madden (2014). All three are somatic movement practices focused on self-awareness, identification of points of tension or blockage, and identifying modes of sustainable embodiment; many actor training programmes engage with all three. 'The Lir' is Ireland's National Academy of Dramatic Art, housed in Trinity College Dublin since 2011.

2 *Qigong* has roots in Chinese medicine. It unifies breathing exercises, moving meditations, and coordinated postures and movements to cultivate holistic wellness in the practitioner.

resistance. With younger actors especially given something to fight against, what they say comes out —

NJ: What they say comes out more forcibly.

CQ: Yes, more forcibly, more grounded, more committed. That's exactly what we mean.

NJ: And you design grounding exercises that are specific to a given writer, or to heightened text?

CQ: To heightened text in general — both for them to be able to manage it and have no fear of it. Then I'll try and do things more catered to the demands of that particular text, and I'll give them a strong intention, of course. For an actor, they always need that. If there's someone standing there actually waiting to die, and that moment could come anytime — if they're ready for it — it is a very strong impulse for them. They get it; they can work with that.

NJ: It's an action. It's specific.

CQ: An *action* of being still.

NJ: Yes. And what would be an example of how, when doing Beckett — what types of things would you gear them towards in terms of those exercises that speak to Beckett or come out of Beckett in some way, for the voice? Is there something specific in his heightened text that you might not do with, say, Shakespeare? Do you have certain types of exercises that would be specific to the Beckett context?

CQ: In terms of grounding, there's an exercise about the idea of 'where is your focus', your point of focus. So — again, it wouldn't be specifically for Beckett, it would be for others as well, but I would try and train it for their exercise, for the particular text we're working there, but — point of focus. So where is your focus now? You focus on outside yourself but also inside yourself at the same time. You can focus on your feet, when you're doing, for instance, *A Piece of Monologue*. Or if you're doing *Not I* and you are holding onto a chair, you focus on your relationship to the chair, grounding yourself as you're speaking out. You're thinking on at least those two different levels at the same time, always remaining grounded whether you're delivering something at high speed or a much lower speed.

NJ: That all makes sense. Does Beckett offer support for the voice in the specific way that he has written the text?

CQ: Certainly. For example, how do you root yourself for the screams in *Not I*? You do this high octane, high-paced delivery all the time, and suddenly there's a scream, and you've got to get ready for that scream. But Beckett does it: he preps you for it anyway in the run-up, and then you have to do the scream as well as you can, and then have that moment of silence before you repeat it. The more grounded you are before the scream, the more effective that scream is going to be, and unsettling for the audience too. And he prepares both you and them for it.

NJ: I think this brings us to the cusp of one of the big issues in Beckett and acting, which has to do with the technical demands on the one side versus the emotional demands on the other, and the ways in which there are different discourses out there about the emotions involved. If you look at Whitelaw's account of rehearsal and the discourse of those who follow in her footsteps explicitly, there is a lot of talk about trauma and difficulty. But if you talk to some other directors and actors who emerge more from a movement-based tradition, there's a lot more emphasis on the *technical* aspect of having breath, having it grounded, being ready for the task. For this group of makers, they operate in a very task-focused kind of way; while there might be negative emotion involved, it is considered a joy to be forced to perform text that is that strong, and that clear, and that rooted. Not a trauma but a joy. I think the voice is interesting in the way that it returns our focus to the music that can be found within technique. Certainly, it combines with emotional pressure, as when you're talking about resistance — how resistance creates intention, how there is a link between the physical and the emotional intensity that comes out. You're not generating the emotion out of some background experience or sense memory, but rather out of the physical pressure that generates this need to speak. It feels like a struggle between Meyerhold's biomechanical approach versus early Stanislavski, or — if we were really to make it a blunt split between internal and external strategies of acting — it seems like the way you're talking about voice is external. But in someone's work like Linklater's, you can see how that connects to things which are very deep, profound, rooted, where an emotional aspect arises within the task.[3] Could you talk about how this binary

---

3   Vsevolod Meyerhold (1874–1940) and Konstantin Stanislavski (1863–1938) are often held up as two polarities of approaching acting, as the former is associated with the physically-based

breaks down for you? Do you think of the voice of something that is a muscle, like a weightlifting task that you have to kind of train and develop, something technical and external, or do you think that it relates mainly to freedom of access to emotions in the body's interior?

CQ: It can't just be the former. You have to work on your technique every single day, but it cannot just be that, because there's no truth then. Then it's just like playing an instrument. And that's fine — the way *you* play an instrument is much more interesting to listen to or look at than someone who is doing it perfectly accurately. I would do a lot of Linklater. I will go into impulses, but I try and make those personal for them. I will give them ideas and images, but they may not work for everybody, so I'll suggest to them that they find their own reasons to sigh, their own reasons to scream at this moment. I will try and get them to do that. Though we've talked about Beckett many times, you know, saying that there's no backstory, or that he's not interested in the backstory — still the actor, if they want to, can make a backstory for themselves. You can talk about *Happy Days* as being a person trapped in a hole as being related to marriage, or ageing, or motor neuron disease — you know, something that hits them — 'Oh, I can relate to that!' But it doesn't *have* to be that at all. But if it works, especially initially just to get going and start committing to what they're saying, great. You then may not need it, because you've actually found yourself in the text and in the moment.

NJ: So that's part of the underpinning: a technique backed by truths?

CQ: Yes. I'll suggest things to them, something that maybe has a resonance for me initially, but they don't have to take it. That's important for me. I'm quite wary of working too emotionally. And yet if it's not there, you're a bit worried. Absolutely, there is a balance between the two. I've said that to them many times, about how you've got to have technique and emotional truth as well. It can't just work for them. It has to work for us.

NJ: You are a performer as well, responding to your own needs or desires to perform Beckett, in addition to offering exemplary training for these students.

'biomechanics' system, while the latter has been received (not always accurately, especially in translation) as based on the use of the more emotionally-based 'sense memory' in creating truthful performances. In reality, the two systems intersect at many points. Kristin Linklater (b. 1936) created a technique predicated on freeing the functions of the vocal mechanism, codified in *Freeing the Natural Voice* (1976, revised 2006).

In your own practice, do you find yourself developing one mode of acting over another, or are you kind of able to practice what you preach with them? Do you also use your own citations in the early part of the process, and then just try to be in the moment in the moment of performance? How do you navigate that terrain as a vocal performer yourself?

CQ: It's a very good point, because I haven't been on stage with Beckett for a couple of years now. But I remember the pain of being in *Play* and getting into those bins that became urns. As the only male in it, my shoulders were broader than others, and they were all made for one fit, so the pain of getting in them was like 'Here we go again, that slog again'. But what I always said to myself is what someone told me before: this has never happened before. I have to get on with it right now. No matter how many times you've done it before, this is brand new for them. And as soon as you get going, as soon as you start trust between each of you, it starts to take off and be new again. And the breath is an enormous contributor and comforter for that. You have to have the breath grounded in order to be calm enough to do it. Because as some have said before, it's like open-heart surgery. I'll use any technique that I can — there's one I've been using recently, the 'four-seven-eight', which is very simple. The breath comes in through the nose for a count of four; you hold it gently for seven, using that seven to visualise or to begin mindfulness, to think positively; out for eight silently. That's an exercise you do ad nauseum, and then you can increase that capacity. It's good for capacity as well, but you can do more with it. It's a great one for me just before I go on or just before it's about to start, if I'm feeling panicky. It's a grounding of the breath. It helps the mind to calm, so the adrenaline is doing the right thing as opposed to taking over. Another one I use for capacity, again for something like *Happy Days*, where she has the gabble, and then the idea — it's very simple, you use a straw while breathing. It's quite a thin straw, and you're breathing out through the straw for thirty seconds. Then the breath comes in, gently held for just a second, and then you try it again. You can get up to 30 or 40 seconds, or you can do it certainly to sense, if you need to take a breath. That really helps, and students have been realising the benefit of that.

NJ: A little bit like marathon runners who train at high altitude. Restricting oxygen, the pinpoint aspect of that straw exercise — it matters that it's going out to a directed point.

CQ: Yes, it's for point-of-focus as well. And if they get bored doing it, I say you can do it in whatever position you want to. Standing, or sitting, or kneeling, or lying, and standing and walking while you're doing it. Some of them use a mirror and actually use their breath to write on the mirror, keeping their mind completely on something else, and they get to 30 seconds or 40 seconds faster. That idea of them taking an exercise and running with it, using their own version of it, is what I want for them to do, so they'll keep using it afterwards. Capacity, grounding, breath support: those are the fundamentals that they need for everything they do, but if you don't have them for Beckett, you're in very big trouble.

NJ: When you talk about things like 'calm' or 'grounding' or 'adrenaline', are you aware of any formal medical studies of the voice that explore this, or is the bulk of your own rooting in this through the practical experience? As this bumps up against the recent discourses in the medical humanities around wellness — people finding simple routines, for example through breath, to care for themselves — is there any dimension of this vocal practice that you would identify as medical?[4]

CQ: No, I haven't gone into the medical side personally, though I know Linklater has. Speaking of wisdom through experience, the Chinese say that the root of all illness is stress. If the actor's breathing is working for them as opposed to against them, they will hopefully have less stress. I don't know all the technical terms, but I know I was the tensest actor in the world. I know how it starts to open or become more supported in time. If you're working with the breath you're working with the mind. I won't be too technical about it, but I'd say that it's common sense that the voice work affects the actor's experience of acting, and the experience of others watching.

NJ: I'm interested in that question, because I feel like there are so many perspectives on the voice which are anatomical or based in speech therapy, and I don't know the extent to which the practical knowledge of your experience as a teacher is valorised as knowledge in that community. I have certainly seen actors develop a vital habitus out of breath work. My story is also from rehearsing *Play*: for actors who are otherwise stressed about the performance, they could gain resilience from the simple strategy of a vocal warm-up, using their breath to build ensemble as well. In the focus phase of a warmup like we had

---

4 A large number of voice-related medical studies can be found online at https://voicefoundation.org/health-science/voice-disorders/resources-related-links/ (accessed 19 February 2021).

for *Ethica*, after breathing together, actors would have done a standard intake for two beats, and then a steadily growing output, from four beats to six and eight — gradually also resonating, starting to warm the vocal cords sequentially.[5] The habit of leading that warm-up created an atmosphere that I felt was gaining control over the energy in the room. And when we were incredibly stressed about technical or timing issues, on tour for example, the actors would use that breath exercise to power through.

CQ: It's very important to atmosphere. But Rodenburg talks about versatility.[6] You may want to try a non-sequential variation — not building 4, 6, 8, but instead 6, 3, 14 — because text is not always going to be growing in order. Sometimes you get to a line with far too much breath left. You have to find your chest voice, opening the pharynx in the chest, rooting right down get the most out of the voice. My students have been struggling with it for over a year.

NJ: Have you noticed a cultural dimension to this? Is there a vocal quality that is specifically related to national origin, or is voice more marked by issues of class?

CQ: It's more about class. I've noticed that over the years — I'm teaching twenty years — class and self-esteem. Often these are interwoven, but if someone is down on themselves, you can hear it in their voice, maybe from being told off. The voice is there, you just have to uncover it. Or the people who are ashamed of their voice: it can be wonderful to celebrate that and open that up. Class is a huge debate as well in training. In many cases, it's only the middle class who can afford to train. I think the arts are suffering from that generally: some of the people best suited haven't had the spare capacity, while others are in schools, are used to expressing themselves in public, have opportunities to *commit* to language and to be exposed to great language early. They're brilliant because they understand the need to stay alive in Beckett. 'I'm not unhappy enough' — that idea — but they may not have it technically. You can never do one exercise that will work for everybody. You must find another way in for some, a different language for others. I spoke with the Irish scholar Gerry Dukes about Beckett's prodigious memory of paintings that he had seen years

---

5   The *Ethica* project included *Play, Come and Go, Catastrophe*, and *What Where*, and was performed in Dublin, Sofia, and Enniskillen in 2012–13.
6   Patsy Rodenburg (b. 1953) is Head of Voice at the Guildhall School of Music and Drama in London and has held positions at numerous international theatre companies, including the Royal Shakespeare Company and Royal National Theatre. See Rodenburg (2015).

ago, reporting it perfectly, and I realised that if I use visual, oral, and kinaesthetic stimuli, I will help people to become less resistant. You can see these things and work physically on something like *Happy Days*, before you work vocally. This woman's in the ground. So physically they feel this thing keeping them down and then having to work against that, they can viscerally connect to the situation that the person's in, and they wouldn't need the backstory. The idea of being weighed down is enough. Another way of getting that resistance was to notice the question 'what do I do when words fail?' We would play a game where every piece of text is coming to close the mouth. Every pause — coming, coming, coming — and it's terrifying. If the actor can see something very simple that forces them to speak with trepidation, we can quickly analogise that situation for any age, any background.

NJ: This puts me in mind of two different situations. When I first started at Trinity College I worked in the disability service, and I tutored a lot of people with dyslexia. We talked in those days about 'learning styles', or people who prefer auditory versus visual-verbal information, or visual-nonverbal versus kinaesthetic. While this four-part division is not well supported scientifically, it is useful pedagogically, and certainly has been validated at least in terms of memory: the ways in which learning is most likely to be retained is when you have more than one of these channels working in the brain. The overlaps between different modes of sensory perception are very strong. If visual information is added to incomplete auditory information, then the brain resolves it. In projects like *The Encounter* or some of the binaural recordings of Pan Pan's *Cascando*,[7] sometimes you can't tell what's happening if you don't look at the visual, but if you're given a visual prompt, you immediately understand both: the brain knows what's happening. It seems there is a pathway for synaesthesia and hyper-sensory awareness that always needs to be engaged that way. If this can be found, it's much easier to work experimentally. It starts the dialogue with actors about connecting between the source text and event, the voice and the audience, much quicker.

---

7 Referring to two so-called 'headphone pieces' of theatre, Complicité's *The Encounter* (2016–17) and Pan Pan's vesion of *Cascando* (2015–16), two audio-based productions much discussed around the time of this dialogue. Binaural microphone technology uses a 'prop-head' microphone that processes the signal of two microphones located roughly where the ears are on a human head, mimicking the spatial nature of audio as experienced inside the head. While *The Encounter* did use binaural technology in its production, Pan Pan ultimately did not, although as dramaturg Johnson was present at some recording experiments using this technique.

CQ: Someone who does a lot of public speaking said to me recently that you can only remember what you see. He had a visual image for every phrase he spoke. That's tough — and I don't fully agree, I think it has to be aural and visual combined. It's so much easier for me.

NJ: When I was doing more acting, I noticed that I often tried to memorise text while walking, and that there's a lot more that connects in rehearsal on your feet than at the table: when you go to your next mark, you just know what line goes with that mark, you're mapping it. The *intention* to move that way opens up that part of the text. I did my first Beckett prose anthology performance in Chicago in 2002, and even though it was a minor project in an undergraduate setting, it blazes back to life when I hear Conor Lovett perform those same lines.[8] I know exactly where I was on stage, in what lighting state.

CQ: I was also thinking about movement when we are learning lines — it's a huge thing. I've always said to actors that if they can wash dishes and clean the floor and go over those lines, then they own them. You have to 'own' the text — it can't be new in front of an audience. Many people think it's restrictive, and it takes an awful lot of work for something like *Happy Days*. But it also probably raises interesting legal questions with the Estate. You're speaking as if you wrote it yourself, as if it's come from you. Your voice is united with the voice of the author.

NJ: Would you find that people who have certain types of voice training, for example as members of a choir or full-blown classical vocal training, flourish differently from novices in the vocal/textual workshops that you do? Is it at all like the problem that movement teachers have, where highly trained students might be less flexible or less free as a result, as a consequence of increased embodied control or the influence of a particular style?

CQ: I think cultural barriers matter more than training. Culture affects voice hugely. I've noticed that some American female students can tend to get stuck in their head voice, that they might be resistant to open up a deeper 'woman' voice and instead use their 'girl' voice in speaking. It takes a long time for students to accept that there's more to their voice — this has happened two or

---

8   Conor Lovett co-founded Gare St Lazare Ireland with Judy Hegarty-Lovett, and performs Beckett's prose worldwide. The 'anthology performance' discussed here is *On Going On*, Wallis Theatre, Northwestern University (December 2002), a Beckett prose anthology performed as part of Johnson's undergraduate senior thesis in performance studies.

three times. Often they are terrific singers, and they think it's going to damage their voice if they open it up lower, but it just gives them the possibility of more range.

NJ: Versatility would clearly be one of the goals you would have if you took three years of vocal training in a conservatory. Are there other words you would apply beyond 'grounding' and 'capacity' that you are trying to help students to build?

CQ: They're all interlinked: grounding, breath capacity, breath support, pitch and pitch range, the pace of delivery, so they're not just doing the same pace all the time. And basically, in the end it's about tone. Articulation of the text, not just technically, but with creativity, versatility, and variety. Beckett is a fantastic training tool, because of the variety of pace that his texts require. One interesting exercise I do is to have three areas on the ground where they speak slower (normal pace), then fast, and then normal. Once they've got that principle, they have degrees of fast, depending on the side of the room, and they choose when they move. They get surprised by something. That simple exercise opens up the text for variety.

NJ: What do you think about containment and Beckett? Are you of the view that Beckett gives you a freedom within the textual box, within the container of the stage event?

CQ: One of our exercises is with a Shakespearean sonnet, which is what I think of when you say 'restriction'. But then, even if you have just fourteen lines and a regular metre, the possibilities are almost endless. Within the restrictions that are in there, your own resistance comes through.

NJ: What do you make of Beckett's stage direction, for Clov and others, that describes the voice as 'toneless'?

CQ: You've got to find tone within the toneless. If you're looking at sound waves on a digital recording, it's astonishing to see how much range is there. It's about the scale: think of the cardiogram. That's one pitch, basically, or each spasm is, but there is so much variety when you visualise the wave.

NJ: How would these exercises be used by you in rehearsal? Do you spend a lot of time on the vocal aspects when you are directing, whether Beckett or something else?

CQ: Only if they need it. They have to learn to do it themselves. Rehearsal time is so precious, as you well know — I will do it if it's absolutely necessary, but the older they are the harder it is to introduce something like that.

NJ: I identify with the challenge of being both a teacher and a director, and even though they inform each other, I certainly see those roles as different in important ways. I have to be on the lookout for when I start to 'teach' an actor or 'direct' a student. As a teacher, you are often alert on day one — you can tell individually which person is already open, which carries a particular barrier, or which one needs more rooting or grounding — you develop your range of prescriptions just from working with them, and you get used to them.

CQ: Yes, and when you get back into the room as a Beckett director fresh from that experience, and you are no longer teaching but observing actors, it can be hard to integrate that experience.

NJ: Something that I've found in a lot of Beckett vocal performances is that directors and actors can take those stage directions like Clov's 'toneless', or reported directions like his 'no colour, no colour' to Whitelaw, incredibly literally, almost legalistically. I think that we frequently mishear that message as needing to create a standard 'Beckettian' vocal quality for a Beckett text. While it's hard to describe in words, I certainly feel that I recognise this 'Beckett voice' when I hear it, even in myself. It takes on a portentous quality, maybe elegiac, but is there a risk of branding Beckett with a strange flatness?

CQ: My theory would be that his idea of 'less colour' is the reaction to the training that people were undergoing in the 1950s and 60s. People used their voices far more to effect, rather than being behind what they were saying. They used much more range. He was writing before kitchen-sink drama came in, before naturalism took over the British theatre. He would listen to the radio, and it was full of these voices. This cracked, strange voice that was coming out of the box: when I was doing radio drama on the BBC, they all sound the same. There's nothing identifying about them.

NJ: I also have a theory about it — I think we share the impulse, but perhaps we differ on the theory. I've identified the 'Beckett voice' more as being about the influence of melodrama and farce, and Beckett wanting to create a different theatre. Just materially, a lot of the actors were moving between his serious shows at the National or the Royal Court and other projects that were highly expressive or dynamic.

CQ: In that field of British and Irish actors, their training would have been more technical. Beckett wanted that technique, but in a different way. It was not as important as the text. It would just arise.

NJ: The voice applied is a by-product of the conditions of body, stage, context.

CQ: Absolutely. The right use of the body will give you the right use of the voice.

Works Cited

Bartenieff, Irmgard with Dori Lewis (1980), *Body Movement: Coping with the Environment*, New York and London: Routledge.

Feldenkrais, Moshe (2011), *Embodied Wisdom: The Collected Papers of Moshe Feldenkrais*, Berkeley, CA: North Atlantic Books.

Germoni, Karine and Pascale Sardin (2012), 'Tensions of the In-between: Rhythm, Tonelessness and Lyricism in *Fin de partie/Endgame*', in SBT/A, 24: *Early Modern Beckett / Beckett et le début de l'ère modern: Beckett Between / Beckett entre deux*, pp. 336–50.

Linklater, Kristin (2006), *Freeing the Natural Voice*, London: Drama Publishers/Quite Specific Media [1976].

Madden, Catherine (2014), *Onstage Synergy: Integrative Alexander Technique Practice for Performing Artists*, Bristol: Intellect Books.

Rodenburg, Patsy (2015), *The Right to Speak: Working with the Voice*, 2nd edition, London: Bloomsbury/Methuen.

Beckett in Performance: The Body of a Beckettian Actor

Melissa Nolan

Abstract

The Beckettian actor has been known to undergo physical and mental suffering in order to fulfil the text. Like the Beckett characters they play, they too are stuck, isolated, cut off, distant, subjected to stimuli, and often tormented. The phrase 'to act' cannot be easily attributed to the Beckettian actor, for they are often at the mercy of the writer. Extending the 'voice' of practice in this volume, this essay explores what happens to the actor's body — that being my own — during the rehearsal and performance process for Samuel Beckett's plays.

1 Beckett-Actor Performing Beckett-Artist

Having performed in many of Beckett's plays to date — up to September 2012, *Not I, Footfalls, Rough for Radio II, Play, Rockaby, Come and Go* and *Teacht Is Imeacht* (Irish language translation of *Come and Go* by Gabriel Rosenstock) — my work as an actor is revealing the patterns of voice and embodiment across his works. The core objective of this chapter is to draw on this experience to explore the actor's body in the theatrical space with the texts of Samuel Beckett.

The vast majority of character-based theatre requires human bodies that are physically, aurally and visually mindful in the space. The mind of an actor undergoes many different psychological states that can allow multiple character types, as it journeys through a variety of emotions in order to support the narrative. To serve, support and present the text, actors are required to be fully open and fully available for the expression of ideas to filter through the conscious and subconscious mind. The actor therefore gains a great sense of liberation and fulfilment. Freeing the whole of the self — body, mind and voice — in context, the actor's body is a means of carrying the narrative; it serves and has a purpose.

However, in the theatre of Samuel Beckett, the body goes through a process of what Pierre Chabert calls 'metamorphosis'. Chabert claims the body is moulded, sculpted, violated, subjected and fragmented as it goes through a difficult process of embodiment. This same dramatic force and principle is also given to that of light, space, object and text. All are simplified and given finite importance in the theatrical space (Chabert, 23–8). To an audience member seeing, or as I prefer to describe it, *experiencing* Beckett's work for the first time, it may seem different, strange, possibly alien in fact. He creates images that are not traditional, despite my belief that the foundations of his work lie in highlighting the human condition. What he does create brings us beyond our everyday, into a place that lights up the darkness.

Beckett's constant use of cyclical patterns, both verbally and structurally, are all shaped with minute precision: a huge challenge for any actor. In my varied experience performing Beckett, this challenge has never ceased to prick my curious artistic mind and soul. His ability to capture sound, light, text, and gesture into a musical score steers me into unchartered waters where I am left stripped naked, and yet I feel completely safe.

Edward Albee says, 'He [Beckett] probably taught me more than anything else: the precision of language' (Knowlson, 2006, 231). A Beckett performance is devoid of free exploration and spontaneous and natural movement. To perform Beckett an actor must leave improvisational skills at the door. Beckett's relationship with the body in space ultimately succeeds and is fulfilled, creating tension and conflict. It is what Chabert claims as the perfect drama; when the actor's body suffers in the theatrical space, it exists all the more powerfully (Chabert, 23–8). If the actor's body is alive, present and mindful, it can therefore appear all the more real, fuller with dimension, understanding and objective. The lack of physical movement in a Beckettian role allows the energy to go somewhere else. Tension and conflict are created within the language. However, the traditional technique of 'finding your character' is not adopted; rather, it is done through fragmentation, restriction, immobilisation, confinement, and impairment, as well as exploring physical and mental difficulties. This is how Beckett creates drama. Each action a Beckettian actor performs must be discovered and played clearly and fully without anticipation or conclusion. Performing Beckett means performing specifically. It is no secret that Beckett did not like actors to 'find their character'; he wanted them to 'play parts as impersonally as possible' (Fletcher, 140). When an actor asked him about meaning regarding a character, his response was always 'don't ask me for any meaning in the thing; it just is what it is' (Knowlson, 2006, 188).

> He simply did not trust actors to get it right. [...] Beckett felt that both directors and actors were an unfortunate necessity and that the ideal dramatic executant would be one totally subservient to the author's ideas about production and prepared to abandon his or her personality and

character in favor of the text. The ideal actor would be, as a person, invisible. (Cronin, 525)

Performing Beckett can create physical and mental suffering; a Beckettian actor in performance may also find similarities between themselves and their characters, as they are stuck, isolated, cut off, distant, subjected to stimuli and tormented. Students who have primarily been taught the Stanislavskian-based approach to acting can find it extremely difficult to 'let go' of character in this way. Jonathan Kalb states that a Beckett performance should follow the simple standard that 'ambiguity [is ...] a positive performance value' (48). Lawrence Held, an Australian writer and former actor with the San Quentin Drama workshop, understood this, stating it as 'not method acting, not Stanislavski; when the characters (if they could be called characters) left the stage, they left the stage' (Knowlson, 2006, 201). For this reason, Julie Campbell contends, 'Beckett's plays are not easy on the audience or easy on the actors' (9).

Beckettian actors like Billie Whitelaw described the state of her spine 'like a corkscrew' after years of working on Beckett; Jack MacGowran commented on his experience of performing *Eh Joe* as 'the most gruelling 22 minutes I have ever had in my life' (Zinman, 56). Siân Philips working on the voice in *Eh Joe* remarked 'we worked like machines' (Haynes and Knowlson, 2003, 109), and Brenda Bruce commented on playing Winnie, 'my heart was hammering so hard that it hurt' (Fletcher, 163).

For the Beckett actor, the text is there; however, what is not written may not be expressed on the printed page — the wonderful echoes or contrasts of voices like musical instruments, the dark and light tones of inflections and words, the exact timing of gestures and expressions, the length of a pause, the urgency of a movement or the pace of dialogue. Finding these are essential to the performance. In this regard, researching Beckett's theatrical notebooks helped me discover what he wanted, his precise vision.

2   *Footfalls*

The posture required for May is echoed by the painting 'Virgin of the Annunciation' by Antonello da Messina, which Beckett had seen in Munich's Alte Pinakothek in 1937. Her sculptural figure shows her arms tightly folded across her awkwardly curved body, as she paces back and forth along the stage. Billie Whitelaw said that 'sometimes I felt as if he were a sculptor and I a piece of clay [...] he would endlessly move my arms and head in a certain way, to get closer to the precise image in his mind' (Haynes and Knowlson, 76). For my

FIGURE 1 Melissa Nolan in *Footfalls*
PHOTO © FUTOSHI SAKAUCHI

own performance of May in *Footfalls* (Focus Theatre, Dublin, April 2012), the pacing back and forth required nine steps within nine seconds, while staying within the lighting strip. This strip is all May has to move within, endlessly walking up and down. On the ninth step I placed my foot at an angle so I could swing my body round to face the opposite direction and start the whole process again. As Geraldine Plunkett (who played V) could not see my movements, my nine footsteps needed to be heard so she would know when to speak. I wanted to find a motivation to turn and through the rehearsal process decided on her believing, or in hope, that the next nine steps would be the last — and then the next and so on — like the voice in *Cascando*, 'one more and I'll be finished', and like dozens of other Beckettian characters from Lucky in *Waiting for Godot* to Mouth in *Not I*, 'on and on' (Beckett, 381), but in paces not words. I found the rehearsal and each performance physically and mentally exhausting. The movements in *Footfalls* are simple, yet require precision, so the smallest inaccuracy has an adverse effect. Rehearsals were certainly not an overnight success. It took several gruelling weeks to become confident and find the exact physical rhythm. I discovered layering each instruction a breakthrough in gaining results. Once I managed to perfect the rhythm of pacing, I could add the taut folded arms. This allowed me to create conflict within the movement: hypnotic pacing juxtaposed with May deathly gripping onto herself. Creating the correct tone and volume of the nine steps was also a challenge. Professor Gerry Dukes, biographer of Beckett, who saw my performance, thought the volume far too subtle, describing them as 'mercifully quiet'. In response to this, we tried attaching sandpaper to the soles of my shoes, which created the right texture of sound, but was too loud and upstaged V when she spoke. To counter this, we added stockings over my shoes and sand paper, and thankfully this achieved the desired result. Each step was subtle but effective, supporting the line 'I must hear the feet however faint they fall' (Beckett, 401–3). Rosemary Pountney describes this movement of May as 'an old-fashioned gramophone running down and needed to be wound up again' (from an interview by Feldman).

Time and again my director (Cathal Quinn) asked me not to drop my tone too low (I was slipping into the voice of *Rockaby*) but to keep it girlish, as an antithesis to the mother's 'white voice', a quality Beckett craved from his actors from *Endgame* on. When I lowered my tone, I sounded too old and masculine. I needed to keep the adult female quality but in a childlike way: a virgin in her forties. Jung's lecture about the young girl that 'had never been born entirely' (Jung, 195–6) stayed with me during the rehearsal process, suggesting a voice absent, distant, removed.

The light that shone on me when I faced front was blinding, which started my eyes to water and my nose to run to the point of dripping from my chin. Of course, I had to carry on. In a naturalistic play a character could simply wipe it as part of the action, but this is Beckett. I was forced to ignore this natural reaction from my body. From my experience the light in *Footfalls* is similar to the spotlight in *Play*: interrogator.

3 *Not I*

The text of *Not I* worried me greatly on my first approach. As a performer I had never come across a piece that left me so dumbfounded. Where was I going to start? How was I going to breathe? Could I remember the entire text? These were just some of the questions that came to me.

Rosemary Pountney states of rehearsing for *Not I*:

> There was no point in trying to research older women in how they breathed, walked, talked when playing Mouth, all this is impossible. Instead empty myself of all preconceptions and try to be open to a new form of communication. Immerse myself into rehearsals with articula-

tion exercise and build the frantic vocal pace required. (from an interview by Feldman)

Reading the text on a daily basis was my starting point. I read it over and over again, no performance, no tones, inflections, nothing, just the text. This simple 'reading' process went on for weeks. I had to get my mouth literally around the text, so that it became clear, articulate and precise. I became a little more confident with the text after four weeks, which allowed me to start working on the speed. I broke the text down into the four movements (sections) as indicated by Beckett. Each movement allowed me to work between boundaries. This provided some comfort despite the ridiculous demands of the text. What became the greatest challenge was my breathing. I began to feel faint and disorientated. To my shock, I had forgotten how to breathe correctly. Billie Whitelaw collapsed at a *Not I* rehearsal, but she never blamed Beckett or the text. I had to go back to each section and find where I could take my breath, that way allowing me full use of speed and articulation without fainting. Breaking the text down into this minute scale was a tedious task, and a case of trial and error. But before I could perform it, I needed to train my breath and voice, much like a distance runner preparing their body to endure a marathon. I had to build up my lung capacity in order for my breath to support the words. It required my mind and body to be extremely flexible, awake and concentrated. Getting eight hours sleep per night was crucial in allowing me to push myself in rehearsals. When I had the text memorised I began to test myself; I spoke the words while moving around, lying down, throwing a ball from one hand to the other, stacking chairs, running frantically about the space. This drove the text deeper into my memory and physical body. The less I thought about the text, the more the mouth worked. Jessica Tandy, who played Mouth, claimed 'you must not think what you are saying; it just has to come out ... it all makes perfectly good sense, musically' (Knowlson, 2006, 236). I became engrained in the text: the breaths, silences and pauses became this fantastic dark musical score, with 'a complex network of interrelated musical or choreographic echoes' (Haynes and Knowlson, 128). I was now ready for performance.

16 March 2010 was the first time I performed *Not I* at Smock Alley Theatre, Dublin, directed by Keith Hughes as part of his MA Directors' showcase. The space was completely black. I sat eight feet in the air on a chair, which was strapped to a large metal frame. I was covered in a large black cloth that also covered the metal frame. I had ear plugs in my ears, dark goggles over my eyes, black make-up around my mouth, and a small light shone on my lips that were painted blood-red. A video camera stood behind the light with its viewfinder facing the audience; this image was projected on to a large stone wall. The

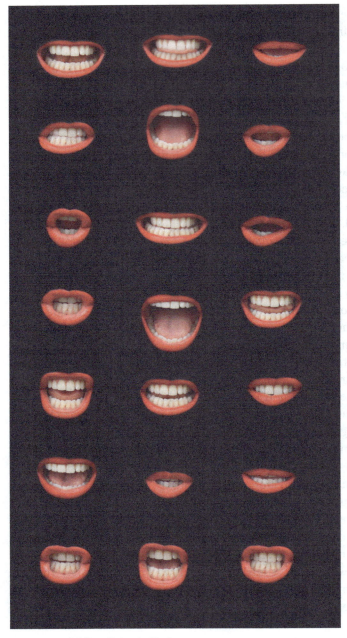

FIGURE 2   Melissa Nolan in *Not I*
PHOTO © BOB DIXON

image of the mouth was now visible in three forms; mine, the viewfinder and the projected image. The Auditor was not used; instead, the video camera on its tripod replaced him. The audience entered a blackened space, Mouth already whispering. After three minutes I began. When I finished speaking the text I went back into a whisper, after which the audience then had to leave. No bow or clap. Keith and I decided that we did not want a definite start nor an end to the piece; we wanted Mouth to be this continuous painstaking babbling aperture of never-ending torture. Feedback from the audience was positive — they liked being brought into the darkened space where Mouth existed, in perpetuity, floating in an unlit abyss.

My next performance of *Not I* was under the direction of Cathal Quinn. This was performed at Powerscourt Gallery, Dublin, September 2010. The space was an art gallery by day, a theatre space by night. It was small, and audience members sat close to me. *Not I* was the second piece of the line-up, which meant I could not be pre-set. Instead I had to walk in the dark to my seat. Due to the restrictions in the space it was not possible to raise me eight feet in the air, so instead I sat on an average-size chair, this time wearing infra-red lipstick. We decided to explore if the infra-red lipstick and infra-red lighting had any bearing on the overall effect of the performance. Audience feedback suggested the infra-red idea made the mouth seem bigger, as if the mouth were dreamlike. Personally, I felt the effect may have diminished the dark undertones in the text. Also, the infra-red lighting picked up other fabrics and objects in the gallery, which did not bring complete focus and attention to my lips.

My overall experience of performing *Not I* was a frightful, painstaking challenge which pushed me to limits and feelings I never thought I could achieve as a performer. I am forever grateful to Beckett for this.

4   *Rough for Radio II*

Mouth on Fire, the theatre company I co-founded with Cathal Quinn, sought permission from the Beckett Estate to perform this radio play on stage. The cast included John Cullen, Jennifer Laverty, Colm O'Brien, Cathal Quinn and myself. We were granted permission with one rule: the performance must be in the dark or as close to it as possible. This meant the actors had to learn the script off by heart. I was cast at a very late stage in the rehearsal process (two weeks until we opened), as the original actress was re-cast in a TV show. Thankfully, as co-founder of the company, I had attended most of the previous rehearsals. Yet the mammoth task of slotting into such a role was daunting at first, considering that they had been working on the text for months. However, like my approach to *Not I*, I broke the script down into sections. Working closely with the director on a daily basis, we organised extra rehearsals with the entire cast, and I caught up as quickly as I could. I recorded the entire text so I could listen to it on my phone or on a CD in the car. The two weeks were taxing. The pressure was on, as I was also producing the entire production, named *Tyranny in Beckett*, which also consisted of *What Where*, *Catastrophe* (I was also cast late in this) and the world premiere of *As The Story Was Told*.

I found *Rough for Radio II* wonderful to work on. I felt the music, the beats, the silences, the pauses and words. Working in the dark was a great challenge, but again like *Not I*, I controlled my breath so as not to faint or become anxious during performance. We moved into the space: Smock Alley Boys School, Dublin, in November 2011. A seventeenth-century theatre, it holds approximately one hundred people positioned on four different levels. The sound effects were performed live by the 'Animator', who stood in the middle of the space with a table in front of him. On this table was positioned a small microphone, a bull whip, a piece of leather, a writing pad and a pencil; these were our sound effect props. On the very top of the wooden structure stood an old-style radio under a small faint spotlight. Prior to performance the audience were informed that this play was just over twenty minutes in duration and they would be in darkness. Next came the sound of a radio being tuned, a faint spotlight on the radio, and I began. My stance during the piece needed to support me for the duration. I had my feet shoulder-width apart, my arms by my side and my face pointing frontwards. Performing in the dark allowed my eyes to become accustomed to the gloom, and after a while I could make out shapes of people and structures. To allow me to remain concentrated and focused, I decided it best to keep my eyes shut. Any movement from the audience would break my concentration and possibly remove me from the piece.

This play is intended as a radio play where actors may have their script in front of them to glance at during performance. However, for this production, all actors had to learn the entire script, which meant all pauses and sound effects also had to be rehearsed too, in the dark. Finding the rhythm of this text was not difficult — in fact, it was one of the few Beckett pieces that prior to opening night I felt at ease and confident. The clipped Received Pronunciation (RP) accent that I used for the 'Stenographer' allowed me to animate with ease. I felt very free performing this text. The production was well received.

5   *Catastrophe*

Catastrophe was another play in the production titled *Tyranny in Beckett*, also performed at Smock Alley Boys School in Dublin, November 2011. The cast

FIGURE 3   Melissa Nolan and Colm O'Brien in *Catastrophe*
PHOTO © CATHAL QUINN

included John Cullen, Cathal Quinn and Colm O'Brien. Jennifer Laverty and I alternated the role of A (Assistant). In rehearsals the director Cathal Quinn and I spoke of the fearful world of *Catastrophe*, how the plight of P (The Protagonist) could so easily fall upon my character should she not perform her tasks to D's (Director) approval. This gave me great impetus in my approach, and the image of a constant hanging guillotine above my head drove me in each performance. I spoke in a clipped RP accent and developed a light and quick way of moving, allowing me to appear flighty and nervous, birdlike. I wore shoes with a small heel. I had my hair tied up and exceptionally neat. All of this created a harsh and practical demeanour. I wore thick black tights and a long bottle-green dress under a buttoned up 'white overall'. The lay of the unique theatre space was exceptionally well suited for this piece. P was positioned up on a raised wooden stage. The steps leading from the main performance space to the top of the wooden structure allowed A to constantly go up and down to carry out her 'final touches' on P. When D left to 'see how it looks from the house', we had the actor playing D physically leave the space, walk up the back-stage steps and re-enter at the very top of the auditorium amid the audience while they are immersed in watching A and P. The time that it took that actor to walk up the back steps allowed me (A) to take 'out a rag, wipes vigorously back and seat of chair, discards rag, sits again' (Beckett, 456–61). The sound of my footsteps punctuated the space beautifully well.

Playing A in *Catastrophe* allowed me to play more in delivering the text, as it was dialogue-driven, and I relished the opportunity to move about the stage compared to the brutal confinement of *Not I* and *Footfalls*.

6   *Come and Go*

Come and Go was part of a production called *Before Vanishing*... that was performed in English and Irish language at Focus Theatre, Dublin, April 2012. The cast were as follows: Jennifer Laverty, Geraldine Plunkett and myself. Geraldine's age, being considerably older than Jennifer and I, did not place any hindrance in the piece nor the rehearsal process; additionally, the text states 'ages undeterminable' (Beckett, 353–7). I was cast as Vi. I found this text to be technically challenging at first. We had to work out a consistency in the length we gave our silences, our pauses, how we moved, sat or stood. Either I was too fast or the others were too slow, often. We chose to have a large mirror in front of us so that we could see the height of one other, how our feet were positioned, how wide our arms were, and also when to lift the hands at the end. Since I was the tallest of the three, I had to bend my torso slightly, which proved to be uncomfortable at times. These technical moves are the key to this play. It needed to be as smooth as possible so that the text is just resting on these movements and gestures.

In performance we entered in the dark. Facing front, we sat as a trio on a small wooden black bench. Our costumes were long heavy coats, and we needed to take care not to trip on the end of them. Blackness remained for twenty seconds. In that time, if need be, we could silently adjust our coat or hat. After lights up (cold, blue tones), we remained still, solid, no movement, like a painting. After twenty seconds, dialogue. Our silences were seven seconds. On leaving the bench, we stood up (five seconds), stood for three seconds, walked three steps and then turned to leave the playing space. The pace of the walk was practised over and over again to harness a rhythm, a synergy between us. At times my nose started to drip (the same as in *Footfalls*). Why my body reacted like this, I have no idea. I could not do anything but let it occur and carry on; even when I was out of the playing space, I did not tend to my running nose, as that would have broken my focus.

From the English version of *Come and Go*, lights went to black. The actors playing Vi and Ru needed to return to original position (i.e. swap sides of the bench). We did this at the same pace and style of movement as in any other period of the play. Then after lights up (different, more sepia colour) and again after twenty seconds silence, this time, the world premiere of *Teacht Is*

FIGURE 4 Geraldine Plunkett, Melissa Nolan, and Jennifer Laverty in *Come and Go/ Teacht Is Imeacht*
PHOTO © FUTOSHI SAKAUCHI

Imeacht (*Come and Go*) in the Irish language, translated by Gabriel Rosenstock. We chose to have the same length for silences, pauses and movements. Working in another language was incredibly difficult; using my tongue and mouth with sounds that I had only uttered in secondary school a decade previous proved strenuous. The only fluent Irish speaker in the group was Geraldine. Jennifer had never even learned Irish in school, so she was starting afresh, which proved at times to be almost impossible. The Irish version, because of the sound, gave the text a new richness, a mystery. In many ways the piece seemed more suitable to the Irish-language version. *Come and Go* in both English and Irish is one of my favourite Beckett pieces, purely because of the beauty that it creates visually, a dreamlike painting.

7   *Play*

Play was the second Beckett text I performed (Powerscourt Gallery, Dublin, September 2010). I was cast as W1; Jennifer Laverty played W2, and Cathal Quinn played M. Having performed *Not I* where I had pushed myself beyond limits I never knew existed, I tackled this text with more confidence. Aware the text was tremendously arduous to grasp, I set about putting structures in place. Constant reading of the text was first and foremost. Finding the rhythms of the language and the musicality of the piece came next. Using an RP accent allowed me to draw out the music in the text, and it was not until complete fluidity that I began to really hear the piece. During rehearsals we focused on small phrases within the text and walked round the rehearsal space reciting these. Whenever I am at a point where I am able to do another task such as play in the space, walk to rehearsals, even drive my car while reciting the text accurately, I feel I am close to knowing it well enough for performance.

When our urns became available, we decided to use them in short rehearsal slots. We needed to build up our physical stamina to last the entire performance. Knees and lower back became increasingly painful during rehearsals, so we opted to wear knee pads, which worked very well. Unfortunately, my lower back began to seriously trouble me, yet I had little choice but to suffer it. Staying completely still in the urns while performing *Play* became a test of endurance. Sweat would build up on my brow; my thighs and lower back became tense as I held myself rigid. Inside our urns were two metal rods, and I held on to these tightly. This helped me to remain completely still. The urns were constructed from metal frames that held bin-bags. They were covered in sacking material that was painted dark grey and green. An opening was cut at the back of them so the actors could crawl inside. We carried our urns onto the stage, each step in sync.

The spotlight role in the piece was given to actor Colm O'Brien, who was required to learn the entire piece. He sat in the stalls of the front row, facing the urns (on stage) with a mobile spotlight and moved it according to the

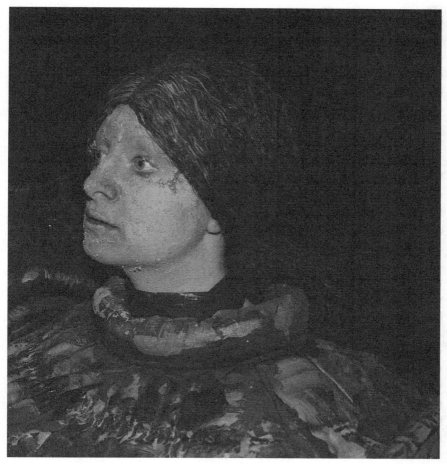

FIGURE 5   Melissa Nolan in *Play* (dress rehearsal)
PHOTO © MATTHEW RALLI

directions in the script. During performances I would listen to the music of the text. Nerves and anxiety meant at times we spoke too fast, and our articulation suffered. During one performance I suddenly forgot what my next line was, when all of sudden the spotlight lit me and without conscious thought the text sprang from my mouth. It was frightening. I spoke to the other actors about my experience, and they too talked of similar experiences.

One performance of *Play* which haunts me was when the spotlight Colm was using stopped working. Everything fell into complete darkness. Instinctively, we continued the text. The stage manager and lighting technician rushed to the back of the theatre, jumped up on the very back row, which was fortunately empty, and started to use a follow-spot light that was on a lighting rig. Colm, seeing what they were doing, began using his arm to direct the lighting technician, who miraculously followed his lead and together they continued the interrogation. Dressed in a long black hooded cloak, the interrogator remained in control. I do not know how we managed to carry on with that performance, but we did, much to the audience's appreciation.

8   *Rockaby*

When I first approached this text, I was apprehensive, as I thought I was too young to play the woman in the chair. I thought I would not be able to get those low tones in the voice that only come with age. Beckett does not give exact age of the character in his text, which thankfully allowed me to perform it. I did not have a rocking chair when we started rehearsals, so instead I would sit on a normal wooden kitchen chair and rock myself back and forth. I rocked forward, said a line of the text, then inhaled a breath on the backward rock. This was my rhythm for the piece, slight and slow, keeping focus on the musicality, finding the rhythms.

Getting the low tone required for this piece was my greatest test. I worked with Cathal Quinn (Cf. previous chapter for a dialogue about his vocal instruction), and found this rewarding as he knew, with correct guidance and monitoring, how I could reach the low register required. Vocal warm-ups prior to rehearsal allowed me to achieve the toneless qualities Beckett wanted. Cathal would constantly tell me, 'Stay low, stay low, find that low tone'. After hours of rehearsal and using the rhythm of the piece, I was able to consistently achieve the low register, but now volume became an issue. I worked harder, strengthened my vocal muscles further until we were ready to record the text. I could not bring the rocking chair into the recording studio, so I had to improvise and go back to my initial moving back and forth on a fixed chair. This aided, and the recording went very smoothly.

The stage direction 'unblinking gaze' was another challenge. I do not have the natural ability to stare for long periods of time without blinking. To combat any soreness in the eyes or eye watering, when my head was in the darkened zone of the rocking, I blinked, unseen by the audience. Every night I would ask Cathal to sit in the front row and check to see if he could see me blink when I rocked back. It worked.

For my performance of *Rockaby* we did not have a mechanically assisted rocking chair due to the company's limited production budget. Instead, we focused the front light above the knees, leaving the feet in complete darkness. The dress was long enough to cover the feet, which allowed me to rock the chair myself. My thighs became stiff and sore a few minutes into the performance because I was holding a lot of tension in them (Beckett, 433–42). My rocking required control without flaw, as if I was being pushed mechanically. This, along with the performance, provided a great test of endurance each night.

9   Coda

Walter Asmus, who worked as an assistant director under Beckett's direction, summarises Beckett's vision: 'To strive for precision, to strive for simplicity' (Fletcher, 147). Asmus witnessed Beckett's perfectionism, being 'always dissatisfied' and would often say 'it's still a long way'. Beckett demanded a 'great deal' from his actors, to be 'word perfect' from the start. Of this, Asmus states, 'nobody can do that'. Rehearsals became 'mechanical', despite perhaps working on a very funny text (Knowlson, 2006, 190–1). In performing Beckett, space and time become very clear. One becomes a channel for the text. The actor discovers that each movement, word, sound, however slight must be taken on its own terms, this is the precision that is ultimately required (Zarrilli, 103–16). Beckett had no problem stopping an actor who said 'it is' when in fact the text read 'it's'. He knew his work precisely (Knowlson, 2006, 201). The actor cannot cheat using tricks, habits or devices as a safety net. Nor can they hide behind props, costumes or scenery. When I understood Beckett's precision and finite detail, I could work within this framework and knew that I would be safe. Many actors may think that Beckett 'ties the actor up' (Knowlson, 2006, 174) in a constrained knot, but if you simply read the text you cannot go wrong. If you 'cut corners' (175) you lose the entire piece. 'Acting' is therefore obsolete. 'Don't act', he would say, 'he wanted the essence of what was in you to come out' (Knowlson, 1996, 553).

The demands I faced performing Beckett's work allowed me to understand physicality, or the lack thereof, through extreme concentration of tension and conflict in gesture, words, movement and stillness. Not only did this strengthen my resolve as a performer, but also as a person, and I thank Beckett for this. The rehearsal process begins this slow takeover of the body and mind. The ego of an actor has no place. These plays are so perfect in construction that they require no adjustments or finer details. They simply stand alone. Why change them? Distort them? When there is 'only one way to perform them: as written' (Fletcher, 173).

Works Cited

Beckett, Samuel (1990), *The Complete Dramatic Works*, London: Faber and Faber.

Campbell, Julie (2005), 'The Entrapment of the Female Body in Beckett's Plays in Relation to Jung's Third Tavistock Lecture', *SBT/A*, 15: *Historicising Beckett/Issues of Performance, Beckett dans l'histoire/En jouant Beckett*, pp. 161–72.

Chabert, Pierre (1982), 'The Body in Beckett's Theatre', *JOBS*, 8, pp. 23–8.

Cronin, Anthony (1996), *Samuel Beckett: The Last Modernist*, London: Harper Collins.

Feldman, Matthew (2009), 'Interview: Dr. Rosemary Pountney on Beckett', available online at: www.soundcloud.com/fred2360.

Fletcher, John (2003), *About Beckett: The Playwright and the Work*, London: Faber and Faber.

Haynes, John and James Knowlson (2003), *Images of Beckett*, Cambridge: Cambridge UP.

Jung, C. G. (1968), 'The Tavistock Lectures', in *Analytical Psychology: Its Theory and Practice*, London: Routledge & Kegan Paul, pp. 195–6.

Kalb, Jonathan (1989), *Beckett in Performance*, Cambridge: Cambridge UP.

Knowlson, James (1996), *Damned to Fame: The Life of Samuel Beckett*, London: Bloomsbury.

Knowlson, James and Elizabeth Knowlson, eds. (2006), *Beckett Remembering/Remembering Beckett: A Centenary Celebration*, New York: Arcade Publishing.

Zarrilli, Phillip B. (1997), 'Acting "at the nerve ends": Beckett, Blau and the Necessary', *Theatre Topics*, 7: 2, pp. 103–16.

Zinman, Toby (1995), '*Eh Joe* and the Peephole Aesthetic', *SBT/A*, 4: *The Savage Eye/L'oeil Fauve*, pp. 53–64.

Translating Beckett's Voices in Different Cultures

Yoshiko Takebe

Abstract

This chapter analyses how Japanese audiences interpret Samuel Beckett's drama by finding its imagery within the context of Japanese society, culture, and traditions. Without deviating from the original texts, the images are transformed through intersemiotic translation. Roman Jakobson argues that 'Interlingual translation or translation proper is an interpretation of verbal signs by means of some other language' and that 'Intersemiotic translation or transmutation is an interpretation of verbal signs by means of signs of nonverbal sign systems' (139). This chapter introduces types of imagery in Samuel Beckett's drama performed in Japan from both verbal and nonverbal viewpoints of interpreting theatre in our contemporary age.

Japanese audiences have responded to Beckett's plays ever since Shinya Ando witnessed the premiere of *Waiting for Godot* at the Théâtre de Babylone in 1953 and introduced it into Japan. While Beckett's plays have been performed by *Shingeki* [New Drama] actors who are familiar with the Western style drama developed in Japan (about a hundred years ago), they have also been performed and even adapted by Japanese Noh and Kyogen actors in the style of Japanese traditional performing art.

This chapter analyses four different Japanese productions of Beckett's plays performed in Japan and Dublin in the 2010s: the New National Theatre Tokyo's *Waiting for Godot*, produced in April 2011 just after the Great East Japan Earthquake in March 2011; the same play adapted and performed in August 2011 on a country road by a tree just over 20 kilometres away from the stricken Fukushima nuclear power plant, both of which revealed post-3.11 images of the devastated areas; *Happy Days*, presented in March 2018 as one of the projects for Theatre Commons Tokyo 2018; and an experimental nonverbal version of the same play in 2013, later invited to Dublin Theatre Festival 2017.

Translating Beckett's drama in a different language and different culture requires and enables translators, directors, actors, and audiences to leave the original text and migrate into a new theatrical environment. Bandia suggests that the 'context of migration, by its very nature, evokes translation and bilingualism as a fundamental condition of being. Translation therefore partakes of the cultural representation of otherness as a primordial instrument' (283).

This concept of 'otherness' is fundamental to translating Beckett's voices and is a feature which draws in global audiences, provoking questions without ever providing clear answers. In addition, Roman Jakobson argues that 'Interlingual translation or translation proper is an interpretation of verbal signs by means of some other language' and that 'Intersemiotic translation or transmutation is an interpretation of verbal signs by means of signs of nonverbal sign systems' (139). Those four productions are valuable to focus on because both pairs (two productions of *Waiting for Godot* and two performances of *Happy Days*) emphasise the contrast between interlingual and intersemiotic translations, between locality and globalism, which will ultimately lead to the discussion of Beckett's understating of otherness through translation.

This chapter examines how the voice of Beckett, both verbally and nonverbally, can be interpreted and translated for contemporary Japanese theatres. The challenge of interpreting his plays from culturally different perspectives possibly enriches the levels of variations.

1   Beckett's Voices between Verbal and Nonverbal Images

Instead of giving his characters specific historical and personal backgrounds, Beckett in turn lets his characters be strangers, who do not belong to a place, floating and rootless. Although Beckett, who chose to emigrate from his homeland, seemed to rejoice in his freedom in a foreign country on the surface, it was his mission to embody in his drama the ache and repentance of being an outsider and refugee situated on the verge of marginality.

If Beckett, who was strict about translating and directing his plays on the stage, were still alive in the twenty-first century, it is doubtful whether he would allow such Japanese adaptations, which do not translate every single word of his source texts. While with the foreignisation strategy, 'the translator leaves the author in peace as much as possible and moves the reader toward him' (Schleiermacher, 49), with the domestication strategy, the translator 'leaves the reader in peace as much as possible and moves the writer toward him' (Schleiermacher, 49). Japanese audiences are better able to savour the delicate aesthetics and complexity of Beckett's theatre when his plays are made to migrate into a new theatrical environment.

Thus, we may define 'Beckett's voices between verbal and nonverbal images' as work that transcends cultural boundaries and acts as a 'mirror that reflects otherness'. Beckett's drama contains both sides of the same coin, maintaining space for a global audience to scrutinise the plays from limitless perspectives to discover one and none. Translating Beckett's voices in different cultures therefore means holding up a mirror to the source text to show a reflection of otherness. It is noteworthy that Beckett himself chose to write in French and translated his oeuvre from non-native French to his native tongue of English. According to the biography by Anthony Cronin,

> For him, an Irishman, French represented a form of weakness by comparison with his mother tongue. Besides English because of its very richness holds out the temptation to rhetoric and virtuosity, words mirroring themselves complacently, Narcissus-like. The relative asceticism seemed more appropriate to the expression of being, undeveloped, unsupported, somewhere in the depths of the microcosm. (360)

Beckett's decision to write in a non-native language in the original text and then to translate into his mother tongue itself symbolises 'Beckett's voices between verbal and nonverbal images' that transcend cultural boundaries. The translation of his oeuvre by the playwright himself is one of the reasons why Beckett's texts are readable and adaptable for global audiences of diverse languages and cultures. Moreover, as mentioned in the biography by James Knowlson,

> It was also easier, Beckett maintained, to write in French 'without style'. He did not mean by this that his French had no style, but that, by adopting another language, he gained a greater simplicity and objectivity. French offered him the freedom to concentrate on a more direct expression of the search for 'being' and on an exploration of ignorance, impotence and indigence. Using French enabled him to 'cut away the excess, to strip away the color' and to concentrate more on the music of the language, its sounds and its rhythms. (357)

In order to become objective towards his homeland and to face unsolved questions of humanity regardless of time and space, Beckett stoically composed his manuscripts in a foreign language in an attempt to situate himself abroad, to experience his life as an alien/other and refugee. Thus, Beckett's theatrical stance itself is alienation, somewhat similar to the foreignisation strategy: 'an ethnodeviant pressure on [target-language cultural] values to register the linguistic and cultural difference of the foreign text, sending the reader abroad' (Venuti, 20). In other words, Beckett, being a writer and a translator, gave his own environment foreign status from the beginning. On the other hand, when Beckett's drama is translated using the domestication strategy: 'an ethnocentric reduction of the foreign text to target language cultural values' (Venuti,

20), those translated versions paradoxically come much closer to the heart of Beckett's own intention. Writing in a foreign language by Beckett enabled a global audience to reflect on and share in the vulnerabilities of humankind. The musicality of each language in the world echoes through translations of Beckett's voices in different cultures.

2   Post-3.11 Voices of Devastated Areas in *Waiting for Godot*

This section discusses how Beckett's voices are reflected and echoed in the performance of *Waiting for Godot* produced just after the Great East Japan Earthquake at the New National Theatre in Tokyo and the adaptation of *Waiting for Godot* by Kamome Machine, performed in Fukushima.

The New National Theatre's *Waiting for Godot*, which was planned long before the earthquake, did not expect that the production would strike a chord with the audience. The devastated area in northeast Japan was deprived of everything, left with debris and radioactivity from the nuclear power plant in Fukushima. Even Tokyo became dysfunctional for several days, and metropolitan residents experienced such inconvenient circumstances as the suspension of transportation, cell phone services, water and electric supplies. The residents in northeast Japan were forced to wait for things to get back to normal. The suspended atmosphere depicted in *Waiting for Godot* became more realistic and heartrending in light of the actualities faced by people in the audience. Even after the lifelines of the metropolitan areas were restored, many theatres were closed, and they cancelled performances in recognition of the darkening of the public mood as the whole nation went into mourning for the disaster victims. Despite this unprecedented condition, the National Theatre Tokyo presented *Waiting for Godot*, which brought an unexpected success in the way the audience responded to the play as if its situation were their own.

For those who felt sympathy with the people in northeast Japan, the empty space where Vladimir and Estragon stood under the tree looked just like the disaster areas shown day after day on TV. Many spectators must have been emotionally engaged in the staging of *Waiting for Godot* under such exceptional conditions, where the aftershock they were still experiencing during the actual show heightened the atmosphere of nothingness and helplessness that pervades the play. 'Performing *Waiting for Godot* under these circumstances means something. This is because it is a play of hope and prayer for those in despair' (Okamuro, 2011, 10; my translation). On the other hand, rather than staging as a mode of comfort and prayer, Mariko Hori argues that the original play is supposed to be standing more on the same level as the victims: '*Waiting for Godot* was born as a result of seeking to the very end what it is like to be on the verge of a status where death is the only solution' (79; my translation). The audiences themselves surrounding the stage from three sides in darkness at New National Theatre Tokyo effectively functioned as the ghosts of the victims; they were aware of the ghostly existence haunting two tramps by seeing other audience members sitting on the other side. The audiences who were fortunate enough to be able to see the play in the aftermath of the earthquake must have felt the uncanny hung in the air as something real, not just as something in a fictional space. According to the interview with the director of this production, 'the Great East Japan Earthquake which took place the day before yesterday has changed our perspectives. We are actually in the midst of bewilderment. In the case of *Waiting for Godot*, there is a much higher possibility for the audiences to perceive something beyond the intentions of the producer' (Mori, 8; my translation).

While this *Waiting for Godot* struck a chord with the audience because it happened to be produced just after 3.11, there is another production of *Waiting for Godot* which, though the original title was used, was appropriated and changed into the context very much different from the original text, but was intentionally presented in the context of the 3.11 image. It was done by a Japanese troupe called Kamome Machine on August 6, 2011 on a country road by a tree just over 20 kilometres away from the stricken Fukushima nuclear power plant. Because they chose that specific zone as a performing space, the audience were very few. Yet they put the video capture on the Internet, which caught the attention of a journalist of *The Wall Street Journal of Japan*, who made the production known to its international readers. The journalist writes, 'The version filmed by the Kamome Machine theatre group begins with thirty seconds of footage of the barrier to the evacuation zone around the ravaged plant, as well as roads crumpled by the force of the March 11 earthquake and tsunami' (Maxwell). Reduced to forty minutes and casting a woman, this version was not strictly faithful to Beckett's play, yet it attempted to represent the atmosphere arising from a sense of hopelessness in Beckett's text. While the two men and a woman seem to be merely hanging around on the road without any purpose by standing, crouching down, or facing all directions in silence, the following key dialogues from Beckett's text take place between them.

>   ESTRAGON: Let's go.
>   VLADIMIR: We can't.
>   ESTRAGON: Why not?
>   VLADIMIR: We're waiting for Godot.
>   ESTRAGON: (despairingly) Ah! (1954, 10)

Performing outdoors near the nuclear power plant enabled these dialogues to efficiently echo as the voices of the victims accompanied by their silence. By situating the characters at the actual location of the devastated area, the image of *Waiting for Godot* expanded in a hard-boiled, visceral sense. The troupe was courageous to perform the play in their casual clothing, despite the danger to be affected by radiation: 'While the group's members had concerns about radiation so close to the reactors, they purposefully wore no masks or special clothing for protection against radiation exposure' (Maxwell). In other words, they risked their lives to wait for Godot, which is truer to the intention of Beckett's original text. Just as Beckett risked his life to participate in the Resistance in France during the Second World War instead of staying in his homeland, the actors in fact experienced being in the hazardous zone in Fukushima to reflect the voices of the victims rather than praying for them in Tokyo from a distance. As Hori suggests, 'Beckett did not depict it as it is even though it was his own real experience. Instead, Beckett "universalised" it by questioning his personal experience as the repeatedly universal experience in fact imposed on the whole humankind' (80; my translation). In this sense, this piece can be said to be more loyal to translating Beckett's true voices compared to the New National Theatre Tokyo's *Waiting for Godot*, because '*Waiting for Godot* was born as a result of seeking to the very end what it is like to be on the verge of a status where death is the only solution' (Hori, 79; my translation). The bodies in *Waiting for Godot* are bodies *in extremis*, and the Kamome Machine production takes this idea even further, staging actual bodily risk, on the edges of a zone of death and destruction.

Under such voluntary restraint pervasive in Japan, these productions of *Waiting for Godot* significantly echoed the voices and reflected the images of Japanese audiences at that crucial time.

3   Floating Voices in *Happy Days*

A Japanese production of Beckett's *Happy Days* depicting the immobilisation of Winnie was performed in March 2018 by the aforementioned troupe Kamome Machine as one of the projects for Theatre Commons Tokyo 2018 held in an area of Minato-ward in Tokyo over the course of three weeks between February and March. The aim of this whole event was to propose a model for future theatres 'by applying theatrical ideas — in the context of everyday life and the urban space' (Shibahara, 3; my translation). The director of the project, Chiaki Soma, explains that it is not just us humans, us adults, who are invited to the collective space. The artists will channel the voices of children, of history's dead, of nature, of animals. In order to see the world in all its gradations, one must increase the resolution. Listen closely. Straddle different axes of time. See those experiences as processes, incomplete. Pick up all these tools and deploy them with subtle gestures. (7; my translation)

Set in a non-theatrical, round room with glass windows located on the upper floor of a building at Mita campus of Keio University in Tokyo, *Happy Days* was translated into more-colloquial modern Japanese. Beckett's source text set in a wasteland migrated into a contemporary urban space in Tokyo. The mound in the source text was represented with shiny silver magnet textiles designed like a shell and covering Winnie's body like a robot. Unlike his partner, Willie emphasised his mobility by walking outside in the garden surrounding the room. The room and the garden exhibiting sculptures by Isamu Noguchi, which were first designed by the architect Yoshiro Taniguchi in 1951, were redesigned by Kengo Kuma to be relocated in 2005.

In this Japanese version of *Happy Days*, the verbal and nonverbal aspects demonstrated by Winnie were accentuated by those of *rakugo*, the traditional Japanese vaudeville of storytelling. *Rakugo* is a traditional performing art of Japan established in the Edo period, which has been used for entertainment for over 400 years and is still widely popular in Japan today. During a show, the lone storyteller (*rakugoka*) dressed in a kimono sits on a small pillow (*zabuton*) and uses only a paper fan (*sensu*) and a cotton hand towel (*tenugui*) as props. A *rakugo* story is told through a conversation among multiple characters. Therefore, *rakugoka* must play each character by changing in pitch, tone, facial expression, gestures and a slight turn of head. The *rakugo* performance always ends with a punch line (*ochi*). Winnie, who was deprived of her mobility, used her limited props and space to express her verbal lines to the fullest. Like the storyteller in *rakugo*, she exaggerated her facial expressions and the modulations of her voice. As the *rakugoka* tapped his paper fan, Winnie tapped her magnet textile costume, syncopating with her rhythmical verbal lines and accompanied by the sound of a traditional Japanese three-stringed lute. These verbal and nonverbal forms accentuated by *rakugo* essence enhanced the atmosphere of nostalgia and ridicule that pervades Beckett's *Happy Days*: 'Indeed Koman [*Rakugoka*] once compared himself to a "time machine" that sent the audience back to the nostalgic old times, pasts that they had never seen and places they had never been' (Brau, 87).

In contrast with the immobilised Winnie, Willie gradually stood up, opening the glass windows and leaving the room to walk around the garden with its commanding night view of urban Tokyo. The open-air night breeze blew in through the window while Winnie inside the room kept on talking against the high-rise buildings lit up with neon lights in the sky. Towards the end of the play, Willie, dressed in a silk hat and a bow tie, reappeared crawling in from the backyard, behind the audience and against the backdrop of the Tokyo Tower. As he re-entered the room, he slid his body awkwardly along the floor, through a pillar between a fireplace and the audiences, reaching Winnie at the conclusion of the last scene. Willie's effort to cling to Winnie's body was reminiscent of an embryo holding on to its mother in the womb, just like the image in Beckett's source text. The sense of floating in the mother's womb was symbolically compared with the whole audience floating in a house in the center of Tokyo. The production implied the suspended, equivocal atmosphere that lies between comfortableness of traditional male–female relationship and uneven division of domestic labour that still affects Japanese society. According to the analysis in 2019 by World Economic Forum, 'Japan's gender gap is by far the largest among all advanced economies and has widened over the past year. The country ranks 121st out of 153 countries on this year's Global Gender Gap Index, down 1 percentage point and 11 positions from 2018' (Schwab, 31). The statistics explains that 'even in advanced economies such as Japan the share of time that women spend is more than four times that of men. Across advanced and developing countries there is a negative relationship between women's relative amount of time they spend on unpaid domestic work and economic participation and opportunity gender gaps' (Schwab, 11).

In spite of the aforementioned statistics, the power balance between men and women has been improved compared to the past, and more Japanese women work outside the house while some men contribute to domestic chores. On the other hand, Japanese women's social advancement caused low birth-rate and an aging population in Japan. The floating image of embryo depicted in this production connoted both the positive and negative sides of Japanese gender issues: how men are embraced like an embryo by women who stay more at home; and how women's social advancement caused low birth-rate, the increase of unborn embryos. The relationship between immovable Winnie and movable Willie reminds contemporary Japanese audiences of the past Japanese society when women were still restricted inside a house and their participation in society was relatively low. Since the traditional male–female relationship between Winnie and Willie was demonstrated in the realistic busy atmosphere of neon, sirens, and wind in contemporary Tokyo through the transparent windows of the house, this performance was particularly effective for accentuating the nostalgia and sentimentality, while Winnie's body itself acted as a kind of 'time machine'. Nevertheless, this performance shared not only reminiscence of the past but also the on-going anxiety, uneasiness, and rootlessness of humankind by questioning whether the traditional male–female relationship is happy or not, and whether the social advancement by women brings happiness or not. The urban people in Tokyo coincided with voices of Winnie and Willie in Beckett's *Happy Days* both verbally and nonverbally. Thus, this production functioned as 'site-specific art' that effectively combined architecture, home-like space in Tokyo, actors, audience and Beckett's floating voices within the performance space.

The musicality of Winnie's monologue was also translated successfully by Kaku Nagashima with Japanese plosive and onomatopoeic sounds. With the aid of *rakugo*-like techniques, Winnie's monologues and gestures became more familiar yet more traditional for Japanese audiences as minimal art: 'Because *rakugo* is done solo, without costumes or extensive props, and has traditionally favored a subtler style of representation, one might describe it as a minimalist performing art' (Brau, 51–2). As a whole, the nostalgia and memory embodied by Winnie's voices 'to speak in the old style' (Beckett, 1986, 147) are reminiscent of those in Japanese *rakugo*.

> *Rakugo* performances often encourage nostalgia, which, though different from heritage, may contributeto its designation as cultural treasure. Perhaps *rakugo*'s valorization of the past functions as a kind of critique. Many stories depict *ninjo*, a warmth and feeling in human relationships, that serves as a counterpoint to the vast, impersonal city in which Tokyo *rakugo* is performed today. Linked with such idealised regional symbols as *edokko* ('child of Edo', Edo native) and *shitamachi* (the 'downtown' low city of townspeople), Tokyo *rakugo* may be deployed in a kind of nostalgic quest for cultural identity. (Brau, 6–7)

The relationship between Winnie and Willie in this performance therefore symbolises both the nostalgia for the traditional male–female relationship that has been lost in Japanese contemporary society, and the nostalgia for the Japanese cultural identity including *rakugo*, and the rootlessness and impersonality of floating Japanese society. While the production reflected a conservative male–female relationship in which women tolerate inequality, it also implied the liberation for women through Winnie's floating voices.

While the Kamome Machine's *Happy Days* demonstrated the verbal voices of Japanese cadence through Winne's translated lines, there is another Japanese production — a dance piece of *Happy Days* which particularly focused on the nonverbal images of the play as if presenting a silent movie. This performance originally created in 2013 by the Japanese troupe Kamome-za directed by Makoto Satoh performed several times in Japan and was invited to Dublin Theatre Festival 2017 as *Her Voice* and performed in Galway and Paris as well. Set in a simple bare stage with a hole from which Winnie's upper body in Act I and her head in Act II stick out, Keiko Takeya, a Japanese dancer, eloquently moves her slim, limber arms and her neck with facial expressions like a ballet dancer without speaking any verbal lines. According to Yasushi Satoh, a researcher of contemporary French theatre, 'It does not matter whether it was a play without dialogue or butoh without dancing. I felt that this piece simply reached a radical human existence' (Satoh; my translation) while Minako Okamuro describes the piece as 'through humour and pain we could feel how physical Beckett's play was' (2017). Moreover, this performance was also acceptable abroad beyond the cultural boundaries and experimental challenges. As explained by Síofra Ní Shluaghadháin,

> Satoh and Takeya look at the play as an internal monologue, giving power to the minutiae of gesture and expression in the absence of the spoken word. It is a piece that crosses boundaries of language and understanding. Although *Her Voice* is another take on *Happy Days*, it is not a prerequisite to have seen the original Beckett play. In this, *Her Voice* finds strength, building on, but not relying on, Beckett to create a work that is as original as it is an homage to a theatrical master.

On the other hand, this performance in silence with nonverbal gestures may not always be comprehensible to those who have never read the original text of Beckett's *Happy Days*.

> The work will obviously not appeal to a wide audience. For one, it would make little sense to anyone not familiar with *Happy Days* itself. It is a play for those who want to delve deeper into Beckett's work and this piece does allow you to view it from a different perspective. (Quinn)

Both verbal and nonverbal images written in Beckett's *Happy Days* were aesthetically and theatrically translated in those two Japanese productions through interlingual and intersemiotic manners to embody Winnie's floating voices and voiceless emotions.

While some years have passed since the Great East Japan Earthquake and the victims of the disaster are almost forgotten on the surface, those two Japanese productions of Beckett's *Happy Days* asked the audiences what it means to live in the twenty-first century global society from the point of translating cultural identities. In other words, the former *Happy Days* performed in the limited area of Minato-ward in Tokyo pursued interlingual translation of Winnie's voices in the old style through locality. The latter *Her Voice* toured abroad and challenged intersemiotic translation of Winnie's nonverbal voices through globalism.

The contrast between Tokyo and Fukushima, discussed in the previous section through the two productions of *Waiting for Godot*, also aimed to highlight the distinction between interlingual translation at New National Theatre Tokyo and intersemiotic translation on a road near the nuclear power plant in Fukushima.

4   Conclusion — Beckett's Understanding of Otherness through Translation

Thus, just as Beckett emphasised the significance of dualism in his dramaturgy (e.g. pairs of characters, the symmetry of the stage, repetition of two acts in *Waiting for Godot* and *Happy Days*), we can define 'Beckett's voices between verbal and nonverbal images' as the 'mirror that reflects otherness'. Beckett's migration from Ireland to France enabled him to observe his homeland and language as well as to experience the Resistance during the Second World War. 'Domesticating' translation was more effective than 'foreignisation' in allowing Japanese dramatists and audiences to take in Beckett's voices of otherness. Two productions of *Waiting for Godot* discussed in this chapter seem to offer novel opportunities for testing how Beckett's work resonates with specific moments in Japan right after the Great East Japan Earthquake.

The two productions of *Happy Days* analysed in this chapter scrutinised the floating voice of Winnie's monologue, 'Strange feeling that someone is looking at me' (Beckett, 1986, 155), which conveys a keen awareness of the perception of her own presence: 'To be is to be perceived'. This doctrine of Berkeley, '*esse est percipi*' (Berkeley, 31), is what Beckett strove to interrogate throughout his plays. Unlike Berkeley who found the ultimate gaze in God, Beckett came to the realisation that the other self cannot be separated from oneself. This essential theme of 'otherness' is what motivated Beckett as a writer, translator and director for his theatre. According to Sinéad Mooney in *A Tongue Not Mine: Beckett and Translation*, 'Beckett's directing work allowed him to self-collaborate, thus, in a manner analogous to the interrelation of his writing and self-translating, which fosters a productive mutual estrangement between writing and translating selves' (186). Beckett's stoicism in the theatre is manifested through translation between French and English, between page and stage. As Mooney writes, 'Translation in this sense also manifests itself in

Beckett's theatre in that his plays were frequently not published until after they had already been performed in their "original" language, and Beckett had reconsidered the text in performance — so that the published text reflects performative experience' (185).

Since Beckett was keenly aware of what it means to be alien to others and in oneself, his drama connotes an unseen or unwritten scene or figure that exists with extra margin, leaving room for multiple interpretations of scenes and characters. Japanese Beckett plays have been transformed into some futuristic or traditional Japanese images representing 'other' voices, transporting their audiences backwards or forwards into the past and future that mirror the 'otherness' of all humankind.

Note

The first part of this article is based on my paper 'Analysis of Post 3.11 Performability for Beckett's Dramaturgy' in *Shujitsu English Studies*, 31, Shujitsu University, 2014.

Works Cited

Bandia, Paul F. (2011), 'Translation, Migration, and Relocation of Cultures', in Sandra Bermann and Catherine Porter, eds., *A Companion to Translation Studies*, Oxford: Wiley Blackwell, pp. 273–84.

Beckett, Samuel (1954), *Waiting for Godot*, New York: Grove P.

Beckett, Samuel (1986), *The Complete Dramatic Works*, London: Faber and Faber.

Berkeley, George (1998), *A Treatise Concerning the Principles of Human Knowledge*, ed. Jonathan Dancy, Oxford: Oxford UP.

Brau, Lorie (2008), *Rakugo: Performing Comedy and Cultural Heritage in Contemporary Tokyo*, Lanham: Lexington Books.

Cronin, Anthony (1996), *Samuel Beckett: The Last Modernist*, London: Harper Collins.

Hori, Mariko (2017), *Revised Versions of* Waiting for Godot*: Beckett as Director*, Tokyo: Fujiwara Shoten.

Jakobson, Roman (2004), 'On Linguistic Aspects of Translation', in Lawrence Venuti, ed., *The Translation Studies Reader*, New York: Routledge, pp. 138–43.

Knowlson, James (1996), *Damned to Fame: The Life of Samuel Beckett*, London: Bloomsbury.

Maxwell, Kenneth (2011), '*Waiting for Godot* — in Fukushima', *The Wall Street Journal Japan*, 6 August.

Mooney, Sinéad (2011), 'Foreign Bodies', in *A Tongue Not Mine: Beckett and Translation*, Oxford: Oxford UP.
Mori, Shintaro (2011), 'Interview: 2011 — Reality of Waiting', *Program for Waiting for Godot*, Tokyo: New National Theatre.
Okamuro, Minako (2011), 'Prayer from the Debris', *Program for Waiting for Godot*, Tokyo: New National Theatre.
Okamuro, Minako (2017), *Audience Feedback 1 for* Her Voice, Tokyo: Kamome-za.
Quinn, Morgan (2017), *'Her Voice* — Samuel Beckett Theatre — Dublin Theatre Festival — Review', *No More Workhorse*, Dublin, 11 October.
Satoh, Yasushi (2017), *Audience Feedback 1 for* Her Voice, Tokyo: Kamome-za.
Schleiermacher, Friedrich (2004), 'On the Different Methods of Translating', in Lawrence Venuti, ed., *The Translation Studies Reader*, New York: Routledge, pp. 43–63.
Schwab, Klaus (2019), *Global Gender Gap Report 2020*, Geneva: World Economic Forum.
Shibahara, Satoko and Mai Hashiba (2018), *Program for Theatre Commons Tokyo 2018*, Tokyo: Theatre Commons Tokyo Executive Committee.
Soma, Chiaki (2018), 'Director's Note: How to see the nuance in the world', in Satoko Shibahara and Mai Hashiba, eds., *Program for Theatre Commons Tokyo 2018*, Tokyo: Theatre Commons Tokyo Executive Committee.
Shluaghadháin, Síofra Ní (2017), *Audience Feedback 2 for* Her Voice, Tokyo: Kamome-za.
Takebe, Yoshiko (2014), 'Analysis of Post 3.11 Performability for Beckett's Dramaturgy', *Shujitsu English Studies*, 31, pp. 55–68.
Venuti, Lawrence (1995), *The Translator's Invisibility: A History of Translation*, London: Routledge.

Performances Cited

Happy Days (February 2016), dir. Makoto Satoh, perf. Keiko Takeya and Togo Igawa, Yokohama: Kawamata Hall, BankART 1929.
Happy Days (March 2018), dir. Yuta Hagiwara, perf. Honami Shimizu and Shin Ito, trans. Kaku Nagashima, Tokyo: Keio University Mita Campus, Ex Noguchi Room.
Waiting for Godot (April 2011), dir. Shintaro Mori, perf. Isao Hashizume, Saburo Ishikura, Fubito Yamano, Kenichi Ishii, and Tokio Emoto, trans. Shoichiro Iwakiri, Tokyo: New National Theatre.
Waiting for Godot (August 2011), dir. Yuta Hagiwara, perf. Honami Shimizu, Shintaro Yokote, and Ichiro Matsubara, filmed Takashi Fujii, Fukushima: National Road 6.

Articulations of Voice and Medium in Beckett's Screen Work

Jonathan Bignell

Abstract

This chapter approaches the topic of voice in three distinct but interrelated ways, adopting the term 'articulation' to bring together analyses of the role of voice and the issue of linkage between media forms in Beckett's media work. The first section addresses how Beckett came to have a voice in radio and television in the 1950s and 1960s in Britain, through dependencies on gatekeepers who could grant or deny access to media institutions for him and his fellow cultural producers. Beckett was given a voice because he was recognised as a writer whose work was worthy of broadcast to a national audience, and onto whom a constellation of meanings and expectations was projected by those who facilitated it at the BBC. However, the significance of voice is complicated by the reflexivity about sound in Beckett's first original work for broadcast, the radio drama *All That Fall* (1957). It already questions the notion of voice as speech authorised by its origins in living things located in real places. The chapter shows how, in subsequent work, this occlusion of voice as a marker of presence develops further at the same time as Beckett's dramatic motifs and interests remain consistent and include relationships between body and voice, voice and place, and voice and time (McMullan). However, because of Beckett's refusal to talk publicly about himself as an artist or about his work, his own voice did not provide a parallel discourse that would explicate them. Beckett's lack of speech did not prevent the development of his authorial voice, however, and indeed made his work seem all the more articulate to others so that, for example, when given the Nobel Prize the awarding committee's press release could summarise his contribution to civilisation in a brief formal citation (Ackerley and Gontarski, 407). Beckett could be easily spoken about even if he did not speak.

The second part of the chapter focuses on the relationship between image and sound in Beckett's work on film, in the cinema project *Film* (1964) and the filmed adaptation of the theatre piece *Play* as *Comédie* (1966). In each of them, though in different ways, voice is dissociated from the performance of the actors on screen. The two film projects explored relationships between image and the spoken word, and the chapter develops this by discussing the dramas Beckett wrote for the television screen, in which a voice addresses or discusses the characters. Those voices have close, if also ambivalent, relationships with camera point of view. Voice and image are joined by music in some of Beckett's screen dramas, and in each case music also has implied relationships, but uncertain ones, with voice and camera. This issue of how voice is related to other audio-visual components develops the concept of articulation further, by expanding on its implication of linkage but also the maintenance of separation between one element and another to which it is joined.

The chapter ends by arguing that Beckett's work gave voice to potentialities in the audio-visual media that questioned ideas of technical progress and development. The circumstances of production of Beckett's television work require an account of its use of studio settings and restricted spaces, because they are so insistently atavistic (Bignell, 2021). Beckett's work speaks about the history of the medium. While Beckett himself was interested in the material practices and technologies of production in each medium because he was keen to understand and use their aesthetic possibilities, as Gaby Hartel (2010) has shown, for example, his screen work consciously returned to aesthetic forms that appeared out of date. The separation of voice from on-screen performance in the television plays is the most prominent of these, alongside decisions like shooting almost all of his work in black and white rather than colour and using very long duration shots (long takes) with little editing. Working in the studio in these ways was anomalous even at the start of Beckett's career in television, though it paralleled styles of non-commercial filmmaking at the time and especially in French radical cinema. The dissociation of voice from bodily presence was both a throwback to early silent cinema but also a gesture towards the self-consciously contemporary *nouvelle vague*, thus making an articulated relationship with cinema past and present, linking and joining again.

1   The Artist's Voice

Access to the channels of distribution is a precondition for the creative work of any artist to find a public and establish a reputation (Williams, 53). Because they are large, complex, collaborative industrial enterprises, television, radio broadcasting and cinema are controlled by gatekeepers who make the decisions about commissioning, adapting and documenting artists' work. The gatekeepers may not always be employees of the institutions that record and broadcast programmes or make and distribute films, since other figures like authors' and actors' agents exercise some of the same kinds of control. But where national organisations invest significant resources in facilities and staff, institutional hierarchies and networks of power form a web of decision-making that combines relatively impersonal policy and planning with the interests and prejudices of individuals. In Britain the BBC radio arts and culture channel had a commitment to giving Beckett a voice on radio from the

1950s onwards because of key BBC staff's respect for his work. The Third Programme (later named Radio 3) had tiny audiences ever since its launch in 1946, but it had a disproportionately large role in British culture (Carpenter) because of its support for contemporary writers, including Beckett. As well as adapting material originally created for the stage or for print publication, the Third Programme's producers commissioned new work and sought out emerging talent. To belong to the informal networks associated with the Third Programme meant inclusion in an elite culture with international reach, and recognition for writers, music composers and intellectuals like Beckett who had interests in experimentation (Whitehead, 16).

However, in Beckett's case, his presence on BBC radio was despite the fact that Val Gielgud, Head of Drama from 1934 to 1963, was prone to take an intense dislike to some members of the avant-garde, including Beckett. As Pim Verhulst explains, Gielgud maintained a policy established in the Second World War that broadcasting should preserve and disseminate a canon of important theatre and literature of the past, with a very selective approach to new, experimental work for the radio or television media. Because he was aware of his own narrowness in relation to new writers, Gielgud appointed a deputy in 1953, the theatre director Donald McWhinnie who subsequently worked on many of Beckett's dramas for BBC radio and television. The BBC producer Michael Bakewell, and the senior script editor Barbara Bray, were also supporters of emerging writers including Beckett and were aware of experimental theatre in France. At the suggestion of Cecelia Reeves, the BBC's Paris liaison and a Francophile who had seen the first theatre production of *En attendant Godot* there, the Controller of the Third Programme, John Morris, went to see Beckett in Paris in 1956 about a possible radio drama commission. This was the year after the London premiere of *Waiting for Godot*, and by this time Beckett had found a place as an emerging voice alongside writers like Eugene Ionesco and Harold Pinter (Bignell, 2020). The presence of Beckett's radio voices was dependent on a network of supporting advocates.

So far, this chapter has used the term 'voice' in a metaphorical sense to mean that Beckett was recognised as a creative figure with a distinctive literary and theatrical style, aesthetic and world-view. This distinctiveness might also be termed his unique vision, but voice is especially apposite because it was on spoken word radio that BBC had found a place for his work, in drama and readings of his prose (Van Hulle). BBC commissioned radio dramas from Beckett: *All That Fall, Embers* (1959), *Words and Music* (1962), *Cascando* (1964) and *Rough for Radio 2* (1976). They were complemented by readings of extracts from his prose piece *From An Abandoned Work* (1957), from his novels *Malone Dies* (1958) and *The Unnamable* (1959), and Beckett's theatre plays *Waiting for*

Godot and *Endgame* were both adapted for radio, in 1960 and 1962 respectively. When BBC television first took an interest in Beckett, he was already established as a literary figure featured on radio, a radio dramatist and a theatre dramatist. This provenance had established him as a significant literary voice through broadcast forms that relied on the possibilities of voice and experimented with the medium of sound (Campbell).

It is not only voice and its broadcast possibilities that interested Beckett and his collaborators, but also non-vocal sound and music. Indeed, as Catherine Laws (2010) shows, there is a complex interplay across Beckett's oeuvre between speech, sound, music and silence in which each does not simply contrast with, replace, or exclude the others. In Beckett's work it often seems as if speech aims to run out into silence, while also the extinguishing of speech is feared because what ensues is the endless silence of death. An over-emphasis on voice as speech, rather than as one of a number of kinds of sound, threatens to bring with it a fetishisation of communication. A radical theoretical challenge is posed to the audio-visual media once voice is no longer naturalised as being the speech of a human body present in a particular time and space. Drawing on work by Jacques Derrida, deconstructive theories of film, for example, question the conventions of the medium by addressing work in which image and sound do not coincide to guarantee each other and re-present univocal subjectivities (Brunette and Wills). Although voice most often calls up a metaphysics of presence and a living relation to an interlocutor, Beckett's media work deconstructs this convention rather than supports it. Beckett was probably aware of the approach to radio developed by Rudolf Arnheim in the 1930s, which attributed an enlivening vitality to sound radio as an artistic medium, in comparison to the exhaustion apparent in literature (Hartel). But for Arnheim, the vitality of radio was not anchored to its referential relationship with voice or human communication, but to the possibilities it offered for exploring the materiality of sound as an artistic medium.

For example, from the beginning of Beckett's work for sound broadcasting with *All That Fall*, speech is put next to other kinds of sound. There are passages of animal noises that remark on the play's rural setting in a stylised way, rather than representing plausible surroundings, as the director McWhinnie explained in his memoir (133–51). Moreover, as it continues, the play introduces further sounds that are all effects, signalling objects and events but in a punctual, declarative tone. There is a loud bicycle bell, a car and a steam train, and later animal noises recur in the form of squawking chickens. Sound becomes a material resource, a token that indicates a source for the sound and marks the presence of that object or creature as part of the fictional world (Frost, 367). But each sound has an independent, functional role to signal the presence of what generates it; each sound is processed, manipulated and distanced from its referent. Thus, sounds become aural quotations from a repository of sounds like one of the BBC's proprietary sound effects compilations, from which, indeed, they derived. Sounds, including voices regarded as one among the many possible kinds of sound, become disarticulated from the persons, things, places, and times from where they might seem to originate.

The aural and the visual counterpoint each other in a similar way in Beckett's screen work, especially in relation to voice, because the dramas dissociate voice from the presence of a speaker. The conceptual, social and technological mechanism for relaying Beckett's literary and theatrical voice was broadcasting (Bignell, 2010), whose structural form has separation, articulation, and the play of presence and absence at its heart. The throwing of seeds by a farmer from a bag across a prepared soil, aiming to scatter the seed with even spacing, is the root of the term 'broadcasting'. It was adopted to mean the transmission of radio and television signals because of the idea of sending out from a central source, such as a transmission aerial, and the awareness that the direction of sending could only be one-way. Dissemination of signals could only be from a broadcaster to an audience, with no return path, and moreover the broadcaster would be unable to determine exactly where the signal would be received nor what effect it might have. Moreover, because of its emergence out of the technologies of telegraphy and telephony (Winston, 67–87), the content of broadcasting was assumed to be voice (though of course music and other sounds were also transmitted). Just as casting seed would be necessarily inexact, and some seeds would germinate while others would not, so broadcast signals would be beamed across a wide area rather than to specific homes, and audiences might respond in a variety of ways to the signals, or not attend to them at all.

It is easy to see how this metaphor can readily adapt when the signals in question are voices, and the broadcaster becomes a speaker to a widely dispersed and differentiated public. The philosopher and media theorist John Durham Peters (210–1) described broadcasting as 'an idealised configuration among speakers and audiences. It conjures visions of the agora, the town meeting, or the "public sphere"'. Radio and television are like public speaking, that might take the form, at their most conservative, of proclamation or announcement, but also, at their best, the form of conversation, discussion and consensus-building (Smith). In media cultures dominated by commercialism the speaker might be thought of as a salesperson and the audience as a market, but in the nations of Western Europe where broadcasting was conceived as a public good during Beckett's lifetime, it was assumed that there should be a plurality of voices, literally and metaphorically, and thus that there would be a place for artistic voices offering innovative ideas, challenging forms and unexpected subjects.

In Germany, the other key national context for Beckett's media work alongside Britain, broadcasting was conceived as a conduit to a mass audience rather than as an art in itself. Since a television production of *Eh Joe* there in 1966, the West German regional broadcaster Süddeutscher Rundfunk (SDR) in Stuttgart repeatedly welcomed Beckett (Hartel et al, 2009). He directed versions of his own original television work commissioned for BBC, and *Nacht und Träume* (1982), his last television play, was commissioned by Reinhart Müller-Freienfels, SDR's head of television broadcasting, who also produced the SDR premiere of Beckett's *Quadrat 1 + 2 (Quad)* (1981). At SDR there was little exploration of the specificities of television as a medium for drama (as opposed to a medium for adapting works created for theatre) until the 1990s after his death, because of debates in Germany about the social function of television. Despite the enthusiasm of Müller-Freienfels, the medium was widely assumed to be a lightweight amusement, aiming to entertain, in which case Beckett's work would be foreign and unpalatable fare that did not belong there (Voigts-Virchow). Starting from the same position, however, some critics argued for the seriousness of television as a medium for the dissemination of art, as a counter to television's vapidity. Beckett could take such a role, offering complex literary and philosophical material that could be showcased on television and might raise the cultural standards of the television audience. In Germany, as in Britain, television was conceived as a medium for Beckett's artistic voice, as a relay mechanism, although opinion was divided about how effective this could ever be. Cultural pessimism did not prevent SDR's investment in Beckett over two decades, however. Unfortunately, Beckett's death and the deregulation and commercialisation of German media in the 1980s coincided to marginalise his work's continuing impact.

The three plays by Beckett that were screened in the BBC's 'Shades' episode of *The Lively Arts* culture documentary in 1977 were disconnected from the living voice of their author. *The Lively Arts* was so called not only because of the programme's engagement with the current scene in literature, visual art and theatre — its vitality — but also because it used interviews with the living contemporary creators whose work it featured. The interview material framed and documented the artwork made by that week's subject, so that the artist's living voice would guarantee, authorise or underpin his or her work. There was no Beckett voice in 'Shades', no interview with him, and no explication of the commissioning of the two original plays presented alongside a filmed version of *Not I* (1975), namely *Ghost Trio* (1977) and *...but the clouds...* (1977). Instead, Martin Esslin and the programme's host, Melvyn Bragg, gave an account of Beckett's life and explained his concerns. Beckett was absent, and the partial, spectral embodiments of identity hinted at by the dramas' titles (ghosts, clouds, and a speaker who is emphatically 'not' an 'I') reinforce the aesthetic of non-appearance. Even the darkly shadowed, black and white images of the plays and the emptiness of the spaces where the action takes place seem designed to create such an impression. 'Shades' has an ambivalent, if not paradoxical, relationship with the meanings of voice so far discussed; this episode of *The Lively Arts* showcased a living author who was absent, documenting and presenting Beckett's work as the product of a distinctive and important artistic voice that was located elsewhere.

2 On Film

Ideas about vision, voice and presence had been explored in Beckett's audiovisual work that preceded his television plays. He had written and shot *Film*, made partly in a studio and partly on location in New York in the summer of 1964. The key structural motif of the production, which even at the time seemed aesthetically unsatisfactory to Beckett and his collaborators, is the separation of points of view between a fleeing man, O, and his pursuer E. Location shots demonstrate E's power to traverse space in pursuit of O, despite the loss of an intended opening sequence in the street that would have embedded the action further into a realistic milieu. There is a sense of tension in the film, created by O's anxiety about exposure in this exterior space and E's freedom of movement through the space. While O is in exterior space, the initially silent film suddenly proclaims the presence of its own soundtrack when two passersby in the street are confronted by the hurrying O, and one of them bids him to be silent with a gesture and the sibilant 'Shhh!' The sound is synchronous with the diegetic action shot by the camera, but the fact that it is the sole sound, and one that asks for silence, undercuts its significance as a voiced sound at the same time as drawing attention to its presence. This use of voice in *Film* is highly rhetorical, deliberate, and prominent. It is also somewhat comic, in that it invites the spectator to join in with a joke that references the long-past experience of silent cinema while refuting that this film belongs to that past or aims to reproduce it (Bignell, 2009, 133–8). The second part of the film is shot in a studio set, representing the apartment where O unsuccessfully seeks refuge from E. The move into this artificial space ought to offer the chance to control visible space more effectively but the film's lighting, from an overhead suspended rig, produces oddly mottled shadows and light on the walls, and the props such as a photograph of an ancient mask, and a pet dog, cat, goldfish, and parrot seem to intrude on this artificial space rather than belonging in it. *Film* is in many ways a flawed experiment, but its dissociations offered resources that were taken up in Beckett's next screen project.

In 1966, Beckett worked on a filmed studio version of a French theatre production of *Play*. Beckett and his collaborators were able to control the studio space much more effectively than in *Film* and did not use exteriors at all. They focused their attention on manipulating voice and questioning the camera's point of view. *Comédie*'s three figures in funerary urns are lit when speaking but merge into the unlit, black surroundings when silent. The single camera's relationship with the space is frontal, matching the orientation of a theatre audience, but Beckett and the director Marin Karmitz also experimented with close-up and extensive cutting between camera shots. Camera point of view does not reproduce the spectator position of a theatre audience, but because of the disorienting cuts and leaps from close-ups to long shots, neither does it use point of view to create a comprehensible cinematic world. The studio was used very differently from *Film*, as a fully abstract space that repudiated a link with theatrical staging and also strained the cinematic technique of montage (Foster). The voices in Beckett and Karmitz's production of *Comédie* are synchronous with the mouths of speakers seen by the camera, but vision and voice are both highly manipulated in order to distance the film from being a representation of dialogue in its conventional sense. Very rapid cutting of the image track, and electronic compression of vocal sounds on the soundtrack, work together to defamiliarise the speakers' dialogue and the articulation of image and voice.

As recent work by Anthony Paraskeva (36) has shown, the disarticulation of image and voice in these film works is in dialogue with experimental (especially French) cinema that Beckett was aware of in the 1950s and 1960s. French *nouvelle vague* directors and writers were going back and revaluing silent cinema in the critical journals associated with European Modernism in the mid-twentieth century (Bignell, 2009, 128–38), when Beckett was casting silent film actor Buster Keaton in *Film* and working with Soviet experimental film-maker Dziga Vertov's brother on the production. Moreover, Paraskeva (34) emphasises Beckett's knowledge of the radio and theatre work of Marguerite Duras, both directly and via the influence of his lover Barbara Bray, who translated Duras' texts into English. Like Beckett, Duras explored intermedial forms that drew on, and deconstructed, the conventions of theatre, film and novel for representing action, character and setting. Duras, like Beckett, directed her own work, the first such foray being the film *Nuit noire, Calcutta* (1964) which she made in collaboration with Marin Karmitz who worked with Beckett on *Comédie*. In her extraordinary *India Song* (1975), which she described as 'texte théâtre film', voice and image are separated and ambivalently articulated with each other, and Beckett developed variants of this technique in his television plays and also in his theatre plays after *Krapp's Last Tape*. Soundtracks became an independent channel of information rather than a subordinate explanatory or accompanying element alongside the visual.

Throughout his audio-visual work, Beckett explored the audio-visual resources that radio, then film and television, offered in terms of the dual meanings of articulation: the creation of a unity founded on the interdependence between two or more distinct components. The production of Beckett's screen work in studios, sound stages (and, in the early days, in *Film*) on location works with and against the opportunities and constraints of technologies and aesthetic conventions in which voice can play quite different roles. Television, radio, theatre and cinema develop Beckett's awareness of each medium's history and specificity.

3   Studio Voices: Conjuring Rooms

All of Beckett's plays for television were shot in studios, with no location shooting, and television studios have their own aesthetic and cultural significance as production spaces. When Beckett was making television dramas, from 1966–88, the television studio was increasingly and pejoratively associated with the linguistic emphasis of scripted drama rather than with a drama of physical dynamism, action and movement (Macmurraugh-Kavanagh and Lacey). For audiences and some reviewers, this made Beckett's dramas seem like voices from a superseded past, coming from elsewhere and potentially irrelevant to the emergent aesthetics of contemporary television at the time (Bignell, 2009, 164–201). The use of studio space and its technologies had impacts on specific aspects of the plays' aesthetics, including performance style, the degree of emphasis on close-up, and on sets and lighting. Beckett's television plays use the intimacy of the studio and exploit the primacy of acted performance, negotiating with conventions for literary, theatrical drama in relation to voice and image.

The champion of the script-focused, studio-bound technique in Britain was the director Don Taylor, who sought to characterise it as the essence of drama for television, whereas shooting on film on location seemed to him like making low-budget cinema, an inevitably inferior achievement: 'True television drama has a quite different aesthetic from film-making. It tolerates, in fact it relishes imaginative, argumentative and even poetic writing in a way the film camera does not' (38). Taylor's reference to 'writing' is to script-writing, and especially dialogue. Television drama offered the chance to craft language that would be spoken by highly trained performers, acting in specially designed settings built in the studio, thus creating an imaginative fictional world in which all elements of the drama could be aesthetically harmonious and controlled. The result would be 'long, developing scenes, where the actors can work without interference from the director's camera', and television drama would be what Taylor described as 'a writers' and actors' medium' (38). Voice is a key component of this ensemble of creative means, and Taylor argues for the affective charge generated thereby, emerging as 'passion that comes from deep wells of feeling plumbed by good words'. What is odd about Beckett's television plays, though, is that the characters on set do not speak any words. Beckett's television dramas do not feature a well-wrought interplay between characters' voices, realising a fictional world through well-delineated personae, places and temporal settings.

The room, and home in general, have connotations of privacy, family and the reproduction of social relations that are associated with theatre naturalism. Raymond Williams described television drama as 'the ultimate realisation of the original naturalist convention: the drama of the small enclosed room, in which a few characters lived out their private experience of an unseen public world' (1990, 56). However, the public world remains unseen in all of Beckett's screen work after *Film*; in *Eh Joe* the exterior beyond the disproportionate and thus visually emphatic windows and doors is never given concrete or representational form because it is never seen by the camera. The room in *Eh Joe* might seem to be a refuge but it is also a bare, unhomely environment. There is voice but no conversation, as the camera closes up on Joe's face, and the female voice whose speaker we never see proclaims her power to enter the space and confront him, via her association with a camera that moves only when she speaks. Dissociated voice and vision, in a setting that references domestic space but is clearly a constructed studio set, destabilises conventions of psychological interiority, social context and the referentiality that television drama can claim.

Voice in *Ghost Trio* is a mediator between the drama and the viewer, and in the first part of the play she establishes the difference and similarity between the represented room on-screen and an actual room such as the domestic viewer's own space. There are still shots of segments of the walls and floor, for example, but they are grey panels such as are used to construct theatre flats for stage sets; they signify a space rather than showing one. Voice's command that the viewer should not raise the volume on the television set is another recognition of the drama as an artifice of the camera and sound recording. Voice conducts the audience, leading the viewer's eye to designated parts of the space. Despite an opening wide shot that takes in the room setting and the

Figure sitting within it, much as in *Eh Joe*, Voice's comments about the space make the audience consider the means of staging itself, and the construction of this fictional space. Rather than focusing attention on the visible performer and the beginning of a narrative centred on the character, attention is focused on the apparatus of television representation and its rendering on the two-dimensional screen. Moreover, it is not the presumed central character who Voice introduces first, but instead the material comprising the set: walls, floor, pallet and door. Figure is the last to engage Voice's and the camera's attention. Figure is also immobile and at some distance from the camera when first observed. Voice has a pedagogic role, as Linda Ben-Zvi (35) has noted, thus acquiring an authorial and interpretive agency that intervenes between the viewer and Beckett's authorial voice, and asserts the control by Voice of the camera and the Figure. In *Ghost Trio* the voice has directorial authority, linked to the camera's agency to visualise the action and thus addresses the relationship between voice and power.

The importance of music to *Ghost Trio* adds another dimension to the role of speech in the drama. Catherine Laws (2003) has analysed the music in *Ghost Trio*, arguing that it draws on the conventions of German Romanticism and might thus offer a kind of lyrical consolation to the on-stage figure who seems to hear it. But in fact, she sees the music as one among the other elements that Beckett introduces in order to deconstruct their conventional significance. Through an extended analysis of the use of Beethoven's music, Laws shows that its role is ambiguous. The relationship between the starting and stopping of music and the movements of the figure, F, holding a box that might be a cassette recorder, do not allow us to be sure that F is playing music that we, the audience are able to hear with him. In relation to Voice, V, the Beethoven never begins at her command, V appears not to control the volume of the music on the soundtrack, and the camera movements that she seems to control for most of the drama do not have a straightforward correspondence with the volume of the music as the camera dollies towards or further away from F. The music seems to come from a source outside the figure and the objects onstage, yet it does not derive from the voice who oversees this space, and moreover it does not function as separate commentary or emotional guideline for the action. Just as image and voice have been separated and recombined in ways that allude to, but question, their priority over each other, music too becomes an ambiguous component that deconstructs its conventional diegetic and non-diegetic functions.

Beckett develops his investigation of off-screen space further in *...but the clouds...*, whose narrator describes his movements in his house and then his walks outside, while thinking of an absent lover. There is an almost immobile male figure at the start of the drama and a static female figure in the closing moments, and the narrator conjures a representation of himself walking into and out of a spotlit area surrounded by empty darkness. Voice calls these personae into existence, it seems, in order that they will carry out the simple actions being described (like the man getting up in his nightclothes, dressing, then leaving the house in order to walk the surrounding roads). Voice and image are separated while remaining connected by the activity of narration, and the only space that the voice makes present for the camera is a small lighted area in which these micro-dramas of leaving and returning are demonstrated. Neither the room in which the figure sits, nor the interior or exterior spaces that he talks about traversing, are shown at all. Again, there is a hint of a distinction, associated with the role of voice in relation to action, between the room and public space in the outside world, but these spatial demarcations are not made present representationally.

Whereas in *...but the clouds...* the figure and the space were claimed for control by Voice, in *Quad* (1982) there is no voice at all. However, as in *Ghost Trio*, there is music that could be understood either as accompaniment or as a prescriptive soundtrack determining the figures' movement. Moreover, there are no faces and minimal expressive gestures. With few faces visible in Beckett's later television plays, following the emphasis on the face in *Eh Joe*, expressivity is further restrained just as voice gives way to music. The viewer is invited to look at the screen as a composition and a surface, more than as a window through which expressive performance is perceived. The whole drama in *Quad* takes place in two long takes, one in colour and the other in black and white. Four shrouded figures of indeterminate sex enter a space seen from above by a fixed camera, and they each shuffle around the vertices of a square demarcated area in the centre of the frame, approaching but walking around a central point. This continues the emphasis on framing produced in *Ghost Trio* by the rectangles of the floor, wall, and F's pallet, which each mirror the square television screen. The unlit and off-screen space is not identifiable, as in *...but the clouds...*, and the even, unchanging lighting in each of the play's two sections makes no reference to the directionality or changing orientation of daylight, nor the highlighting of specific characters or passages of action that lighting does in theatre or dance performance.

In his last play for television, Beckett developed this use of music and also returned to questions of communication by focusing on gesture. *Nacht und Träume* is set in a room, dimly lit and with a single male figure seated at a table. Since the figure seems to be asleep with his head and arms resting on the table, when a wipe effect is used to replace the image of the apparently 'real' space of the room by another space, almost identical to the first, the second seems to be a dreamt image. Beckett's screenplay refers to the identical images of the figure as A and his dreamt self, B. There is no voice in the drama, but as in passages from *Ghost Trio*, it is not clear whether the music represents what A dreams he hears, or whether it is from an external agency that supplies the music as an accompaniment to the action. But the similarity highlights the difference between the two scenes, since A is enveloped in darkness while B is surrounded by light. It is also significant that the visual space of the dream is in some respects parallel to the space of the television screen itself, because of its vignette shape. The manipulation of the visual field to produce window-like effects questions the television screen as a revelatory 'window' and suggests that it might purvey dreams or other kinds of illusory representations.

There is voice in Beckett's television plays, but the voices are not, it seems, uttered by the figures seen by the camera. The questions that the dramas pose for viewers, therefore, are how, or even whether, the voice is synchronous with the physical action in a shot, and the related issue of whether voice has an agency that might cause, describe or be affected by the action. What is in question is the relationship between embodiment and articulation. Embodiment denotes the fact that there can be no voice without a body to utter it. Yet the embodied personae on screen, who are not the speakers of the voices the audience hears, have an implied relation to voices because the voices are present at the same time as the figures on screen. There is a link between the seen and the spoken, so that they comprise an articulation. Voice and body join as two things that yet remain distinct. Questions of relationship, causality, and temporal and spatial presence are raised but also complicated and deferred in ways that work on the medial conventions with which dramatists, actors, directors, and viewers must negotiate.

Works Cited

Ackerley, C. J. and S. E. Gontarski (2006), *The Faber Companion to Samuel Beckett*, London: Faber and Faber.

Arnheim, Rudolf (1936), *Radio*, London: Faber and Faber.

Ben-Zvi, Linda (1985), 'Samuel Beckett's Media Plays', *Modern Drama*, 28: 1, pp. 22–37.

Bignell, Jonathan (2009), *Beckett on Screen: The Television Plays*, Manchester: Manchester UP.

Bignell, Jonathan (2010), 'Into the Void: Beckett's Television Plays and the Idea of Broadcasting', in Daniela Caselli, ed., *Beckett and Nothing: Trying to Understand Beckett*, Manchester: Manchester UP, pp. 125–42.

Bignell, Jonathan (2020), '"Random dottiness": Samuel Beckett and Harold Pinter in 1958', in Anita Rákóczy, Mariko Hori Tanaka, and Nicholas E. Johnson, eds., *Beckett Influencing/Influencing Beckett*, Budapest and Paris: Károli Gáspár UP/ L'Harmattan, pp. 61–74.

Bignell, Jonathan (2021), 'Screen and Stage Space in Beckett's Theatre Plays on Television', in Amanda Wrigley and John Wyver, eds., *Theatre Plays on British Television*, Manchester: Manchester UP.

Brunette, Peter and David Wills (1989), *Screen/Play: Derrida and Film Theory*, Princeton: Princeton UP.

Campbell, Julie (2013), 'Beckett and the BBC Third Programme', in *SBT/A*, 25: *Beckett in the Cultural Field / Beckett dans le champ culturel*, pp. 109–22.

Carpenter, Humphrey (1997), *The Envy of the World: Fifty Years of the BBC Third Programme and Radio 3*, London: Weidenfeld and Nicolson.

Chignell, Hugh (2017), 'British Radio Drama and the Avant-garde in the 1950s', *Historical Journal of Film, Radio and Television*, 37: 4, pp. 649–64.

Foster, David (2012), 'Spatial Aesthetics in the Film Adaptation of Beckett's *Comédie*', *Screen*, 53: 2, pp. 105–17.

Frost, Everett (1991), 'Fundamental Sounds: Recording Samuel Beckett's Radio Plays', *Theatre Journal*, 43: 3, pp. 361–76.

Hartel, Gaby (2010), 'Emerging out of a Silent Void: Some Reverberations of Rudolf Arnheim's Radio Theory in Beckett's Radio Pieces', *JOBS*, 19: 2, pp. 218–27.

Hartel, Gaby, Kraus Völker and Thomas Irmer (2009), 'The Reception of Beckett's Theatre and Television Pieces in West and East Germany', in Mark Nixon and Matthew Feldman, eds., *The International Reception of Samuel Beckett*, London: Continuum, pp. 75–96.

Herren, Graley (2009), 'Different Music: Karmitz and Beckett's Film Adaptation of *Comédie*', *JOBS*, 18: 1–2, pp. 10–31.

Laws, Catherine (2003), 'Beethoven's Haunting of Beckett's *Ghost Trio*', in Linda Ben-Zvi, ed., *Drawing on Beckett: Portraits, Performances, and Cultural Contexts*, Tel Aviv: Assaph, pp. 197–214.

Laws, Catherine (2010), 'Beckett and Unheard Sound', in D. Caselli, ed., *Beckett and Nothing: Trying to Understand Beckett*, Manchester: Manchester UP, pp. 176–91.

Macmurraugh-Kavanagh, Madelene and Stephen Lacey (1999), 'Who Framed Theatre?: The "Moment of Change" in British TV Drama', *New Theatre Quarterly*, 57, pp. 58–74.

McMullan, Anna (2010), *Performing Embodiment in Samuel Beckett's Drama*, London: Routledge.

McWhinnie, Donald (1959), *The Art of Radio*, London: Faber.

Paraskeva, Anthony (2017), *Samuel Beckett and Cinema*, London: Bloomsbury.

Peters, John Durham (1999), *Speaking into the Air: A History of the Idea of Communication*, Chicago: U of Chicago P.

Smith, Anthony (1998), 'Television as a Public Service Medium', in Smith, ed., *Television: An International History*, Oxford: Oxford UP, pp. 38–54.

Taylor, Don (1998), 'Pure Imagination, Poetry's Lyricism, Titian's Colours: Whatever Happened to the Single Play on British TV?', *New Statesman*, 6 March, pp. 38–9.

Van Hulle, Dirk (2017), 'The BBC and Beckett's Non-radiogenic Plays in the 1950s', in David Addyman, Matthew Feldman and Erik Tonning, eds., *Samuel Beckett and BBC Radio: A Reassessment*, New York: Palgrave Macmillan, pp. 43–58.

Verhulst, Pim (2017), 'The BBC as Commissioner of Beckett's Work for Radio', in David Addyman, Matthew Feldman and Erik Tonning, eds., *Samuel Beckett and BBC Radio: A Reassessment*, New York: Palgrave Macmillan, pp. 81–102.

Voigts-Virchow, Eckart (1998), 'Exhausted Cameras: Beckett in the TV-zoo', in Jennifer Jeffers, ed., *Samuel Beckett: A Casebook*, New York: Garland, pp. 225–49.

Whitehead, Kate (1989), *The Third Programme, A Literary History*, Oxford: Clarendon.

Williams, Raymond (1981), *Culture*, London: Fontana.

Williams, Raymond (1990), *Television, Technology and Cultural Form*, London: Fontana.

Winston, Brian (1998), *Media, Technology and Society — A History: From the Telegraph to the Internet*, London: Routledge.

All That Fall as a Case Study in the Possibilities and Problematics of Re-routing Samuel Beckett's Radio Plays for Performance in Other Media

Everett C. Frost

Abstract

Beckett insisted that his radio plays were specific to the medium for which they were intended, having been written for voices, not bodies. Re-routing them to other media is a problem he could not have foreseen but one that is now made exigent by the subsequent advent of new technologies and the virtually total absence of radio as a medium for drama. Adaptations of them for stage and digital technologies can increasingly be expected to happen and need to be encouraged. But how to revive them and under what circumstances? I have no answers, but will use his first radio play, *All That Fall* to set a framework for discussing the issues in the spirit of John Cage's remark in another context: 'Permission granted, but not to do anything you want'.

The radio play began as itself an adaptation of drama to a new broadcast technology. But radio producers quickly began to discover that the new medium was not merely a means for transmitting an ancient artform but an opportunity to use the new medium to create original forms of specifically aural drama more akin to music than to its theatrical origins. Adapting the radio plays for the stage and for contemporary forms of multimedia performance rescues them from oblivion by returning their dormant voices to drama's origins in the theatre. It is not a displacement, but a revival.

By placing Beckett's insistence on their genre specificity as radio drama in this historical and theoretical perspective, I will not eliminate the intractable problems of extracting them from their broadcast specificity, but might contribute to a more general understanding of the problematics of cross-genre productions that extend beyond either radio or Beckett.

∙ ∙ ∙

Permission granted, but not to do anything you want.
JOHN CAGE[1]

---

[1] While writing this essay for the Beckett Working Group's plenary session at the 2013 IFTR–FIRT Convention in Barcelona, this advice from the master of chance operations con-

⋯

All That Fall is a specifically radio play, or rather radio text, for voices, not bodies. I have already refused to have it 'staged' and I cannot think of it in such terms. A perfectly straight reading before an audience seems to me just barely legitimate, though even on this score I have my doubts. But I am absolutely opposed to any form of adaptation with a view to its conversion into 'theatre'. It is no more theatre than *End-Game* is radio and to 'act' it is to kill it. Even the reduced visual dimension it will receive from the simplest and most static of readings [...] will be destructive of whatever quality it may have and which depends on the whole thing's *coming out of the dark.* [...] [F]rankly, the thought of *All That Fall* on a stage, however discreetly, is intolerable to me.²

⋰

Understanding Beckett's resistance to staging his first radio play begins, but does not end, by placing this oft-quoted letter into its historical and biographical context.³ Radio's extraordinary potential as a medium for transmitting drama was recognised from its earliest beginnings. In the United Kingdom, this potential was initially understood to mean, as the BBC liked to put it, extending the proscenium arch of the West End to the living rooms of the nation and the world. In doing so it provided much sought after opportunities (and, not incidentally, income) for playwrights and performers. Radio, along with early silent film, extracted drama from the exclusive domain of the theatre: plays now occurred on movie screens and, via radio, in living rooms (and later, in cars, on the beach, iThings, Blackberries, etc.). But, as David Wade, an early radio author-critic argued: 'In acting [...] as a theatre substitute, it seems to me that the BBC is engaged not so much in radio drama as in drama by means of radio' (219). Enthusiastic radio producers like Donald McWhinnie,

---

cerning the American broadcast of the Westdeutscher Rundfunk production of his *Hörspiel*, *Roaratorio: An Irish Circus on Finnegans Wake*, seemed to summarise epigrammatically what I was attempting to say. I include it as an homage to Julie Campbell who was, herself, adept at such gentle, puckish concisions.

2   Samuel Beckett to his American publisher, Barney Rosset, 27 August 1957, which appears as the frontispiece to Zilliacus, 1976.

3   I explore that context in greater detail in Frost, 2014, 251–65.

who directed many of Beckett's radio and television plays, wanted to demonstrate that radio was not merely a means for *transmitting* drama, but also an opportunity to create a unique, radio-specific, form of it — an acoustic genre that, along with silent film, could stand on equal footing with its theatrical predecessor.

The need for such validation increased in the early 1950s with television replacing radio as the primary form of home entertainment and its steady drain of audiences, talent, budgets, and — perhaps above all — of prestige. Radio drama was defended as the genre most closely aligned with music, which — on theories derived directly and indirectly, from Schopenhauer — was recognised as the premiere artform speaking directly and non-referentially to and through the emotions. Schopenhauer had argued that since it 'reproduces the emotions of our innermost being, but entirely without reality and remote from its pain [...] music is so very much more powerful and penetrating than is that of the other arts, for these speak only of the shadow, but music of the essence of the thing itself' (Schopenhauer, 257).[4]

The wide regard for Schopenhauer's view of music is reflected by its influence on Walter Pater's *Renaissance*:

> It is the art of music which most completely realises this artistic ideal, this perfect identification of matter and form. In its consummate moments, the end is not distinct from the means, the form from the matter, the subject from the expression: they inhere in and completely saturate each other; and it is to the condition of its perfect moments, all the arts may be supposed constantly to attend and aspire. [...] [T]he arts may be represented as continually struggling after the law or principle of music to a condition which music alone completely realises. (114)[5]

The fact that radio consisted of sound alone was not considered a deficiency but an advantage that television lacked. It justified the continuing survival and developing aesthetic of radiophonic drama as a unique artform that created the intimate emotional immediacy of a dramatic experience taking place in the privacy of the listener's own head without the reductive externalising distraction of visuals. Drama specifically written to exploit the particular character of the radio medium became the *sine qua non* of broadcasting, and

---

4 Partially quoted in Pilling, p. 177.
5 Beckett read Pater as early as his undergraduate years at Trinity College Dublin, and drew upon Schopenhauer's conception of music in his monograph on Proust.

writers were sought, encouraged, and economically incentivised, to not merely supply stage plays in search of a theatre, but to devise radio-specific works.

When, after more than a year's deliberation, BBC radio advised Beckett that it was rejecting *Waiting for Godot* on grounds that it was not sufficiently radiophonic, and invited him to write something that was, it felt confident that, as John Morris, Controller of the BBC third programme wrote to the Head Radio Drama, 'I got the impression that he has a very sound idea of the problems of writing for radio and that we can expect something pretty good' (Knowlson, 385). Beckett, however, was less confident:

> [...] am told that [Val] Gielgud [Head of BBC Radio] wants a play for the 3rd Programme. Never thought about Radio play technique but in the dead of t'other night got a nice gruesome idea full of cartwheels and dragging of feet and puffing and panting which may or may not lead to something. (Beckett, 2011, 631)

It led to something pretty good, and Beckett became identified as one of radio drama's principal innovators:[6]

> We are not so ready to believe the radio play to be different from the stage play, yet the blind medium of radio in its unique power upon the ear of stimulating the imagination makes for a kind of drama which can embrace subjects film and theatre may never approach. Its subtle and mercurial manipulation of sounds and words, allied to its quality of immediacy and intimacy with the listener, give it possibilities of development that await only the right dramatist. We think now of the poetic plays of Mr Louis MacNeice, of Dylan Thomas's *Under Milk Wood*, and of Mr Samuel Beckett's *All That Fall* as tentative but real steps towards the discovery of radio drama's proper form. (Styan, 287)

It is in this context that Clas Zilliacus, in his seminal study of Beckett's media plays, describes Beckett's 27 August 1957 letter to Barney Rosset as 'the

---

6 Even before broadcast or publication when the question of adaptation for stage or film had not yet come up, Beckett had replied to a film critic with whom he was in correspondence, 'No, the script for the 3rd [BBC Radio 3], *All That Fall* [...] is specifically radio' (Beckett, 2011, 678). After the success of *All That Fall*, McWhinnie and the BBC were confident that they had recruited Beckett as one of their stars, committed to radiophonic drama. McWhinnie in an internal BBC memorandum 21 February, 1957: 'My impression is that if he [Beckett] is to write at all in the near future, it will be for radio, which has captured his imagination' (qtd. in Knowlson, 388).

most substantial document available on Beckett's views on converting for one medium works conceived for another'. But his discussion of 'The Plays Out of Their Element', which concludes that 'these works by Beckett have little or nothing to gain and much to lose if transposed for other media', (Zilliacus, 169), could not have anticipated how radically the technologies and conventions of how radio is produced, programmed, transmitted, and heard have changed. The genre specificity of Beckett's radio plays needs to account not only for their radiophonic intentionality, but also for radio's radically altered nature and its diminished use as a medium for drama. Periodic repeat broadcast of the original productions are rare, and new radio productions of them virtually non-existent. The historic productions become artefacts difficult to hear. The absence of new professional radio productions sentences Beckett's radio plays to performative oblivion. They are specific not only to a medium but also to a lost place and time, neither of which, as Beckett reminds us that Proust reminds us, can be recovered except in memory.

It is ironic that what makes adaptation of Beckett's radio plays at once so appealing and so difficult is that he so successfully made them radiophonic that something is lost in extracting them from the medium for which they were intended and remain best suited. But something is also lost in *failing* to adapt them. Categories of genre such as radio drama, like the plays included in them, change over time, and also change their affiliations to other genres. Pushing their boundaries — as Beckett had done by combining tragedy and comedy into tragicomedy in *Waiting for Godot* — has for literature and drama been a source of innovation and re-invention: 'Thus in the course of history works gradually change their generic affiliations in such a way as to preserve their interest for each new generation. Yet the genre's tradition embodies a compensating continuity that may keep readers in touch with older meanings and values' (Fowler, 1989, 216). Adapting Beckett's radio plays for the stage rescues them from oblivion by returning them to drama's theatrical origins. It is not a displacement but a re-union.

Further, just as radio changes over time, and genre changes over time, so too do Beckett's radio plays and our understanding of them. Not to examine possibilities for re-routing Beckett's radiophonic drama in the light of contemporary circumstances is to impose parameters inherited from the past without bothering with an inquiry into the present. The radio plays are part of the total body of Beckett's work, and we encounter them in the context of a half-century of the innovations in theatre, drama, and broadcasting of which Beckett was among the significant architects. We have learned much about how to respond to Beckett's work in the half-century since the original production of *All That Fall*. First responders to it had not seen *Not I* or *Happy Days* and could not see

Maddy Rooney and her husband Dan in the context of Winnie and Willie. Few original listeners would have read *Molloy, Malone Dies,* and *The Unnamable*; and none could have read *The Lost Ones*. Nor had they access to the impressive body of Beckett scholarship, biographies, productions, letters, notebooks, and manuscript drafts that assist interpreters in making sense of his work (provide your own aspirin, he once suggested).

Enoch Brater observes that 'Critics who have followed the performance history of Beckett's work for the stage and the mechanical media have been from the start heavily influenced by the force of these plays in their original productions', aptly concluding that 'This is, perhaps, as it should be' (183). But perhaps not *all* as it should be. The original productions give an invaluable indicator of how Samuel Beckett thought things should be done at the time they were done — an indispensable resource for enriching and imagining new productions. But a consequence of not adopting strategies for adapting Beckett's radio plays to contemporary circumstances is that the original productions become embalmed in an iconic aura that deprives them of alternative versions with which to compare them. As Druid Theatre artistic director Garry Hynes, noted in an interview with Peter Crawley about her productions of Synge, 'No audience is going to thank you by saying: "That was really rather interesting to see that historical curiosity". They want to be engaged and provoked within the context of their lives at the present moment. *That* is the job' (Crawley, 1).

Donald McWhinnie's conception of *All That Fall* is no more 'definitive' for being first than subsequent productions, including mine, can claim to be. There is never going to be a definitive approach to the intractable questions of adaptation. The problem lies in choosing from among what counts as adequate and inadequate forms of it — according to whom, and towards what ends. It is within these complex, inter-related, and sometimes contradictory variables that performative strategies for Samuel Beckett's radio plays need to be imagined.

Rigid insistence on faithful adherence to original intentionalities, even on the assumption that they are recoverable, turns them into exercises in karaoke. Insistence that original intentionalities are irrelevant transforms them into something that is no longer Beckett.[7] Either way, what gets lost is the play.

---

7 Kevin Branigan asserts that, 'the critic in an age influenced by Roland Barthes's literary theory [of the death of the author], cannot afford to be restricted in his interpretations by the directions or protestations of the author' (59). Neither can she 'afford' to ignore them, however immersed in Barthes's literary theory she might be. While not being 'restricted', she might well be advised. Why would any critic or director, seeking to get it right, be anything other than grateful for any help she could get, including help from an author — even a

Finding it might well begin by understanding *why* the play is radiophonic — not to impede the adaptation but to improve it: 'Beckett's view of *All That Fall* — a view that is borne out by the work itself — makes clear that interpretation of it must take into account its condition as a radio text; must see this condition as an essential aspect of its nature and meaning' (Van Laan, 39). It contributes to what Iain Bailey has described as getting the tone of the production right (206–9). Not only Beckett's use of the form but also his dialogue with it needs to be considered in any transposition of genre. For, as Linda Ben-Zvi has observed, 'Essential ... to any appraisal of Beckett's writing — fiction, drama, or media plays — is an awareness of the specific form in which Beckett conceived the work, since for him, more than for most writers, the work is not only predicated on the form, but invariably becomes a critique of its form' (24).

1 Acoustic Scenography: What Makes *All That Fall* Radio-Specific?

All Beckett's performance works — whether for stage, screen, or radio — were written with minute attention to their staging, genre, and production requirements incorporated into the text. As Joslin McKinney and Philip Butterworth note in their introduction to scenography:

> Perhaps the most scenographically inventive playwright, Samuel Beckett, has concerned himself with space and image to the extent that words and scenograpy are inextricably intertwined from the start of the play. Beckett's concern is with staging plays and not just the text on the page. The operation of scenographic elements, particularly spatial ones, is deliberately mobilized by Beckett's texts. Stage directions and descriptions of the settings of his plays [...] are seen to be as fundamental to the text as the words given to the characters. For him use of stage space is a primary element in dramatic construction. (88)

In *All That Fall*, Beckett's integration of scenographic elements into the text of the play is no less operative than in his stage plays. In it he designs an acoustic

---

posthumous one? 'The writer's business is to make excessive demands of his interpreters' (McWhinnie, 103). The ultimate arbiter is the work itself. On Barthian grounds not only is the author and author's text (and its drafts and variants) contextualised, so is the director, scenographer, and critic (including Branigan, including this one). We are ineluctably held in infinite mobiles of reflecting mirrors, seeking to make something palpable out of ephemeral images. That is the challenge, and what makes it interesting: the extraordinary pleasure of it all.

scenography — that creates vivid visual dimension out of text and sound as well as an acoustic one.[8] They place Maddy in the world she experiences. The soundscape — a 'gruesome idea full of cartwheels and dragging of feet and puffing and panting' — is part of the radiophonic conceptual origins of the play. A fascination with the ghostly, ghastly, and the macabre is a staple of radio drama,[9] and Beckett's play exploits radio's awareness that unseen and imagined horrors are far scarier than seen ones. As Hugh Kenner has noted, Beckett did not begin by writing a script for *All That Fall* and then try to find a place for it, because, as the suggestion that he write something specifically for radio 'specified a medium, not a subject, [Beckett] has allowed the novel medium to generate its fit subject, achieving thus [...] a symbiosis between the theme of the work and the kind of experience the audience is having' (159).

In his influential essay on 'Samuel Beckett and the Art of Broadcasting', Martin Esslin correctly grasps the fact that the listener experiences the play entirely from Maddy's point of view — 'from which subjective viewpoint, he is witnessing the action, and indeed inside whose mind he is supposed to be' — but mis-states the consequences:

> Thus by the use of stylized and distorted sounds, radio can create a subjective reality halfway between the objective events experienced and their subjective reflection within the mind of the character who experiences them — halfway between waking consciousness and dreamlike states, halfway between fact and fantasy, even hallucination [...] It might be a bad dream. (Esslin, 131)

While there are notable radio dramas that are set 'halfway between' interior and exterior points of view, it will not do for *All That Fall*. We are not 'supposed to be' in her mind, we are entirely in her mind and never anywhere else. The play adheres to the Aristotelian unity of space as well as time. There are no half-ways.

Contrary to the assumption that '[We] do not [always] hear what she hears, any more than we see what she sees' (Cleveland, 276; also see Campbell, 147–68 and Kalb, 128), we hear only what she hears, experience only what she experiences, and in the skewed way appropriate to her character and consistent with her state of mind. Nor is she having a bad dream or hallucination — something created in or by her mind. It would be out of character for Maddy to make-up

---

8   Just as stage and television plays are given distinctive acoustic features, and even *Film* has a single (and dramatically significant) 'Shhhh!' that distinguishes it from a silent movie.
9   It also anticipates the spectral images that haunt plays still to come: notably *Footfalls*, *Eh Joe*, and the ghostly greys of the television plays.

or conjure Mr. Barrell, and there is no reason to believe that Mr. Slocum is not her former admirer and does not 'really' give her a lift in his automobile, etc. Listeners experience all the action of the play entirely by witnessing the volatile, disoriented, mind of its protagonist, Maddy, as she makes the laborious journey to the station, awaits her husband Dan, and returns home with him. As Robert Pinget's heartwarming hour-long television adaptation of *Tout ceux qui tombent* makes clear, staging or filming these external events requires Maddy's physical, external, presence which obliterates the locational interiority. While the play is not Maddy's hallucination or bad dream, neither does it take place on the road to and from the Boghill railroad station and on its platform, but in the consciousness of Maddy coming into existence for the audience experiencing her journey by means of the mental soundscape experiencing that landscape. The audience experiences Maddy in the mental act of experiencing herself in the physical world — including the existence of her own often erotic body — coming into being in the act of perception. Louise Cleveland insightfully sees that *All That Fall* 'is a record of an excruciatingly physical journey. Maddy's body is not abstracted from the drama by being rendered invisible. Her concrete existence is a continual embarrassment — breathing, shuffling, requiring ministrations of others' (268).

In emphasising Maddy's experience of physical embodiment, Anna McMullan and Ulrika Maude contribute a welcome corrective to the critical imbalance set in motion by Esslin's often insightful essay. In adding the body to the audio experience of 'Hearing Beckett', Maude notes 'that the special relevance the acoustic has to issues of embodiment in Beckett's work has been overlooked. [...] Beckett's experiments with sound [...] ultimately bear witness to the persistence with which Beckett grounds subjectivity firmly in a material context' (48). 'Indeed', as McMullan clearly demonstrates in her chapter on 'Radiophonic Embodiments', 'from Maddy's point of view, her body is both a material encumbrance which weights every step and a protean material which shifts its shape to match her affective and psychic state' (70), the tragicomic, and often erotic, dramatic consequences of which are fully exploited throughout the play.

Beckett shares what he once said of Proust's narrator:

> [T]he radiographical quality of his observation. The copiable he does not see. He searches for a relation, a common factor, substrata. Thus he is less interested in what is said than in the way in which it is said. [...] [T]he exact quality of the weather, temperature, and visibility, is transmitted to him in terms of sound, in the chimes and the calls of the hawkers. (Beckett, 1987, 83)

And so it is with Maddy and the sounds she hears and the way she hears them. The footsteps, for example, meticulously specified throughout the script, which in the second half of the play are a nonverbal punctuation to the dialogue between Maddy and Dan, are heard in that exaggerated way by Maddy.[10] As Julie Campbell has noted, radio has no difficulty preserving the unities of space and time while tracking Maddy's continuous walk to and from the railroad station, but in the theatre 'movement is generally restricted to the stage space in front of the audience' (147), and so has trouble following her travels.

Additionally, in *All That Fall*, there are radio gags that depend upon being heard unseen and depend for full effect on the voyeuristic delight of knowing that the play is being broadcast to a general audience. Radio announcers dread the canard in which some wag has replaced a program's intro theme music with something jarring — a cacophony of animal sounds, such as the rural sounds that open the play, being one April Fool's Day favourite — that can be exploited as a sure way to grab an audience's attention.

Unseen, the scene in which Maddy's former admirer, Mr. Slocum (pun intended), helps her into his automobile, has delicious erotic overtones that lampoon radio's prurience and in doing so creates one of the most outrageously funny moments in the play. Performed on stage the visible presence of the automobile however much deconstructed — as in the staging of the recent Jermyn Theatre production discussed below — diminishes the scene into seeing that all that is going on is that she has a helluva time getting into the car.

These are among the reasons that, 'Even the reduced visual dimension it will receive from the simplest and most static of readings ... will be destructive of whatever quality it may have and which depends on the whole thing's *coming out of the dark*'. The exploitation of point of view from which the action is experienced is fundamental to the genre specificity of all Beckett's radio plays. The genre has been so inextricably written into the play, that while the play can be extracted from its genre, the genre cannot be so easily extracted from the play.

Beckett's reluctance to allow stage productions of his radio plays often stemmed from his apprehension that adaptation really meant *adaphatrôce*: his bi-lingual pun for adapting them for reasons that he found unsuitable

---

10   This presents no formidable difficulty on radio because the footsteps are not generated by the performers' feet but by a sound effects technician with a box of gravel. If staged as if the audience is witnessing a radio performance, with the sound effects, technicians, characters, they become a distraction that upstages Beckett's play.

(Beckett and Schneider, 1998, 324). *Adaphatrôcities* included such things as using the plays for stylised performances, making them more plausible or 'realistic', eliminating their 'teasers' and ambiguities, updating them to make them 'relevant', or upstaging them into crowd pleasers for trendy performances from auteur directors and scenographers, or vehicles for star talent.

The 2012 Jermyn Theatre production, directed by Trevor Nunn and starring Michael Gambon and Aileen Atkins,[11] made *All That Fall* into an interesting and enjoyable evening of theatre while remaining technically loyal to the text by muting the play's stoic pessimism and leaving the stars at liberty to exploit its potential for crowd-pleasing humour, thus, so the press spin gave it out, liberating poor Beckett from clueless intellectuals. Although staged to suggest the concept of witnessing a broadcast of the play, it added costumes appropriate to the characters. Making the action visible on stage, it was argued, improved the play by resolving the ambiguity surrounding the death of a child at the end, incorrectly supposing that this was something the radio could not do. But erasing Beckettian enigmas never improves his work no matter where performed. The production moved the play in the direction of pantomime and got the tone wrong. It diminished the play's dark pessimism and changed its genre not so much from radio to stage as from tragicomedy to whodunnit, thereby gaining laughs at the expense of the pathos embedded in the Beckettian reminder that there is nothing funnier than unhappiness.

Concerns such as these prompted Beckett to write the oft-cited letter refusing to allow a theatrical performance of *All That Fall*. He was responding to a request to stage it from Herbert Berghoff, whose 1956 production of *Waiting for Godot* Beckett found irritatingly problematic partly because it had been misdirected as a star turn for the 'top banana', Burt Lahr. Refusing permission was motivated by the fear that *All That Fall* would be similarly falsified. But Beckett relented a few weeks later: 'I cannot hold out against a simple reading of *All That Fall*, so let it be. But no frills, for the love of God'. And Berghoff did indeed mount a no-frills staged reading with actors seated upstage and approaching a pair of downstage lecterns to read their parts. A half-year later Beckett wrote to Barney Rosset that 'Mary Manning, old friend, is welcome to do *All That Fall*' in a staged reading that ran for a fortnight at the Poet's Theatre in Cambridge, Mass., USA, in April 1958. In March 1963, having recently finished two intensely radiophonic pieces, *Words and Music* and *Cascando,* Beckett left it to his publishers to discriminate between staging and upstaging his radio plays, writing

---

[11] Opened at the Jermyn Street Theatre, London 11 October, 2012; continued at the Arts Theatre, London 6–24 November, 2012. See Frost, 2013 for my review.

to Grove press: 'Confirm no staging of radio plays. O.K. for genuine readings. If you have doubt don't authorize. Leave it to your discretion' (Zilliacus, 169–70; Knowlson, 421–2).

A decade later resisting celebrity appropriations of his plays created an awkward situation. Adamantly refusing 'a hot offer for [staging] *All That Fall* at [London's] National [Theatre]' from Sir Laurence Olivier and Joan Plowright, risked alienating a major institution. The couple had flown to Paris to persuade Beckett, when the routine request for permission from Kenneth Tynan (managing scripts at the National) was, to the consternation of one and all, turned down. 'Larry kept saying', Beckett wrote to Alan Schneider, '"It'd make a GREAT SHOW!" However said no again. Impossible in the light. They had worked out some idea with players moving from stage onto screen. They were a bit fed up with me but very nice' (Beckett and Schneider, 214; Zilliacus, 179–80). Having become the poster boy for the phenomenon dubbed 'Theatre of the Absurd' by Martin Esslin in 1961 and 'damned to fame' by the Nobel Prize in 1969, Beckett could foresee that the pressure to stage the radio plays would continue to increase, and to mean anything goes — from Heidelberg students turning *All That Fall* into an *unterkühltes* [supercool] multimedia dance and pantomime, to the Living Theatre's inclusion of *All That Fall* and *Embers* in an evening of Beckett, prompting the *Village Voice* reviewer to lament that, 'Samuel Beckett is a great enough writer for us to believe that when he writes a play for radio, he intends it and designs it to be spoken and not acted' (Zilliacus, 171). In a staging of *All That Fall* and *Embers*, André Gregory wanted props and sets for the latter because, while the former had a lot of characters, the latter had only two characters, one of which was not there very much and so needed some jazzing up.

In this context Beckett's refusal to allow staged productions of his radio plays was a desperate — and often futile — response to the fact that needless liberties were being taken in the stagings that turned the plays into something they were never meant to be. It is arguably the case that Beckett finally withdrew permission for anything other than a radio production of *All That Fall*, not because a staged reading was unacceptable to him but in exasperation over 'a quality common to most projects for staging *All That Fall*: [while] none of them aims at unstinted realism; many find the task of transposition an opportunity for formal experiment' (Zilliacus, 171). Beckett was simply fed up with struggling against actors, producers, directors, scenographers, and post-Barthian (death of author) theorists wanting to commit '*adaphatrôce*' on his play for their own agenda in ways not congenial to its spirit or consonant with its essence and that would compromise its texture, tone, or spirit.[12] His

---

12   See Zilliacus, pp. 169–82 for *adaphatrôcities* up to 1971.

response to having repeatedly to deal with these difficulties led to a generic statement of conditions for staging the radio plays that reflects Beckett's impatience with them:

> Mr. Beckett has specifically stated that these are meant to be radio plays and should therefore be read, not acted. They are plays for voices and he has given permission for stage readings, but he definitely does not want the 'readers' to be costumed, to use any props, to move around the stage any more than is necessary to get to the microphone, or to use any movements even when standing still. They should be read just as if it were being done over the radio and there were no audience to see the performers. If your plans are different from those specified above, I'm afraid that we cannot give you permission to do the play. If you feel that you can accept these restrictions, we'll certainly be happy to permit you to give a production. (Zilliacus, 175)

One way to stage them without destroying their radiophonic quality is to produce them in audio form and simply play them for live audiences. I have often done so with the Beckett Festival productions for radio, and found no difficulty with audiences sitting quietly in the dark or near-dark, listening intently for 90 minutes. The touring Pan Pan staging of the play (from 2012–19, directed by Gavin Quinn) provided an interesting variation of this strategy. Beckett's drama was pre-recorded and played over monitors in a space with controlled acoustics and lighting and with comfortable seating distributed throughout. Sound Design (Jimmie Eadie) and Lighting and Set Design (Aedín Cosgrove) won *Irish Times* 'Best' awards for 2011. The acting is very fine indeed, and aside from following the BBC production with the rural sounds of animals performed by actors (to which Beckett consistently — and in my view, correctly — objected; see Frost, 1994, 192–7), the *bruitage* is well done. Staging the play was marred, however, by the deliberately intrusive lighting used to accent the dramatic climaxes — mistakenly treating the absence of visuals as something to be overcome — and so burying the play in the lighting effects. The intent would seem to have been to inflict Maddy's disorientation on the audience, notably in the railroad platform confusion, and in the storm of wind and rain that concludes the play. Since we see the action from Maddy's point of view the intention makes sense. When heard, however, the audience does not itself actually experience what Maddy experiences. It overhears her experiencing at one remove, and experiences her experience vicariously. But the auditor does not replace her; is not subjected to her experience, is not disoriented, as if it were she. In phenomenological terms, she is an experiencing subject whom we experience as object. Instead of drawing the audience into

Maddy's point of view its attention was drawn to the intrusive lighting taking over and running amuck. Maddy did not get lost in the wind and rain as the script requires, she got upstaged by the lighting which replaced my experience of her disorientation with my own.

In the Beckett centenary year, 2006, I was invited by Emma Jordan to direct a reading of *All That Fall* for Prime Cut Productions in Belfast, Northern Ireland.[13] Provided with excellent actors I sought a concept for an onstage performance of the disembodied voices and sounds that Maddy experiences. We were neither reading the play on stage before an audience nor making it into a theatrical performance. Instead we staged a performance of the act of reading the play. The distinction is important, and not, I hope, merely a matter of elaborate word-play. Actors performed not the roles in the play but played the role of actors reading that portion of the play that is contained in the words that their characters say in *All That Fall* (i.e. the dialogue), leaving most of the sounds they make to the *bruitage*. Maddy, for example, is made up not only of the words she says but is also woven out of the web of sounds that she hears or thinks she hears, and makes and hears herself making. Her footsteps were very much a part of the performance but did not actually emanate from the feet of Stella McCusker, the actress playing the role — a conventional matter on radio, but a formidable conundrum on stage. Almost all the sound effects were prepared in advance and fed on cue over speakers into the performance. The physical presence of the script became not an impediment to a performance but a 'prop' — not only something to lean on, but a *property* signifying the actor performing the role of reader. The convention was re-enforced by the presence on stage of two music stands, which served as props in both senses of the word: a support for the script that would disencumber the hand, and a property whose semiotics said, 'staged reading'. Ironically, this seems also to have been the strategy adopted by the Berghoff reading discussed above (and identified as a 'concert reading', which might well be a better term than my 'staged reading'). Maddy's music stand was placed centre stage and that of the other characters to stage left and slightly upstage from Maddy's, in keeping the dynamic of the interaction of characters while arguing against the realistic or plausible. A slight movement of the music stands during the arrival of Dan's train left Maddy and Dan flanking each other. The palpably visible presence of these two simple props — script and music stands — reframed the play we performed into not *All That Fall*, but the staging of a reading of the radio play Beckett had written. I suppose they were also a visual way of conveying our

---

13   Waterfront Studio Theatre, Belfast, 6 February, 2006. More fully described in Frost, 2007.

indebtedness to Beckett's script and its radiophonic origins — re-routing without being imprisoned by them: and trying to understand in theatrical practice the problematic that inform this essay's theorising.

Works Cited

Bailey, Iain (2013), 'Sounds Worthy of the Name: Tone and Historical Feeling in Beckett's Drama', in Peter Fifield and David Addyman, eds., *Samuel Beckett: Debts and Legacies: New Critical Essays*, London: Bloomsbury, pp. 191–214.

Beckett, Samuel (1987), *Proust and Three Dialogues with Georges Duthuit*, London: John Calder.

Beckett, Samuel (2009a), *The Letters of Samuel Beckett, Vol. I: 1929–1940*, ed. George Craig, Martha Dow Fehsenfeld, Dan Gunn and Lois More Overbeck, Cambridge: Cambridge UP.

Beckett, Samuel (2009b), *All That Fall and Other Plays for Radio and Screen*, preface and notes by Everett C. Frost, London: Faber and Faber.

Beckett, Samuel (2011), *The Letters of Samuel Beckett, Vol. II: 1941–1956*, ed. George Craig, Martha Dow Fehsenfeld, Dan Gunn and Lois More Overbeck, Cambridge: Cambridge UP.

Beckett, Samuel, and Alan Schneider (1998), *No Author Better Served: The Correspondence of Samuel Beckett and Alan Schneider*, ed. Maurice Harmon, Cambridge: Harvard UP.

Ben-Zvi, Linda (1985), 'Samuel Beckett's Media Plays', *Modern Drama*, 18: 1, pp. 22–37.

Branigan, Kevin (2008), *Radio Beckett: Musicality in the Radio Plays of Samuel Beckett*, Oxford: Peter Lang.

Brater, Enoch (2004), 'Billie Whitelaw's TV Beckett', in Linda Ben-Zvi, ed., *Drawing on Beckett: Portraits, Performances, and Cultural Contexts*, Tel Aviv: Assaph Book Series, pp. 183–96.

Bryden, Mary, ed. (1998), *Samuel Beckett and Music*, Oxford: Oxford UP.

Campbell, Julie (2009), '"A Voice Comes to One in the Dark. Imagine": Radio, the Listener, and the Dark Comedy of *All That Fall*', in Steven Barfield, Matthew Feldman and Philip Tew, eds., *Beckett and Death*, London: Continuum, pp. 147–68.

Cleveland, Louise (1969), 'Trials in the Soundscape: The Radio Plays of Samuel Beckett', *Modern Drama*, 11: 3, pp. 267–82.

Crawley, Peter (2006), 'The Crystal Heart of Druid: Garry Hynes', *Irish Times* 'Weekend Review', 11 March, pp. 1–2.

Esslin, Martin (1982), 'Samuel Beckett and the Art of Broadcasting', in *Mediations: Essays on Brecht, Beckett, and the Media*, New York: Grove P, pp. 125–54.

Fowler, Alistair (1989), 'Genre', in Erik Barnouw, et al. eds., *International Encyclopedia of Communications*, Oxford: Oxford UP, pp. 215–7.

Frost, Everett C. (1994), 'A "Fresh Go" for the Skull: Directing *All That Fall*, Samuel Beckett's Play for Radio', in Lois Oppenheim, ed., *Directing Beckett*, Ann Arbor: U of Michigan P, pp. 186–219.

Frost, Everett C. (2007), '"No Frills for the love of God": Reading a Staged Reading of Beckett's *All That Fall*', *The Beckett Circle*, 30: 2, pp. 9–13.

Frost, Everett C. (2013), 'Performing the Jermyn Street Theatre's Staging of *All That Fall*: A Review Essay', *JOBS*, 22: 2, pp. 245–58.

Frost, Everett C. (2014), '"The Sound is Enough": Beckett's Radio Plays', in S. E. Gontarski, ed., *The Edinburgh Companion to Samuel Beckett and the Arts*, Edinburgh: Edinburgh UP, pp. 251–65.

Kalb, Jonathan (1994), '"The Mediated Quixote: The Radio and Television Plays, and Film', in John Pilling, ed., *The Cambridge Companion to Samuel Beckett*, Cambridge: Cambridge UP, pp. 124–44.

Kenner, Hugh (1973), *A Reader's Guide to Samuel Beckett*, London: Thames and Hudson.

Knowlson, James (1996), *Damned to Fame: The Life of Samuel Beckett*, New York: Simon & Schuster.

Maude, Ulrika (2009), *Beckett, Technology and the Body*, Cambridge: Cambridge UP.

McKinney, Joslin and Philip Butterworth (2009), *The Cambridge Introduction to Scenography*, Cambridge: Cambridge UP.

McMullan, Anna (2010), *Performing Embodiment in Samuel Beckett's Drama*, London: Routledge.

McWhinnie, Donald (1959), *The Art of Radio*, London: Faber and Faber.

Pater, Walter (1919), *The Renaissance*, New York: Boni and Liveright.

Pilling, John (1998), 'Proust and Schopenhauer: Music and Shadows', in Mary Bryden, ed., *Samuel Beckett and Music*, Oxford: Oxford UP, pp. 173–8.

Schopenhauer, Arthur (1969), *The World as Will and Representation*, trans. E. F. J. Payne, New York: Dover.

Styan, John L. (1963), *The Elements of Drama*, Cambridge: Cambridge UP.

Van Laan, Thomas F. (1986), '*All That Fall* as "a Play for Radio"', *Modern Drama*, 19: 1, pp. 38–47.

Wade, David (1981), 'British Radio Drama since 1960', in John Drakakis, ed., *British Radio Drama*, Cambridge: Cambridge UP, pp. 218–24.

Zilliacus, Clas (1976), *Beckett and Broadcasting: A Study of the Works of Samuel Beckett for and in Radio and Television*, Abo: Abo Akademi.

Bibliography

Works by Samuel Beckett

Beckett, Samuel (1953), *Watt*, New York: Grove P.
Beckett, Samuel (1954), *Waiting for Godot*, New York: Grove P.
Beckett, Samuel (1957), *Proust*, New York: Grove P.
Beckett, Samuel (1963), *Watt*, London: John Calder.
Beckett, Samuel (1964), *How It Is*, London: John Calder.
Beckett, Samuel (1965), *Proust and Three Dialogues with Georges Duthuit*, London: John Calder.
Beckett, Samuel (1965), *Three Novels*, New York: Grove P.
Beckett, Samuel (1967), *Stories and Texts for Nothing*, New York: Grove P.
Beckett, Samuel (1973), *Murphy*, London: Picador.
Beckett, Samuel (1980), *Company*, New York: Grove P.
Beckett, Samuel (1983), *Worstward Ho*, London: John Calder.
Beckett, Samuel (1983), *Disjecta: Miscellaneous Writings and a Dramatic Fragment*, London: John Calder.
Beckett, Samuel (1984), *Disjecta: Miscellaneous Writings and a Dramatic Fragment*, ed. Ruby Cohn, New York: Grove P.
Beckett, Samuel (1984), *The Collected Shorter Plays of Samuel Beckett*, New York: Grove P.
Beckett, Samuel (1984), *The Collected Shorter Plays of Samuel Beckett*, London: Faber and Faber.
Beckett, Samuel (1986), *Catastrophe et autres dramaticules*, Paris: Les Éditions de Minuit.
Beckett, Samuel (1986), *The Complete Dramatic Works*, London: Faber and Faber.
Beckett, Samuel (1987), *Proust and Three Dialogues with Georges Duthuit*, London: John Calder.
Beckett, Samuel (1990), *Le Monde et le pantalon suivi de Peintres de l'empêchement*, Paris: Minuit.
Beckett, Samuel (1992), *Dream of Fair to Middling Women*, ed. Eoin O'Brien and Edith Fournier, Dublin: Black Cat P.
Beckett, Samuel (1992) *The Theatrical Notebooks of Samuel Beckett*, Vol. III, ed. James Knowlson, London: Faber & Faber.
Beckett, Samuel (1993), *Dream of Fair to Middling Women*, London: John Calder.
Beckett, Samuel (1993), *Samuel Beckett's Company/Compagnie and A Piece of Monologue/Solo: A Bilingual and Variorum Edition*, ed. C. Krance, New York: Garland Reference Library of the Humanities.

Beckett, Samuel (1994), *Three Novels: Molloy, Malone Dies, The Unnamable*, New York: Grove P.
Beckett, Samuel (1995), *The Complete Short Prose, 1929–1989*, ed. S. E. Gontarski, New York: Grove P.
Beckett, Samuel (1996), *Nohow On*, with an introduction by S. E. Gontarski, New York: Grove P.
Beckett, Samuel and Alan Schneider (1998), *No Author Better Served: The Correspondence of Samuel Beckett and Alan Schneider*, ed. Maurice Harmon, Cambridge: Harvard UP.
Beckett, Samuel (1999), *Proust and Three Dialogues with Georges Duthuit*, London: Calder.
Beckett, Samuel (1999), *The Theatrical Notebooks of Samuel Beckett: The Shorter Plays*, ed. S. E. Gontarski, New York: Grove P.
Beckett, Samuel (2006), *The Complete Dramatic Works*, London: Faber and Faber.
Beckett, Samuel (2006), *The Grove Centenary Edition*, ed. Paul Auster, 4 vols, New York: Grove P.
Beckett, Samuel (2009), *All That Fall and Other Plays for Radio and Screen*, ed. Everett C. Frost, London: Faber and Faber.
Beckett, Samuel (2009), *Company, Ill Seen Ill Said, Worstward Ho, Stirrings Still*, ed. Dirk Van Hulle, London: Faber and Faber.
Beckett, Samuel (2009), *Krapp's Last Tape and Other Shorter Plays*, ed. S. E. Gontarski, London: Faber and Faber.
Beckett, Samuel (2009), *Murphy*, ed. J. C. C. Mays, London: Faber and Faber.
Beckett, Samuel (2009), *The Letters of Samuel Beckett, Vol. I: 1929–1940*, eds. Martha Dow Fehsenfeld and Lois More Overbeck, Cambridge: Cambridge UP.
Beckett, Samuel (2011), *The Letters of Samuel Beckett, Vol. II: 1941–1956*, eds. George Craig, Martha Dow Fehsenfeld, Dan Gunn and Lois More Overbeck, Cambridge: Cambridge UP.
Beckett, Samuel (2016), *The Letters of Samuel Beckett, Vol. IV, 1966–1989*, eds. George Craig, Martha Dow Fehsenfeld, Dan Gunn and Lois More Overbeck, Cambridge: Cambridge UP.
Beckett, Samuel (n.d.), 'Watt, Composite T and Tccms/inc with A revisions and A note S', The Harry Ransom Humanities Research Center at the University of Texas at Austin.

Criticism and Other Sources

Abbott, H. Porter (1996), *Beckett Writing Beckett: The Author in the Autograph*, Ithaca, New York: Cornell UP.

Abram, David (1996), *The Spell of the Sensuous: Perception and Language in a More-than-Human World*, London: Vintage Books.
Ackerley, C. J. and S. E. Gontarski (2006), *The Faber Companion to Samuel Beckett*, London: Faber and Faber.
Addyman, David, Matthew Feldman and Erik Tonning, eds. (2017), *Samuel Beckett and BBC Radio: A Reassessment*, Basingstoke: Palgrave Macmillan.
Adler, Alfred (1921), *The Neurotic Constitution (Outlines of a Comparative Individualistic Psychology and Psychotherapy)*, New York: Moffat, Yard and Company.
Adorno, Theodor (1991), 'Trying to Understand Endgame', *Notes to Literature*, ed. and trans. Shierry Weber Nicholson, New York: Columbia UP, pp. 241–75.
Adorno, Theodor (2005), *Minima Moralia: Reflections on a Damaged Life*, trans. E. F. N. Jephcott [1974], London: Verso.
Albright, Daniel (2003), *Beckett and Aesthetics*, Cambridge: Cambridge UP.
Ali, Khaleem Nafeez Mohammed (2014), 'Impossible Voices: Phenomenologies of Sound in Beckett', PhD diss., Harvard University.
Alvarez, Alfred (1992), *Samuel Beckett*, London: Fontana.
Arikha, Avigdor (2006), 'Avigdor Arihka on Beckett and Art', in James and Elizabeth Knowlson, eds., *Beckett Remembering/Remembering Beckett: Uncollected Interviews with Samuel Beckett & Memories of Those Who Knew Him*, London: Bloomsbury, pp. 143–5.
Arnheim, Rudolf (1936), *Radio*, trans. Margaret Ludwig and Herbert Read, London: Faber and Faber.
Arnheim, Rudolf (1957), *Film as Art*, Berkeley: U of California P.
Arnheim, Rudolf (1997), *Film Essays and Criticisms*, trans. Brenda Benthien, Madison, WI: U of Wisconsin P.
Asmus, Walter D. (1977), 'Rehearsal Notes for the German Première of Beckett's *That Time* and *Footfalls* at the Schiller-Theater Werkstatt Berlin (directed by Beckett)', trans. Helen Watanabe, *JOBS*, 2, pp. 82–95.
Atik, Anne (2001), *How It Was: A Memoir of Samuel Beckett*, London: Faber and Faber.
Avikunthak, Ashish (2013a), 'In Search of a Genealogy: Experimental, Avant-Garde or Prayōga?', *Deep Focus*, 1: 4, pp. 32–6.
Avikunthak, Ashish (2013b), 'East by Northwest', Interview by Michael Guarneri, *Débordements*, 31 March, 2013.
Bailey, Iain (2013), 'Sounds Worthy of the Name: Tone and Historical Feeling in Beckett's Drama', in Peter Fifield and David Addyman, eds., *Samuel Beckett: Debts and Legacies: New Critical Essays*, London: Bloomsbury, pp. 191–214.
Bakhtin, Mikhail (1984), *Problems of Dostoevsky's Poetics*, ed. and trans. C. Emerson, Minneapolis/London: U of Minnesota P.
Balázs, Béla (1931), *Theory of the Film*, trans. Edith Bone, London: Dennis Dobson.

Balázs, Béla (2010), *The Early Film Theory: Visible Man and the Spirit of Film*, ed. Erica Carter, trans. Rodney Livingstone, New York: Berghahn Books.

Bandia, Paul F. (2011), 'Translation, Migration, and Relocation of Cultures', in Sandra Bermann and Catherine Porter, eds., *A Companion to Translation Studies*, Oxford: Wiley Blackwell, pp. 273–84.

Barnard, G. C. (1970), *Samuel Beckett: A New Approach: A Study of the Novels and Plays*, New York: Dodd, Mead & Co.

Bartenieff, Irmgard with Dori Lewis (1980), *Body Movement: Coping with the Environment*, New York and London: Routledge.

Barthes, Roland (2002), *Oeuvres Complètes*, Tome I, ed. Éric Marty, Paris: Éditions du Seuil.

Beckett, Edward (1998), 'Foreword', in Mary Bryden, ed., *Samuel Beckett and Music*, pp. v–vi.

Beiser, Frederick C. (2008), *Schiller as Philosopher*, Oxford: Oxford UP.

Ben-Zvi, Linda (1985), 'Samuel Beckett's Media Plays', *Modern Drama*, 28:1, pp. 22–37.

Ben-Zvi, Linda (1987), 'Phonetic Structure in Beckett: From Mag to Gnaw', in Alan Warren Friedman et al eds., *Beckett Translating/Translating Beckett*, University Park, PA: Pennsylvania State UP, pp. 155–64.

Ben-Zvi, Linda, ed. (1990), *Women in Beckett: Performance and Critical Perspectives*, Urbana and Chicago: U of Illinois P.

Ben-Zvi, Linda, ed. (2003), *Drawing on Beckett: Portraits, Performances, and Cultural Contexts*, Tel Aviv: Assaph Book Series.

Benjamin, Walter (1969), 'The Storyteller', in Hannah Arendt, ed., *Illuminations*, New York: Schocken, pp. 83–110.

Bergson, Henri (2004), *Memoria y Vida*, Madrid: Alianza Editorial.

Berkeley, George (1998), *A Treatise Concerning the Principles of Human Knowledge*, ed. Jonathan Dancy, Oxford: Oxford UP.

Bernold, André (2015), *Beckett's Friendship: 1979–1989*, Dublin: The Lilliput P.

Besbes, Khaled (2007), *The Semiotics of Beckett's Theatre: A Semiotic Study of the Complete Dramatic Works of Samuel Beckett*, Boca Raton, Florida: Universal Publishers.

Bignell, Jonathan (2009), *Beckett on Screen: The Television Plays*, Manchester: Manchester UP.

Bignell, Jonathan (2010), 'Into the Void: Beckett's Television Plays and the Idea of Broadcasting', in Daniela Caselli, ed., *Beckett and Nothing: Trying to Understand Beckett*, Manchester: Manchester UP, pp. 125–42.

Bignell, Jonathan (2020), '"Random dottiness": Samuel Beckett and Harold Pinter in 1958', in Anita Rákóczy, Mariko Hori Tanaka, and Nicholas E. Johnson, eds., *Beckett Influencing/Influencing Beckett*, Budapest and Paris: Károli Gáspár UP / L'Harmattan, pp. 61–74.

Bignell, Jonathan (2021), 'Screen and Stage Space in Beckett's Theatre Plays on Television', in Amanda Wrigley and John Wyver, eds, *Theatre Plays on British Television*, Manchester: Manchester UP.

Biswas, Tapu (2006), *Samuel Beckett's* Waiting for Godot: *Indian Interpretations through Critical and Analytical Studies, Translations and Stage Productions*, Kolkata: Avantgarde.

Bixby, Patrick (2009), *Samuel Beckett and the Postcolonial Novel*, New York: Cambridge UP.

Bourdieu, Pierre (1993), *The Field of Cultural Production: Essays on Art and Literature*, ed. Randal Johnson, New York: Columbia UP.

Branigan, Kevin (2008), *Radio Beckett: Musicality in the Radio Plays of Samuel Beckett*, Oxford: Peter Lang.

Brater, Enoch (1974), 'The "I" in Beckett's *Not I*' *Twentieth Century Literature*, 20: 3, pp. 189–200.

Brater, Enoch (1987), *Beyond Minimalism: Beckett's Late Style in the Theater*, Oxford: Oxford UP.

Brater, Enoch (2004), 'Billie Whitelaw's TV Beckett', in Linda Ben-Zvi, ed., *Drawing on Beckett: Portraits, Performances, and Cultural Contexts*, Tel Aviv: Assaph Book Series, pp. 183–96.

Brater, Enoch (2010), 'The Seated Figure on Beckett's Stage', in S. E. Gontarski, ed., *A Companion to Samuel Beckett*, Chichester: Wiley-Blackwell, pp. 346–57.

Brau, Lorie (2008), *Rakugo: Performing Comedy and Cultural Heritage in Contemporary Tokyo*, Lanham: Lexington Books.

Briscoe, Donald and Roy Curtis-Bramwell (1983), *The BBC Radiophonic Workshop: The First Twenty-Five Years*, London: The British Broadcasting Corporation.

Brook, Peter (2008), Interviewed by Paul Taylor, *The Independent*, 5 September 2008, rpt. http://www.newspeterbrook.com/tag/fragments/.

Brown, Llewellyn (1998), 'La Voix, signe de l'impossible chez Samuel Beckett', *SBT/A*, 7: *Beckett Versus Beckett*, pp. 165–76.

Brown, Llewellyn (2013), 'Voix et illimité dans *L'Innommable*', *SBT/A*, 25: *Beckett in the Cultural Field/Beckett dans le champ culturel*, pp. 239–52.

Brown, Llewellyn (2016), *Beckett, Lacan and the Voice*, Stuttgart: Ibidem.

Brunette, Peter and David Wills (1989), *Screen/Play: Derrida and Film Theory*, Princeton: Princeton UP.

Bryant-Bertail, S. (1995), 'The True-Real Woman: Maddy Rooney as Picara in *All That Fall*', *Assaph: Studies in the Theatre*, 11, pp. 1–17.

Bryden, Mary, ed. (1998) *Samuel Beckett and Music*, Oxford: Clarendon P.

Bryden, Mary, ed. (2013), *Beckett and Animals*, Cambridge: Cambridge UP.

Bull, Michael and Les Back (2003), *The Auditory Culture Reader*, Oxford: Berg.

Burn, Gordon, George Poste and Damien Hirst (2000), *Theories, Models, Methods, Approaches, Assumptions, Results and Findings*, New York: Gagosian Gallery.

Burrows, Rachel (1989), 'Interview with Rachel Burrows', with S. E. Gontarski, Dougald McMillan and Martha Fehsenfeld, *JOBS*, 11–12, pp. 1–15.

Butler, Brad, and Karen Mirza (2006), *Cinema of Prayōga: Indian Experimental Film & Video, 1913–2006*, London: No.w.here.

Büttner, Gottfried (1999), 'Samuel Beckett as a Modern Initiate' in Bruce Stewart, ed., *Beckett and Beyond*, Gerrards Cross: Colin Smythe, pp. 42–52.

Cage, John (1961), *Silence: Lectures and Writings*, Middletown, CT: Wesleyan UP.

Campbell, Julie (2005), 'The Entrapment of the Female Body in Beckett's Plays in Relation to Jung's Third Tavistock Lecture', *SBT/A*, 15: *Historicising Beckett/Issues of Performance, Beckett dans l'histoire/En jouant Beckett*, pp. 161–72.

Campbell, Julie (2009), '"A Voice Comes to One in the Dark. Imagine": Radio, the Listener, and the Dark Comedy of *All That Fall*', in Steven Barfield, Matthew Feldman and Philip Tew, eds., *Beckett and Death*, London: Continuum, pp. 147–68.

Campbell, Julie (2013), 'Beckett and the BBC Third Programme', *SBT/A*, 25: *Beckett in the Cultural Field/Beckett dans le champ culturel*, pp. 109–22.

Campbell, Julie (2013), 'Close your eyes: *Embers* and the Difficulties of Listening', in Peter Fifield and David Addyman, eds., *Samuel Beckett: Debts and Legacies*, London and New York: Bloomsbury Methuen Drama, pp. 133–52.

Carpenter, Humphrey (1997), *The Envy of the World: Fifty Years of the BBC Third Programme and Radio 3*, London: Weidenfeld and Nicolson.

Caruth, Cathy (1995), *Trauma: Explorations in Memory*, Baltimore: Johns Hopkins UP.

Caruth, Cathy (1996), *Unclaimed Experience: Trauma, Narrative, and History*, Baltimore: Johns Hopkins UP.

Casanova, Pascale (2004), *The World Republic of Letters*, Cambridge: Harvard UP.

Casasanto, Daniel and Katinka Dijkstra (2010), 'Motor Action and Emotional Memory', *Cognition*, 115, pp. 179–85.

Caselli, Daniela (2005), *Beckett's Dantes: Intertextuality in the Fiction and Criticism*, Manchester: Manchester UP.

Castagnino, María Inés (2012), 'El espejo de dos caras: relaciones entre algunas piezas teatrales de Samuel Beckett y las artes pictóricas', in *VIII Congreso Internacional de Teoría y Crítica Literaria Orbis Tertius*, Centro de Estudios de Teoría y Crítica Literaria — IdIHCS/CONICET Facultad de Humanidades y Ciencias de la Educación Universidad Nacional de La Plata, http://citclot.fahce.unlp.edu.ar/viii-congres, accessed June 2015.

Cavecchi, Mariacristina (2009), 'Samuel Beckett, Visual Artist', in D. Guardamagna and R. Sebellin, eds., *The Tragic Comedy of Samuel Beckett: 'Beckett in Rome', 17–19 April 2008*, Rome: Università degli Studi di Roma «Tor Vergata» — Gius. Laterza & Figli, pp. 122–42.

Chabert, Pierre (1982), 'The Body in Beckett's Theatre', *JOBS*, 8, pp. 23–8.
Chakraborty, Thirthankar (2020), 'Samuel Beckett and the World Republic of Letters', *Journal of World Literature* 5:2, pp. 222–39.
Chattopadhyay, Arka (2011), '"From inner to outer shadow": Reading the Obscure Object of Anxiety in the "Dramaticules" of Samuel Beckett', *Miranda*, 4, https://miranda.revues.org/1902, accessed 7 October 2015.
Chattopadhyay, Arka (2015), 'The Politics of Non-Arrival: Avikunthak Waiting for Kalki', available online at: www.avikunthak.com.
Chignell, Hugh (2017), 'British Radio Drama and the Avant-garde in the 1950s', *Historical Journal of Film, Radio and Television*, 37: 4, pp. 649–64.
Cleveland, Louise (1969), 'Trials in the Soundscape: The Radio Plays of Samuel Beckett', *Modern Drama*, 11: 3, pp. 267–82.
Cohn, Ruby (2001), *A Beckett Canon*, Ann Arbor: U of Michigan P.
Connor, Steven (1988), *Samuel Beckett: Repetition, Theory and Text*, Oxford: Basil Blackwell.
Connor, Steven (1992), 'Between Theatre and Theory: *Long Observation of the Ray*', in John Pilling and Mary Bryden, eds., *The Ideal Core of the Onion: Reading Beckett Archives*, Reading: Beckett International Foundation, pp. 79–98.
Connor, Steven (2003), 'Beckett's Atmospheres', a paper given at the 'After Beckett / Après Beckett' conference in Sydney, January 2003, available online at: http://stevenconnor.com/atmospheres-2.html, accessed 11 March 2018.
Connor, Steven (2007), 'Whisper Music', available online at: stevenconnor.com/whisper-music.html.
Connor, Steven (2008), '"On Such and Such a Day ... In Such a World": Beckett's Radical Finitude', *SBT/A*, 19: *Borderless Beckett/Beckett sans frontières: Tokyo 2006*, pp. 35–50.
Connor, Steven (2014), *Beckett, Modernism and the Material Imagination*, Cambridge: Cambridge UP.
Crawley, Peter (2006), 'The Crystal Heart of Druid: Garry Hynes', *Irish Times* 'Weekend Review', 11 March, pp. 1–2.
Cronin, Anthony (1996), *Samuel Beckett: The Last Modernist*, London: Harper Collins.
Curtius, Ernst Robert (1928), *Marcel Proust*, Paris: Les Éditions de la Revue Nouvelle.
Damrosch, David (2009), *How to Read World Literature*, Chichester: Wiley–Blackwell.
David, Heather and Étienne Turpin (2015), *Art in the Anthropocene: Encounters Among Aesthetics, Politics, Environments and Epistemologies*, London: Open Humanities P.
Davies, Paul (2006), 'Strange Weather: Beckett from the Perspective of Ecocriticism', in S. E. Gontarski and Anthony Uhlmann, eds. *Beckett after Beckett*, Gainesville: UP of Florida.
Davis, Robin J. and Lance St J. Butler (1988), *'Make Sense Who May': Essays on Samuel Beckett's Later Works*, Gerrards Cross: Colin Smythe.

De Vos, Laurens (2011), *Cruelty and Desire in the Modern Theater: Antonin Artaud, Sarah Kane, and Samuel Beckett*, Madison, NJ: Fairleigh Dickinson UP.

Deleuze, Gilles (1986), *Cinema 1: The Movement Image*, trans. Hugh Tomlinson and Barbara Habberjam, Minneapolis: U of Minnesota P.

Deleuze, Gilles (1995), 'The Exhausted', trans. Anthony Uhlmann, SubStance, 24: 3, pp. 3–28.

Deleuze, Gilles (1998), 'The Exhausted' in *Essays Critical and Clinical*, trans. Anthony Uhlmann, London: Verso, pp. 152–74.

Deleuze, Gilles (2013), *Cinema I: The Movement-Image*, trans. Hugh Tomlinson and Barbara Habberjam, London: Bloomsbury.

Deleuze, Gilles (2017), *The Movement-Image: Bergsonian Lessons on Cinema*: Lecture 4, 1 December 1981, Purdue University Research Repository, doi:10.4231/R7319T3M, available online at: https://purr.purdue.edu/publications/2734/1.

Dennett, Daniel C. (1991), *Consciousness Explained*, Boston: Little, Brown & Company.

Derrida, Jacques (1976), *Of Grammatology*, Baltimore: Johns Hopkins UP.

Derrida, Jacques (1983), 'The Principle of Reason: The University in the Eyes of Its Pupils', *Diacritics*, 13: 3, pp. 3–20.

Derrida, Jacques (1998), 'To Unsense the Subjectile', in Jacques Derrida and Paule Thévenin, eds., *The Secret Art of Antonin Artaud*, Cambridge (Massachusetts): MIT P, pp. 59–157.

Derrida, Jacques (2001), 'What Is a "Relevant" Translation?', trans. Laurence Venuti, *Critical Inquiry*, 27: 2, pp. 174–200.

Derrida, Jacques (2001), *Writing and Difference*, London: Routledge.

Descartes, René (1965), *Discourse on Method, Optics, Geometry, and Meteorology*, trans. Paul J. Olscamp, Indianapolis, IN: Bobbs–Merrill.

Dijkstra, Katinka, Michael P. Kaschak and Rolf A. Zwaan (2007), 'Body Postures Facilitates Retrieval of Autobiographic Memories', *Cognition*, 102, pp. 139–49.

Dolar, Mladen (1996), 'The Object Voice', in Renata Salecl and Slavoj Žižek, eds., *Gaze and Voice as Love Objects*, Durham: Duke UP, pp. 10–31.

Dolar, Mladen (2006), *A Voice and Nothing More*, Cambridge, MA: MIT P.

Doll, Mary A. (1988), 'Walking and Rocking: Ritual Acts in *Footfalls* and *Rockaby*', in Robin J. Davis and Lance St J. Butler, eds., *'Make Sense Who May': Essays on Samuel Beckett's Later Works*, Gerrards Cross: Colin Smythe, pp. 46–55.

Doll, Mary A. (1989), 'The Demeter Myth in Beckett', *JOBS*, 11/12, pp. 109–22.

Ducrot, Oswald (1994), *Le dire et le dit*, Paris: Minuit.

Eisenstein, Sergei (1988), *S. M. Eisenstein Selected Works, Vol. I: Writings, 1922–1934*, ed. and trans. Richard Taylor, London: BFI Publishing.

Eliot, T. S. (1971), *Four Quartets*, Orlando: Harcourt Inc.

Esslin, Martin (1982), 'Samuel Beckett and the Art of Broadcasting', in *Mediations: Essays on Brecht, Beckett, and the Media*, New York: Grove P, pp. 125–54.

Esslin, Martin (1991), 'Telling it How It Is: Beckett and the Mass Media', in J. E. Smith, ed., *The World of Samuel Beckett*, Baltimore: The Johns Hopkins UP, pp. 204–16.

Esslin, Martin (2006), 'On his debt to Joyce' in James and Elizabeth Knowlson, eds., *Beckett Remembering/Remembering Beckett: A Centenary Celebration*, New York: Arcade Publishing, pp. 47–9.

Feldenkrais, Moshe (2011), *Embodied Wisdom: The Collected Papers of Moshe Feldenkrais*, Berkeley, CA: North Atlantic Books.

Feldman, Matthew (2006), *Beckett's Books: A Cultural History of Samuel Beckett's 'Interwar Notes'*, London: Continuum.

Feldman, Matthew (2014), 'Beckett's Trilogy on the Third Programme', *SBT/A*, 26: *Revisiting* Molloy, Malone meurt / Malone Dies *and* L'Innomable / The Unnamable, pp. 41–62.

Fink, Bruce (1995), *The Lacanian Subject: Between Language and Jouissance*, Princeton: Princeton UP.

Flahault, François (1978), *La parole intermédiaire*, Paris: Seuil.

Fletcher, John (2003), *About Beckett: The Playwright and the Work*, London: Faber and Faber.

Fonteneau, Françoise (1999), *L'éthique du Silence: Wittgenstein et Lacan*, Paris: Seuil.

Foster, David (2012), 'Spatial Aesthetics in the Film Adaptation of Beckett's *Comédie*', *Screen*, 53: 2, pp. 105–17.

Foucault, Michel (1969), 'What is an Author?', available online at: http://www.generation-online.org/p/fp_foucault12.htm.

Foucault, Michel (1984), 'Of Other Spaces: Utopias and Heterotopias', trans. by Jay Miskowiec, *Architecture/Mouvement/Continuité*, October (originally 'Des Espaces Autres', March 1967), available online at: http://web.mit.edu/allanmc/www/foucault1.pdf.

Fowler, Alistair (1989), 'Genre', in Erik Barnouw, et al. eds., *International Encyclopedia of Communications*, Oxford: Oxford UP, pp. 215–7.

Freud, Sigmund (2006), *The Penguin Freud Reader*, ed. A. Phillips, Penguin Books, epub format.

Friedman, Susan Stanford (2012), 'World Modernisms, World Literature, and Comparativity', in Mark Wollaeger and Matt Eatough, eds., *The Oxford Handbook of Global Modernisms*, Oxford: Oxford Handbooks Online.

Frost, Everett (1991), 'Fundamental Sounds: Recording Samuel Beckett's Radio Plays', *Theatre Journal*, 43: 3, pp. 361–76.

Frost, Everett (1997), 'A "Fresh Go" for the Skull: Directing *All That Fall*, Samuel Beckett's Play for Radio', in Lois Oppenheim, ed. *Directing Beckett*, Ann Arbor: U of Michigan P, pp. 186–219.

Frost, Everett (1998), 'The Note Man on the Word Man: Morton Feldman on Composing the Music for Samuel Beckett's *Words and Music* in *The Beckett Festival of*

Radio Plays', in Mary Bryden, ed., *Samuel Beckett and Music*, Oxford: Clarendon P, pp. 47–55.

Frost, Everett C. (2007), '"No Frills for the love of God": Reading a Staged Reading of Beckett's *All That Fall*', *The Beckett Circle*, 30: 2, pp. 9–13.

Frost, Everett (2009), 'Preface', Samuel Beckett, All That Fall and Other Plays for Radio and Screen, ed. Everett Frost, London: Faber and Faber, pp. vii–xxiii.

Frost, Everett C. (2013), 'Performing the Jermyn Street Theatre's Staging of *All That Fall*: A Review Essay', *JOBS*, 22: 2, pp. 245–58.

Frost, Everett C. (2014), '"The Sound Is Enough": Beckett's Radio Plays', in S. E. Gontarski, ed., *The Edinburgh Companion to Samuel Beckett and the Arts*, Edinburgh: Edinburgh UP, pp. 251–65.

Garrard, Greg (2012), '*Endgame*: Beckett's Ecological Thought', *SBT/A*, 23: *Filiations & Connexions/Filiations & Connecting Lines*, pp. 383–97.

Geneste, Bruno (2017), 'Samuel Beckett, l'"entre" vivifiant de lalangue et l'hiatus sinthomatique: contrer ces vérités du surmoi', in Brown, ed., *La Violence dans l'œuvre de Samuel Beckett: entre langage et corps*, Paris: Lettres modernes Minard, 'La Revue des Lettres modernes; Série Samuel Beckett', no. 4, pp. 89–116.

Genette, Gérard (1980), *Narrative Discourse: An Essay in Method*, trans. Jane E. Lewin, New York: Cornell UP.

Germoni, Karine and Pascale Sardin (2012), 'Tensions of the In-between: Rhythm, Tonelessness and Lyricism in *Fin de partie/Endgame*', in *SBT/A*, 24: *Early Modern Beckett/Beckett et le début de l'ère modern: Beckett Between/Beckett entre deux*, pp. 336–50.

Gibson, Andrew (2010), *Samuel Beckett*, London: Reaktion Books.

Gontarski, S. E. (1985), *The Intent of Undoing in Samuel Beckett's Dramatic Texts*, Bloomington: Indiana UP.

Gontarski, S. E. (1986), *On Beckett: Essays and Criticism*, New York: Grove P.

Gontarski, S. E. (1995), 'Editing Beckett', *Twentieth Century Literature*, 41: 2, pp. 190–207.

Gontarski, S. E. (2006), 'Viva, Sam Beckett, or Flogging the Avant-Garde', *JOBS*, 16: 1, pp. 1–10.

Graver, Lawrence, and Raymond Federman, eds. (1997), *Samuel Beckett: The Critical Heritage*, London: Routledge and Kegan Ltd.

Grossman, Évelyne (2008), 'À lalimite...: lecture de *Cette fois* de Samuel Beckett', *SBT/A*, 19: *Borderless Beckett/Beckett sans frontières: Tokyo 2006*, pp. 51–66.

Hale, Jane Alison (1987), *The Broken Window: Beckett's Dramatic Perspective*, West Lafayette, Indiana: Purdue UP.

Hartel, Gaby (2010), 'Emerging Out of a Silent Void: Some Reverberations of Rudolf Arnheim's Radio Theory in Beckett's Radio Pieces', *JOBS*, 19: 2, pp. 218–27.

Hartel, Gaby, Kraus Völker and Thomas Irmer (2009), 'The Reception of Beckett's Theatre and Television Pieces in West and East Germany', in Mark Nixon and Matthew

Feldman, eds., *The International Reception of Samuel Beckett*, London: Continuum, pp. 75–96.

Harvey, Lawrence (1970), *Samuel Beckett: Poet and Critic*, Princeton: Princeton UP.

Haynes, John and James Knowlson (2003), *Images of Beckett*, Cambridge: Cambridge UP.

Heilbron, Johan (1999), 'Towards a Sociology of Translation: Book Translations as a Cultural World-System', *European Journal of Social Theory*, 2: 4, pp. 429–44.

Herren, Graley (2009), 'Different Music: Karmitz and Beckett's Film Adaptation of *Comédie*', *JOBS*, 18: 1–2, pp. 10–31.

Homan, Sidney (1984), *Beckett's Theaters: Interpretations for Performance*, Lewisburg: Bucknell UP.

Hori, Mariko (2014), 'Beckett's Struggle with His Traumatic Memories', *The Economic Review*, 6, Institute of Economic Research, Aoyama Gakuin University, pp. 1–20.

Hori, Mariko (2017), *Revised Versions of Waiting for Godot: Beckett as Director*, Tokyo: Fujiwara Shoten.

Hutchings, Williams (1986), 'Abated Drama: Samuel Beckett's Unbated *Breath*', *Ariel*, 17: 1, pp. 85–94.

Ihde, Don (1976), *Listening and Voice: A Phenomenology of Sound*, Ohio: Ohio UP.

Ihde, Don (2007), *Listening and Voice: Phenomenologies of Sound*, Vol. 2, Albany: State U of New York P.

Jakobson, Roman (2004), 'On Linguistic Aspects of Translation', in Lawrence Venuti, ed., *The Translation Studies Reader*, New York: Routledge, pp. 138–43.

Janvier, Ludovic (2012), 'Entretien réalisé par Martin Mégevand', *Littérature*, 167: '*Samuel Beckett*', September, 2012, pp. 7–22.

Juliet, Charles (2007), *Rencontres avec Samuel Beckett*, Paris: P.O.L.

Juliet, Charles (2009), *Conversations with Samuel Beckett and Bram van Velde*, trans. Tracy Cooke et al., Dublin: Dalkey Archive P.

Jung, C. G. (1968), 'The Tavistock Lectures', in *Analytical Psychology: Its Theory and Practice*, London: Routledge & Kegan Paul, pp. 195–6.

Kalb, Jonathan (1989), *Beckett in Performance*, Cambridge: Cambridge UP.

Kalb, Jonathan (1994), '"The Mediated Quixote: The Radio and Television Plays, and Film", in John Pilling, ed., *The Cambridge Companion to Samuel Beckett*, Cambridge: Cambridge UP, pp. 124–44.

Kelleher, Joe (2015), 'Recycling Beckett', in Clare Finburgh and Carl Lavery, eds., *Rethinking the Theatre of the Absurd: Ecology, the Environment and the Greening of the Modern Stage*, London: Bloomsbury, pp. 127–46.

Kendrick, Lynne and Roesner David, eds. (2011), *Theatre Noise: The Sound of Performance*, Cambridge: Cambridge Scholars Publishing.

Kennedy, Seán (2004), '"A Lingering Dissolution": *All That Fall* and Protestant Fears of Engulfment in the Irish Free State', in Linda Ben-Zvi, ed., *Drawing on Beckett: Portraits, Performances, and Cultural Contexts*, Tel Aviv: Assaph Book Series, pp. 247–61.

Kenner, Hugh (1973), *A Reader's Guide to Samuel Beckett*, London: Thames and Hudson.

Kim, Rina (2010), *Women and Ireland as Beckett's Lost Others*, Basingstoke: Palgrave Macmillan.

Kiuchi, Kumiko (2005), 'Against Autobiography: Samuel Beckett's *Company/Compagnie* as an Autobiographical Writing of Another', *Interdisciplinary Cultural Studies* 8, pp. 143–160.

Knowlson, James (1996), *Damned to Fame: The Life of Samuel Beckett*, London: Bloomsbury.

Knowlson, James and Elizabeth Knowlson, eds. (2006), *Beckett Remembering/Remembering Beckett: A Centenary Celebration*, New York: Arcade Publishing.

Knowlson, James and John Pilling (1979), *Frescoes of the Skull: The Later Prose and Drama of Samuel Beckett*, London: Calder.

Lacan, Jacques (1966), *Écrits*, Paris: Seuil.

Lacan, Jacques (1973), *Le Séminaire, Livre XI, Les quatre concepts fondamentaux de la psychanalyse*, Paris: Seuil.

Lacan, Jacques (1977), *Seminar XI: The Four Fundamental Concepts of Psychoanalysis*, New York: W.W. Norton & Co.

Lacan, Jacques (1981), *The Seminar of Jacques Lacan: Book XI: The Four Fundamental Concepts of Psychoanalysis*, ed. Jacques-Alain Miller, New York: Norton.

Lacan, Jacques (1991), *Le Séminaire, Livre VIII, Le Transfert*, Paris: Seuil.

Lacan, Jacques (2001), *Autres écrits*, Paris: Seuil.

Lacan, Jacques (2001), *Écrits: A Selection*, London: Routledge.

Lacan, Jacques (2004), *Le Séminaire, Livre X, L'Angoisse*, Paris: Seuil.

Lacan, Jacques (2005), *Le Séminaire, Livre XXIII, Le Sinthome*, Paris: Seuil.

Lacan, Jacques (2011), *Le Séminaire, Livre XIX, ...ou pire*, Paris: Seuil.

Lacan, Jacques (2013), *Le Séminaire, Livre VI, Le Désir et son interprétation*, Paris: Seuil.

Lacan, Jacques [1978] (2015), *Le Séminaire, Livre II, Le Moi dans la théorie de Freud et dans la technique de la psychanalyse*, Paris: Seuil.

Lamont, Rosette (1990), 'Beckett's *Eh Joe*: Lending an Ear to the Anima', in L. Ben-Zvi, ed., *Women in Beckett: Performance and Critical Perspectives*, Urbana and Chicago: U of Illinois P, pp. 228–35.

Lamport, Francis (2005), 'Schiller and Euripides: The Translations of 1788 and Schiller's Later Plays', *German Life and Letters*, 58: 3, pp. 247–70.

Lavery, Carl (2018), 'Ecology in Beckett's Theatre Garden: Ways to Cultivate the *Oikos*', *Contemporary Theatre Review*, 28: 1, pp. 10–26: a special issue on Staging Beckett and Contemporary Theatre and Performance Cultures, ed. Anna McMullan and Graham Saunders.

Lawley, Paul (1994), 'Stages of Identity: From *Krapp's Last Tape* to *Play*', in John Pilling, ed., *The Cambridge Companion to Beckett*, Cambridge: Cambridge UP, pp. 88–105.

Laws, Catherine (2003), 'Beethoven's Haunting of Beckett's *Ghost Trio*', in Linda Ben-Zvi, ed., *Drawing on Beckett: Portraits, Performances, and Cultural Contexts*, Tel Aviv: Assaph Book Series, pp. 197–214.

Laws, Catherine (2010), 'Beckett and Unheard Sound', in Daniela Caselli, ed., *Beckett and Nothing: Trying to Understand Beckett*, Manchester: Manchester UP, pp. 176–91.

Laws, Catherine (2017), 'Imagining Radio Sound: Interference and Collaboration in the BBC Radio Production of Beckett's *All That Fall*', in David Addyman, Matthew Feldman, and Erik Tonning, eds., *Samuel Beckett and BBC Radio: A Reassessment*, Basingstoke: Palgrave Macmillan, pp. 103–38.

Libera, Antoni (1980), 'Structure and Pattern in *That Time*', *JOBS*, 6: Autumn, pp. 81–9.

Linklater, Kristin (2006), *Freeing the Natural Voice*, London: Drama Publishers/Quite Specific Media [1976].

Locatelli, Carla (2000), 'Unwording beyond Negation, Erasures and Reticentia: Beckett's Committed Silence', in Henry Sussman and Christopher Devenney, eds., *Engagement and Indifference: Beckett and the Political*, Albany: SUNY P, pp. 19–42.

Logie, Robert H., and Michel Denis, eds. (1991), *Mental Images in Human Cognition*, Amsterdam: Elsevier Science Publishers.

Lyons, Charles (1964), 'Beckett's *Endgame*: An Anti-myth of Creation', *Modern Drama*, 7: 2, pp. 204–9.

Lyons, Charles R. (1983), *Samuel Beckett*, London: Macmillan Education.

Lyons, Charles R. (1990), 'Male or Female Voice: The Significance of the Gender of the Speaker in Beckett's Late Fiction and Drama', in Linda Ben-Zvi, ed., *Women in Beckett: Performance and Critical Perspectives*, Urbana and Chicago: U of Illinois P, pp. 150–61.

Lyotard, Jean-François (1993), 'Oikos', in *Political Writings*, trans. Bill Readings and Kevin Paul Geiman, London: UCL P., pp. 96–107.

Mackay, Donald G. (1992), 'Constraints on Theories of Inner Speech', in Daniel Reisberg, ed., *Auditory Imagery*, Hillsdale, NJ: Lawrence Erlbaum, pp. 121–49.

Macmurraugh-Kavanagh, Madelene and Stephen Lacey (1999), 'Who Framed Theatre?: The "Moment of Change" in British TV Drama', *New Theatre Quarterly*, 57, pp. 58–74.

Madden, Catherine (2014), *Onstage Synergy: Integrative Alexander Technique Practice for Performing Artists*, Bristol: Intellect Books.

Malkin, Jeanette R. (1999), *Memory-Theatre and Postmodern Drama*, Ann Arbor: U of Michigan P.

Margolin, Uri (2003), 'Cognitive Science, the Thinking Mind, and Literary Narrative', in D. Herman, ed., *Narrative Theory and the Cognitive Sciences*, Chicago: CLSI (U of Chicago P.), pp. 271–94.

Mason, Bruce (2015), 'Death *is not* an End: It is just another way of dealing with life', in Melissa McCarthy, ed., *Momentum: Research and Innovation*, U of Rhode Island, pp. 50–5.
Maude, Ulrika (2008), '"Hint of Jugular and Cords": Beckett and Modern Medicine', SBT/A, 19: *Borderless Beckett/Beckett sans frontières: Tokyo 2006*, pp. 281–91.
Maude, Ulrika (2009), *Beckett, Technology and the Body*, Cambridge: Cambridge UP.
Maxwell, Kenneth (2011), '*Waiting for Godot* — in Fukushima', *The Wall Street Journal Japan*, 6 August.
Mayberry, Bob (1989), *Theatre of Discord: Dissonance in Beckett, Albee, and Pinter*, Rutherford: Fairleigh Dickinson UP.
McAuley, Gay (1966), 'Samuel Beckett's *Come and Go*', *Educational Theatre Journal*, 18: 4, pp. 439–42.
McDonald, Rónán (2006), *The Cambridge Introduction to Samuel Beckett*, Cambridge: Cambridge UP.
McKinney, Joslin and Philip Butterworth (2009), *The Cambridge Introduction to Scenography*, Cambridge: Cambridge UP.
McMillan, Dougald and Martha Fehsenfeld (1988), *Beckett in the Theatre*, London: John Calder.
McMullan, Anna (1993), *Theatre on Trial: Samuel Beckett's Later Drama*, London: Routledge.
McMullan, Anna (2010), *Performing Embodiment in Samuel Beckett's Drama*, London: Routledge.
McWhinnie, Donald (1959), *The Art of Radio*, London: Faber and Faber.
Mendelyte, Atene (2015), 'The Image of a Mind-Skull: Samuel Beckett's *...but the clouds...* and Television-Philosophy', *Film-Philosophy Journal*, 19, pp. 325–43.
Milner, Jean-Claude (1978), *L'Amour de la langue*, Paris: Seuil, 'Connexions du champ freudien'.
Mitchell, Breon (1976), 'Art in Microcosm: The Manuscript Stages of Beckett's *Come and Go*', *Modern Drama*, 19: 3, pp. 245–54.
Mitchell, Juliet (1998), 'Trauma, Recognition, and the Place of Language', *Diacritics* 28:4, pp. 121–33.
Mooney, Sinéad (2011), 'Foreign Bodies', in *A Tongue Not Mine: Beckett and Translation*, Oxford: Oxford UP.
Moorjani, Angela (1982), *Abysmal Games in the Novels of Samuel Beckett*, Chapel Hill, NC: U of North Carolina P.
Moorjani, Angela (2004), '"Peau de chagrin": Beckett and Bion on Looking Not to See', SBT/A, 14: *After Beckett/D'après Beckett*, pp. 25–38.
Moretti, Franco (1994), 'Modern European Literature: A Geographical Sketch', *New Left Review*, 1: 206, pp. 86–109.
Moretti, Franco (2000), 'Conjectures on World Literature', *New Left Review*, 1, pp. 54–68.

Mori, Shintaro (2011), 'Interview: 2011–Reality of Waiting', *Program for* Waiting for Godot, Tokyo: New National Theatre.
Morin, Emilie (2014), 'Beckett's Speaking Machines: Sound, Radiophonics and Acousmatics', *Modernism/modernity*, 21: 1, pp. 1–24.
Morrison, Kristin (1985), 'The Rip Word in *A Piece of Monologue*', *Modern Drama*, 1: 1, pp. 349–54.
Morton, Timothy (2010), *The Ecological Thought*, Cambridge, MA: Harvard UP.
Müller, Jürgen (1996), *Intermedialität. Formen moderner kultureller Kommunikation*, Münster: Nodus Publikationen.
Nemoto, Misako (2004), *Nemuri to Bungaku* [*Sleep and Literature*]: *Proust, Kafka and Tanizaki*, Tokyo: Chuko-shinsho.
Nguyên, Albert (2010), 'Les Clefs de lalangue: Beckett, Cixous, Joyce et... Lacan', *L'En-je lacanian*, 2:15: 'Rencontre et répétition', pp. 67–111.
Nguyên, Albert (2014), *Le Désir à l'heur du réel: Séminaire de Bordeaux 2013–2014*, École de psychanalyse des Forums du Champ lacanien.
Nicholson, Simon, and Sikina Jinnah (2016), *New Earth Politics: Essays from the Anthropocene*, Cambridge, MA: MIT P.
Nietzsche, Friedrich (1967), *The Birth of Tragedy and the Case of Wagner*, trans. Walter Kaufmann, New York: Vintage.
Nightingale, Benedict (1997), 'Benedict Nightingale in New Stateman', in Lawrence Graver and Raymond Federman, eds., *Samuel Beckett: The Critical Heritage*, London: Taylor and Francis, pp. 370–5.
Nixon, Mark (2010), 'Chronology of Beckett's Journey to Germany 1936–37', *JOBS*, 19: 2, pp. 245–72.
Nixon, Mark (2011), *Beckett's German Diaries 1936–1937*, London: Continuum.
Ojrzyenska, Katarzyna (2014), 'Music and Metamusic in Beckett's Early Plays for Radio', in Sarah Bailes and Nicholas Till, eds., *Beckett and Musicality*, London: Routledge, pp. 47–62.
Okamuro, Minako (2011), 'Prayer from the Debris', *Program for* Waiting for Godot, Tokyo: New National Theatre.
Okamuro, Minako (2017), *Audience Feedback 1 for* Her Voice, Tokyo: Kamome-za.
Oppenheim, Lois (2000), *The Painted Word: Samuel Beckett's Dialogue with Art*, Ann Arbor: U of Michigan P.
Ost, Isabelle (2008), *Samuel Beckett et Gilles Deleuze: cartographie de deux parcours d'écriture*, Bruxelles: Facultés universitaires Saint-Louis.
Ovadija, Mladen (2013), *Dramaturgy of Sound in the Avant-garde and Postdramatic Theatre*, Montreal: McGill–Queen's UP.
Paraskeva, Anthony (2017), *Samuel Beckett and Cinema*, London: Bloomsbury.
Pater, Walter (1919), *The Renaissance*, New York: Boni and Liveright.

Pattie, David (2000), *The Complete Critical Guide to Samuel Beckett*, King's Lynn: Biddles.
Pearce, Damien (2008), 'Actor slits his own throat as knife switch turns fiction into reality' in *The Guardian*, 11 December 2008. http://www.guardian.co.uk/world/2008/dec/11/actor-slits-throat, accessed 25 February 2016.
Pennebaker, D. A. and C. Hegedus (1982), *Rockaby, a play by Samuel Beckett* (film), New York: Pennebaker Associates.
Perloff, Marjorie (1982), 'Between Verse and Prose: Beckett and the New Poetry', *Critical Inquiry*, 9:2, pp. 415–33.
Perloff, Marjorie (1998), 'The Silence That Is Not Silence: Acoustic Art in Samuel Beckett's *Embers*', in Lois Oppenheim, ed., *Samuel Beckett and the Arts: Music, Visual Arts, and Non-print Media*, New York: Garland.
Peters, John Durham (1999), *Speaking into the Air: A History of the Idea of Communication*, Chicago: U of Chicago P.
Piette, Adam (1996), *Remembering and the Sound of Words: Mallarmé, Proust, Joyce, Beckett*, Oxford: Clarendon P.
Pilling, John (1998), 'Proust and Schopenhauer: Music and Shadows', in Mary Bryden, ed., *Samuel Beckett and Music*, Oxford: Oxford UP, pp. 173–8.
Pilling, John (2006), *A Samuel Beckett Chronology*, Basingstoke: Palgrave Macmillan.
Porge, Erik (2015), *Le Ravissement de Lacan: Marguerite Duras à la lettre*, Toulouse: Érès.
Porter, Jeff (2016), *Lost Sound: The Forgotten Art of Radio Storytelling*, Chapel Hill: U of North Carolina P.
Pountney, Rosemary (1988), *Theatre of Shadows: Samuel Beckett's Drama 1956–76*, Gerrards Cross: Colin Smythe.
Proust, Marcel (1971), *Contre Saint-Beuve précédé de Pastiches et mélanges et suivi d'Essais et articles*, ed. Pierre Clarac, Paris: Gallimard.
Proust, Marcel (1987), *À la recherche du temps perdu* t.1, eds. J.-Y. Tadié et al., Paris: Les Éditions Gallimard.
Proust, Marcel (2005), *In Search of Lost Time I: Swann's Way*, trans. C. K. Scott Moncrieff and T. Kilmartin, revised by D. J. Enright, London: Vintage Books.
Quinn, Morgan (2017), '*Her Voice* — Samuel Beckett Theatre — Dublin Theatre Festival — Review', *No More Workhorse*, Dublin, 11 October.
Reisberg, Daniel, ed. (1992), *Auditory Imagery*, Hillsdale, NJ: Lawrence Erlbaum.
Reisberg, Daniel, Meg Wilson, and J. David Smith (1991), 'Auditory Imagery and Inner Speech', in Robert H. Logie and Michel Denis, *Mental Images in Human Cognition*, Amsterdam: Elsevier Science Publishers, pp. 59–81.
Robertson, John G. (1902), *A History of German Literature*, New York: G. P. Putnam's Sons.
Rodenburg, Patsy (2015), *The Right to Speak: Working with the Voice*, 2nd edition, London: Bloomsbury/Methuen.

Roloff, Volker (1994), 'Einleitung: Buñuels reflektierte Intermedialität', in Ursula Link-Heer and Volker Roloff, eds., *Luis Buñuel: Film, Literatur, Intermedialität*. Darmstadt: Wissenschaftliche Buchgesellschaft, pp. 1–12.

Sass, Louise A. (1992), *Madness and Modernism: Insanity in the Light of Modern Art, Literature, and Thought*, Cambridge: Harvard UP.

Satoh, Yasushi (2017), *Audience Feedback 1 for* Her Voice, Tokyo: Kamome-za.

Schiller, Friedrich (1967), *On the Aesthetic Education of Man in a Series of Letters*, trans. Elizabeth A. Wilkinson and L. A. Willoughby, Oxford: Clarendon P.

Schiller, Friedrich (2006), *Mary Stuart*, trans. Joseph Mellish, *Project Gutenberg*, 26 October, 2006, available online at: http://www.gutenberg.org/files/6791/6791-h/6791-h.htm.

Schleiermacher, Friedrich (2004), 'On the Different Methods of Translating', in Lawrence Venuti, ed., *The Translation Studies Reader*, New York: Routledge, pp. 43–63.

Schneider, Alan (1986), *Entrances: An American Director's Journey*, New York: Viking P.

Schopenhauer, Arthur [1818] (1966/1969), *The World as Will and Representation*, trans. E. F. J. Payne, New York: Dover.

Schwab, Klaus (2019), *Global Gender Gap Report 2020*, Geneva: World Economic Forum.

Sharpe, Lesley (1991), *Schiller: Drama, Thought and Politics*, Oxford: Oxford UP.

Sharpe, Lesley (1995), *Schiller's Aesthetic Essays: Two Centuries of Criticism*, Columbia, SC: Camden House.

Shibahara, Satoko and Mai Hashiba (2018), *Program for Theatre Commons Tokyo 2018*, Tokyo: Theatre Commons Tokyo Executive Committee.

Shluaghadháin, Síofra Ní (2017), *Audience Feedback 2 for* Her Voice, Tokyo: Kamome-za.

Skowronski, John J., Richard W. Walker and Andrew L. Benz (2004), 'Who Was I When That Happened? The Timekeeping Self in Autobiographical Memory', in Denise R. Beike, Jmaes M. Lampinen, and Douglas A. Behrend, eds., *The Self and Memory*, New York: Hove Psychology P, pp. 183–207.

Smith, Anthony (1998), 'Television as a Public Service Medium', in Smith (ed.), *Television: An International History*, Oxford: Oxford UP, pp. 38–54.

Smith, David J. (1991), 'The Auditory Hallucinations of Schizophrenia', in Daniel Reisberg, *Auditory Imagery*, Hillsdale, NJ: Lawrence Erlbaum, pp. 151–78.

Soma, Chiaki (2018), 'Director's Note: How to see the nuance in the world', in Satoko Shibahara and Mai Hashiba, eds., *Program for Theatre Commons Tokyo 2018*, Tokyo: Theatre Commons Tokyo Executive Committee.

Sontag, Susan (1988), 'Artaud', in Antonin Artaud, *Selected Writings*, Berkeley: U of California P, pp. xvii–lix.

Stewart, Paul (2011), *Sex and Aesthetics in Samuel Beckett's Work*, Basingstoke: Palgrave Macmillan.

Styan, John L. (1963), *The Elements of Drama*, Cambridge: Cambridge UP.

Takebe, Yoshiko (2014), 'Analysis of Post 3.11 Performability for Beckett's Dramaturgy', *Shujitsu English Studies*, 31, pp. 55–68.

Taylor, Don (1998), 'Pure Imagination, Poetry's Lyricism, Titian's Colours: Whatever Happened to the Single Play on British TV?', *New Statesman*, 6 March, pp. 38–9.

Thompson, Geoffrey, no date. Recorded talk on Samuel Beckett. MS4985. Beckett International Foundation, University of Reading.

Tilghman, Benjamin R. (1991), *Wittgenstein, Ethics and Aesthetics: The View from Eternity*, Albany, NY: SUNY P.

Tubridy, Derval (2010), 'Beckett's Spectral Silence: *Breath* and the Sublime', *Limit(e) Beckett*, 1, pp. 102–22.

Uhlmann, Anthony (2006), *Samuel Beckett and the Philosophical Image*, Cambridge: Cambridge UP.

Van Hulle, Dirk (2010), 'En écrivant Godot: Beckett et la peine d'écrire', in Llwellyn Brown, ed., *Samuel Beckett 1: 'L'Ascèse du sujet'*, Caen: Lettres modernes Minard, 'La Revue des Lettres modernes: Série Samuel Beckett', pp. 71–83.

Van Hulle, Dirk (2017), 'The BBC and Beckett's Non-radiogenic Plays in the 1950s', in David Addyman, Matthew Feldman and Erik Tonning, eds., *Samuel Beckett and BBC Radio: A Reassessment*, New York: Palgrave Macmillan, pp. 43–58.

Van Laan, Thomas F. (1986), '*All That Fall* as "a Play for Radio"', *Modern Drama*, 19: 1, pp. 38–47.

Venuti, Lawrence (1995), *The Translator's Invisibility: A History of Translation*, London: Routledge.

Verhulst, Pim (2017), 'The BBC as Commissioner of Beckett's Work for Radio', in David Addyman, Matthew Feldman and Erik Tonning, eds., *Samuel Beckett and BBC Radio: A Reassessment*, New York: Palgrave Macmillan, pp. 81–102.

Verlaine, Paul (2005), *Œuvres poétiques complètes*, Paris: Robert Laffont.

Voigts-Virchow, Eckart (1998), 'Exhausted Cameras: Beckett in the TV-zoo', in Jennifer Jeffers, eds., *Samuel Beckett: A Casebook*, New York: Garland, pp. 225–49.

Wade, David (1981), 'British Radio Drama since 1960', in John Drakakis, ed., *British Radio Drama*, Cambridge: Cambridge UP, pp. 218–24.

Wajcman, Gérard (1998), *L'Objet du siècle*, Lagrasse: Verdier.

Wardle, Irving (1968), *New English Dramatists 12: Radio Plays*, Harmondsworth: Penguin Books.

Watson, David (1991), *Paradox and Desire in Samuel Beckett's Fiction*, New York: St. Martin's P.

Weller, Shane (2008), 'Not Rightly Human: Beckett and Animality', *SBT/A*, 19: *Borderless Beckett/Beckett sans frontières: Tokyo 2006*, pp. 211–21.

Weller, Shane (2009), '"Some Experience of the Schizoid Voice": Samuel Beckett and the Language of Derangement', *Forum for Modern Language Studies*, 45:1, pp. 32–50.
Weller, Shane (2013), 'Forms of Weakness: Animalisation in Kafka and Beckett', in Mary Bryden, *Beckett and Animals*, Cambridge: Cambridge UP, pp. 13–26.
Wessler, Éric (2009), *La Littérature face à elle-même: l'écriture spéculaire de Samuel Beckett*, Amsterdam: Rodopi.
Wessler, Éric (2017), 'La Violence comme métaphore de l'écriture dans l'œuvre de Beckett', in Llewellyn Brown, ed., *La Violence dans l'œuvre de Samuel Beckett: entre langage et corps*, Paris: Lettres modernes Minard, 'La Revue des Lettres modernes; Série Samuel Beckett', no. 4, pp. 263–81.
West, Sarah (2010), *Say It: The Performative Voice in the Dramatic Works of Samuel Beckett*, Amsterdam: Rodopi.
White, Harry (2008), *Music and the Irish Literary Imagination*, Oxford: Oxford UP.
Whitehead, Kate (1989), *The Third Programme, A Literary History*, Oxford: Clarendon P.
Whitelaw, Billie (1990), 'Interview', in Linda Ben-Zvi, ed., *Women in Beckett*, Urbana: U of Illinois P.
Whitelaw, Billie (1996), *Billie Whitelaw...Who He?*, New York: St. Martin's P.
Williams, Raymond (1981), *Culture*, London: Fontana.
Williams, Raymond (1990), *Television, Technology and Cultural Form*, London: Fontana.
Winston, Brian (1998), *Media, Technology and Society — A History: From the Telegraph to the Internet*, London: Routledge.
Worth, Katharine (1998), 'Words for Music Perhaps', in Mary Bryden, ed., *Samuel Beckett and Music*, pp. 9–20.
Worth, Katharine (1999), *Samuel Beckett's Theatre: Life Journeys*, Oxford: Clarendon P.
Yates A., Francis (1966), *The Art of Memory*, London: Routledge.
Zarrilli, Phillip B. (1997), 'Acting "at the nerve ends": Beckett, Blau and the Necessary', *Theatre Topics*, 7: 2, pp.103–16.
Zilliacus, Clas (1976), *Beckett and Broadcasting: A Study of the Works of Samuel Beckett for and in Radio and Television*, Abo: Abo Akademi.
Zinman, Toby (1995), '*Eh Joe* and the Peephole Aesthetic', SBT/A, 4: *The Savage Eye/L'oeil Fauve*, pp. 53–64.
Žižek, Slavoj (1989), *The Sublime Object of Ideology*, London: Verso.
Žižek, Slavoj (1991), *Looking Awry: An Introduction to Jacques Lacan through Popular Culture*, Cambridge, MA: MIT P.
Žižek, Slavoj (1996), '"I Hear You with My Eyes"; or, The Invisible Master', in Renata Salecl and Slavoj Žižek, eds., *Gaze and Voice as Love Objects*, Durham: Duke UP, pp. 90–126.
Žižek, Slavoj and Renata Salecl, eds. (1996), *Gaze and Voice as Love Objects*, Durham: Duke UP.

Zourabichvili, François (2012), *Deleuze: A Philosophy of the Event: Together with The Vocabulary of Deleuze*, trans. Kieran Aarons, Gregg Lambert, and Daniel W. Smith, Edinburgh: Edinburgh UP.

Performances and Multimedia

Avikunthak, Ashish (2010), *Ashish Avikunthak, 1995–2010*, DVD, Calcutta: Ashish Avikunthak Productions.

Beckett, Samuel (2007), 'Breath', Online video clip, *YouTube*, http://video.google.com/videoplay?docid=-8915465772259371796#, accessed 21 January 2021.

Beckett, Samuel (2007), 'Breath', Online video clip, *YouTube*, http://www.youtube.com/watch?v=vw6HWwPEQm8, accessed 21 January 2021.

Beckett, Samuel (2008), 'Breath', Online video clip, *YouTube*, http://www.youtube.com/watch?v=1rZ8xParVmE&feature=player_embedded#at=77, accessed 21 January 2021.

Beckett, Samuel (2010), 'Breath', Online video clip, *YouTube*, http://www.youtube.com/watch?v=S2K9LA0f064, accessed 21 January 2021.

Feldman, Matthew (2009), 'Interview: Dr. Rosemary Pountney on Beckett', available online at: www.soundcloud.com/fred2360.

Happy Days (February 2016), dir. Makoto Satoh, perf. Keiko Takeya and Togo Igawa, Yokohama: Kawamata Hall, BankART 1929.

Happy Days (March 2018), dir. Yuta Hagiwara, perf. Honami Shimizu and Shin Ito, trans. Kaku Nagashima, Tokyo: Keio University Mita Campus, Ex Noguchi Room.

Ricks, Christopher (2014), 'Lecture on T. S. Eliot's Auditory Imagination', Harvard College, 2 September, 2014, available online at: https://www.youtube.com/watch?v=zhkcrQo9YdU.

Waiting for Godot (April 2011), dir. Shintaro Mori, perf. Isao Hashizume, Saburo Ishikura, Fubito Yamano, Kenichi Ishii, and Tokio Emoto, trans. Shoichiro Iwakiri, Tokyo: New National Theatre.

Waiting for Godot (August 2011), dir. Yuta Hagiwara, perf. Honami Shimizu, Shintaro Yokote, and Ichiro Matsubara, filmed Takashi Fujii, Fukushima: National Road 6.

Index

A

Abbott, H. Porter   204n., 206
Abram, David   159n.4, 172
Ackerley, C. J.   2, 3, 10, 99, 107, 109, 193n., 206, 280, 292
acousmatic(s)   67, 160, 160n.6, 163, 212
acoustic(s)   129, 131–2, 134–5, 138, 141, 164, 209–11, 213, 215, 217, 297, 301–9
Act Without Words II   159n.2, 229
adaptation   2, 7, 9, 99, 187, 208–19, 221, 225, 232, 268, 270, 280, 295–6, 298n., 299–301, 303–4
Adler, Alfred   128n., 134, 138, 141
Adorno, Theodor   175, 179, 180, 181, 183, 184, 189, 214, 216, 219
aesthetic(s)   8–9, 70, 76, 116, 162, 175–7, 179, 181–9, 221, 224, 229, 268, 276, 281–2, 286, 288–9, 297
'Afar a Bird'   31–2
Albee, Edward   121, 251
Albright, Daniel   48, 55
Aldwych Theatre. *See* productions
Alexander, F. Matthias   237n., 238n.1
Ali, Khaleem   31n.
Allen, Keith   209
All That Fall   8, 11, 28, 36n., 46, 158–72, 280, 282–3, 295–309. *See also Tout ceux qui tombent*
Alte Pinakothek   252
Alvarez, Alfred   212, 219
Ando, Shinya   267
Antaral (Endnote)   221, 224–5, 227, 230–2
Anthropocene   161n.8, 167
Antropova, Svetlana   8, 127–42
A Piece of Monologue   9, 37, 108–09, 193–207, 238–9
appropriation   3, 91, 93, 306
Arikha, Avigdor   34, 144, 156
Aristotle / Aristotelian   26–28, 47, 153, 225, 302
Arnheim, Rudolf   160, 172, 197, 199, 201, 204, 206, 283, 292
Arsonist Productions. *See* productions

Artaud, Antonin / Artaudian   26, 39, 85–6, 94–5
articulation   77, 79, 128, 209, 247, 255, 263, 280–92
Arts Theatre (London). *See* productions
Asmus, Walter   97–8, 101, 105, 107, 109, 226, 265
'Assumption'   25, 27–31, 38
As The Story Was Told   258
Atik, Ann   34, 39, 108–9
Atkins, Aileen   305
Attali, Jacques   28
Auschwitz   216. *See also* World War II
Avikunthak, Ashish   221–34

B

Battersea Arts Centre (BAC). *See* productions. *See* theatres
Bacon, Francis   27, 145
Bailey, Iain   301, 309
Bakewell, Michael   282
Bakhtin, Mikhail   56, 63
Balázs, Béla   194, 198, 200, 202–6
Balzac, Honoré de   176, 178, 181, 185
Bandia, Paul F.   267, 278
Barnard, G.C.   14, 21
Barr, Richard   121
Bartenieff, Irmgard   237, 237n.
Barthes, Roland   222, 233, 300n.
BBC (British Broadcasting Corporation)
   Radio   2, 2n., 46, 48n., 61, 163, 164n., 165, 165n., 169, 170n.10, 170n.11, 248, 281–2, 296, 298, 298n., 307
   Radiophonic Workshop   163n., 284
   Television   280–94
   Third Programme   2n., 33, 46, 158, 163n., 164, 164n., 282, 298
Beckett, Edward   34
Beckett Estate   7, 246, 257
Beckett, John   48n.
Beckett on Film   81, 208–9, 216
Bedlam. *See* Bethlem Royal Hospital

Beethoven, Ludwig van   28, 34, 43, 44, 46, 210, 290
Before Vanishing...   260
Beiser, Frederick   183–4, 189
Benjamin, Walter   210, 220
Benz, Andrew L.   140, 142
Ben-Zvi, Linda   7, 25–41, 144, 156–7, 173, 290, 292–3, 301, 309
Berceuse
   painting (Van Gogh)   146*n*., 146–7
   play (Beckett)   151. *See also Rockaby*
Berghoff, Herbert   305, 308
Bergson, Henri   106*n*., 112, 121, 130, 132–3, 142
Bernold, André   33, 40
Bertail, Sarah Bryant   167, 173
Bethlem Royal Hospital   14
betweenness   8, 11, 112–8
Bhabha, Homi   231
Bible   166
   Deuteronomy   33*n*.
   Genesis   166–7
Bignell, Jonathan   9, 280–94
bilingual(ism)   97–109, 304
Bion, Wilfred   4, 15, 136
Biswas, Tapu   228, 233
Bixby, Patrick   231–3
Blake, William   119
Blin, Roger   35–6, 117–8
Bois, Elie-Joseph   106
Bollmann, Horst   36
Bollywood   224
Bourdieu, Pierre   223–4, 233
Boyle, Kay   168
Bragg, Melvyn   285
Branigan, Kevin   300*n*., 301*n*.
Brater, Enoch   2, 74, 82, 120, 122, 132–3, 142, 144, 155–6, 300, 309
Bray, Barbara   99, 163, 163*n*., 282, 287
Breath   5, 9, 38, 208–20
Briscoe, Desmond   163, 173
Brook, Peter   39, 40, 118
Brown, Llewellyn   3, 8, 10, 67–84
Bruce, Brenda   252
Bryden, Mary   33, 39–40, 46, 55, 158–9, 162, 166, 173–4, 309–10
Buggy, Niall   81
Burn, Gordon   217, 220
Burrows, Rachel   176, 178, 181, 189

Butterworth, Philip   301, 310
...but the clouds...   115, 122, 285, 290–1
Büttner, Gottfried   176–7, 185, 189
Byron, Lord George Gordon   26–7, 31

C

Cage, John   27, 220, 295
Campbell, Julie   2*n*., 3, 7, 10–22, 63, 97, 158, 160, 173, 252, 266, 283, 293, 296*n*.1, 302, 304, 309
Carroll, Lewis   230
Cartesian. *See* Descartes, René
Caruth, Cathy   213, 220
Casanova, Pascale   222–3, 233
Casasanto, Daniel   128, 142
Cascando   6–7, 42–3, 46, 48, 51–4, 171, 245, 253, 282, 305
Caselli, Daniela   166*n*., 173, 292–3
Castagnino, María Inés   146, 156
Catastrophe   110, 145, 244*n*.5, 258–60
Cavecchi, Mariacristina   144, 148, 157
Cette fois   8, 83, 97–110. *See also That Time*. *See also Damals*
Chabert, Pierre   250–1, 266
Chakraborty, Thirthankar   9, 221–34
Chekhov, Anton   224
Chion, Michel   28
Chopin, Frédéric   34
Cinema of Prayōga   221, 223–5, 229
cinematographic   112, 221–33
circular/circularity   133, 148, 227
Clément, Bruno   76
Cleveland, Louise   302–3, 309
Cohn, Ruby   29, 32, 40, 48, 51, 55, 130, 136*n*.4, 142, 144*n*.2, 197*n*.4, 206, 219, 233
Cold War   161, 161*n*.9
Come and Go   9, 39, 120, 221–34, 244*n*.5, 250, 260–2. *See also Kommen und Gehen*. *See also Teacht is Imeacht*
Comédie   280, 287, 293. *See also Play*
Comment c'est   159*n*.1. *See also How It Is*
Company   31–2, 39, 75, 82, 86, 108–10
Connor, Steven   3, 29, 32, 47, 52–4, 89–90, 96, 159, 173, 185–6, 189, 195, 206
Conradt, Gerd   208–9, 217
Corneille, Pierre   178

Cosgrove, Aedín 307. *See also* Pan Pan Theatre
Coveney, Michael 120*n*.
Crawley, Peter 300, 309
Cronin, Anthony 181, 189, 252, 266, 269, 278
Cullen, John 257, 259
Curtius, Ernst Robert 106, 106*n*.

D

Damals 98, 100, 105. *See also Cette fois. See also That Time*
Dante Alighieri 114, 132–3, 166*n*.
D'Aubarède, Gabriel 188
Davies, Paul 158–61, 173
deconstruction 3, 4, 85, 93–4, 130, 228, 283, 287, 290, 304
Deleuze, Gilles 8, 111–3, 116–21, 145, 184, 205
Democritus 69
Dennett, Daniel C. 12, 22
Dépeupleur, Le 159*n*.2. *See also The Lost Ones*
Derrida, Jacques 47, 52–3, 55, 85–6, 93–6, 234, 283
Descartes, René 27, 40, 93
   Cartesian 93, 119
Devlin, James Gerard 170
De Vos, Laurens 1–10, 26*n*., 40, 85–96
Dijkstra, Katinka 128–9, 142
Divine Dignities 134, 134*n*.
Dolar, Mladen 31, 40, 209, 211–3, 215, 219–20
Doll, Mary A. 151, 153–5, 157
Dostoevsky, Fyodor 56
Dream of Fair to Middling Women 11, 22, 43, 55, 71, 82
Druid Theatre. *See* productions
Dublin Theatre Festival. *See* productions
Ducrot, Oswald 7, 56–7, 63
Dukes, Gerry 244, 254
Duras, Marguerite 76*n*.10, 287
Dwan, Lisa 38, 120*n*.

E

Eadie, Jimmie 307
ecocriticism 8, 158, 161*n*.8
ecology 162
Éditions de Minuit 224
Eh Joe 5, 48, 113, 115–6, 154, 157, 252, 266, 285, 289–91, 302*n*.9
Eisenstein, Sergei 201–2, 206
Eliade, Mircea 155
Eliot, T. S. 35, 41, 138*n*., 142
Embers 7, 46, 56–64, 69, 88–90, 96, 130, 132, 171, 282, 306
embodiment 2, 6, 33, 37, 45, 62, 74–5, 85–6, 89, 111–3, 115, 121, 127, 135, 156, 159, 169, 171, 182, 185, 212, 214, 231, 238, 246, 250–1, 268, 275–6, 286, 292, 299, 303, 308
En attendant Godot 32, 67, 71, 224, 282. *See also Waiting for Godot*
Encounter, The (Complicité) 245, 245*n*.
Endgame 33, 35–7, 69, 86, 90–1, 139, 148, 159, 159*n*.1, 161, 166, 200, 200*n*., 214, 254, 283. *See also Fin de partie*
enunciation 7, 9, 56–60, 62, 70, 77–8, 81, 88, 231
Esposito, Bianca 133*n*.
Esslin, Martin 12–3, 22, 144, 185, 189, 285, 302–3, 306, 309
Ethica (2012–13 project) 244, 244*n*.5
ethic(s) 9, 113, 119, 183, 186*n*., 221
Ethics (Geulincx) 150, 150*n*.
Euripides/Euripidean 177–80
Even-Zohar, Itamar 223

F

failure 5, 16, 20–1, 28–9, 31, 42, 49–50, 53–4, 56–8, 61–2, 76, 87, 92, 95, 115, 134, 139, 162, 175, 177, 178*n*.3, 179*n*., 180–5, 210, 215–6, 222, 245, 299
Fehsenfeld, Martha 22, 33, 35, 36*n*., 40, 55, 110, 122, 142, 172–3, 189, 309
Feldenkrais, Moshé 237, 249
Feldman, Matthew 2*n*., 10, 134–5, 137, 142, 172–3, 195, 206, 254–5, 266, 293–4, 309
Feldman, Morton 33, 131
Ferguson, Adam 183
Film 149, 152, 222, 227
Fin de partie 36, 117, 159*n*.1, 249. *See also Endgame*

Fischer-Lichte, Erika   26
Flahault, François   57n., 62
Focus Theatre. *See* productions. *See* theatres
Footfalls   6, 109, 113, 117–8, 127–42, 145, 250, 252–4, 260, 302n.9. *See also Tritte*
Foucault, Michel   113, 115–7, 119, 122
fragmentation   3–4, 78, 127, 129–30, 187, 251
Fragments   39
frame/framing   15, 17, 26, 71, 143, 146–7, 193–4, 198, 202–5, 285, 291, 308
Freud, Sigmund   3–4, 76n.9, 83, 85, 128, 135
    pre-oedipal   86–7, 90–1
    oedipal   86, 179
Friedrich, Caspar David   144n.2
From an Abandoned Work   33, 70, 282
Frost, Everett C.   9, 33, 40, 158, 160, 164, 167, 169, 170, 173, 283, 293, 295–310

G

Gambon, Michael   305
Gangar, Amrit   223
Gare St. Lazare Ireland   246n.
Garrard, Greg   158, 160–1, 173
gender   168, 274. *See also* sexuality
Geneste, Bruno   77–8, 83
Genest, Gudren   36
Genette, Gérard   104, 110
German Diaries of 1936–37   175–7, 185
'German Letter' of 1937   5, 28–9, 31, 42–3, 71, 182, 210, 232. *See also* 'literature of the unword'
Geulincx, Arnold   149–52
Ghost Trio   202, 285, 289–93
Giacometti, Alberto   144
Gibson, Andrew   161n.9, 173
Gielgud, Val   282, 298
Giorgione   146
globalisation   222, 268, 277
Godard, Jean-Luc   112
Goethe, Johann Wolfgang von   177–9, 185
Gontarski, S. E.   2–3, 8, 10, 38n.12, 39–40, 75, 83, 99, 107, 109–23, 156, 173, 186–7, 189, 193n., 206, 224, 226–7, 232–4, 280, 292, 310
Gooch, George Peabody   177
Gregory, André   306
Grossman, Évelyne   76, 80n., 83

Grüner, Gustav   138
Guildhall School of Music and Drama   244n.6

H

Haerdter, Michael   36–7
Hale, Jane Alison   155, 157, 193n., 198, 206
Happy Days   34, 37, 159, 161, 168, 200n., 241–2, 245–6, 267–8, 272–7, 279, 299
Harry Ransom Humanities Research Center   14
Hartel, Gaby   160n.7, 173, 281, 283, 285, 293
Harvey, Lawrence   117, 122
Haydn, Joseph   34
Hegarty-Lovett, Judy   246n. *See also* Gare St. Lazare Ireland
Hegedus, Chris   144n.1, 155, 157
Held, Lawrence   252
Her Voice   276–7, 279
heterotopia   116–8, 121
Higgins, Aidan   11
Hirst, Damien   208–9, 216–7, 220
Hoevels, Daniel   178n.3
Hölderlin, Friedrich   15
Hori Tanaka, Mariko   1–10, 193–207, 270, 272, 278, 293
Howe, Mary Manning   185, 305
How It Is   1, 75, 159–60, 166, 172. *See also Comment c'est*
Hughes, Keith   255
Humboldt, Wilhelm von   188
Hutchings, William   217, 219, 220
Hynes, Garry   300. *See also* Druid Theatre

I

Ibsen, Henrik   153
Ihde, Don   12–3, 22, 25, 27, 32–3, 35, 40
Ill Seen Ill Said   52, 82
Imagination Dead Imagine   159n.2
Imagination morte imaginez   159n.2
Innommable, L'   67, 83. *See also The Unnamable*
intersemiotic. *See* semiotic
invisibility   1, 6, 17, 44–5, 108, 116, 130, 139, 200, 204, 211, 214, 238, 303

Ionesco, Eugene   282
Irish Free State   161*n*.9
'iteratism'   26, 104, 120*n*.

J

Jakobson, Roman   267–8, 278
Jermyn Street Theatre. *See* productions. *See* theatres
Johnson, Nicholas E.   1–10, 237–49
Jordan, Emma   308
Joyce, James   12, 26–7, 30, 95, 113, 185, 222
Joyce, Lucia   128
Juliet, Charles   25, 33, 40, 75, 83
Jung, Carl   136*n*.5, 141, 254

K

Kafka, Franz   118
Kalb, Jonathan   2, 34, 40, 128, 142, 252, 266, 302, 310
Kamome Machine. *See* productions. *See also* Her Voice
Karmitz, Marin   287, 293. *See also* Comédie
Kaun, Axel   28–9, 31, 71, 182, 210, 232. *See also* 'German Letter' of 1937
Keaton, Buster   287. *See also* Film
Keio University   273
Kelleher, Joe   161, 173
Kendrick, Lynne   25, 40
Kennedy, Seán   161*n*.9, 173
Kenner, Hugh   49, 55, 302, 310
Kiuchi, Kumiko   8, 97–110
Knowlson, James   14, 22, 33, 40, 71*n*., 73, 83, 97, 110, 127–8, 130–1, 133*n*., 134, 138, 140–1, 144–6, 148, 151, 156–7, 176, 189, 212, 214, 220, 251–2, 255, 265–6, 269, 278, 298, 306, 310
Kommen und Gehen   226. *See also* Come and Go. *See also* Teacht is Imeacht
Krapp's Last Tape   4, 6, 8, 32–3, 35, 37, 48, 50, 85–90, 93, 95–6, 110, 115, 133, 145, 153*n*., 159*n*.1, 160, 200*n*., 288
Kuma, Kengo   273
Kyogen   267

L

Labeille, Daniel C.   155*n*., 156
Lacan, Jacques   3–4, 7, 9, 67–8, 70, 72, 75, 76*n*.10, 77, 79, 81–3, 86–7, 91–4, 96, 138–9, 211, 218, 220
Lacanian   3, 9, 79*n*., 87
lalangue   67, 75–82
objet (petit) a   4, 9, 70, 72, 82*n*., 208, 211, 214–5, 218
Lahr, Burt   305
lalangue. See Lacan, Jacques
Lamonte, Rosette   154
Lamport, Francis   179*n*., 189
Laverty, Jennifer   257, 259–62
Lavery, Carl   158, 160, 162, 172–4
Lawley, Paul   87–88, 90, 96
Laws, Catherine   43, 55, 158, 160, 164*n*., 165–6, 170*n*.17, 174, 283, 290, 293
Lehmann, Hans-Thies   26
Letters of Samuel Beckett   22, 55, 110, 122, 142, 172–3, 176–7, 182, 189, 309
Levy, Eric   2
Libera, Antoni   74, 83
light   16, 27, 30, 37, 46, 49, 72, 75*n*.7, 100, 105, 113, 129, 130–1, 135, 137, 139, 141, 145–7, 166, 195–6, 197*n*.3, 198–200, 205, 212, 214, 223, 227–8, 251–2, 254, 286, 292
lighting (stage)   5, 8, 72, 75, 100, 129–30, 133, 136*n*.4, 145, 246, 253, 255, 257–8, 260, 262–4, 286, 288, 291, 307–8
linguistics   1, 3–4, 7, 48, 57*n*., 62, 91–2, 100, 102, 137–8, 197*n*.3, 221, 288
Linklater, Kristin   240–1, 243, 249
Lir, The   237, 238*n*.1
'literature of the unword'   5, 7, 29, 43, 182, 222. *See also* 'German Letter' of 1937
Living Theatre   306. *See* productions
Llull, Ramon   134
Locatelli, Carla   218, 220
Losey, Joseph   99
Lost Ones, The   159, 171, 300. *See also* Le Dépeupleur
Lovett, Conor   246. *See also* Gare St. Lazare Ireland
Lyons, Charles   143, 152–3, 155, 157, 166, 174
Lyotard, Jean-François   162, 174

M

MacGowran, Jack   170n.16, 252
MacGreevy, Thomas   14, 178, 185
Machiavelli, Niccolò   183
Mackay, Donald G.   12, 19, 22
MacNeice, Louis   298
Madden, Catherine   238n.1, 249
Magee, Patrick   2, 33, 36, 170n.16
'Magee Monologue'   33
Malkin, Jeanette   129–30, 142
Malone Dies   10, 32, 222, 282, 300. See also *Malone meurt*
Malone meurt   10, 32, 67. See also *Malone Dies*
Manning, Mary   185, 305
Margolin, Uri   12n., 22
Marxism   183
material/immaterial   6–8, 10, 14, 25, 28, 30–32, 37, 42–55, 71, 75, 106, 111–4, 116, 118, 129–30, 133, 136, 162, 210, 212, 226–7, 248, 262, 281–3, 285, 290, 303
Maude, Ulrika   158, 160, 174, 186–7, 189, 212, 220, 303, 310
Mayberry, Bob   212, 220
McAuley, Gay   224, 234
McCusker, Stella   308
McDonald, Rónán   46–7, 55
McKinney, Joslin   301, 310
McMillan, Dougald   33, 35, 36n., 40, 189
McMullan, Anna   8, 143, 154–5, 157–74, 185, 187, 189, 194, 202, 204n., 206, 280, 293, 303, 310
McWhinnie, Donald   33, 36n., 97, 158, 160n.7, 163–5, 168n.14, 169–70, 174, 282–3, 293, 296, 298n., 300, 301n., 310
Meagher, Robert Emmet   228
media/medium   1–2, 5–7, 9–10, 18, 32, 46–48, 63, 88, 94, 111, 113, 115–6, 158–60, 162–4, 172, 193, 195, 203, 217, 222, 224, 229, 232, 280–5, 288–9, 295–302
memory   1, 8, 13, 19, 45n.3, 48, 61, 80n., 88, 106–7, 109, 112, 114, 116, 118, 120, 127–32, 134, 136–8, 140–1, 143, 155n., 193n., 203, 221, 225–6, 233, 240, 241n., 244–5, 255, 275, 299
Mendelyte, Atene   116
Mercier et Camier   67, 71

Messina, Antonello de   252
Metz, Christian   28
Meyerhold, Vsevolod   240
Mihalovici, Marcel   145
Milner, Jean-Claude   68n.2, 77, 83
Mitchell, Breon   136, 142, 229, 234
Molloy   1, 10, 21, 33, 300
Monde et le pantalon, Le   71, 75, 82
Montesquieu, Baron de   183
Mooney, Sinéad   277, 279
Moorjani, Angela   20–22
Moretti, Franco   223, 234
Morin, Emilie   158, 160, 163, 164n., 174
Morris, John   164n., 282, 298
Morrison, Kristin   193, 195n., 204n., 207
Mouth on Fire. See productions. See also Nolan, Melissa and Quinn, Cathal
Müller-Freienfels, Reinhart   285
Müller, Jürgen   116, 122
Murphy   12, 15, 22, 50, 82, 149, 152
musicality   1, 6–7, 25–6, 34–6, 48–9, 73, 78, 81, 117, 164, 165n., 171, 215, 229, 237, 251–2, 255, 262, 264, 270, 275

N

Nacht und Träume   285, 291
Nagashima, Kaku   275
National Gallery, London   146
National Theatre. See Royal National Theatre
National Theatre School Canada. See productions
Nazism   181
'neither'   33, 131. See also Feldman, Morton
Nemoto, Misako   104
New National Theatre Tokyo. See productions. See theatres
Nguyên, Albert   77–8, 81–4
Nicolás, Teresa Rosell   8, 143–57
Nietzsche, Friedrich   119, 178–9, 190
Nightingale, Benedict   214–5, 220
Ní Shluaghadháin, Síofra   276, 279
Nixon, Mark   16, 175–9, 181, 185, 190, 293
Nobel Prize   280, 306
Noguchi, Isamu   273, 279
Noh   267

INDEX   337

Nolan, Melissa   9, 250–66. *See also* Mouth on Fire
Northwestern University   246*n*.
nothing   4–5, 17–18, 25–6, 30, 33*n*., 43–4, 61, 75, 91, 93, 114, 118, 196, 200, 202, 204, 211–2, 232, 255, 270
Not I   25, 37–8, 71, 74, 81, 85, 90–4, 98–9, 109, 120, 122, 187, 196, 218–19, 239–40, 250, 253–8, 260, 262, 285, 299
Nunn, Trevor   305

O

objet a. *See* Lacan, Jacques
O'Brien, Colm   257, 259, 262
oedipal. *See* Freud, Sigmund
O'Farrell, Mary   170
Ohio Impromptu   80, 98, 113, 195
oikos   158, 161–3, 170–2
Ojrzyenska, Katarzyna   167, 174
Okamuro, Minako   270, 276, 279
Olivier, Sir Laurence   306
On Going On   246*n*.
Ost, Isabelle   76*n*.11, 80, 84
Ovadija, Mladen   25–6, 40

P

Pan Pan Theatre. *See* productions
Paraskeva, Anthony   287, 293
Pater, Walter   297, 310
Pearce, Damien   178*n*.3, 190
Pennebaker, D. A.   144*n*.1, 155–7
performativity   2, 6, 26, 117, 130, 143, 209, 278, 299, 300
Perloff, Marjorie   25*n*., 40, 57, 58*n*., 64
Peters, John Durham   284
Phalke, Debasaheb   224
phenomenology   1, 7, 32, 129, 166, 224, 307
Philips, Siân   252
Piette, Adam   26–7, 41
Pilling, John   44, 55, 71*n*., 83, 96–8, 110, 127, 140–2, 212, 297*n*.4, 310
Pinget, Robert   303
Pinter, Harold   99, 282

Play   37, 81, 121, 164, 242–3, 244*n*.5, 250, 254, 262–4, 280, 287
Plowright, Joan   306
Plunkett, Geraldine   253, 260–1
Pochade radiophonique   46, 171. *See also Rough for Radio II*
polyphony   56–7, 62, 175
Porge, Erik   76*n*.10, 84
Porter, Jeff   28, 41, 204*n*., 206, 278
postcolonial   9, 224, 231–2
postmodern   130
poststructuralist   3
Pountney, Rosemary   38*n*.11, 41, 71, 73, 84, 194, 200, 207, 254, 266
powerlessness   76, 149–50, 152
Powerscourt Gallery. *See* productions
pre-oedipal. *See* Freud, Sigmund
Prime Cut Productions. *See* productions
productions (of Beckett works)
    Aldwych Theatre   33
    Arsonist Productions   208–9, 216
    Arts Theatre   305*n*.
    Battersea Arts Centre (BAC)   120*n*.
    Belfast   308, 308*n*.
    Berlin   100*n*., 144*n*.2. *See also* Schiller-Theater Werkstatt
    Chicago   246. *See also* Wallis Theatre
    Druid Theatre   300
    Dublin   201, 237–67, 276. *See also* Focus Theatre and Smock Alley
    Dublin Theatre Festival   267, 276
    Enniskillen   120*n*., 244*n*.
    Focus Theatre   253, 260
    Fukushima   267, 270–2, 277
    Galway   276. *See also* Druid Theatre
    Jermyn Street   304–5, 305*n*.
    Kamome Machine   270–2, 275
    Kolkata   226
    Living Theatre   306
    Mouth on Fire   201, 201*n*.7, 257
    National Theatre School Canada   208–9, 215
    New National Theatre Tokyo   267, 270–2, 277
    Pan Pan Theatre   245, 245*n*., 307
    Paris   276
    Powerscourt Gallery   257, 262
    Prime Cut Productions   308

productions (of Beckett works) (cont.)
  Royal Court Theatre 33, 36n., 120n., 248
  RTF (Paris) 46
  Schiller-Theater Werkstatt 36, 97–8, 226
  Smock Alley Theatre 255, 258
  Sofia 244n.5
  Southbank Centre 120
  Städtische Bühnen 145
  Stuttgart (SDR) 285
  Theater X (Cai) 201n.7
  Theatre Commons Tokyo 267, 272
  Théâtre de Babylone 35, 267
  Théâtre des Bouffes du Nord 39
  Tokyo 201, 267, 270–7
  Voices International 170
  Wallis Theatre 246n.
  Westdeutscher Rundfunk 296n.1
Proust 21, 44, 47, 55, 115, 117, 221, 225, 229
Proust, Marcel 8, 44, 97, 99, 103–6, 110, 225, 297n.5, 299, 303
pseudocouple 69
pseudo-fusion 127, 138
psychoanalysis 1, 3–4, 10, 14–5, 127–8, 137.
  See also Freud and Lacan
psychology 14–5, 127–8, 135, 137

Q

Qigong 238, 238n.2
Quad / *Quadrat 1 + 2* 74, 186, 285, 291
Quinn, Cathal 9, 201–2, 237–49, 254, 257, 259, 262, 264. *See also* Mouth on Fire
Quinn, Gavin 307. *See also* Pan Pan Theatre
Quinn, Morgan 276, 279
Quoi Oú 176, 185–7. *See also* What Where

R

Racine, Jean 178–9, 181
Rakugo 273–5
Rank, Otto 128n., 134
Ray, Sukumar 230
Reavey, George 99
Reeves, Cecelia 282
Reisberg, Daniel 13n., 22
religion(s) 180

Hinduism 224
Judaism 33
Protestantism 181–2
Roman Catholicism 140n., 181–2, 184
Rembrandt 146–7
repetition 3, 21n., 25–6, 28, 31, 35, 36n., 53–4, 79, 82, 90, 106, 114, 127, 129–32, 137–8, 148, 151, 155, 208, 221, 223, 229–30, 233, 277
Ricks, Christopher 35, 41
rhythm(ic) 25–6, 29, 30n., 33, 35–6, 38–9, 70, 89, 97, 106–7, 127, 129, 131–2, 143, 151, 153, 155, 165–6, 171, 203, 205, 215–6, 237, 253, 258, 260, 262, 264, 269
ritual(istic) 155, 223, 226, 228–30
Robertson, John G. 177, 180–1, 183–4, 190
Rockaby 6, 8, 37, 39, 120, 143–57, 250, 254, 264–5
Rodenburg, Patsy 244, 244n.6
Roe, Annie 148
Roesner, David 25, 40
Roloff, Volker 116, 122
Rose, Arthur 8, 175–90
Rosenstock, Gabriel 250, 261. *See also* Mouth on Fire
Rosset, Barney 296n.2, 298, 305
Rough for Radio I 46
Rough for Radio II 46, 250, 257–8, 282. *See also* Pochade radiophonique
Rousseau, Jean-Jacques 183
Royal Court Theatre. *See* productions. *See* theatres
Royal National Theatre. *See* theatres
Royal Shakespeare Company. *See* theatres
RTF (Radiodiffusion-Télévision Française). *See* productions

S

San Quentin Drama workshop 252
Sass, Louise A. 13–4, 16, 22
Satoh, Makoto 276
Satoh, Yasushi 276, 279
Saussure, Ferdinand de 3
Schauspielhaus, Berlin. *See* theatres
Schiller-Theater, Berlin. *See* theatres
Schiller, Friedrich 8, 9, 145, 175–90

schizophrenic   13–5
Schmahl, Hildegard   128, 130
Schneider, Alan   73, 82, 99, 107, 110, 120–2, 156, 305–6, 309
Schopenhauer, Arthur   7, 42, 44–6, 51, 54–5, 297, 310
Schroeder, Ernst   36
Schubert, Franz   34
Searle, Humphrey   51*n*.6
Second World War. *See* World War II
semiotic / intersemiotic   3, 98, 100, 109, 267–8, 276–7, 308
sexuality   137, 155. *See also* gender
shadow   12, 20, 30, 131, 145, 147, 201, 227, 286, 297
Shaeffer, Pierre   160*n*.6
Shafer, Murray   28
Shakespeare, William   27, 39, 200, 231, 239, 247
Sharpe, Lesley   178, 182–3, 188, 190
Shelley, Mary   26–7, 31, 34, 38
Shingeki (New Drama)   267
Siess, Jürgen   7, 56–64
Sigg, Anna   9, 208–20
silence   2, 5–8, 17, 25, 29, 34–5, 43, 46, 53, 63, 69, 73, 77, 81, 85–96, 100, 105, 107, 109, 139, 167, 200*n*., 202, 208–11, 213–9, 221, 223, 225, 228, 231, 233, 240, 255, 258, 260–1, 271–2, 276, 283, 286
Silverman, Kaja   3
Simond, Charles   177*n*.
Sinclair, Peggy   204*n*.
'singularism'   1, 43*n*., 70–1, 77, 102, 104, 115–6, 136, 140, 155
Skowronski, John J.   140, 142
Smith, Anthony   284, 294
Smith, David J.   13, 18–20, 22
Smock Alley Theatre. *See* productions. *See* theatres
Soma, Chiaki   272, 279
Sontag, Susan   85, 96
Southbank Centre. *See* productions. *See* theatres
space   2, 9, 21, 31, 44, 47, 49, 57, 62, 71, 73, 85, 101, 116–8, 130, 133, 145, 158, 160–3, 169, 172, 176, 186, 213, 222–7, 232–3, 250–1, 255, 257–62, 265, 268–75, 281, 283, 286–92, 301–2, 304, 307

Spivak, Gayatri Chakravorty   231
Städtische Bühnen. *See* productions. *See* theatres
Stanislavski, Konstantin   240, 252
Stekel, Wilhelm   134
Stewart, Paul   168*n*.15, 174
Stock, Werner   36, 199
subjectivity   67, 70–2, 76*n*.9, 77, 108, 183, 185, 283, 302–3
Süddeutscher Rundfunk (SDR). *See* productions
Swann, Charles   104

T

Takebe, Yoshiko   9, 267–79
Takeya, Keiko   276, 279
Tandy, Jessica   38, 120, 217–8, 255
Taniguchi, Yoshiro   273
Tarkovsky, Andrei   225
Tavistock Clinic   128, 136*n*.5
Taylor, Don   288–9, 294
Teacht Is Imeacht   250, 260–1. *See Come and Go*. *See Kommen und Gehen*
technology   6–9, 48, 88, 158–74, 217, 245*n*., 281, 284, 288, 295, 299
temps retrouvé, Le   99
tension   10, 47, 53, 131, 143, 145, 148, 151, 153, 163, 165, 183, 186, 188, 203, 212, 238*n*.1, 251, 265, 286
Textes pour rien   67. *See also Texts for Nothing*
Texts for Nothing   4, 5, 10, 26, 46, 113, 160, 215
Thass-Thienemann, Theodor   27
That Time   4, 8, 37, 67, 71–2, 75–8, 80, 82–3, 97–110, 145. *See also Cette fois*. *See also Damals*
theatres (venues)
    Aldwych Theatre   33
    Arts Theatre   305*n*.
    Battersea Arts Centre (BAC)   120*n*.
    Focus Theatre   253, 260
    Jermyn Street   304–5, 305*n*.
    Royal Court Theatre   33, 36*n*., 120*n*., 248. *See* productions
    Royal National Theatre   244, 244*n*.6, 248

theatres (venues) (cont.)
    Royal Shakespeare Company   238,
        244n.6
    Schiller-Theater Werkstatt   36, 97–8, 226
    Southbank Centre   120
    Städtische Bühnen   145
    Theater X (Cai)   201n.7
    Theatre Commons Tokyo   267, 272
    Théâtre de Babylone   35, 267
    Théâtre des Bouffes du Nord   39
    Wallis Theatre   246n.
Theater X (Cai). *See* productions. *See* theatres
Theatre Commons Tokyo. *See* productions.
    See theatres
Théâtre de Babylone. *See* productions. *See*
    theatres
Théâtre des Bouffes du Nord. *See*
    productions. *See* theatres
Thomas, Dylan   298
Thompson, Dr. Geoffrey   14–5, 22
tone / toneless   32–8, 50, 73, 107, 115, 138, 194,
    204, 212, 237, 247–8, 252, 254–5, 264,
    273, 283, 301, 304–6
Toury, Gideon   223
Tout ceux qui tombent   303. *See also All That
    Fall*
translation   4, 8, 61, 97–100, 103, 106, 109, 177,
    221–3, 229–30, 232, 241n., 250, 267–70,
    277
'transmission'   2, 77, 284
trauma(tic/tised)   4–5, 7–9, 127, 129, 134–5,
    195, 203–4, 208–19, 227, 240
Trinity College Dublin   133n., 178, 238n.1,
    245, 297n.5
Tritte   128. *See also Footfalls*
Tsushima, Michiko   7, 42–55
Tubridy, Derval   216, 220
Tynan, Kenneth   306
Tyranny in Beckett   258

U

Uhlmann, Anthony   122, 145, 149, 150, 152,
    157, 173, 189
uncanny   6, 193, 201, 215–6, 227, 271
University of Reading   14
Unnamable, The   1, 2, 5, 53, 71, 99, 119, 282,
    300

V

Van Gogh, Vincent   8, 146–7
Verbatim/The Voice   108
Verhulst, Pim   282, 294
Verlaine, Paul   68–9, 84
Vertov, Dziga   287
Voices International. *See* productions
void   4, 8, 75, 77, 82, 86, 91, 108, 145, 176
von Humboldt, Wilhelm. *See* Humboldt
von Schiller, Friedrich. *See* Schiller

W

Wade, David   296, 310
Waiting for Godot   5–6, 30n., 35–7, 67–8, 71,
    82, 119, 144n.2, 148, 228–9, 253, 267–8,
    270–2, 277–9, 282–3, 298–9, 305
Walker, Richard W.   140, 142
Wallis Theatre. *See* productions. *See* theatres
Wardle, Irving   163
Ward, Shiela   170
Warrilow, David   34
Was Wo   185–7. *See What Where*. *See Quoi Où*
Watt   3, 7, 11–22, 28
Webern, Anton   34
Weller, Shane   14–5, 22, 159, 174
Welsh, Irvine   13n.
Wessler, Éric   70, 72, 84
Westdeutscher Rundfunk. *See* productions
West, Sarah   2, 31n., 41, 194–5, 207
What Where   38, 74–5, 115, 121, 185–7, 189,
    244n.5, 258. *See also Was Wo*. *See also
    Quoi Où*
Whistler, James McNeill   8, 146–7
White, Harry   34n., 41
Whitelaw, Billie   9, 33–4, 36–7, 41, 117, 120,
    127, 131, 151, 156, 240, 248, 252, 255
Wilder, Clinton   121
Williams, Raymond   281, 289, 294
Wilson, Meg   13, 22
Windelband, Wilhelm   177
Wittgenstein, Ludwig   186n., 190, 220
Woolf, Virginia   69
Words and Music   6–7, 33, 42–3, 46, 48, 51–4,
    115, 171, 282, 305
World War II   3, 11, 161, 214, 216, 272, 277, 282
Worstward Ho   10, 28

INDEX

Worth, Katharine 51*n*.6, 55, 131, 133, 140*n*., 142

Y

Yates, Francis A. 134, 142
Yeats, Jack 146
Yeats, William Butler 115–6

Z

Zilliacus, Clas 48*n*., 50–3, 55, 163, 164*n*., 170*n*.16, 174, 296*n*.2, 298–9, 306–7, 310
Žižek, Slavoj 3, 92, 93, 96, 211, 212, 213, 215, 220

Printed in the United States
by Baker & Taylor Publisher Services